Between 1939 and 19[...] [...]s 200,000 mentally ill or physical[...] unworthy of life'. This complex a[...] [...]uthanasia' programme. It provide[...] [...]rtise later deployed in the 'Final S[...]

This is the first full-[...] [...]ramme. It begins by establishing t[...] [...] [...]uring and after the First World War [...] [...]st-cutting concerns, but also by th[...] [...]ame more receptive to occupational therapy and experiments in community care. However, the former only served to underline the problem presented by chronic patients, while the latter raised the spectre of uncharted depths of mental illness in the population at large. Many psychiatrists became receptive to drastic 'eugenic' solutions long before 1933.

The advent of the National Socialist government brought further reductions in the care of the asylum population. Many inmates were now compulsorily sterilised in the interests of racial fitness; and while psychiatrists enthusiastically deployed the new somatic therapies such as ECT to treat acute cases, many of them subscribed to the Nazis' policy of killing chronic or unproductive cases. There was thus no conflict between psychiatric reform and extermination. As a result, hundreds of thousands of men, women and children were gassed, starved or murdered with lethal injections in a series of ever-widening programmes.

Uniquely, this book considers the role of *all* those involved in these policies: bureaucrats, doctors, nurses, health officials, lawyers, clerics, and also parents, relatives, and the patients themselves. Using a wealth of original archival material, it highlights many of the moral issues involved in a way that is profoundly disquieting. The book concludes by showing the ease with which many of the perpetrators filtered back into German society after 1945.

DEATH AND DELIVERANCE

DEATH
AND
DELIVERANCE

'Euthanasia' in Germany
c. 1900–1945

MICHAEL BURLEIGH

*Reader in International History, London School of Economics
and Political Science*

CAMBRIDGE
UNIVERSITY PRESS

Published by the Press Syndicate of the University of Cambridge
The Pitt Building, Trumpington Street, Cambridge CB2 IRP
40 West 20th Street, New York, NY 10011–4211, USA
10 Stamford Road, Oakleigh, Melbourne 3166, Australia

First published 1994
Reprinted (twice) 1995

Printed in Great Britain by Redwood Books, Trowbridge, Wiltshire

A catalogue record for this book is available from the British Library

Library of Congress cataloguing in publication data
Burleigh, Michael.
Death and deliverance: 'euthanasia' in Germany c. 1900–1945 /
Michael Burleigh.
p.   cm.
Includes bibliographical references and index.
ISBN 0–521–41613–2 (hardback)
1. Euthanasia – Germany – History – 20th Century. 1. Title.
R726.B87 1994
179'.7 – dc20 93–48229 CIP
ISBN 0 521 41613 2 hardback
ISBN 0 521 47769 7 paperback

CE

for Linden

Problem 97:

A mental patient costs about 4RMS a day to keep, a cripple 5.50 RMS, a criminal 3.50 RMS. In many cases a civil servant only has about 4 RMS, a salaried employee scarcely 3.50 RMS, an unskilled worker barely 2 RMS for his family. (a) illustrate these figures with the aid of pictures. According to conservative estimates, there are about 300,000 mental patients, epileptics etc., in asylums in Germany. (b) What do they cost together per annum at a rate of 4 RMS per person? i) how many marriage loans at 1,000 RMS each could be awarded per annum with this money, disregarding later repayment?

(From Adolf Dörner [ed.], *Mathematik im Dienste der nationalpolitischen Erziehung mit Anwendungsbeispielen aus Volkswissenschaft, Geländekunde und Naturwissenschaft* [Frankfurt am Main 1935], p. 42.)

Assuming an average daily outlay of 3.50 RM there hereby results:

1.   a daily saving of RM 245.955
2.   an annual saving of RM 88.543.980
3.   assuming a life expectancy of ten years

   RM 885.439.800

in words eight hundred and eighty-five million four hundred and thirty-nine thousand eight hundred Reichmarks,

i.e. this sum will have been, or has already been, saved by 1 September 1951 by reason of the disinfection of 70.273 persons which has been carried out to date

(T–4 internal statistical digest found at Schloss Hartheim in 1945. National Archives Washington, T 1021, Heidelberger Dokumente, Roll 18, Item Nr 000–12–463, Exhibit 39, p. 4.)

CONTENTS

Contents

ILLUSTRATIONS

ACKNOWLEDGEMENTS

SELF-EVIDENTLY, researching and writing this book has sometimes been a gloomy task, although one does not want to make too much of this. There has been a major consolation in the shape of the many German friends and colleagues, most of whom are seriously expert in these fields, and friends in England who have been kind enough to tolerate my amateurish ventures into their disciplines, or who took time out from their own books to read mine. I would like to express my warm appreciation to Götz Aly, State Prosecutor Willy Dressen, Ernst Klee, Jonathan Glover, Alice and Georg Herrnleben, Desmond King, Ludwig Rost, Armin Trus, Paul Weindling and Wolfgang Wippermann.

Stewart Lansley, Waldemar Januszczak, Joanna Mack, Karl Laabs, Georg Pahls and Richard MacQueen brought their very considerable creative talents to bear on what became the film 'Selling Murder', contributing more than they realise to my thinking on the chapter which bears the eponymous title. Recutting some of the Nazi film material provided several insights into how it had actually been made in the first place. Their generosity of spirit and intelligence made a pleasant change from what one has come to experience in the universities. I am also grateful to audiences at Birkbeck College, London, the University of Sussex and the Open University Psychological Society for their comments on lectures on this subject between 1991 and 1993, lectures which perforce tended to spread the gloom of Hegesias.

The British Academy, Leverhulme Trust, London School of Economics and Nuffield Foundation generously contributed to the long periods of research upon which this book is based. Richard Evans, Ian Kershaw and Donald Cameron Watt were very supportive of the entire project. The staff of the various archives listed in the bibliography facilitated my researches, as did the Fellows of the Royal Society of Medicine in London by allowing me to work in their magnificent library. As always, William Davies at Cambridge University Press was an interested and sympathetic commissioning editor, although I suspect that, twelve years on now, he wishes the telephone had never been invented.

Finally, there are some very personal debts, for which mere words are inadequate recompense. Helmut Heinze, Klara Nowak, Paula S. and Josef Simon were trusting enough to share raw memories, in the last case regarding issues which had never much exercised someone who is a non-believer. The emotional links formed will always stay with me. Without Josef Simon I would not have been to virtually every place mentioned in this book, nor managed to interview some of the perpetrators. Being of a sceptical cast of mind, the latter experience at least served to remind me of several recurring gaps in the record. Although the legal depositions and witness statements grow denser with detail each time someone is interviewed (and some of those discussed in this book have been interviewed by German police or prosecutors on twenty separate occasions), I am conscious of gaps and deliberate omissions on many issues of substance. The same caveat also obviously applies to the historical written record, where not all that was done was committed to paper.

The final words of acknowledgement should necessarily go to the person who has had to live for five years with what is a grim subject. My wife Linden has no special interest in Germany, having been born in India. Although our version of 'uxoriousness' is not based upon shared card indices, she has read and discussed every draft of this book from the point of view of an interested, and perhaps less desensitised layman, putting up with some prolonged separations while I researched or filmed in Germany. The dedication is an inadequate way of saying thank you to her, and at least as far as the subject goes, 'nie wieder'.

For legal reasons, and because of German data protection laws, the surnames of victims and perpetrators have been given in the form of initials, except in cases where the identity of the person has been in the public domain for so long that this precaution is superfluous. This seemed a more satisfactory approach than having to invent several hundred surnames in the interests of readability. The concluding bibliographical essay and discussion of source materials are primarily designed to assist anyone who might wish to take these subjects further. The discussion of Peter Singer demonstrates the enduring relevance of some of these questions.

Michael Burleigh
December 1993

INTRODUCTION

THIS IS a long book on a bleak subject. Moving from the local to the general, this brief introduction will explain both the historiographical context and the book's explicit objectives. In 1988, I published *Germany Turns Eastwards*, a study of the relationship between various kinds of academics who studied Russia and eastern Europe and the National Socialist dictatorship. I then co-authored a more wide-ranging study of the National Socialists' attempts to realise a racial dystopia. The intention was to redress some of the theoretical excesses of academic writing about National Socialism in the 1960s and 1970s, by deliberately going back to basics, albeit with the benefit of the outstanding research on (for example) foreign forced labour, the persecution of the socially marginal, and the roles of gender and generation produced, mainly in Germany, during the last two decades. Parts of this second study of the Nazi 'Racial State' stimulated my interest in the present project, while making it superfluous to retrace the development of racist ideologies in the present work.

This research agenda very much reflects my own intellectual dissatis-faction with the range of questions posed during what has increasingly become the 'classically modern' era of writing about inter-war Fascism and National Socialism, i.e. questions formulated upon the basis of one or other kind of (practically redundant) Marxism. Living at the end of what some of my more radical students term Marxism's 'century of failure', there seems no reason, beyond mere faith or dogmatic obduracy, to approach the past armed with Marxism's rapidly rusting analytical equip-ment. We may not have quite reached the 'end of history', for ersatz Communism, illiberal xenophobic nationalism and 'ethnic cleansing' seem to be enjoying something of a renaissance; but we have probably come to one of those times of opportunity when people need to address and formulate a new set of questions.

The questions raised in the present book also reflect a certain amount of unease about the impact of 'market forces' upon historical knowledge. With some notable exceptions, particularly in Germany where there is a

· 1 ·

thriving 'alternative', or freelance, historical culture (not to be confused with the left-wing academic 'counter'- Establishment), historians combine research with teaching. Although this is mainly a happy arrangement, there are a few drawbacks. The past is increasingly rendered more accessible to students by being construed as a series of controversies, debates and problems, more or less 'in' or 'out' of focus. Articles and short books are produced to cater for that market. Indeed, being consumer-driven, the market virtually dictates a fresh supply of 'controversies', including ones based on subjects that would strike an uninvolved lay observer as profoundly uncontroversial. This industry in turn effectively sets the parameters for further research, with major, and sometimes justified, scholarly reputations being established on the basis of what are essentially contributions to historiography. The process is no doubt less circular, mechanical and solipsistic than the above remarks suggest, but there is some degree of veracity in any caricature. Thus, in the case of the Third Reich, much of this pedagogical product concentrates upon the origins of the 'Final Solution' or whether the regime had an intentional or unintentional 'modernising' effect upon German society. Since these are not the areas in which the most interesting research has been done in the last decade or so, they inevitably lend themselves to the reiteration of dogma: particularly in Germany where professors represent schools and a ramified academic clientele, but also in Britain where students are invited to evaluate secondhand and sometimes partial accounts of debates in Germany which are themselves divorced from the cutting edge of research on this period, which increasingly functions outside the universities.

Although the 'euthanasia' programme and the Holocaust are intimately related, this book is thus not a contribution to the debate between intentionalists and functionalists about the origins of the 'Final Solution', a debate which peaked in the late 1970s. In this book the reader approaches, and is then led around, the various entrances to that nightmare, without venturing any further. On a rough calculation, the Holocaust occupies about a dozen pages. This conscious evasion is partly a matter of rendering the whole project feasible, and partly because it would be otiose to try to improve on the very impressive scholarship of Yehuda Bauer, Gerald Fleming, Saul Friedländer, Raul Hilberg, Eberhard Jäckel, Helmut Krausnick, Michael Marrus or Isaiah Trunk, severally the acknowledged masters in this area. There is a vast English-language literature on the Holocaust, whereas to date this is the first full-scale English study on the 'euthanasia' programme. The latter raises enough disturbing questions in its own right, without being treated as merely the antechamber of the greater, and subsequent, humanly willed atrocity.

What questions does *Death and Deliverance* seek to raise, if not always answer? In a narrow sense, this is an attempt to study the relationship between psychiatric reform, eugenics and government cost-cutting policies during the Weimar Republic and Nazi periods. As we all know, eugenic solutions to real, or perceived, social ills had widespread currency long before the Nazis came to power – and by no means exclusively in Germany. Being modern, 'progressive' and 'scientific', they were not bereft of devotees over the whole political spectrum. Just as many of the most innovative features of 'Weimar culture' – notably in painting – actually predate the First World War, so some of the most inhumane policies pursued by the Nazis had their origins in developments during the Weimar period. This was the case with discussions of the desirability of chucking overboard 'dead ballast' from the 'Ship of Fools' in the interests of enhanced national efficiency, which in Germany took on renewed saliency in the context of the multiple crises following the Versailles treaty. It was also the case with the initially optimistic brush between a reformed psychiatric sector and social problems whose scale had not been anticipated, and which hence engendered profound pessimism and the search for drastic rethinking of the viability of all expenditure in this area, with many psychiatrists calling for radical eugenic solutions and the killing of incurables. All of these developments predated the advent of a National Socialist government, and illustrate rather well the adverse sides of what the late Detlev Peukert called Weimar's experiment in classical modernity.

Although the advent of the National Socialist regime had very deleterious effects upon people living in asylums – i.e. conditions worsened, patients were compulsorily sterilised, and the regime's propaganda none too subtly disputed their human personality – the decision to kill people had complex origins. The so-called 'children's euthanasia' programme undoubtedly reflected the desire of some parents to rid themselves of the 'burden' represented by severely handicapped offspring, this being an element in the equation often conveniently overlooked by research on the subject. Some parents wanted to concentrate their flagging energies upon their other healthy children; others wanted to remove any 'taint' which might affect the purity of their family pedigree. These attitudes were hardly surprising, since they were largely in line with what limited opinion polls on these matters had revealed in the mid 1920s, polls which actually reveal parents anticipating the precise course of Nazi policy. Opinion-sounding undertaken by the SD (the SS security service) during the 'euthanasia' programme also reveals that people were far from unanimous in condemning these policies.

The 'euthanasia' programme for adults was very much bound up with clearing the decks in order to wage war. Hitler and his subordinates did not slither into it through contingent circumstances; nor did bureaucratic mechanisms assume a life of their own in the way that some historians imagine was the case with the 'Final Solution'. The 'euthanasia' programme was a carefully planned and covertly executed operation with precisely defined objectives. Those responsible believed in the necessity of what they were doing. Mentally and physically disabled people were killed to save money and resources, or to create physical space for ethnic German repatriates and/or civilian and military casualties, both in 'Aktion T-4' and through shootings carried out by the SS in Pomerania and Poland, and in the 'euthanasia' programme's various continuations. In other words, these policies reflected a non-medical agenda, even if some psychiatrists belatedly tried to give them some *ex post facto* medicalised rationalisation in order to defend their little beleaguered professional empires. The idea of 'modernising' psychiatric provision came to them after they had cold-bloodedly murdered tens of thousands of people, while recreating scenes of 'medieval' desolation in the asylums, with skeletal patients lying on straw or locked in vermin-infested bunkers.

Again, one has to bear in mind that most people affected had been placed in asylums by their families (state committals were exceptional, even under a regime which used inflationary definitions of insanity), and that there is little evidence of the latter exercising themselves to retrieve their relatives even when it was very obvious what fate was in store for them. Instead of concentrating upon well-known instances of individual outrage at these killings, historians might ask how far silent collusion facilitated the vast majority of them. One of the reasons this subject was so conspicuously neglected in post-war Germany is probably that its real secrets lie buried for ever in the consciences of many ordinary German families. The ways in which the state, and many members of the medical profession, systematically betrayed the trust of those who consigned their relatives to their care are unfortunately only part of the story. The gradual hardening of a particular moral climate – though this is admittedly a rather nebulous, albeit vital, analytical category – and the slow seepage of a post-Christian and illiberal ideology into the thoughts and actions of the generality are equally striking. Why did many plain people abandon concern for the 'weak', in favour of a vulgar Social Darwinist ideology which entailed a reversion to the laws of the farmyard or jungle? Did they imagine that they would always be on the side of the lions and wolves? Why did the rights of individuals collapse in front of such collectivist goals as the good of the economy, race or nation? What factors explain why some people were so susceptible to this ideology, and what explains those who rejected it?

From what has gone before, it should be obvious that this is not just another book about the moral vacancy of what are demotically and snobbishly known as profs, shrinks and eggheads (a matter that should hardly surprise in a culture which has elevated venality into the cardinal academic virtue), although it does have things to say about the relationship between social ambition, professionalisation and an absence of moral inhibition, things which some may find unfashionable. It gives equal, if not more, attention to senior health and political functionaries both in Berlin and the regional capitals, the latter a relatively understudied group of perpetrators. These men recommended personnel suited to work in an extermination programme, helped find appropriate places to carry it out in, and generally expedited matters through the pressure they could exert upon the staff of hundreds of ecclesiastical, private and state institutions. Venturing into the latter, the book also tries to give the range of possible responses to a state-sponsored programme of mass murder. The book also takes a dispassionate look at the lower echelons of involvement in mass murder. Dispassionate, because some historians tend to become misty-eyed whenever they write about the horny-handed sons and daughters of toil. Many of the most devious and pernicious individuals in this book were 'ordinary' working-class people, e.g. agricultural labourers, builders, cooks or lorry-drivers, some of whom went on via the 'euthanasia' programme to command extermination camps. This is the story of a sort of social mobility from cook to camp commandant. There is also the matter of women perpetrators. This aspect of Nazism, the chance for bullies to lord it over others, tends to be neglected.

All societies have people supposedly professionally concerned with law and moral values, notably lawyers, judges and clerics, to spread the net no further. In this case, most of those people turned a blind eye towards – or worse, actively colluded in – these policies, as can be seen from the fact that half of the victims in the first phase of the 'euthanasia' programme came from ecclesiastical asylums. Down on the ground, in those asylums, a certain degree of haggling over the fate of individuals was permitted by the bureaucrats responsible for the policies, in order to promote collusive involvement, but also to cater for the element of human bad conscience. Protests from the churches came too late to be effective, were easily circumvented, and ran parallel with discussions between the Roman Catholic hierarchy and sections of the Protestant charitable network on the one side, and the regime on the other, about how the 'euthanasia' programme could be rendered more palatable to their sensitive consciences. I make no apologies for being dismissive of their so-well-documented agonising, and their high-level networking with men who were fundamentally contemptuous of them. It is a distortion of reality to highlight the odd individual, such as Bishop Galen, who – no doubt with great courage – decided to protest against these matters despite the possible deleterious consequences. Such individuals were not typical.

Any book on a subject like this should make the authorial viewpoint fairly explicit. Hence I should say at the outset that I have no axes to grind regarding contemporary discussions about euthanasia (if anything I am sympathetic to its voluntaristic implementation), but like many people, feel uneasy about both right-to-die, Dr-Death-style fanatics and their counterparts in the 'Abortion-Holocaust' (*sic*), right-to-life movements. Nor, despite the subject of the book, do I have any particular animus against psychiatrists, the complexities and frustrations of whose job must engender a certain respect and humility in a mere historian.

Obviously, this book does not deny the reality of mental illness, nor seek to reduce very complex issues to a series of comfortable Leftish clichés about psychiatry as a form of intellectualised policing on behalf of the middle classes – even supposing that mental illness is as class-specific, or related to industrialisation, as that discredited model automatically suggests. As this book makes clear, there was not one form of Goffmanesque 'total' psychiatric institution, but instead a dense variety of confessional, private and state homes and asylums, whose responses to these policies were manifold, albeit universally ineffective. My approach has been to study the individuals who lived, worked and died in them rather than to dilate upon power structures, instrumental rationality or totalising institutions, and all the other blunt analytical equipment some people bring to the study of infinitely complex realities. In that sense I have learned something from recent English work, notably by Roy Porter, on the rich variety of containment and treatment of madness in remoter centuries; less from Foucault, Goffman and their various German disciples.

Any book on National Socialist Germany should be concerned with the victims and bystanders as well as the perpetrators, although, as should have already become evident, this conventional triad bears little relationship to the complex reality of the German historical experience. Many of the victims became victims because the bystanders could not cope, or did not want them. I can see no ultimate point in rehearsing the details of, say, murderous experiments with human subjects, or how one went about constructing a gas van or chamber, to the exclusion of the people who died as a consequence. Such work reflects a terrible poverty of the imagination and easily slides into a sort of technical prurience. This book therefore attempts to recapture what fitful signals there are regarding the people murdered. Fitful, because the victims only live on in vague memories, or more often as random entries in various kinds of official documentation. Occasionally one hears their own voices through items of their own correspondence.

This subject is difficult, and one I am not sure I have resolved very satisfactorily. Visiting memorial exhibitions in Germany devoted to these events has brought home the dangers of 'reselecting' one's own 'victims'. Too often those killed are depicted as being 'normal', as if normality somehow promotes empathy. Some of the people described in this book were quite clearly as much of a handful as some of the deranged individuals that get on some people's nerves on the streets of contemporary London or New York. I have tried not to deny (or exaggerate) that fact, while not making some cheap contemporary right-wing point out of it. Without being sententious about it, our societies stand judged by the degree of tolerance we evince towards their most distressed or weakest members. The minor inconvenience they caused others did not justify killing them, least of all by people trained and paid to look after them. To question *that* is merely distasteful rather than a manifestation of intellectual radicalism. The same goes for recent 'liberal' philosophical attempts to question our received and instinctual respect for the sanctity of human life through sophistries based on the capabilities and 'rights' of animals.

It goes without saying that I do not expect this book to promote enhanced democratic awareness, or even more sensitive treatment of the disturbed or disabled, categories one should be careful not to conflate. Those individuals who across Europe are involved in subverting democracy, or who occasionally throw people in wheelchairs down subway stairs for amusement's sake in Germany (a country which, incidentally, has enviable provision for disabled people), would be as much interested in the subject of this book as a flat-earthist in the theories of Bohr or Einstein. Attempts to convince such people of what 'actually happened' are faintly ridiculous, since denial of reality is bound up with their political agenda. The solution to their problem is not more history books – let alone cheaply sensationalist accompanied filmic visits to Auschwitz with neo-fascists pitted against Holocaust survivors – but a properly enforced legal system and an electorate indisposed to vote for the parties such people support.

Finally, this book does insist that the events it describes were unique to Nazi Germany, although the Vichy regime also decimated the asylum population. Of course, the degrading treatment of mental patients is a phenomenon of our time and place too. To take a couple of glaring examples: very recently, the Greek authorities turned a blind eye to a Goyaesque concentration camp for the mad on the island of Leros until western European television made an issue of it; and in Britain, where trade unions protect the rights of prison officers of a fascistic disposition, patients in secure hospitals such as Ashworth or Rampton have been regularly and systematically abused, particularly if they are of Afro-Caribbean origin. We all know that the regime in the former Soviet Union was also notorious for declaring dissidents insane and then maltreating them. However, to my knowledge, Nazi Germany was unique in attempting to exterminate the chronically mentally ill and physically disabled in the interests of economy and racial fitness.

PART ONE

SAVING MONEY, SPENDING LIVES

CHAPTER 1

WINTER LANDSCAPES: PSYCHIATRIC REFORM AND RETRENCHMENT DURING THE WEIMAR REPUBLIC

DURING THE First World War, 140,234 people died in German psychiatric asylums.[1] Assuming an average peacetime mortality rate of 5.5% per annum, this means that 71,787 people died as a result of hunger, disease or neglect: about 30% of the entire pre-war asylum population.[2] Psychiatrists watched and recorded mortality rates, weight loss and the progress of epidemic diseases, impotent in the face of governmentally decreed wartime rationing. In the asylums of Saxony alone, 6,112 people died between 1914 and 1918, compared with 1,784 between 1911 and 1914. At the Saxon asylum of Colditz, to put these statistics in humanly comprehensible terms, this meant that 560 people died during the four years of war, compared with a pre-war peacetime average of twenty-two deaths per annum.[3] At Emmendingen near Freiburg, the average annual mortality rate between 1913 and 1915 was ninety-five per year. In 1916 this rose to 162, a year later to 285 as tuberculosis decimated the asylum population.[4] Overcrowding engendered communicable diseases; patients who regularly fouled themselves were left lying on sawdusted floors.[5] Diet was poor, indigestible, and normally devoid of cereals, meat or fats. By definition, asylum inmates had no opportunities to augment rations through hoarding or purchases on the black market.[6] At Berlin-Buch, the calorific value of the patients' daily diet fell from 2,695 calories in July 1914 to 1,987 calories in January 1918. Whereas some 302 patients had passed away in the course of 1913, by 1917 the number had climbed to 762.[7] In his opening address to the annual conference of the German Psychiatric Association in May 1920, the chairman, Karl Bonhoeffer, perceived a shift in the moral climate:

It could almost seem as if we have witnessed a change in the concept of humanity. I simply mean that we were forced by the terrible exigencies of war to ascribe a different value to the life of the individual than was the case before, and that in the years of starvation during the war we had to get used to watching our patients die of malnutrition in vast numbers, almost approving of this, in the knowledge that perhaps the healthy could be kept alive through these sacrifices. But in emphasising the right of the healthy to stay alive, which is an inevitable result of periods of necessity, there is also a danger of going too far: a danger that the self-sacrificing subordination of the strong to the needs of the helpless and ill, which lies at the heart of any true concern for the sick, will give ground to the demand of the healthy to live.[8]

Bonhoeffer was and remains a controversial figure, and this passage from his address is open to several interpretations. Around the turn of the century he conducted dubious degenerationist studies concerning beggars and tramps, and went on in the mid 1930s to give lecture courses to those officially charged with implementing the compulsory sterilisation policies introduced by the National Socialists.[9] What were these 'changes in the concept of humanity' to which Bonhoeffer was alluding?

Until the end of the nineteenth century, the term 'euthanasia' retained its original, classical, meaning of a 'fine' or 'gentle' death, as exemplified by Suetonius' account of the death of Augustus. In the early seventeenth century, Francis Bacon, who was responsible for the Latin transcription of the word, significantly modified the concept by according doctors the exclusive right to alleviate the suffering of the dying.[10] This did not extend to actively or passively terminating a person's life. As one German medical dissertation crisply had it: *Mortem accelerare medico non licet*.[11] Several nineteenth-century German commentators were aware of the inflationary potentialities – what moral philosophers would nowadays call the slippery slope argument – inherent in extending the doctor's powers to include euthanasia.[12] To take one example from among many, in 1806 the distinguished Berlin physician Christoph Wilhelm Hufeland wrote:

[the doctor] should and must do nothing other than maintaining life; it is not up to him whether that life is happy or unhappy, worthwhile or not, and should he incorporate these perspectives into his trade the consequences would be unforeseeable and the doctor could well become the most dangerous person in the state; if this line is crossed once, with the doctor believing he is entitled to decide upon the necessity of a life, then it only requires a logical progression for him to apply the criteria of worth and, therefore unworth, in other instances.[13]

In the 1890s this received view on euthanasia was drastically modified by the polemicist Adolf Jost to include both 'the right to die', i.e. voluntary euthanasia, and the concept of negative human worth, i.e. not only the life-negating suffering of a dying person, but also the negative burden placed upon relatives or the community by the incurably ill and mentally defective. Jost believed that the latter could be killed regardless of the fact that they were sometimes not in a position to articulate their wishes. Other writers, such as Wilutsky, who introduced the unfavourable comparison between prolonged human suffering and how humans dispose of dying animals which recurs several times in subsequent debates, also erased the distinction between voluntary euthanasia and the involuntary killing of what he and others regarded as 'life unworthy of life' (*vita non jam vitalis*). Considerable authority was given to these ideas by the zoologist and populariser of Darwin, Ernst Haeckel, who fused the notion of killing as an act of mercy with the crudely materialistic argument that this would save a great deal of public and private money.[14] An enthusiastic exponent of the idea that one could steer the process of natural selection, Haeckel wrote approvingly of what he alleged to be the ancient Spartan practice of selective infanticide.[15] On the eve of the First World War, the official organ of Haeckel's Monist League became the forum for a brief but intense debate about 'euthanasia'. In May 1913, *Das monistische Jahrhundert* published an open letter from Roland Gerkan, who at the time was dying from a lung disease which made breathing let alone writing very onerous. As he pointed out, these were no longer merely matters of academic contemplation for him. Gerkan's choice of forum for his draft euthanasia law was no accident, for by 'destroying' the consolations of an afterlife, the Monist natural philosophy had removed any religious justifications for suffering in the present: 'Why, instead of permitting us to die gently today, do you demand that we embark upon the long martyr's road, whose final goal is certainly the same death which you deny us today?'[16]

Gerkan's essential predicament was that while he wasted away (aware that behind the blandly valedictory 'following a long, serious illness he gently went to sleep' would be the reality of his choking to death), a few feet away stood a pharmacy, where for a few pfennigs he could have the means to final 'peace and salvation': 'But no, that is not for me: I am not a domestic animal! I am a human being and must endure to the end because that is the way things are. Doctors and judges do not allow themselves to be bribed.'[17]

Gerkan outlined a draft law sanctioning euthanasia:

§1 Whoever is incurably ill has the right to assisted death (euthanasia).

§2 The right to assisted death will be established by the patient's petition to the relevant judicial authorities.

§3 On the basis of the petition, the court will instigate an examination of the patient by the court physician in association with two qualified specialists. Further doctors can be involved in the examination at the request of the patient. This examination must take place no later than one week after the submission of the petition.

§4 The record of the examination must show whether the examining doctors were scientifically convinced that the illness was more likely to follow a terminal course than that the patient would recover permanent ability to work.

§5 If the examination finds that a terminal outcome is the most probable one, then the court should accord the patient the right to die. In contrary cases, the patient's request will be firmly denied.

§6 Whosoever painlessly kills the patient as a result of the latter's express and unambiguous request is not to be punished, provided that the patient has been accorded the right to die under clause 5 of the law, or if posthumous examination reveals that he was incurably ill.

§7 Whosoever kills the patient without his express and unambiguous request will be punished with hard labour.

§8 Clauses 1 to 7 are equally applicable to the elderly and crippled.[18]

Within a week of despatching his draft law, Gerkan was dead.[19]

The ensuing debate was not merely about the desirability of euthanasia, but also concerned what the League's chairman, the Nobel-Prize-winning chemist Wilhelm Ostwald called the ongoing project of 'codifying a secular ethics':[20] in itself a perfectly respectable project. The most vehement case in the Monist debate about Gerkan's draft law was put by Wilhelm Börner. Most obviously, Börner drew attention to the indeterminate, and hence inflationary scope of Gerkan's proposals, and to the subjectivity of pain. People suffering from colic, neuralgia or gallstones might be in extreme pain, but one would hardly comfortably accord them the right to die on this basis. There were also problems with Gerkan's stress on probable outcomes, for the course of an illness could not be predicted apodictically. Carefully distancing himself from Christianity's insistence upon bearing one's cross, Börner took Socrates and Giordano Bruno as examples of a 'secularised' and heroic form of suffering, arguing that a Monist ethic towards caring for the sick would seek to fan the 'little Promethean flame' residing in all of us. Although Gerkan's proposed law was fundamentally wrongheaded, nonetheless Börner generously conceded that the exertions of drafting it certainly distinguished Gerkan himself as a prototypical Monist hero.[21]

Wilhelm Ostwald, who supported Gerkan, attempted systematically to refute Börner's arguments. Specifically, he claimed that 'in all circumstances suffering represents a restriction upon, and diminution of, the individual and capacity to perform in society of the person suffering'.[22] Moreover, Galileo was a better model than Giordano Bruno, since the survival of his 'heretical' teachings was more important to human society than Bruno's gesture of refusing to recognise the Church's formal authority. In addition to these as yet rather academic concerns, other commentators also drew attention to the inflationary and radicalising potential inherent in Gerkan's proposals. The Bielefeld judge Alfred Bozi noted that nothing stood in the way of extending Gerkan's law to encompass people who could not express their wishes, which meant incurable mental patients who 'pass their lives without profit to the community'. This would mean the revival of older collectivist legal notions whereby the interests of the majority could override those of the individual. This would result in a form of *Staatsabsolutismus*, for which, he rather complacently claimed, 'there is no foundation today'.[23] The doctor M. Beer concurred in this slippery slope argument, saying:

I also believe that this would the first step, but whether it would be the last appears to me to be very doubtful ... Once respect for the sanctity of human life has been diminished by introducing voluntary mercy killing for the mentally-healthy incurably ill, and involuntary killing for the mentally ill, who is going to ensure that matters stop there?[24]

Although in many respects it simply developed the arguments used by Jost, by far the most influential contribution to the debate on euthanasia was a tract published in 1920 and entitled 'Permission for the Destruction of Life Unworthy of Life', by Karl Binding (1841–1920) and Alfred Hoche (1856–1944). The subject was no longer merely a matter of academic contemplation; millions of people had died in the recent war, and hard choices about resources had been made. The fact that one of those choices involved the mass starvation of mental patients not only went unmentioned, but was consciously denied. It is difficult to decide whether the tract was prescriptive or an uneasy and evasive ethical rationalisation of what had already taken place. Building, at least in Binding's case, upon a series of unimpeachably liberal premises, the tract systematically rehearsed a series of illiberal and crudely materialistic arguments in favour of involuntary euthanasia. Binding was the senior partner, although he did not actually live to see the fruits of his cogitations beyond proof stage. One of Germany's leading specialists in constitutional and criminal jurisprudence, Binding had retired to Freiburg after distinguished appointments at the universities of Heidelberg, Freiburg, Strassburg and Leipzig.[25] His positivistic theory of legal norms based on social requirements and historical precedents accorded the state paramount rights, overriding the claims of individuals or morality. Alfred Hoche was a more mediocre figure, a professor of psychiatry at Freiburg, better known for his sharp critical interventions and stylistic elegance than for the scientific import of his neuropathological studies of how electricity was conducted by the spinal cords of people who had been decapitated.[26]

He lost his only son at Langemark and wrote rather bad poetry about the experience of grief.[27] He was clearly a difficult character, and a number of his obituarists took the opportunity to speak ill of the dead.[28] Because of his marriage to a Jew, he took early retirement from his post at Freiburg when the National Socialists came to power. Ironically, he was privately critical of the National Socialist eugenic laws, pointing out that they would have precluded the birth of (*inter aliis*) Goethe, Schopenhauer and Beethoven; and he opposed the 'euthanasia' programme, after it claimed one of his relatives, even though much of its rationale derived from his own writings.[29]

Binding's starting point was the idea that every individual had sovereign

Plate 1. Karl Binding and Alfred Hoche. The joint authors of the influential tract 'Permission for the Destruction of Life Unworthy of Life' which was first published in 1920.

powers to dispose of his or her own life as he or she saw fit; specifically, to commit suicide.[30] The only argument he could muster against the legality of suicide was the loss to society of potentially valuable members.[31] Legal problems inevitably multiplied when people tried to assign this sovereign right to third parties in the case of assisted suicide or voluntary euthanasia. He had no problems with euthanasia in its 'pure' form, regarding it as an 'act of healing' for the doctor to use artificial means to bring about a person's death, if it spared that person protracted suffering. Only a 'pedant' would regard this as curtailing a person's life in any meaningful sense; rather it was merely a question of substituting a painless, shorter-term death for longer terminal suffering.[32] Since the person dying was often unconscious, Binding apparently regarded questions of consent as being academic and marginal. Pointing to others (principally Adolf Jost) active in rolling back the state's monopolistic and limited control of killing (i.e. war and capital punishment), Binding finally broached the question which transparently most exercised him: 'Is there human life which has so far forfeited the character of something entitled to enjoy the protection of the law, that its prolongation represents a perpetual loss of value, both for its bearer and for society as a whole?'[33] He invited the reader to compare battlefields littered with the corpses of young soldiers, or a mine after a terrible accident, with the profligate care allegedly currently expended upon 'idiots' in institutions, described here as 'not merely worthless, but actually existences of negative value'.[34] There could be no doubt that some lives were a 'burden' upon state and society as well as to the individuals themselves. Should one protect such life or license its destruction?

Temporarily recovering his liberal respect for the rights of individuals, Binding introduced the rather feeble caveat that such measures would have to be consensual, or would be prohibited in the case of feebleminded persons who appeared to enjoy their lives.[35] Three groups of people would be affected by the new legal measures he was proposing. First, terminally ill or mortally wounded individuals who unequivocally expressed the wish to accelerate the act of dying. Hopelessness would augment the more customary criterion of unendurable pain. Secondly, 'incurable idiots' – for there was little concern with precise categories, regardless of whether the idiocy was congenital or of relatively recent provenance. Since these people allegedly had no will to live, killing them could not be regarded as an infringement of their will. 'Their life is absolutely pointless, but they do not regard it as being unbearable. They are a terrible, heavy burden upon their relatives and society as a whole. Their death would not create even the smallest gap – except perhaps in the feelings of their mothers or loyal nurses.' They were a 'travesty of real human beings, occasioning disgust in anyone who encounters them'. In more heroic times, the state would have had no qualms in doing away with them.[36] In a footnote, Binding actually claims that death would spare idiots the humiliation of 'having to run the gauntlet of other people's cruel jokes and obloquy'.[37] The third and final group consisted of mentally healthy people who, having been rendered unconscious through accident of battle, would be appalled to see their own condition in the event of their regaining consciousness. Others should simply anticipate their wishes for them, by the dubious method of projecting what their own rational response to such a condition might be. Who were these 'others', and indeed, how did Binding view the practicalities of extending the range of permissible killing? Proceedings were to be instigated either by the person concerned, or his or her relatives or doctor. A state authority would then determine whether that person was dying or incurably mentally ill. In the first case this body – which was to consist of a doctor, a lawyer and a psychiatrist under a non-voting chairman – would also ascertain whether the person was articulating a genuine and sustained wish or giving voice to temporary despair. This panel would then recommend that nothing stood in the way of killing the supplicant; the act of killing would be done by a doctor with the aid of powerful drugs. The 'permitting committee' would be obliged to keep detailed records.[38] The possibility of error was brushed aside with the remark: 'what is good and reasonable must happen despite every risk of error ... humanity loses so many of its members on account of error, that one more or less hardly counts in the balance'.[39]

Hoche, arguing from decades of practical experience – presumably other than with the spinal columns of executed criminals – began his 'medical comments' by highlighting the virtual absence of an accessible body of work on medical ethics which could constitute a 'code of practice'. Instruction in medical ethics was *ad hoc* and informal, a matter of gleaning pearls of wisdom from one's superiors during the long medical apprenticeship. There were inevitably exceptions to the Hippocratic oath, of which the most obvious was abortion when the mother's survival was at stake. Everything was relative, including codes of medical ethics 'which are not to be regarded as something which remains the same for eternity'.[40]

Like his colleague, Hoche turned quickly to the subject of the incurably mentally ill. Hoche distinguished between those whose mental defects were congenital and those who acquired them later in life. The former resembled a scattering of stones which had never been shaped by a creative hand; the latter the rubble of a building that had suddenly collapsed. The first group had no emotional ties either with their surroundings or with others; the second group could exert a very considerable emotional purchase upon other people. 'Full idiots' represented a considerable burden for the community, their relatives and the state. They were 'mentally dead', without human personality or self-consciousness, 'on an intellectual

level which we only encounter way down in the animal kingdom'.[41] Pity
was a totally misplaced emotion in these cases, since 'where there was no
suffering, there can also be no pity' (*wo kein Leiden ist, ist auch kein
mit-Leiden*).

He next moved swiftly from questions of personality to the question of
cost and numbers. These vulgar economistic arguments should not be
confused with philosophical utilitarianism. Hoche claimed to have contacted every German asylum in order to establish an average annual cost of
1,300RMS for the care of each idiot. Although he did not bother to do the
arithmetic, Hoche claimed that 20–30 idiots with an average life
expectancy of fifty represented 'a massive capital in the form of foodstuffs,
clothing and heating, which is being subtracted from the national product
for entirely unproductive purposes'.[42] This was before one started calcu-
lating such indirect costs as wages and salaries for the personnel in
asylums, interest payments in the case of private establishments, and so on.
The question of 'ballast existences' had become acute in these times of
national crisis. The nation resembled a difficult expedition, in which there
was no room for 'half- quarter- or eighth forces'.

In a key passage, Hoche claimed that people had allegedly ceased to
think of the state in organic terms, with the corollary that any single part of
the 'body' that had become either useless or harmful ought to be removed.
It would take time for these new ethical perspectives to become general
currency. Only a few exceptional individuals were at present capable of
thinking in those terms. The sort of sentiments which would have to
become general were exemplified by the examples of the explorer Greely,
who shot a fellow member of his expedition in the back of the head because
by surreptitiously taking more than his fair share of food, he was growing
stronger than the rest; or Scott, who watched stoically as one member too
many of his expedition walked out of a tent to a death in the snow in the
interests of his fellows.[43] These examples of extreme choices in situations
in which the explorers had entered voluntarily were supposed to sanction
throwing overboard dead 'ballast' from the Ship of Fools. Speaking very
much *de haut en bas*, Hoche claimed that only a layman would be concerned
about the potential for serious error of the sort that can occur in capital
cases. Doctors would be in no doubt that there was 'one hundred per cent
certainty in selection'. He concluded with Goethe's metaphor of civili-
sation ascending in the manner of steadily ascending spirals. Just as the
present time condemned as barbaric earlier eras in which killing defective
infants was allegedly customary, so future epochs would regard the
'over-exaggerated notions of humanity and over-estimation of the value of
existence' in the present as their own barbaric past.[44] Rather like critics of
the 'rational-totalitarian' aspiration represented by modern prisons, Hoche
evidently believed the progression lay in regression to simpler times.

The ensuing intense debate involving doctors, lawyers and theologians continued fitfully throughout the 1920s. A few of the main positions will be rehearsed here. Commenting upon the tract, the Tübingen psychiatrist Robert Gaupp made explicit connections between the carnage of the First World War, the 'economic prison' Germany had become in the wake of Versailles, and the need for commensurate adjustments to normative ethical values. As an asylum psychiatrist during the terrible winter of 1916–1917, Gaupp had often wondered why he was bothering to provision his patients when people 'of full value' were starving to death in the world outside. His only criticism of the authors was that they had been timid in directly confronting their Christian critics.[45] Another favourable response to Binding and Hoche came from the Berlin judge Karl Klee, who in a lecture to the Society for Forensic Medicine in November 1920 recommended augmenting capital punishment, which was controversial because of its undercurrents of satisfying a lust for revenge, with the elimination of all 'parasitic existences' in the interests of the collective.[46] He advocated a *via media* between the barbaric customs of antiquity or contemporary primitive peoples and the 'abstract-Christian extreme' embodied in the doctrine of the sanctity of human life.[47]

Other commentators or authors of theses tried to give the practical proposals of Binding and Hoche greater definition. If some writers (for example, F. Pelckmann) tried to give equal consideration to voluntary euthanasia and the 'destruction of life unworthy of life', the Liegnitz councillor Borchardt's draft legislation focussed exclusively upon the latter issue. Apart from questions of technical convenience, the reason for this lay in the disproportionate costs occasioned by 'incurable idiots'. With considerable pedantry, and no greater display of statistical rigour than Hoche, Borchardt calculated that 15,000 'incurable idiots' cost about 115 million marks in upkeep. Rather oddly, he suggested that these sums could be better expended upon old people's homes, institutions for cripples, schools and orphanages. His modifications to Binding and Hoche's proposals included altering and extending the composition of the 'permitting committees'; attaching them to the higher courts located in university towns; introducing majority as opposed to absolute voting; and last but not least, permitting the welfare services to initiate 'euthanasia' proceedings, since they would be more cost-conscious and less emotionally involved than a person's nearest relatives.[48]

Gerhard Hoffmann (alias Ernst Mann), used a fictional form for his eugenic dystopias in which roving commissions of doctors, armed with police powers and abetted by denunciation, would select the unfit, including those suffering from organic diseases such as cancer or tuberculosis, to be eliminated. In 1922 he sent the following cryptic demands to the Reichstag: '1. Extermination of the mentally ill. 2. Mercy killing for the terminally ill. 3. Mercy killing for the exhausted. 4. The killing of crippled and incurably ill children.'[49] In his writings, 'euthanasia' was at once an act of 'mercy', a means of eugenic prophylaxis, and a chance to disburden the economy. In the 1920s this was an aberrant and extreme view; a decade later it became official policy.

Critics of Binding and Hoche, and by extension of Borchardt or Mann, were numerous and vocal. Some clearly despised the 'utilitarian shop-keeper' mentality which appeared to inform the tract,[50] although this was a little unjust to philosophical utilitarians. Others worried about the inflationary, slippery-slope potentialities latent in the whole enterprise. A few had doubts regarding the inherent arbitrariness and perniciousness of value judgements regarding the quality of human life. The Berlin–Buch psychiatrist Waschkuhn, who was concerned with the elasticity of notions of incurability, made ironic reference to the two authors marching out under the banner of 'a profound love of humanity' in order to eliminate a defenceless army of mental patients.[51] Others pointed more pragmatically to the sheer terror (and higher incidence of persecution mania) which was bound to accompany quite routine committals to asylums.[52]

The most sustained refutation of the arguments advanced by Binding and Hoche, as well as Borchardt and Mann, was contained in a book published in 1925 entitled 'The Problem of Curtailment of Life Unworthy of Life' by Ewald Meltzer, the director of the Katharinenhof asylum at Grosshennersdorf in Saxony. Written in an accessible and attractive style, the book is as much a testament to the wide literary, philosophical and scientific culture of the German bourgeoisie as it is a humane and important contribution to the debate on euthanasia. He was the sort of man who provokes the question '*ubi sunt?*'

Meltzer evidently regarded the arguments of Binding and Hoche as a challenge to everything he stood for.

In addition to condemning the inflationary and totalitarian potentialities in Mann's proposals, Meltzer hotly disputed the claim that people with mental handicaps had lost the last vestiges of human personality, stressing instead their capacity and will to enjoy life.[53] Most of his criticisms took the form of a defence against the charge that the sort of work he and others did was pointless and a waste of national resources. He disputed the heroic qualities which Binding and Hoche claimed for their new morality, regarding it 'as far more heroic to accept these beings to the best of one's abilities, to bring sunshine into their lives, and therewith to serve human-ity' than to kill them for utilitarian reasons.[54] Checking his Plutarch, Meltzer dismissed the alleged Spartan practice of killing defective infants as an historical aberration, simultaneously questioning its efficacy as an artificial means of selection.[55] A wide variety of sources, including Carlyle, Dostoevsky, Hellenbach, Kant, Kropotkin, Novicow and Rousseau, was arrayed to demonstrate that altruism was humanity's distinguishing feature, and that therefore the 'problem' discussed by Binding and Hoche 'could not be dealt with in a few lines'.[56] Asylums for handicapped people were not only valuable centres of scientific research, but also tangible manifestations of Christian charity.[57] Regardless of any superficial feelings of revulsion, visitors to asylums invariably took away vivid impressions of practical manifestations of human altruism.[58] Explicitly endorsing Oswald Bumke's claim that all manifestations of 'degeneration' were of social origin, Meltzer made a passionate attack upon the materialism of the times, suggesting that industrialists might re-direct their ill-gotten gains into the upkeep of asylums filled with the children of their own underpaid workforce. Many social problems could be resolved by a greater sense of community, wealth taxes, decent wages and a fair distribution of labour.[59]

Prompted by the publication of Binding and Hoche's tract, Meltzer began to ask the parents of his mentally handicapped charges in the Katharinenhof about their attitudes towards these questions. He was struck by the fact that powerful emotional bonds with the children were apparently not incompatible with a 'positive' attitude towards killing them. Naively assuming that any future legislation in this field would automatically hinge upon parental consent, Meltzer decided to carry out a formal survey of opinion among his asylum's parental constituency.[60] The questions he asked either by letter or in face-to-face encounters with visiting fathers were:

1   Would you agree to the painless curtailment of the life of your child if experts had established that it was suffering from incurable idiocy?
2   Would you grant your consent only in the event that you were no longer in a position to care for your child, for example in the case of your own demise?
3   Would you grant your consent only if your child was suffering from severe physical or mental pain?
4   What does your wife think about questions 1 to 3?

Significantly, he felt it necessary to append a footnote saying: 'Your child is perfectly well and happy. Should these questions be the cause of some concern to you regarding your child's life, then we would like to reassure you that the children in our care will continue to receive the same conscientious degree of attention that they have received in the past.'[61]

That this was not very reassuring can be seen from the fact that one child was actually removed from the asylum and in two further cases, influential third parties were induced to contact the asylum to establish that nothing untoward was taking place in connection with Meltzer's survey.[62]

Aware that one can use statistics to prove whatever one will, Meltzer began by questioning the typicality of his sample, pointing to the general economic and political uncertainties of the time and problems local to an industrialised and densely populated region like Saxony. However, responses to the poll were virtually unrelated to political affiliation, except in the case of supporters of the Roman Catholic Centre Party, who were a minority in predominantly Protestant Saxony. The poll also reflected an intense period in the on-going debate about euthanasia, and by the time the book was actually published, Meltzer suggested, opinions might have become quite otherwise.[63] Nonetheless, the results of the poll evidently came as a surprise to the author. Of the 200 people polled, 162 responded to the questions. Of these, 119 (or 73%) said 'yes' to all the questions and 43 (or 27%) said 'no'.[64] The reasons for 'yes' votes included a desire to offload the burden of a handicapped child, with many of them wishing this to be done without their knowledge. Some parents actually wanted to be deliberately deceived, by, for example, being told that their child had died of 'x-manner of illness', i.e. in line with the practice later used in the National Socialist 'euthanasia' programme.[65]

Meltzer reproduced two letters to illustrate the thinking of those who had voted 'yes'. The first was from an industrial white-collar worker with feebleminded twins, who claimed that these questions were being debated among the people to a greater degree than was imagined by experts. He reported almost general approbation towards the idea of changing the law, and 'was of the opinion that death would be an act of kindness for all these children'.[66] A miner and his wife were also strongly in favour of extending to incurably ill humans what anyone would do for a sick animal. The 'mentally dead' were 'a burden for the state, society and for their own relatives'.[67] They claimed that only those who had direct personal experience of the difficulties of bringing up a handicapped child were entitled to air their views on the subject. Only 20 of the 43 who polled 'no' rejected the propositions contained in all four questions. For example, ten respondents approved killing their children in the eventuality of their own deaths. Ironically enough, one set of parents would only contemplate having their child killed in the eventuality of its transfer to another asylum.[68] Most of those who responded negatively to the question did so either because of powerful emotional bonds with their child, or from ethical or religious convictions. Only a few wanted to keep the child alive for the base motive of wishing to continue drawing the benefits which accrued to this category of parent.

Meltzer himself was not an unqualified supporter of the rights of mentally handicapped people. His own views were neither fundamentalist nor unambiguous. In 1934, he publicly admitted that, like the Saxon 'apostle of sterilisation', Boeters, he had instigated sterilisations at a time when they were illegal. On other occasions he wrote that it would be wrong for a doctor to interfere in cases where a mentally handicapped person became fatally ill. In an address to an Inner Mission conference on 'racial hygiene' in 1937, Meltzer acknowledged that there were conditions of national emergency when, because of food shortages or the need for bedspace for military casualties, 'the patient too must pay his dues to the Fatherland' through some form of 'mercy killing'.[69] Twenty-five of the 250 handicapped people in the Katherinenhof survived the 'euthanasia' programme.[70]

Professional medical and psychiatric discussions of these issues resulted in majorities against sanctioning both voluntary euthanasia and the destruction of 'life unworthy of life'. The legalisation of euthanasia was discussed and rejected at the 1921 Karlsruhe Ärztetag (medical convention).[71] In the summer of 1922, the subject occupied one of the sessions of the Dresden conference of the Society for Forensic Psychiatry. Moving the motion 'should doctors kill?', Hans Haenel argued that the sums expended upon 'idiots' could be better used to prevent tuberculosis in childhood. Pity was misplaced where there was no subjective sense of suffering.[72] He was opposed by Ganser, who employed the slippery slope argument, while highlighting the danger to public morality should the killing of mental patients be permitted. Other speakers, the majority of whom rejected the motion, drew attention to the terms of the Hippocratic Oath, or such factors as the possible brutalisation and corruption of the nursing staff in asylums in the event of such measures being adopted.[73]

Apart from the lawyers and doctors whom we have been considering, these weighty issues inevitably involved that section of opinion professionally concerned not only with upholding the doctrine of the sanctity of human life, but also with running ramified networks of charitable institutions. Both major churches had umbrella organisations responsible for representing (and to some extent controlling) an upsurge in lay piety and concern for the 'social question', whose tangible manifestations were a host of lay nursing fraternities, youth associations and institutions for the disadvantaged. The controlling bodies were respectively the Protestant Central Committee for the Inner Mission of the German Protestant Church, and the Roman Catholic Caritas Association for Catholic Germany.[74] Opinions of the work of Binding and Hoche among professional theologians and heads of ecclesiastically administered asylums were not as straightforward as one might imagine. Certainly, some theologians, such as Martin Ulbrich, director of the asylum at Magdeburg-Cracau, took the view that the ideas of Binding and Hoche were symptoms of a general moral collapse into unalloyed egotism.[75] It was up to God and not mankind to stop the clock of lives which God alone had started.

We are indebted once again to Ewald Meltzer for the most comprehensive survey of theological opinion, since he took it upon himself to contact several Protestant thinkers to gauge opinion on these questions. Some took the position that the absence of a spiritual life constituted an absence of personality, or in other words, that the mentally defective were merely a *massa carnis*. Professor Karl Weidel of Magdeburg ventured somewhat further by comparing care for mentally handicapped children with the practice of certain ancient desert ascetics who deliberately planted and watered dead twigs in order to reaffirm daily the futility of all terrestrial endeavour.[76] Rejecting the fundamental pessimism that informed Binding and Hoche, Weidel suggested that more attention be paid to 'positive' eugenic measures, including improved maternity care, child benefits in the form of tax concessions, sterilisation of the hereditarily ill, and stringent control of marriage. The religious pedagogue Karl Ernst Thrandorf, whom Meltzer unhelpfully described as a disciple of the Leibniz-Hebart school of pluralistic realism(!), essentially tried to fuse Weidel's insistence on the presence or absence of spiritual life with neuropathological criteria. Defective brains ruled out spiritual awareness.[77] Those theologians who rejected the ideas of Binding and Hoche tended either to point to the prospect of general moral brutalisation, or to stress that the handicapped had been put here by God to remind us of the consequences of sin.[78] None of them seemed to be capable of challenging the stereotypical images of the mentally handicapped employed by Binding and Hoche; on the contrary, many either resorted to the same language or used the biblical imagery of 'not casting pearls before swine' (read 'idiots') to convey the same sentiment.[79]

After a half century or so of institutional expansion, in which the number of public asylums rose from ninety-three in 1877 to 226 in 1913, psychiatrists were confronted by sudden contraction. Over a hundred private asylums were forced to close. Others were turned over to other uses, becoming convalescent homes, hostels for refugees, or tubercular sanatoria. The number of patients treated, which had risen from 47,228 in 1880 to 239,583 in 1913, fell sharply to 172,870 in 1919.[80] Entire buildings stood empty, or were occupied by nursing staff rather than patients, a nursing staff moreover which had multiplied because of the statutory eight-hour day.[81] Expenditure upon asylums was cut in favour of areas of medicine where a cure could be anticipated or it was possible to return the patient rapidly to the labour process. Conditions within the asylums were dire. Before the war, patients were given meat, sometimes twice a day, or at least cheese or sausage. By 1922 meat had become a luxury for Sundays only. Before the war, patients were given five hundred grammes of bread a day; by 1922 they were fortunate to get half that amount of bread made from adulterated flour. There were no potatoes to make up the calorific deficit. The food issue was creating an atmosphere among the patients like the oppressively sultry weather before a thunderstorm. Bedding and clothing were not being renewed, and hygiene was sacrificed to the need to economise on heating and soap. Expenditure on drugs, instruments, medical periodicals and books had all been cut back. Essential building work was being postponed; unpainted woodwork rotted, and the floors cried out for oil and wax. Antiquated and inefficient heating or kitchen equipment was being constantly repaired rather than replaced.[82]

A decaying physical fabric was accompanied by a public climate critical of psychiatry in general. A vociferous anti-psychiatric lobby had developed in the 1880s, including both aggrieved former psychiatric patients and such public figures as court chaplain Adolf Stöcker: a lobby essentially concerned with medicalised curtailments of civil liberties. On 9 July 1892 the conservative newspaper *Kreuzzeitung* thundered 'in no other area of our legal existence is such latitude accorded to error, arbitrariness or evil intent as in declarations of insanity'. A number of associations were formed to promote reform of mental health laws. The First World War, with psychiatrists actively asserting their relevance by systematically abusing victims of shell-shock, and the critical climate of the 1918–1919 revolution, gave added impetus to demands for reform. German psychiatrists were denounced as 'venal whores' who would willingly incarcerate anyone the state regarded as a nuisance. In August 1919, the League for Reform of the Mental Health Laws presented the government with a list of demands, including a consolidated national mental health law, a tightening of grounds for committal to an asylum, more stringent penalties for false confinement or maltreatment, the abolition of forensic refereeing, the closure of private institutions, and the creation of an effective institutional inspectorate.[83] In so far as members of the soldiers' and workers' councils did not simply enjoin patients to leave the asylums, there was serious discussion of enhancing patients' rights and giving them the vote, as well as a new-found militancy among the asylums' medical and nursing personnel.

Establishment psychiatrists, notably Emil Kraepelin, responded by propounding a psychiatric version of the 'stab-in-the-back legend'. Thus the exhausted, hysterical and suggestible masses were seen as a prey for psychopathic or sexually deviant revolutionary leaders such as the Munich Räterepublik revolutionaries E. Mühsam and Robert Eglhofer, described as respectively 'a fanatic psychopath' and 'an anti-social psychopath'; or the 'Red Flag' reporter Hilde Kramer, summed up by the psychiatrist Helenefriderike Stelzner as 'a two-metre-tall dyke with short cropped hair'.[84]

Psychiatrists of a more reflective, if not quite 'progressive', persuasion, notably Gustav Kolb of Erlangen (1870–1938), tried to counteract popular confusion of asylums with prisons by recommending the expansion of outpatient provision to establish a sort of dialogue between asylum and wider community. Doctors would come to be seen as 'friends and helpers' rather than 'dungeon keepers'. Special courts, including laymen and a token woman, would be established to protect the interests of the insane and to watch over the asylums.[85] There was an element of preventive strike involved here; and Kolb cannot simply be described as an isolated reformer battling against entrenched conservative professional interests. He had himself carried out dubious therapies on wartime 'neurotics', and had participated in the psychiatric evaluation of the Munich revolutionaries.[86] Since his reform proposals effectively gave the lay concern with individual civil rights primacy over the doctors' concern with prognosis, treatment or the degree to which the patient might affect the rights of others, and hence threatened the medical monopoly of madness, they were rejected by his colleagues.[87] They were looked at afresh when public expenditure concerns in the early 1920s threatened to make it harder to put people in asylums. Countering lay demands to restrict hospitalisation to those who menaced public order, the psychiatric profession rapidly discovered the merits of Kolb's notion of ramified outpatient provision. That it was cheap at the price can be demonstrated by the fact that the 'welfare and advice centre' which was established in Munich in 1924 as the societal extension of the asylum at Eglfing-Haar had annual overheads of 2,000RMs at a time when it cost 1,277RMs to keep one patient in the asylum for a year.[88]

Economic imperatives and professional self-interest were both reflected in Hans Roemer's remark that 'In future an impoverished state will be unable to bear the type of mental asylum provision which developed extensively in most of the regions of Germany before the war ... In any case, the general situation confronts the asylum doctor with the task of participating from the start in the drastic simplification of asylum provision, so that this comes about *with* him and in accordance with his expert recommendations, rather than without, or even against, him.'[89] The fact that regional authorities were sometimes taking it upon themselves to establish facilities without psychiatric involvement added to the psychiatric profession's interest in Kolb's proposals.

Outpatient care had been pioneered by Kolb at Erlangen shortly before the First World War.[90] Elsewhere, for example at the asylum of Emmendingen, it had been essayed decades before, principally because of overcrowding in the asylum.[91] At Erlangen, Valentin Faltlhauser assumed full-time responsibility for outpatient care in 1922, which meant, *inter alia*, supervising two full-time community mental nurses situated in the industrial towns of Nuremberg and Fürth. Families applied to have their relatives released into outpatient care, usually because of the stigma attached to having a relative in an asylum. Precise checks were made on the family's circumstances, and then the patient was released for a three-month probationary period. Other 'mentally abnormal' persons living freely in the community were referred to the outpatient services by the authorities. By 1922, Faltlhauser was dealing with 682 outpatients, of whom the largest groups were manic depressives (24.7%); schizophrenics (19.2%); and 'psychopaths' (25%).[92] Outpatient provision essentially consisted of a form of psychiatric social work which filled the gap between asylum and society. It relied upon the cooperation of the local authorities for premises and publicity, and of local employers who agreed to provide former patients with employment. Females were usually employed as domestics; males by such firms as M.A.N. Schuckert.[93] Given the prevailing popular hostility towards psychiatry, doctors were careful to eschew anything which seemed like compulsion or interference: 'We do not regard it as our task to be spies or guardians, ascertaining when the patient is ready to be readmitted to the asylum; rather we want to be friends of both the patient and his family, who will help him to remain outside the asylum, provided no paramount interests are endangered in the process.'[94] Outpatient work required tact and discretion. In rural Baden, where psychiatrists had to locate former patients in small villages where curtains quickly parted or heads turned in the narrow streets, they went to some lengths to avoid being conspicuous: by, for example, refraining from asking for directions or by parking their vehicles at some distance from the person's residence. They did their best to overcome what were often the 'medieval' notions of mental illness held by the patient's relatives, and tried to humanise the image of psychiatric asylums.[95]

It has often been said that Weimar's expanding health and welfare apparatus was Janus-faced: a generalised, and above all, medicalised version of the nineteenth-century's sterner but more limited concern with policing contagious diseases or public morals.[96] This ambivalence is perfectly mirrored in the measures we have been considering. Inevitably, outpatient provision meant an extension of the range of people who came within the purview of psychiatrists, as the latter discovered abnormal psychological conditions in the families of their outpatients.[97] This led them to construct psychiatric genealogies of the sort pioneered by Ernst Rüdin in Munich.[98] In other words, increased psychiatric contact with the milieu of their patients did not result in psychiatrists manning the barricades against socio-economic deprivation (how could it, for, *contra* Foucault, as mere professionals they had little power) but rather in the view that the people in asylums were merely the tip of a societal iceberg. Mental illness was no longer the result of individual organic dysfunctioning, but rather about the dysfunctioning of entire groups of people. Psychiatric counselling in such matters as marriage or reproduction fell on deaf ears, and was bitterly resented. Although doctors like Faltlhauser regarded outpatient care with justifiable pride, contact with the patients' social milieu only seemed to magnify the order of mental illness, making their prophylactic powers seem totally ineffectual.[99]

Psychiatrists who undertook outpatient work were confronted with two major issues which had profound implications for how they thought about mental illness. Firstly, in the course of finding employment or housing for former patients in an often hostile climate, they were forced to consider an entire socio–economic context rather than a sick individual. Since it was a context they were effectively unable to alter, depending as it did on such variables as the business cycle, they withdrew into exclusively medicalised explanations of mental disorder. They might have been able to tell schizophrenics to stop talking or writing nonsense, but – a fact often overlooked by parochial medical historians – they were really rather small change in relation to the major political players who set the nation's economic parameters. Secondly, through their former patients they encountered a new range of 'abnormal people, who despite having been ill for a long time have never been admitted to an asylum'.[100] Given the scale and intractable nature of the problem, the social work side of outpatient care gave way to monitoring and registering: in other words, essentially control functions.[101] Some psychiatrists began to think in more radical prophylactic terms, for (as is often the case when cost is at stake) nature seemed potentially less intractable than nurture.

In 1928 some two hundred psychiatrists and civil servants met at the inaugural conference of the Society for Mental Hygiene which had been founded three years earlier. In a declaration of intent published in the newly founded *Zeitschrift für psychische Hygiene* (which thenceforth appeared as a supplement to the main professional journal, the *Allgemeine Zeitschrift für Psychiatrie*), the Society announced a wide-ranging agenda, which included the introduction of prophylactic eugenic measures to prevent alcoholism, mental illness and criminality in society at large, and the reorganisation of the asylum network to incorporate outpatient facilities. There were also enthusiastic paeans to the Soviet mental and social hygiene movements. In other words, the Society was a sort of arena for rival (and indeed overlapping) reformist approaches to mental illness: approaches which could be authoritarian or libertarian, or (like many types of reform in these areas) an ambivalent synthesis of both ambitions, nowhere more clearly manifest than in the fact that data collected on families through the outpatient services was being systematically relayed to the genealogists.[102]

Between 1924 and 1929 the number of psychiatric patients rose dramatically, from 185,397 to more than 300,000. There was no commensurate increase in bed capacity, since while forty public asylums were reopened, eighteen private establishments were closed. Over the same period, the average length of time people spent in the asylums was cut from 215 days in 1923 to 103 in 1929. This was not achieved by more effective therapy, but rather by simply increasing the 'throughput', i.e. the tempo at which people were released back into the community. However, sheer pressure of numbers meant a steady build-up of longterm patients, with (for example) the percentage of schizophrenics hospitalised at Erlangen rising from 41.9% of the total patient body in 1925 to 55.8% in 1929.[103] Given the existence of powerful economic constraints, which set firm limits to institutional expansion, the only way to prevent the system gradually silting up was both to extend outpatient provision and to adopt forms of therapy which were designed to return the patient to the community as rapidly as possible.

A possible solution to the latter problem was first comprehensively essayed by Hermann Simon (1867–1947), the pragmatic and sympathetic director of the provincial asylum at Gütersloh. In a series of detailed articles, Simon explained how he developed his 'active therapy' – although, being a modest man, he gave due credit to such precursors as the French reformer Pinel, and Koeppe at Altscherbitz.[104] He deliberately refrained from calling his practices a 'system', since the word conjured up precisely the sort of rigidity that his flexible type of therapy was intended to move away from. Simon began by describing the dire conditions which he consciously set out to change:

I shall never forget the images I saw on a visit to a major asylum some years ago: the proximity of a city meant a considerable number of agitated patients, who gathered together in the corresponding ward. Isolation was frowned upon. Even as I and the colleagues who were guiding me came towards the secure ward for disturbed women, we began to hear much noise, loud laughter, squeals and cries. Upon entering the secure ward (which consisted entirely of patients confined to bed!) we were confronted by what looked like a winter landscape in a snowstorm in the entire room: several younger, excited patients were staging a pillow fight, and the pillows had burst. One's visual impressions can easily be imagined, and the auditory ones can easily be augmented: the fight was accompanied with loud cries, laughter, deranged leaping around (the entire company was dressed in night-shirts). Other patients wailed, screamed, and swore from their beds, partly egging on those who were fighting, partly protesting about the noise. The nurses stood about totally impotent. Directly nearby were the therapeutic baths, some of which were occupied. There was another battle going on here, but this time a naval engagement, fought out with showers of water, naturally with the corresponding din of battle. The nurse stood helplessly in the middle, decked out with a long rubber coat and bathcap. The whole thing was not particularly disconcerting, to a certain extent it was even rather comic; and if I had been a small boy, I would probably have wanted to join in the fun.[105]

According to his own account, Simon stumbled upon 'active therapy' almost by accident:

When in 1905 we began to fill the asylums at Warstein which had been built entirely to my specifications, we expected there to be a considerable percentage of patients who would require stationary bed treatment, to which end we had included the normal provision of suitable wards and balneological facilities (i.e. for about 15% of the total patient cohort). As it happened, we took over the large asylum site in a very derelict and unfinished condition, and the initial quota of patients was very small. The effort of trying to finish off the building works, which included considerable earthmoving, the creation of park facilities, pathways etc., from our own resources forced us to coopt more and more of the patients who were either sitting around the wards or lying in bed, which eventually meant ever bolder resort to really dubious, agitated and disturbed elements. The result was surprising, in that soon a noticeably improved atmosphere emerged in the asylum: it became much quieter and more orderly than it had been before, and the normal ugly manifestations of illness gradually receded. Fears that enhanced freedom of movement or the equipping of very dubious cases with all sorts of tools would result in acts of violence or accidents proved unfounded. On the contrary, it was precisely those patients characterised earlier by extreme excitement, or who were prone to acts of violence, who seemed to improve the most; sometimes the symptoms disappeared entirely in the case of those patients who before had been feared the most. Others, who before were always noisy, refractory or inaccessible, became friendly and approachable; the liveliness of previously impassive patients rose, together with the performance of entire work details. Up to my departure from Warstein in 1914, we were gradually able to occupy nine-tenths of our patients on a regular basis, and at the same time the whole asylum became as good as totally calm; by 1910 this had gone so far that (for example) a foreign psychiatrist who had spent two hours being conducted through what had become an asylum for a thousand patients, including the wards for the most difficult cases, finally expressed the wish to go on to see the 'insane asylum', since he had now seen the 'sanatorium'; it was scarcely possible to make clear to him (given the difficulties he had with the language) that he had been viewing the insane asylum for the previous two hours.[106]

Simon's starting point was that treatment of mental illness was akin to the socialisation of a child or – for he was a convinced Darwinian – to the processes whereby animals either adapt to their habitat or perish. The object of the child's training was to repress those instincts which threatened order in the community, while encouraging those capacities and talents which promoted that community's wellbeing. Commencing with the analogy of infants who ceaselessly cried in the night, it had to be made clear to the individual that the community – in this case the sleepless parents – would not tolerate anti-social behaviour: 'fundamentally, all training must be a struggle: a struggle to subordinate the biologically refractory individual being to the necessities of life in the community'.[107] Likewise, psychiatric therapy was a question of making the patient conform to the 'necessities of existence'.[108] 'Active therapy' involved the careful identification of the therapeutic possibilities available to an individual, and the removal of any environmental conditions in the asylum which were likely to impede recovery. This involved a capacity for self-criticism on the part of the staff from the director downwards, and a rapid clampdown on any patient who disturbed the calm of the institution. The justification for Simon's methods was that they appeared to work. Only a small percentage of patients proved beyond the reach of 'active therapy', and at least patients were being prevented from falling any further into 'conditions unworthy of human beings' in line with the usual degenerative course of their illness.[109]

One of the primary components of Simon's essentially pedagogical method was occupational therapy: 'successful activity creates satisfaction, inner and outer calm; inactive loafing around produces bad moods, moroseness, excitability; these in turn lead to frequent conflicts with those around them, to verbal and physical conflicts, and to prolonged exchanges of insults and perorations'.[110] All therapy should be geared to returning the patient to life in the community, by nurturing the residual parts of a formerly healthy being. Life was literally activity; therefore all patients would have to be mobilised into activity too. The activities had to be purposeful; madmen who would be kings could no longer manufacture their own golden crowns.[111] Upon admission they were to be assigned work immediately on an ascending scale of difficulty and individual responsibility. Level one included carrying things or pushing wheelbarrows under close supervision, or simple mechanical activities such as weaving matting. The patient then progressed to the second level, which might include spreading compost on the gardens, housework, or sealing envelopes. The next level consisted of sewing, vegetable peeling, ironing, and so forth; the fourth level, more advanced gardening (planting, work in the greenhouses), mowing, or office work. The final stage was to be equivalent to employment on the outside, with the patient's responsibilities including running errands, answering the telephone, supervising patient work parties, or portering.[112] After their morning rounds, the doctors were to confer with the senior nursing staff to allot the patients to each of these five levels and the corresponding work party. The patients' names were then attached to the relevant section of a wallchart. Private patients from the 'better' classes were encouraged to pursue such hobbies as gardening, music, painting, photography or foreign languages.[113] Satisfactory performance by all groups was to be rewarded with confectionery, tobacco or enhanced freedom of movement under relaxed supervision. The asylum environment was to be characterised by calm and order. Day-to-day dealings with the patients consisted of discouraging any manifestations of insanity. Force was replaced by a sort of aggressive reasonableness, for 'the only weapon which the psychiatrist can really rely upon in all circumstances is his personal superiority, which he must never surrender'.[114]

Sedatives and short spells in isolation rooms were used as the final sanction. The motto was 'observe – think – act'.

This no-nonsense approach meant that when, for example, a female schizophrenic insisted that Simon post a letter consisting of illogical ravings, he would inform her that he was refusing to post it, but that 'she could write another letter about her affairs, if she wrote like a normal woman and not like a mental patient'. Another schizophrenic who could not recall who Simon was, and whose rambling discourse consisted of the words 'Fritz' and 'uncle', was offered a bar of chocolate if she could answer the question 'Annemarie, who am I?'. The answer 'Doctor Simon' came promptly.[115] Even elderly patients whose habitual belching, coughing, or groaning disturbed others were not tolerated as 'poor old dears', but were moved into empty rooms until they had got the message.[116]

In sum, Simon's reforms meant the normalisation of life in the asylum, with enhanced liberties and responsibilities for those who conformed. They necessarily entailed the diminution of the (metaphorical) space left to the mad, and the subordination of individual rights to that of the asylum community. They also introduced capacity to work as an indicator of recovery – or in other words, actual and potential categories of differential human value within the asylum population. When first publicised at the 1924 psychiatric congress in Innsbrück, Simon's reform proposals received a lukewarm reception from meanminded colleagues bent upon proving his lack of originality: 'what was good in it was not new; what was new was no good'. Three years later the response was more favourable, as one psychiatrist remarked: 'there is no doubt that clinical psychiatry – thanks to Simon – is today in the process of thoroughgoing changes. Finally we psychiatrists have once again become what our name implies: psychotherapists.'[117] This was rather over-optimistic. In the process of widespread diffusion, Simon's 'reforms' merely became a form of 'modernisation', i.e. an economically driven quest for enhanced efficiency and rationalisation.

The Depression intensified on-going debates about the ways in which the Weimar Republic's burgeoning welfare state had outstripped national resources. What had once been a means of diffusing acute political conflict now became its object. Conservative critiques of the ways in which indiscriminate welfarism sapped individuals of their sense of responsibility, and of the evils associated with anonymous bureaucratisation and 'professionalisation', were accompanied by a renewed emphasis on collective national interests and prophylactic solutions as the cheaper option.[118] Drastic public expenditure cuts carried out by a succession of *dirigiste* governments afforded enhanced saliency to such negative eugenic measures as sterilisation or 'eugenically targeted' selective benefits.[119] The onset of the Depression also set effective limits to the reforms associated with Kolb and Simon. However, it is important to emphasise that an era of reform was not simply superseded by one of eugenics and 'euthanasia'. What happened was far more complex, namely the gradual fusion of a reformist dynamic, which (as we have seen) had many inherently economistic and selectionist features, with the hitherto relatively marginal movement in favour of radical eugenic solutions. The contrasts are therefore not between black and white, but rather between subtle shades of grey.

General economic calamity meant that the asylums had to admit more and more patients requiring full-time care and attention as their relatives were no longer in a position to look after them.[120] This meant an end to the reformers' dream of a rapid turnover of admissions and discharges, and a reversion to the asylum as custodial institution for the 'incurable'. This was reflected in the official view of asylums, which ignored the efforts of the reformers to make psychiatric institutions approximate to general hospitals:

The activity of the doctors and nursing staff in mental asylums is entirely different from work in a hospital. Since there is no treatment for mental illness, one can scarcely speak of medical activity. The latter merely consists of a certain regulation. Apart from the administration of baths, exposure to rays, massage, sedatives, and occasionally malarial therapy, which are the customary forms of treatment, there is hardly any other form of medical or nursing activity.[121]

The purely custodial function of the asylums was underlined by decrees issued in 1931 and 1932 which reaffirmed the exclusive right of the police to commit people to asylums in the interests of public safety.[122] Expenditure cuts were recorded from virtually every region. In Brandenburg all budgetary headings excepting drugs were cut by 20%; in Upper Silesia, clothing costs per patient were reduced from 60RMs per year to 45RMs; daily food costs per patient sank from 0.75RMs to 0.55RMs. In Saxony, essential building maintenance work was cut by 10%, clothing bills by 8%, equipment by 10% and food bills by 4%. In Pomerania, patients received ersatz coffee, margarine and a bit of bread for breakfast; patients needing salvarsan or other drugs had to pay for them. In Westphalia the authorities cut all non-essential outgoings by up to 20%, including expenditure on heating, light, power, and water. Everywhere, posts were frozen or a certain proportion of office staff made redundant.[123] Faced with indiscriminately savage cuts, psychiatrists tried to salvage some of the reforms of the preceding years in their own proposals for economies. They did not dispute the need for savings, but rather wanted to make sure that they did not damage the green shoots of their reformist endeavours. In 1931 the German Psychiatric Association organised a prize essay competition on the theme 'How can provision for mental health care be more cheaply reorganised?' First prize went to Emil Bratz (1868–1934) the director of Berlin's Wittenauer Heilstätten, a specialist in the field of alcoholism and author of a collection on humour in neurology and psychiatry.[124] In Berlin, Bratz presided over what was known as the 'Wittenauer' or 'Staffelsystem' ('echelon system'), i.e. a differentiated network of ambulatory and stationary treatment centres which included such specialist facilities as sanatoria for alcoholics, cocaine and morphium addicts.[125] The prize for best runner-up went to Erich Friedländer, director of the Lindenhaus in Lippe. Friedländer had already cautioned against throwing the reformist baby out with the cost-cutting bathwater in an article published a year earlier. He categorically rejected the idea that psychiatry was virtually impotent in the face of mental illness, or that such recoveries as did occur were either accidental or the natural result of the course of an illness.[126] Like Friedländer, Bratz did not quarrel with economies in a time of national emergency. He pedantically detailed how money could be saved, under various cost headings. Schizophrenics could be given a second wool blanket as the heating was turned down; thermometers in every ward would counteract any complaints about the cold with irrefutable proof of the adequacy of the temperature. Power bills could be cut by using low-wattage light bulbs; or, more simply, the patients could have an extra hour in bed on dark winter mornings. If one washed down the walls, it would only be necessary to whitewash the ceilings occasionally. Uneaten food could return to the kitchen for further consideration rather than being consigned to the swillbins. Patients could wear their own clothes rather than a uniform. The cost of drugs was to be shown clearly in the books doctors used to order them from the pharmacists. Patients could replace staff in the kitchens or washhouse, and (notwithstanding problems of confidentiality) as clerks and secretaries in the administration.[127] Instead of the authorities' strategy of choking off the flow of admissions, with its corollary of an increase in incurable cases and hence the reversion of asylums to a purely custodial function, Bratz recommended what was essentially a two-tier system. The hospitals which first admitted patients were to be centres of research and places where modern therapies were designed to achieve as rapid a rate of discharge as possible. Those who did not respond to therapy were to be spun off, in the interests of economy, into a sort of nether world of minimalist, low-cost facilities where they received merely basic attention. Ideally, patients would be discharged into the care of their own families after a few months in the asylum, a policy which cost virtually nothing. If their own family was unwilling to receive them, then further options included paid family fostering (a quarter or a third cheaper than institutional care), or if they required more intensive supervision, hostels for ten to fifteen patients. Schizophrenics could be placed in charitable or ecclesiastical institutions where nursing sisters effectively worked for nothing.[128] Finally, the authorities could concentrate chronic cases in large asylums, which could be distinct from the hospital-like asylums for acute cases, or just a separate part of the same facility.[129] Instead of these asylums being the final destination for an undifferentiated army of outcasts, doctors were to separate the curable and the incurable, a process of discrimination reflected in subsequent levels of care and therapy. Some would benefit from medical progress; others (whose very presence cast a long shadow over its pretensions), would to all intents and purposes be excluded from its orbit. This was to create the psychiatric equivalent of the dividing line between a hospital and a hospice, and the conceptual framework which at the very least sought to diminish the number of 'incurable' patients. Interestingly enough, psychiatrists who advocated such a division of the patient body made explicit connections between having to assign patients to the categories 'curable' or 'incurable' and the decisions doctors made in the case of patients who were terminally ill or experiencing extreme suffering:

Who will be bold enough, even in cases where schizophrenic dementia has only been manifested for a few years, to pronounce the final spiritual death sentence and order transfer to an asylum for the incurable? That would truly be a difficult and portentous decision for both the patient himself and his family, like the controversial tribunals in the case of the destruction of life unworthy of life.[130]

Colleagues of Friedländer's began to argue that caring for chronic or geriatric patients was a 'luxury that Germany could not afford'. A financially constrained nation was in the process of 'caring itself to death'.[131] One way of drastically countering the alleged threat posed by the physically and mentally defective, while at the same time cutting the sums expended on institutionalisation, was eugenic sterilisation. In the early 1920s, Heinrich Boeters, the Saxon 'apostle of sterilisation' and district medical officer in Zwickau, forced the issue on to the agenda by publicising sterilisation operations which he had instigated and which were carried out by the surgeon Heinrich Braun. Obsessive and probably mentally unbalanced, Boeters formulated a series of proposals, known as the *Lex Zwickau*, which would sanction the compulsory sterilisation of (*inter aliis*) idiots, the feebleminded, the blind, deaf and dumb, and illegitimate mothers of low eugenic value.[132] Although this led the authorities in various German states to consider the question of sterilisation, uncertainties in the scientific basis of the proposals and the opposition of legal experts and officials meant that this first wave of proposals got nowhere. Among psychiatrists, the case for sterilisation was comprehensively put by Robert Gaupp of Tübingen at the meeting of the German Psychiatric Association in Cassel in September 1925. Gaupp began by extolling the modern, pioneering spirit which had informed Boeters, and what had already been achieved in this area in both the United States (where Mears, Ochsner and Sharp had pioneered vasectomies and X-ray sterilisation) and Switzerland, where such legislation already existed. Lawyers and a legal code inherited from the late 1860s and early 1870s had yet to take cognisance of the latest eugenic tidings, namely the qualitative eugenic crisis occasioned by the First World War.[133] The peace of Versailles had left Germany with a diminished economic base for a population which was still growing. Using evidence thrown together from Chicago, England, Rostock and New York, Gaupp claimed that there were differential (and hence deleterious) fertility rates between the upper and lower classes: 'the less valuable are reproducing more rapidly than the more valuable'.[134] This was particularly the case with those less serious cases of mental disorder not encompassed by the asylums. It was time to remove 'the burden of the parasites', whose cost to the nation was strikingly demonstrated. These 'statistics' were backed up with lurid anecdotal evidence of a sexual offender – a self-confessed 'beast in human form' – vowing to reoffend upon release, and of a homosexual 'violater of small boys' threatening to shoot himself on the doorstep of the author's home unless Gaupp would have him castrated.[135] Environmental explanations of crime and the risk of diagnostic error were brushed aside, as indeed was the need for scientific certitude regarding the hereditary character of, for example, alcoholism or psychopathic disorders. Although there was no hard evidence regarding the longterm biological damage caused by alcoholism, nonetheless, since the 'entire drunken milieu' was 'poor soil in which to raise children', the wives of alcoholics should be permitted to have themselves sterilised.[136] Concluding with the practicalities of how such procedures would operate, Gaupp left his audience with a quotation from Herbert Spencer to mull over: 'A people consisting of hereditarily valuable individuals is the first condition for the wellbeing of the nation.'[137]

These ideas assumed a new salience and urgency in the straitened economic climate of the late 1920s and early 1930s. Several psychiatrists began to advocate a synthesis between eugenics and the individually focussed reforms we have been considering. One did not supersede the other; they simply converged. Noting that unfavourable prognoses were the most 'racially' favourable outcome, for they would effectively 'eradicate' degenerate hereditary properties, Hans Luxenburger nonetheless sought to combine individual therapy with collectivist eugenic measures. Sterilisation would ensure that the 'personal wellbeing' of the individual would not eventuate in 'disaster for the race'.[138] Emil Bratz's advocacy of returning patients as rapidly as possible to the community, in the interests of enhanced economic efficiency, was accompanied by demands for the sterilisation of 'hereditary' oligophrenics and schizophrenics before their release. Bratz hoped that the Reichssparkommissar would use economic arguments to overcome political or moral objections to projected legislation.[139] In a lecture entitled 'The eradication of the less valuable from society', published in the *Allgemeine Zeitschrift für Psychiatrie* in 1932, Berthold Kihn from Erlangen rehearsed the sort of arguments used by Gaupp in a more starkly economistic fashion. The burden of an exaggerated welfarism was bearing down upon the shoulders of the hard-pressed tax payers of a nation whose resource base Versailles had depleted.[140] While a minority of responsible people apparently trembled with the onset of every new day, others simply signed on, and reproduced regardless, in the knowledge that the social services would pick up the tab for their fecklessness. The counter-selective effects of modern medicine were also 'keeping beings alive whose value to society is at least regarded as very debatable'.[141] There were four possible means of raising the quality of the population: eugenic marriage counselling and prohibition of unions between the 'unfit'; the 'destruction of life unworthy of life'; the isolation in asylums of people deemed unfit to reproduce; and castration or sterilisation for those whose progeny society deemed undesirable.[142] The first option held out little hope, since counselling services tended to be used by 'over-anxious persons of high value' rather than by the mass of the population. Moreover prohibiting marriages was not the same as preventing eugenically undesirable sexual relations. Cost considerations ruled out an increase in the number of people confined in asylums, and in any case, it was unlikely that the less serious, and therefore more eugenically deleterious, cases would be encompassed by such a policy.[143] A crisis in public finance militated in favour of the remaining 'radical measures against the less valuable'. Citing Alfred Hoche, Kihn claimed that expenditure upon 'ballast existences' was unnecessary. Thirty thousand institutionalised idiots cost the Reich forty-five million Reichsmarks a year. He estimated that total expenditure upon the mentally ill was in the region of a further one hundred and fifty million Reichsmarks. Killing these people would remove the burden on the tax payer and release considerable reserves of labour tied up in their care. Throwing in a few 'examples' from antiquity, Kihn passed rapidly to the ideas of Binding and Hoche regarding the killing of chronic mental patients. There were practical problems. The panels which made these decisions would soon come to be regarded as 'murder commissions', and their deeds would acquire the same sort of popular opprobrium as 'the psychiatric padded cell or the hypnotic gaze of the mad doctor'. On balance, this option was not realistic in the current ethical and legal climate: 'I believe we are far away from the feasibility of implementing these demands, and I do not believe that we can anticipate a change in either the legal position or in somewhat over-developed ethical sensibilities in the near future, and for these reasons one must also regard these questions with the greatest scepticism'.[144] That left the 'relatively humane' option of eugenic sterilisation. But would it really have the desired effect? Recessive patterns of inheritance would make this unlikely in the case of schizophrenia; and in any case, the age at which the illness manifested itself, and the alleged lack of sexual appetency evident in many of those affected, suggested that sterilisation would be tilting at windmills. There was a similar problem in the case of epilepsy, where the state of current research precluded any certainty about its hereditary character. Since many idiots were either infertile, had no apparent sexual drives, or were permanently institutionalised, sterilisation was effectively irrelevant. There was no need, either, to sterilise people suffering from forms of manic depression, since their hypermanic offspring were often very gifted. This left the less acute cases of oligophrenia, who, living outside the asylums, constituted 'the root of much suffering, and [who] signified an immense danger for our future'.[145] The vast range of abnormalities subsumed under the rubric 'psychopathic' made general sterilisation impossible, except where criminals, prostitutes or sexual perverts were concerned. Far better to try to counsel these individuals into voluntary sterilisation. Despite these cautionary stipulations, Kihn ended on a modestly optimistic note:

Every measure is permissible which appears cheap and effective in the struggle against the less valuable. There will never be firm legal or humanitarian norms according to which one should proceed in this area. Experience shapes law and humanity, just as law shapes experience. And although today the social benefit flowing from our efforts seems rather slight, so much so that it hardly seems worth it – nonetheless, gentlemen, we do not know what time and future generations will make of these measures, whether from these small endeavours necessity will one day create more drastic steps, before whose success all our know-it-alls will fall silent.[146]

It would be misleading to suggest that these ideas won universal approval from the psychiatric profession. Sterilisation was discussed at some length at the twenty-fifth annual conference of Bavarian psychiatrists in July 1931. Valentin Faltlhauser detected three main camps: those who opposed sterilisation on ethical or theoretical grounds; psychiatric attentists who remained to be convinced of the scientific fundaments underpinning negative eugenic measures; and finally, 'the group of those who really know, as a result of their research' that many mental disorders (including Huntington's Chorea, certain 'core groups' of schizophrenia, manic depression, genuine epilepsy, psychopathic disorder, alcoholism and habitual offenders!) were *au fond* hereditary.[147] Since scepticism was no longer warranted, 'we must find ways to eradicate bad hereditary properties'. Careful propaganda campaigns would pave the way for legally secure forms of voluntary sterilisation, although Faltlhauser did not rule out compulsion in the case of the congenitally feebleminded or criminals. In the ensuing discussion, Oswald Bumke, Kraepelin's successor as professor of psychiatry at Munich and a critic of degenerationist ideologies and racial theories, cautioned that (as in the case of marriage counselling) only intellectuals or people with a high sense of moral responsibility would contemplate voluntary sterilisation. To be effective, sterilisation would have to be compulsory.[148] He also questioned the value of sterilising individual schizophrenics, epileptics and manic depressives, given recessive patterns of inheritance. The alternative of indiscriminate sterilisation of the families of those suffering from these illnesses would leave a world populated, as he dryly observed, by 'a few dessicated bureaucrats – and the schizophrenics'. In his view, the only groups where sterilisation might have some impact were cases of hereditary feeblemindedness and anti-social psychopathic disorders. The remainder of his contribution was striking for its degree of political awareness, sense of responsibility and, as things turned out, remarkable prescience. Here was an intelligent and internationally recognised scientist of a nationalist, conservative persuasion, who could see exactly which way things were tending and who asked his colleagues to make certain ethical choices. Questions like that of sterilisation, he insisted, were too complex to be decided under the pressure of contingent economic circumstances:

if we can prevent the occurrence of mental illnesses with the aid of sterilisation, then certainly we should do so – but not because the state is saving money, but because every mental illness signifies perpetual suffering for both the patient and his relatives. In this case, economic perspectives are not just inappropriate but dangerous. One only needs to take the idea to its logical conclusion – that one should do away with all those people who at the time seem dispensable for financial reasons – in order to arrive at the rather monstrous result: we must kill not merely all the mentally ill and the psychopaths, but every cripple, including wounded war veterans, all the old maids who are not working, all the widows who no longer have children to raise, and all the invalids and old-age pensioners. That would certainly save us money, but I suspect we would not do it.[149]

Bumke also noted that the current political atmosphere, with its political instrumentalisation of 'scientific theories' of race, was not conducive to calm consideration of these questions. With a political awareness and degree of self-restraint absent among many of his colleagues, Bumke observed:

if one were to drag the discussion regarding sterilisation into today's arena of political struggle, then one would probably pretty soon hear less talk about the mentally ill, but more regarding Aryans and non-Aryans, and of the blond Germanic race and the less valuable round-skulls. It is certainly unlikely that anything positive would arise from this; on the contrary, both science in general and genealogy and eugenics in particular would be damaged in ways from which they would not easily recover.[150]

Given the ways in which our contemporary discussions of genetics are still haunted by the shadow of Nazi atrocities, this had a singular prescience. As one leading geneticist has recently remarked apropos the entire eugenic project: 'its blemished past means that human genetics is marked by the fingerprints of its own history'.[151] Inevitably, prominent among those who did not heed his own warning was Bumke himself, for within a decade he became an enthusiastic exponent of the National Socialists' eugenic legislation, although knowledge of the causal relationship of heredity to psychiatric disorders had not advanced one iota in the intervening decade.[152] While Bumke was still sounding a note of caution, the spirit of the age manifested itself in the form of Hans Luxenburger. Any scientific doubts about the hereditary origins of various mental illnesses, and hence the possibility of serious diagnostic error, were subordinated to the interests of the racial collective:

Firstly, occasional mistakes are unavoidable, but they can be tolerated in view of the grave crisis in which our race currently finds itself. It is clear that we cannot fully prevent the transmission of recessive hereditary properties through sterilisation; but they will certainly be considerably contained, and it is impossible to see why one should sit back and do nothing only because a radical eradication of degenerate hereditary properties is still not possible today. Nowadays one is content with partial success in the combating of syphilis and tuberculosis in the hope that the future will bring further help.[153]

In a particularly sinister moment, Luxenburger observed that concrete proof of the hereditary character of certain illnesses was a purely academic affair, and that 'eugenics must not shrink from a certain naivety in the way it looks at things, unless it wants its demands postponed in perpetuity (*ad kalendas graecas*)'. Propaganda would swing the population behind eugenic sterilisation, and the popular will would then be transformed into the appropriate legislation. In the near future, doctors would become 'the executors of the eugenic will of the nation'.[154] Psychiatric eugenics also occupied the second general meeting of the German Society for Mental Hygiene held in Bonn in 1932. Ernst Rüdin gave a keynote address in which he insisted that 'People who are themselves mentally ill or hereditarily feebleminded should not have children.'[155] Luxenburger called for changes in the laws on assault to permit eugenic sterilisation.[156] Rainer Fetscher openly boasted that he had inveigled fifty-three people into having themselves sterilised in his eugenic counselling sessions pointing out that while it cost a mere 120–150RMS to perform the operation, it would cost 10–12,000RMS to educate a deaf and dumb child.[157] The Protestant position was put by Hans Harmsen, chairman of the Inner Mission's standing conference on eugenic questions. Harmsen personified Protestant subscription to hereditarian biology. The latter ideology also had a certain cost-cutting appeal, since it would allow the Inner Mission to replace universal charity with biologically determined selective benefits.[158] Rejecting vulgar utilitarian arguments, Harmsen, who was also medical director of the Inner Mission's network of asylums, described sterilisation as 'a moral duty, which can be explained as love of one's neighbour and responsibility towards future generations'.[159] In other words, Protestants should no longer think in terms of God's individual creations, but rather in terms of the continuum of future creations. Not for the first or last time, an institution supposedly concerned with the eternal adapted its outlook to the prevailing secular ideologies. Although certain Roman Catholics were similarly tantalised by eugenic solutions to social problems – notably the former Jesuit Professor Hermann Muckermann, who was in charge of eugenics at the Kaiser Wilhelm Institute for Anthropology, Human Genetics and Eugenics until he was dismissed for referring to Hitler as an 'idiot' – the 1930 papal encyclical *Casti connubii* represented something of an obstacle to the adoption of negative, if not of positive, eugenic measures. The authoritarian and totalitarian aspects of Roman Catholicism proved its saving grace. Its emphasis on family life and individual salvation – children are put here in order that body and soul may be reunited in eternity – meant a denial of the paramountcy of such terrestrial collectives as race, state or nation.[160] *Casti connubii* did not prevent individual Roman Catholic figures from airing dissident views. Indeed, Joseph Mayer, the Paderborn theologian and editor of the journal *Caritas*, who was to play a controversial role in the 'euthanasia' programme, cited the encyclical as the official Vatican line on sterilisation, but then pointed out that the Church had taken no active steps to obstruct such measures in Denmark, Switzerland or the United States of America.[161] Writings of his which tried to justify compulsory sterilisation by pointing to the spiritual, as opposed to the procreative, blessings of marriage, or the benefits which would accrue to the collective, received the ecclesiastical *imprimatur* notwithstanding their subversion of the Church's teaching on this question.[162]

At the 1932 conference, the official view was put by a Dr Struve of the Prussian Council of State. He argued that 'our state welfare provision must become more discriminating; we must not expend more on the hopeless cases than we spend upon healthy people. We have become a poor people, much poorer than we already care to admit today.'[163] In 1932 the issue of sterilisation was thrashed out in the Prussian Health Council. A year later, the National Socialists dropped the consensual features of the Prussian draft law and quietly changed the law governing assault.[164] The Law for the Prevention of Hereditarily Diseased Progeny was presented to the cabinet on 14 July 1933, and published on 26 July, six days after the signing of the Concordat with the Vatican.[165]

CHAPTER 2

HOPE AND HARD TIMES: ASYLUMS
IN THE 1930s

IN THE mid 1930s the walls of many German asylums were deliberately rendered transparent, in the interests of acquainting a wider public with negative eugenic measures at first hand. Put starkly, this meant that asylums became hortatory freakshows. In 1935, the authorities in the Rhineland reported that over two thousand people had trooped through one of the province's asylums: their ranks included members of the SA and SS, leaders of the Hitler Youth and League of German Maidens, the Nazi Women's organisation, doctors, midwives, nurses, lawyers and teachers.[1] At Eglfing-Haar, Munich, parties consisting of over a hundred people were regularly conducted through the asylum from 1934 onwards. Pandering somewhat to their paymasters, the asylum authorities wrote that these visits were a direct result of the public interest in asylums generated by the regime's racial legislation.[2] In 1936, the asylum was visited by, *inter aliis*, forty persons from the Reich Leadership School of the SA; two hundred SS race experts from the SS Upper Section-Munich South; fifty leaders and instructors of the SS-Standarte 'Julius Schreck'; and several parties from the German Labour Front. A visit by thirty-eight members of the Hitler Youth unit 'Hochland' was disallowed, since it included persons under eighteen years of age.[3] Between 1933 and 1939 over 21,000 people took part in conducted tours of Eglfing-Haar alone. Nearly 6,000 of these visitors were members of the SS.[4] Each tour culminated in a lecture by the asylum authorities illustrating, with the aid of human subjects, the symptoms of the principal psychiatric illnesses, and hence the necessity for the regime's negative eugenic measures. This afforded the asylum directors and doctors an opportunity to stress their own importance within the on-going struggle 'for race and nation'. Public interest was fanned by a sensationalist press. In February 1934 the Munich press was invited to Eglfing-Haar by the Bavarian desk of the Reich Propaganda Ministry, for the explicit purpose of disseminating racial-hygienic propaganda to a wider audience.[5] Censoriously countering the popular tendency to make jokes about 'loony-bins', the *Münchner neueste Nachrichten* noted that life in the asylums was no laughing matter, and that 'one would be lost for words to describe what one had experienced there'.[6] In a piece entitled 'Alive Yet Dead', another visiting journalist was not bereft of words – most of them lurid – to convey to the readers of the *Münchener Zeitung* what he had experienced:

Wild eyes stare out of contorted faces. Others glow with a feverish sheen. Grinning grotesques, who bear scarcely any resemblance to human beings. Those who enter are assailed by shrill cries. Fearful screams and mad laughter. A group of madmen have pressed together at a table by the wall like a herd of frightened beasts. Personal contact with the outside world seems to have been completely broken. Their movements are aimless, purposeless. Typical cases of schizophrenia. Bent and clenched hands in mad movement. Epileptics subject to attacks, with jerking bodies. One walks through a room with bedridden patients, the sick insane. Frequently they are just skeletons covered with skin. Others are lying in impossible positions, mumbling in a confused, dreamlike fashion. They vegetate in a twilight throughout the day and night. What do time or space mean to them? Ideas, action, will, are all confused. Connections between ideas have ceased to exist. A raving maniac hammers on an iron door ... One also sees more amiable scenes. Rooms in which those who are semi-recovered devote themselves to their work. They make a totally normal impression. The asylum environment, a period among people like themselves, have had a beneficial effect. But returned to a freer way of life, many of them will relapse.[7]

Publications of the regime's many formations gradually moved from description to prescription. The *Völkische Beobachter* used waves of rhetorical questions to propagate utilitarian reasons for sterilising the patients, while countering Christian, humanitarian and legal objections to this course of action.[8] Ever in the avant garde, the SS organ *Das schwarze Korps* published in March and June 1937 a pair of human-interest stories which explicitly advocated the 'mercy killing' of the mentally ill and disabled. In the first, entitled 'A Courageous Step', the journal sang the praises of a farmer who had shot his mentally handicapped son in the dead of night. By sentencing the farmer to three years' imprisonment, minus the period he had already spent in investigative custody, the judges had demonstrated a sensitivity to the healthy instincts of the people as distinct from a pedantic adherence to the letter of the law. Naturally, it was intolerable that an individual should arrogate to himself the role of 'judge over life and death', and the historic compromise achieved by the judges of Weimar in this case between popular sentiment and the 'paragraph logic' of the law was merely a provisional solution in such cases. 'Future generations, who will cleanse the laws of life of the detritus of a false belief in pity and liberal humanitarian stupidity, will arrive at other solutions.'[9] A reader's letter published a week later on what had become the topical theme of 'mercy killing' addressed the subject of killing defective infants and the need for a legal and humane way of doing what it was alleged nature herself would do.[10]

Information on the responses of the visitors to asylums is sparse. According to one psychiatrist, Enge of Strecknitz, young people were particularly vicious in their attitudes towards the mentally ill and handicapped. There were also many who sought to affirm their 'racial heroism' by calling for the 'destruction of the mentally ill as lives unworthy of life'.[11] Judging from essays they wrote afterwards, schoolchildren who visited the asylum at Emmendingen in 1938 expected that the nation would soon be liberated from these 'human ruins with bestial instincts' and that 'the doctor would soon become superfluous'. A minority of them objected to the use of human beings as exhibits, or drew attention to the ways in which conditions in asylums manufactured lunatics.[12] At Eglfing-Haar, the object of such tours had apparently been achieved when the bolder among the visitors would ask why the patients were kept alive. After one such visit, a young SS officer from Bad Tölz brought a smile of recognition to the face of Eglfing-Haar's director, Hermann Pfannmüller, when he observed that one might as well set up a machine gun at the asylum entrance to clear away the inmates.[13] That Pfannmüller already had the matter well in hand can be demonstrated by Ludwig Lehners's retrospective account of a visit to Eglfing-Haar in the autumn of 1939, which also reveals that reactions to what was taking place in asylums were sometimes negative, even if in this case the conclusions drawn by the woman visitor he mentioned are in themselves disturbing:

During that time, the public had the opportunity to visit madhouses. Since I had studied psychology in 1934/1935 as part of my professional training, and therefore had some specialised knowledge, I was naturally particularly interested in how a madhouse functioned. For these reasons I took part in a conducted tour through a madhouse.

After we had visited a number of other wards, the asylum director, who was called Pfannmüller, led us into a children's ward. The ward made a clean and cared-for impression. In about fifteen beds there were as many children, all aged between about one and five years old. In this ward, Pfannmüller explained his intentions at some length. I remember the following as a condensed account of the sense of what Pfannmüller had to say: 'As a National Socialist, these creatures (he meant the aforementioned children) naturally only represent to me a burden upon the healthy body of our nation. We don't kill [he may have used a more circumlocutory expression instead of the word 'kill'] with poison, injections etc., since that would only give the foreign press and certain gentlemen in Switzerland new hate-propaganda material. No: as you see, our method is much simpler and more natural.' With these words, and assisted by a nurse who worked in this ward, he pulled one of the children out of bed. As he displayed the child around like a dead hare, he pointed out, with a knowing look and a cynical grin, 'This one will last another two or three days.' The image of this fat, grinning man, with the

Plate 2. Hermann Pfannmüller.

whimpering skeleton in his fleshy hand, surrounded by other starving children, is still clear before my eyes. Furthermore, the murderer declared that they were not suddenly withdrawing food, but rather gradually reducing the rations. A lady who also took part in the tour asked, with an outrage she had difficulty suppressing, whether a quick death aided by injections would not be more merciful. Pfannmüller sang the praises of his methods once more, as being more practical in terms of the foreign press. The openness with which Pfannmüller announced the methods of treatment mentioned above can only be explained as the product of cynicism or foolishness. Furthermore, Pfannmüller made no secret of the fact that among those children who were to be murdered were some who were not mentally ill, namely the children of Jewish parents.[14]

Doctors and psychiatrists worked within parameters set by (*inter aliis*) politicians, and health and financial administrators. In some official quarters there was resentment at the costs of psychiatric provision, and indeed a high degree of cynicism towards the whole psychiatric enterprise. For example, in August 1933 an official in the Ministry of Finance in Württemberg recommended ways of curtailing expenditure in this sector. He wrote:

Sums of money are being disbursed on asylums in Württemberg which bear no relationship to the aims and purposes of the asylums. One has the impression that personal interests, principally those of the medical profession, have assumed far more importance than those of the community as a whole. Psychiatry itself is still in its infancy, and it would be hard to come up with even one instance in which the doctors have succeeded in making a mental patient well again. In every case in which recovery has occurred, this can be attributed to the natural course of the illness.

He recommended that the asylums revert to being 'custodial institutions', and that expenditure on both patients and staff be drastically cut.[15] Writing in 1936 on the reasons for a shortage of psychiatrists, Eglfing-Haar's director Fritz Ast noted that in 'influential circles' the view was abroad that care for the mentally ill was a waste of time and money, for the patients were regarded as being 'of lesser value, useless dead-weight existences'.[16] In studying the professions it is often easy to take them at their own self-estimation, overlooking the not insignificant views of those who paid their salaries.

The idea of actually killing the mentally ill was being canvassed in the late 1930s among senior provincial officials directly responsible for the overall administration of the asylums. According to Dr Wilhelm Hinsen, who resigned in 1938 as director of the Eichberg asylum near Eltville in the Rheingau, these sentiments were articulated by both Wilhelm Traupel, the Landeshauptmann of Cassel and Wiesbaden, and Fritz Bernotat, the desk officer responsible for asylums in the Wiesbaden area:

In 1936 or 1937 Landeshauptmann Traupel said to me at least twice, but perhaps three times, in terms which were not entirely easy to grasp, that it would be better if a law existed which made it possible to kill the mentally ill, since they were all ballast existences – something along these lines. It could have been expressed more sharply. Traupel said this two or three times. I took the opportunity to oppose him. At a conference of directors in Schloss Dehrn, which must have been in about 1936, Bernotat told the circle of assembled directors: 'If I was a doctor, I would do away with these patients.' I told him publicly in the same forum: 'German medicine can congratulate itself that you are not a doctor.' After that there was a pregnant silence.[17]

In an address to a conference of asylum directors on 24 September 1937, Bernotat summarised the impact of his policies upon the asylums of Hesse-Nassau. The only criterion that mattered now was 'what serves the German nation'. To this end he had augmented what he modestly called 'piecemeal' economy measures with a radical rationalisation of existing institutions. A number of the latter, including an asylum at Waldmann-hausen, an institute for the deaf and dumb in Camberg and a school for the blind in Wiesbaden, had been closed down and their patients and pupils sent elsewhere. Their buildings had been either sold off or leased out to organisations involved with youth. In order to screw down expenditure on the mentally ill to an absolute minimum, Bernotat was eager to abandon the 'outmoded notion' of 'optimum' capacity: 'As a drastic example of this I would like to take the asylum at Weilmünster whose "highest occupancy" was fixed at about 1,000 in the pre-war period, but which houses almost 1,500 patients today.' This had not been accompanied by a commensurate increase in staffing, for according to Bernotat, the desired ratio of doctors to patients should be 1:300 and of nursing staff to patients 1:9 or 1:10. Economies had also been achieved in the sums expended per patient. The amount devoted to each patient per day had fallen from 2.80RMs in 1933 to 2.55RMs a year later, rising fractionally to 2.60RMs in 1935. He indicated that these sums now included all ancillary costs, including expenditure on administration and maintenance of the premises, rather than what was spent directly on the patients.[18]

Bernotat's critics and enemies suspected that these rigorous economy measures were in reality a pretext for 'doing business'. The line between ideological fervour and self-interest was a fine one. On 15 October 1943, Dr Friedrich Mennecke, himself by that time responsible for thousands of 'euthanasia' killings, used the opportunity afforded by a spell in hospital to record the genesis of what had become a major feud with Bernotat regarding Mennecke's desire to establish a convulsive therapy unit at Eichberg; his misuse of his car for non-essential journeys; and his alleged mishandling of the case of one of his staff who had sexually assaulted a patient. Although this was clearly a case of the kettle calling the pot black, Mennecke objected to Bernotat's lay dismissal of all mental patients as 'idiots', and hence his total unconcern for their welfare or treatment. Bernotat simply wanted 'as many of them to die as possible'. Endeavouring to find the first signs of a rift, Mennecke latched on to Bernotat's eagerness in 1937 and 1938 to fill the asylums of Hesse-Nassau not simply with patients from ecclesiastical or private asylums in that province, but with patients scooped up from the Rhineland or Saarland. With a daily expenditure of merely forty to forty-five pfennigs per patient, Bernotat's office could pocket the difference on the 1.20 to 2.50RMs they were charging the authorities of the other provinces who were responsible for paying the patients' maintenance.[19] A penny saved was a penny earned. At his trial, Mennecke recalled that when he had protested to Bernotat about overcrowding, the latter had replied 'strike them all dead and then you'll have space'.[20]

The overcrowding that resulted from these policies can be seen from the following figures giving the average number of patients in the Eichberg asylum for each year between 1934 and 1940: 793 (1934); 825 (1935); 891 (1936); 890 (1937); 963 (1938); 1,137 (1939); 1,236 (1940). Over roughly the same period, the ratio of doctors to patients deteriorated from 1:162 in 1935 to 1:300 in 1938.[21] This took no account of the volume of admissions and discharges. As Dr Hinsen pointed out, 'the patient who is admitted and then discharged naturally occasions more work than an elderly patient who has been there for a long time. I regard a ratio of 1:150 as tolerable.'[22] Similar economy measures and overcrowding occurred in other asylums within the region. At Hadamar near Limburg, which was to become one of the major centres for killing patients, actual expenditure per patient fell from 0.47RMS per day in 1936 to 0.44RMS per day a year later.[23] By May 1939 the asylum was regularly occupied by nearly six hundred patients, despite the fact that its maximum capacity had been fixed at 370 three years earlier.[24] At Weilmünster in 1938, 1,515 patients occupied facilities which in 1934 had housed 656.[25] Between 1937 and 1938, some 385 patients were removed from half a dozen private and ecclesiastical asylums and transferred to the state facilities of Haina and Merxhausen. These two asylums were already experiencing difficulties in dealing with approximately 900 patients per asylum, yet the authorities were recommending that they maximise their capacities by each accommodating a further two hundred persons. A number of smaller or specialist facilities were 'rationalised' out of existence in the interests of more effective use of state institutions. Expenditure on food in the state institutions was cut in turn. At Haina, the sum allocated for feeding each patient fell from 0.69RMS per day in 1932 to 0.56RMS in 1933, 0.55RMS in 1934 and 0.54RMS in 1935. These sums should be contrasted with pre-Depression expenditure of 0.93RMS in 1931 and a post-war figure of 1.50DMS in 1954.[26]

Lest it be imagined that these measures were forced upon unwilling asylum administrations, it is simply necessary to refer to the latter's annual reports or publicity materials to demonstrate a high degree of enthusiastic complicity. Thus, in 1936 the administrators of the asylum for backward juveniles at Idstein trumpeted the achievements of 'three years of National Socialist leadership'. Graphs showed how the number of trainees had risen from 614 in 1933 to 737 in 1935, while expenditure per patient had fallen from 2.38RMS per day in 1932 to 1.83RMS two years later. This had resulted in a net saving of 312,524RMS over the same period, this last sum being 'made available to hereditarily healthy people'. Considerable amounts had been spent on housing for the nursing staff, and the asylum's debts had been reduced by 109,400RMS.[27] Psychiatrists put much mental energy into working out what asylums could save in the context of the 'battle for food' or the economies enjoined by the Four-Year Plan.[28]

Asylums administered by the charitable networks of the two churches were informed that transfers to state institutions were being effected 'simply for reasons of enhanced economic efficiency, and not for any political or other reasons', which last disclaimer was hardly reassuring. They were instructed to adopt the 'Führer principle', which in this case meant recognising the immediate authority of the regional health authorities or, failing that, to surrender their charges.[29] The SS organ *Schwarze*

Korps viewed the transfers as a conflict between ultimate objectives. Whereas the Roman Catholic charities saw their function in terms of 'educating people to be children of God', the regime's agents – such as Traupel – thought that 'educating people to be German was the highest imperative'. No amount of special pleading that their expenditure per patient was lower than in state institutions; that their institutions were bulwarks against Bolshevism; that they had lobbied for the introduction of compulsory sterilisation; or that they sang 'Now thank we all our God' to celebrate Hitler's annexation of the Sudetenland, served to deflect state designs upon their charges.[30]

What impact did these economy measures have upon the daily life and health of the patients? In 1938, Professor Kleist of the psychiatric clinic at the University of Frankfurt, who had hitherto inspected the asylums of Hesse-Nassau and the Rheingau on an annual basis, made his final round of inspection after what had been a four-year interval. Kleist had to offer his resignation before he was allowed to perform his statutory duties as an inspector. Following an all-too-obvious row with Bernotat during these inspections, the professor was thenceforth not allowed to return. At Eichberg, which he visited in March 1938, Kleist was appalled by a doctor–patient ratio of 1:446, which was actively threatening the health of the patients. The derisory sum of 0.49RMS was notionally expended upon each patient's daily food. Unhygienic straw bedding was in common use. There were no signs of the new active therapies.[31]

Things at Herborn and Weilmünster were not much better. Kleist noted that the newly reopened asylum at Weilmünster was filling up with chronic patients removed from ecclesiastical institutions. Again, there was one doctor to 503 patients. By contrast, there were nine administrative staff. The chronically feebleminded patients were left without any form of examination or therapy. In the previous year 157 patients had died, including twenty-four of tuberculosis. Kleist noted that the bedding and clothing looked suspiciously clean, as if it was a put-up job for the inspectors. Bernotat, who accompanied the inspectors, waxed perversely lyrical about charitable and private homes for chronic patients where the doctor–patient ratio was 1:900. Kleist thought that this was irresponsible. When Kleist became angry about the straw bedding, Bernotat responded by pointing to a neighbouring labour service camp where the officers had similar sleeping arrangements. The professor also took offence at Bernotat's constant talk of 'idiots' and 'the asocial'.[32]

Drastic economy measures and institutional rationalisation were but two of the measures to affect asylums in the Nazi period. These were accompanied by the introduction of the 'Führer principle', i.e. the overt politicisation of institutional life, commencing in some cases with enforced changes in personnel. At the Kalmenhof asylum in Idstein, the creation of

enlightened clerics and philanthropic Jewish businessmen, the introduction of the 'Führer principle' meant the dismissal of the director, Emil
Spornhauer, and the replacement of its circle of well-to-do sponsors with
local lower-class Nazi fanatics. This was done by lowering the fee for
membership of the association from 20RMS to 1RM, which facilitated the
election of the ubiquitous Fritz Bernotat as the association's chairman.[33]
Spornhauer was ejected by a squad of SS men, while the new director,
Müller, looked on holding appropriately enough a revolver.[34] Among
Müller's earliest initiatives was the introduction of the provisions of the
Law for the Restoration of the Professional Civil Service and a new set of
'works decrees'. Under the rubric 'tasks of the works', staff were informed:
'The principal task of the works is to manage the asylum in such a way that
the outgoings of the National Socialist state on the propagation of unsuitable national comrades will be reduced to an absolute minimum. That will
be made possible through increased occupancy and the greatest economies
in all of the houses of the asylum.' Jewish doctors and nurses were
dismissed, the Hitler salute became obligatory, and staff were obliged to
belong to the Nazi works cell organisation, and to participate in Nazi
parades and celebrations.[35]

Ecclesiastical asylums, too, reflected the mood sweeping the land. From
the Protestant asylum Stetten in Württemberg it was reported: 'For us all
the celebrations ensuing from the national revolution were among the
nicest events of the year: our smallest and biggest children enjoyed the
fluttering flags and the joyous bustle.' The director of the asylum at
Schwäbisch Hall noted: 'We cannot be thankful enough that we have a
Führer who has demonstrated his authority before his people and to the
world at large. Christian charity would have had no place in a bolshevised
nation.' Life in these asylums took on a military character. At Mariaberg
on summer evenings, the handicapped pupils marched 'in neat order
through the asylum courtyard and out into the grounds. From there one
Hitler song after another rang out until the onset of night put an end to the
singing.' Visitors to the classrooms were greeted with a loud 'Heil Hitler!',
for the pupils 'wanted to be real Hitler Youths'. Even the 'weakest'
endeavoured to raise their arms in the German greeting.[36]

The medical staff of ecclesiastical asylums began to include people
whose attitudes towards the mentally ill or physically handicapped were
distinctly un-Christian. In 1937, Dr Rudolf Boeckh, an NSDAP member
since 1932, and from 1936 chief doctor at the Lutheran Neuendettelsau
asylum in central Franconia, gave a talk to the local Nazi Party group on
'the destruction of life unworthy of life'. It is worth considering what he
had to say in some detail. Briefly reviewing the alleged propensity of
primitive peoples, the Chinese, and the Spartans to eliminate 'idiots' at
birth, Boeckh passed swiftly on to the alleged explosion of state welfare

provision for the sick in Germany during the nineteenth century. He claimed that during the First World War, more money was made available to keep a person in an asylum than was used to maintain a soldier at the front. Introducing the apparently telling detail, he alleged that epileptic and feebleminded persons who had fallen over, damaging their teeth, were provided with expensive dental treatment, including gold bridgework, courtesy of the state, while workers went about with decayed teeth. Palaces and villa quarters (he meant pavilion-system asylums) were built to house the mentally ill.

Condemning the 'individualistic' mentality reflected in the 'exaggerated welfare' provided by state institutions, Boeckh extolled the stark virtues of ecclesiastical charitable institutions, a form of 'simplicity' under threat (alas) from state inspectors concerned with such academic issues as the cubic breathing space statutorily required for each patient. The church asylums could cram them in more cost-effectively. Passing on to the burden of his argument, Boeckh claimed that ordinary people resented expenditure on the mentally ill, asking instead 'why one did not simply exterminate these creatures who had no worth, indeed who were a burden, in the interests of the healthy parts of the nation?' Boeckh said that any official doctor would have heard questions like these again and again from the public. These sentiments found a ready response from the National Socialist state, which was ideologically in sympathy with all that was 'positive, healthy, productive and life-affirming', and which regarded 'all that is ill and which cannot be brought back to health as a burden'. The decision regarding whether to 'exterminate life unworthy of life', which had hitherto rested in the hands of God, now lay exclusively with his representative on earth, i.e. 'the Führer'. Boeckh then outlined the likely *modus operandi*, with comprehensive registering of likely cases, a version of the existing Hereditary Health Courts, and advisory panels of medical and legal experts. Since the proceedings were to involve relatives of the people to be killed, Boeckh thought that a little emotional suasion might not go amiss on the population in general, by stressing the deleterious genetic effects upon families of an 'idiot' or two in their number. Anticipating objections from the religious-minded, Boeckh concluded with the observation, expressed in one tortuous German sentence which tries to reconcile the language of eugenics with that of the Bible, that:

although the Creator had certainly imposed illness upon the destiny of mankind, the most severe forms of idiocy and the totally grotesque disintegration of the personality had nothing to do with the countenance of God, and that the Creator had set a warning in our hearts in the form of our feeling for the affirmation of life, that we should not maintain these travesties of human form through an exaggerated and therefore false type of compassion, but rather that we should return them to the Creator.[37]

Although the asylum authorities took the different view that there was no such thing as 'life unworthy of life', they met their colleague Boeckh half way by acknowledging that there was 'naturally life of lesser value', which it was in the collective's interest to sterilise. The state was one of the forces maintaining the world, and Lutherans should respond positively to the state's dispositions. Given this mentality, it is hardly surprising that the Boeckhs of this world should have had their way, and that in 1941 1,911 of Neuendettelsau's 2,137 inhabitants should have been taken away to their deaths.

In many asylums, the ability of the directors to choose their personnel began to be circumscribed. At Eichberg, for example, director Hinsen recalled that in 1936 he was informed: 'in future you will only get SS doctors; they know best how to go around with the needle'.[38] This meant principally Dr Friedrich Mennecke, whose rapid medical advancement ran parallel with his promotions in the SS. Within two years, Mennecke had edged Hinsen out, setting himself and his young wife Eva up in the director's quarters at Eichberg.

Psychiatry had never been a branch of medicine capable of attracting intellectual highflyers or people who equated success with earning the large amounts of money available in general practice or the public health service. Psychiatrists were regarded as second-class doctors.[39] Even within the profession the view was held that psychiatry got the dross. Perennial problems of recruitment, connected with the remote location of most asylums and the authoritarian career structures that prevailed within them, were compounded by the National Socialist regime's relentless negative eugenic propaganda. Psychiatrists were regarded as societal failures who lived, impotent and isolated, cheek by jowl with people who were officially stigmatised. As director Ast put it in an article lamenting the profession's problems of recruitment, psychiatry was increasingly becoming a refuge for 'elements ... who don't feel adequate to the struggle for existence in the free professions'.[40]

However, it would be seriously misleading to attribute the new climate within the asylums to a change in either the age, the political outlook, or indeed the intellectual calibre of the men in charge. The old guard had few difficulties in adjusting to the new order. Fritz Ast (1872–1956), whose views we have been considering, was director of the combined asylum at Eglfing-Haar from 1931 until 1937. Having studied at Munich, Vienna and Berlin, Ast worked continuously in asylums from 1899, except for periods tending the mentally ill King Otto of Bavaria, and subsequently as a military doctor at the front during the First World War. A member of every association, board and committee that mattered, Ast was one of the most respected asylum psychiatrists in the Bavaria of his day.[41] His successor, Pfannmüller, whom we last encountered swinging a child about like a dead hare, devoted considerable space in his first annual report to a valedictory salute to his distinguished predecessor. Ast was a dedicated exponent of Simon's occupational therapy and of Kolb's outpatient care in both Munich and the outlying countryside. He had created facilities for the practice of insulin-coma therapy, so that schizophrenics 'would not have to become longterm asylum inmates, and thereby costly ballast existences'. In 1931, Ast had successfully carried through the merger of Eglfing-Haar into one asylum complex. He managed the transition to conditions after 1933 without having to over-exert his ethical faculties. 'Ast was a convinced exponent of the necessity for racial legislative measures, and the introduction to the asylum of the Hereditary Health Laws presented him with new challenges, which he mastered in an exemplary manner.' Using a certain amount of circumlocution, Pfannmüller commented: 'the hereditarily ill within the asylum were rapidly registered on a card index, and dealt with in terms of the Law'. This meant opening a new surgical department to sterilise patients from both Eglfing-Haar and surrounding private and charitable institutions. Ast was also 'called upon' to act as a judge in the Munich Hereditary Health Court. In 1935, Ast had taken the initiative in setting up a unit to systematically monitor the hereditary health of both his patients and, by extension, their relatives. Respected by his colleagues, Ast was also regarded as 'sympathetic and valued advisor' by his patients. Pfannmüller wished his esteemed predecessor a long and peaceful *otium cum dignitate*, in which 'far from the cares and woes of his office he could devote himself entirely to his personal inclinations as a scientist and human being'.[42]

Changes in the medical personnel were accompanied by an influx of unsuitable people into the nursing profession. The dross was evident here too. Economic exigencies and political patronage usurped the idea of a vocation. Pressure was brought to bear on the asylums to find jobs for unemployed members of National Socialist formations such as the SA, Nazi Women's organisation or League of German Maidens.[43] At Strecknitz, staff who were active trade unionists or members of the SPD were suddenly dismissed, with members of the SA being recruited to take their places.[44]

Detailed studies of the nursing personnel in asylums suggest that the nurses and male orderlies were a far cry from the idealistic and highly motivated young people shown in Nazi propaganda films. The nurses tended to be of petty bourgeois origin, having spent the years between primary school and the commencement of their nursing careers in domestic service or light industry. Nursing seems to have afforded them secure employ until they lighted upon their future marriage partners.[45] The male orderlies tended to be older and from a lower social class, arriving in the nursing profession via such jobs as carpenter, farm labourer and lorry driver. Most of them had been severely affected by the Depression. Becoming an orderly was a route out of longterm unemployment and social declassification, with membership of the National Socialist Party regarded as a sort of work permit, a way of securing permanent employment in the public sector.[46] Rarely was there anything in their background to suggest any particular competence in caring for the sick. They had washed up in the asylums because they had failed to be something else. A former nurse recalled:

My father was a shopkeeper. He had a grocer's shop with a boarding house and did a little farming on the side. He died in 1918. After the war, my homeland became part of Poland; we chose to go to Germany. My mother had to sell up, and I spent the next three years in a refugee camp in Saxony, where I also attended a school. That was between 1921 and 1924. Then we moved to Ingolstadt, where I went to school until I finished. Then I attended a domestic science college run by the deaconesses in Munich and then became a domestic servant. I would have preferred to have been a teacher. But we had lost all of our savings and my mother earned very little, so I could not afford training. Therefore until 1936 I was a servant. When my brother had also left school, my mother took us to north Germany. She leased a business near Neuruppin. I helped out there. But since things did not work out, my mother had to give it up again after two years. I was then faced with the necessity of working again. I would have preferred to have worked in a hospital, but the climate was unfavourable. Then one day I happened upon an advert in a newspaper for trainee nurses; the training was free of charge, and indeed one got pocket money too. I decided to apply to the asylum at Neuruppin. I started work there on 1 January 1938.[47]

Paul R. was born in the village of Wolfenhausen in 1907, becoming a trainee gardener after finishing elementary school. The onset of the Depression badly affected wages in this sector, forcing Paul R. to switch to agricultural labouring. He worked for a farmer in the nearby village of Flach until Christmas 1930. Returning home in that year, Paul R. found occasional work on government work schemes. He joined the NSDAP in 1930 with the explicit intention of improving his employment prospects. In 1936, after several years of occasional work or unemployment, Paul R. became a trainee orderly at the Weilmünster asylum.[48]

People either in, or who had been discharged from, institutions were particularly vulnerable to the National Socialists' Law for the Prevention of Hereditarily Diseased Progeny. As we saw in the previous chapter (p. 42), this Law was agreed at a cabinet meeting on 14 July 1933, coming into force on 1 January 1934. The Law sanctioned the compulsory sterilisation of those suffering from a number of allegedly hereditary diseases: congenital feeblemindedness; schizophrenia; manic depressive illness; hereditary epilepsy; Huntington's Chorea; hereditary blindness; hereditary deafness; serious physical malformation.[49] Between 1934 and

May 1945, about 400,000 people were actually sterilised – about 1% of the population capable of producing children.[50] Some 220 Hereditary Health Courts, each consisting of a judge and two doctors, were established, with a series of Higher Hereditary Health Courts to deal with appeals.[51] These courts simply scrutinised the evidence and reached decisions; they were not fora for legal argument and counter-argument. The presence of the person whose sterilisation was being considered was regarded as being of limited value.[52] The doctors who served on these courts were not necessarily neurologists or psychiatrists, but rather could include dermatologists or surgeons, with no special competence in psychiatric illnesses.[53]

In the case of asylum inmates, who comprised 30 to 40% of those compulsorily sterilised between 1934 and 1936, proceedings were initiated by the asylum medical staff, who often sat on the panels which made the decision to sterilise them. Thus, Valentin Faltlhauser, who initiated the sterilisation of his patients from Kaufbeuren-Irsee, was also one of the judges at the Hereditary Health Court in Kempten which decided their cases.[54] This was to compound conflict of interest with a total breach of the rules of medical confidentiality. Judging from his writings on the subject, these ethical issues never actually seem to have occurred to him. Applications for sterilisation were usually merely accompanied by extracts cobbled together from medical records, which, of course, were not produced to deal with such questions. In the case of former patients, there was also extensive resort to the eugenic wisdom of laymen, as the authorities drew upon the 'expertise' of such people as mayors, social workers and teachers.

The official doctor or asylum director who instigated the sterilisation hearings was obliged, with the aid of an eleven-line 'Merkblatt' (instruction sheet), to inform the person concerned of the nature and purpose of the operation, reassuring him or her that there would be no deleterious consequences for either their general health or their capacity to enjoy sexual intercourse.[55] Paragraph twelve sanctioned the involvement of the police up to and including actually getting the victim on to an operating table.[56] In June 1935 the period allowed for appeals was reduced from a month to fourteen days.[57] The operation involved ligation of the fallopian tubes in the case of women, and vasectomy for men.[58]

At Eglfing-Haar, the operations were conducted by a surgeon and gynaecologist brought in from Munich on a generous *pro rata* basis. Together they were frequently able to sterilise up to five women or twelve men per morning, using respectively general and local anaesthetics.[59] At Kaufbeuren-Irsee patients were sterilised in the municipal hospital. Admission to the asylum came to be popularly regarded as being a certain route to sterilisation.[60] In February 1936, radium and X-ray sterilisation ('Strahlenbehandlung') was introduced for women over thirty-eight or those for whom tying the fallopian tubes might be life-threatening.[61]

Plate 3. Klara Nowak. The founder and current head of the League of those harmed by compulsory sterilisation and 'euthanasia', the Detmold-based self-help group which endeavours to overcome the isolation often experienced by these people, and which collectively represents their interests vis-à-vis government and parliament.

Formal recovery times varied between a week and fourteen days. At Eglfing-Haar, complications and fatalities began to occur from 1935 onwards. Of the 350 people sterilised that year, two women, one thirty-six, the other forty, died as a result of the operation, with the elder of the two bleeding to death because of a botched attempt to combine sterilisation with a caesarean abortion.[62] In 1936 a thirty-one-year old schizophrenic woman died of bronchial pneumonia a week after the operation.[63] Predictably enough, reports summarising each year's quota of sterilisations failed to mention adverse psychological effects on the victims, consequences which can only be gauged indirectly from the fact that in 1933 a patient attempted to castrate himself with a breadknife 'out of fear of sterilisation'.[64] During the first year of these policies at Kaufbeuren-Irsee, two patients experienced serious post-surgical complications, and another committed suicide shortly after the operation. Connections between the two events were fastidiously denied.[65] Articles dealing with the after-effects of compulsory sterilisation, and published in reputable psychological journals, claimed that the operation had no deleterious consequences, and that 'most of the hereditary ill regarded sterilisation with indifference, and sometimes even euphorically'.[66]

Those who had the operation recall neither indifference nor 'euphoria', but rather a painful invasion of their bodies and longterm physical and psychological problems. The following is an extract from a recent interview in 1991 with Klara Nowak, the present chairman of the League of Victims of Compulsory Sterilisation and 'Euthanasia', who was herself compulsorily sterilised in 1941:

QUESTION Were you in pain?

NOWAK Yes, indeed. In the beginning, the wound did hurt, and I also remember that I had to start work very shortly afterwards, fourteen days I think. When we were discharged there was no car or taxi. I remember very well that my legs gave way as I was going to get on the tram. It was so strange, I had never known anything like that. I always used to walk a lot, always out and about.

QUESTION How has the operation influenced your attitude?

NOWAK Well, there was not much to influence. You could not go against it, you had to come to terms with the facts. It was very depressing, of course. There were some critical moments, of course, simply to understand it all, that they had done that. You just could not do anything about it.

QUESTION Were any future plans influenced?

NOWAK Yes, certainly. I had always wished for a large family. I was always thinking what I would do better in the upbringing of my children, different from how my parents had done it. That was my big wish, to have a lovely, healthy family.

QUESTION You wanted to have a family of your own then?

NOWAK Definitely, it was my natural wish; that is why I combined my job plans with family plans. I wanted to become a community nurse and to marry a farmer.

QUESTION How do you regard the operation nowadays?

NOWAK Well, I still have many complaints as a result of it. There were complications with every operation I have had since. I had to take early retirement at the age of fifty-two – and the psychological pressure has always remained. When nowadays my neighbours, older ladies, tell me about their grandchildren and great-grandchildren, this hurts bitterly, because I do not have any children or grandchildren, because I am on my own, and I have to cope without anyone's help.

QUESTION There are always dreams?

NOWAK I have had dreams for a long time. Now I am almost seventy, and they are all buried. How could I start a new life now? It is simply too late for that.[67]

Most of Klara Nowak's post-war career was as a psychiatric nurse.

Leaving aside opportunities for the articulation of social or sexually determined prejudices (which were well to the fore in the original diagnoses) and the supplementary evidence gleaned from such people as employers, schoolteachers and social workers (not to speak of the judgements of the Hereditary Health Courts themselves), the criteria which led to people being categorised as 'hereditarily ill', both in the Law itself and subsequent commentaries, exhibited a number of worrying features. Most of these were actually rehearsed in the contemporary psychiatric literature, although the aim here was clearly to cut off escape routes rather than to prevent miscarriages of this peculiar form of 'justice'.

Many of these problems stemmed from the fact that the hereditary character of all of the diseases specified in the Law was a declaration of faith rather than a matter of scientific certitude; or from the fact that the terms used – notably 'schizophrenia' and 'oligophrenia' – were catchall conveniences of recent historical provenance used to encompass a vast and mysterious range of human experience. Of course, no professionalised 'expert' has an interest in circumspect doubt once all legal safeguards have been eradicated.[68]

Only a few of the most glaring inconsistencies can be highlighted here, since to deal with this literature at any length would be extremely tedious. Apart from the fact that haemophilia, one of the few incontestably hereditary diseases, was quietly omitted, a number of crucial acts of terminological legerdemain were used to paper over the inherent scientific shoddiness of the entire enterprise.[69] Although alcoholism was not regarded as an hereditary illness, its 'chronic' forms suggested 'evidence of mental and moral inferiority' sufficient to warrant sterilisation.[70] Tautological exegetics justified sterilising people who were moderate drinkers, reformed abstainers, and indeed people whose families had no history of hereditary disorders:

The sense of the Law will have been properly understood if the alcohol-intolerant, who are often habitual criminals or asocial psychopaths, are sterilised, even if they are not always addicted to drink, or if the quantity of alcohol enjoyed is relatively moderate.... Certainly, if it can be demonstrated that the father or grandfather (or other close blood relatives) were also chronic drinkers, then this may be an obvious basis for coming to a judgement. On the other hand, the absence of any form of hereditary burden or the presence of any form of mental abnormality in the family concerned in no way detracts from the existence of a hereditarily determined addiction to alcohol.[71]

For the sake of convenience, alcoholism was to be regarded as evidence of an underlying asocial or psychopathic disorder, although neither 'asociality' nor 'psychopathy' were themselves specified in the legislation.

The prefix 'hereditary' was omitted from the term 'schizophrenia', in order to keep open the possibility of sterilising people where the causes of the illness were exogenous. The periods of remission which frequently characterise sufferers from this illness did not constitute grounds for exemption from sterilisation. The same was true in the case of cyclothymia or manic depression, where remission or recovery were regarded as being 'most dangerous' from a racial-hygienic perspective, a feature which had several bearings on the sterilisation of discharged former asylum inmates.[72]

What exactly constituted 'serious physical malformation'? Did it include people with congenital dislocated hips?[73] Was the child of a blind mother with impaired vision because of childhood cataracts hereditarily ill? Were a woman who was only 140cm tall, or people with hare-lips or cleft palates, cases of 'serious physical malformation'? What did one do with a forty-eight-year-old man suffering from muscular dystrophy, for whom sexual intercourse was all but impossible? The answer in all these cases was affirmative, and the people concerned were sterilised, in the last case because the man's partner – and they acknowledged that there was slim chance of his finding one – might have been able to facilitate the act.[74]

The term 'congenital' replaced 'hereditary' in the case of feeblemindedness, to cover cases where the hereditary origins could not be ascertained. Commentaries on the Law argued that since the illness was 'congenital' it must be hereditary, even though reputable psychiatrists were 'by no means entirely certain whether there was actually such a thing as inherited imbecility or (more correctly) debility'.[75] Persons who could satisfactorily answer the intelligence tests designed to ascertain 'feeblemindedness' were usually shipwrecked on such subjective grounds as their way of life or alleged 'moral insanity'; or indirectly, via the frequency of instances of 'feeblemindedness' within their families. Again, recondite articles took care of feebleminded persons with exceptional talents of the sort evinced by autistic savants, by simply arguing that while it was unlikely their skills at drawing or music would be handed down to the next generation, their feeblemindedness would be.[76] The total illogicality of this claim is as noteworthy as the desire to cut any possible escape route for those persons who defied simple categorisation. Alternatively, one might point to the relativity of such notions as 'being gifted', by highlighting the 'twilight of the Gods' which had befallen the 'November artists' of the Weimar Republic following the Nazi seizure of power. Artists like Beckmann or Kirchner were geniuses one minute; puerile daubers the next.[77] More deviously, ever more elaborate intelligence tests were devised to frustrate those enterprising patients who mastered, and shared with their fellows, the answers to the standard variety.

Some of the more obvious pitfalls in drawing the line between common stupidity and the various conditions subsumed under the term 'feebleminded' were voiced by the deputy Reich Doctors' Leader, Fritz Bartels, in the context of debates about whether simpleminded members of the National Socialist Party could or should be sterilised – debates which were dampening initial activist enthusiasm for the policies concerned.[78] The arguments became surprisingly 'environmentalist' when one of their own was under scrutiny:

For example, when a peasant boy from Masuria, who has hardly had any experience of schooling because he has always had to work in the fields, comes to

Berlin and joins some formation or other, and then while drunk commits some sort of stupidity, then there soon comes an application to have him examined with a view to eventual sterilisation. Then there is the famous questionnaire, for example, 'When was Columbus born?' and the boy answers 'no' to everything, saying 'I don't know anything about that', and he does this quite possibly because he has never had an opportunity to learn these things. But the doctor who has examined him once certainly cannot come on this basis to a final verdict that the subject is of lesser value, because perhaps his abilities have never been able to come to fruition. If here and there attempts are made to overlook these questions, which however are very germane to the verdict, then I have to say that the good intentions of the movement are being misused.[79]

The psychiatrists acknowledged that the intelligence tests were next to useless. A study of 'normal' and 'backward' schoolchildren in Samland, the area around Königsberg in East Prussia, revealed equal measures of ignorance about the identity of Bismarck or who had discovered America. Sixty per cent of the 'normal' children could not work out how much interest would accrue on 300RMS at 3% over three years (one of the 'backward' group could), and only 7% of them could tell the difference between a lawyer and public prosecutor (two of the 'backward' group could).[80]

An estimated 30–40% of those sterilised in the years 1934–1936 were patients in asylums. Beginning with mere numbers and global categories, who was affected at ground level? The asylum at Eglfing-Haar had a total of 2,264 patients on 19 September 1933, the date by which all candidates for sterilisation had to be registered. Some 1,552 patients were exempted, either because their illnesses were not among those specified by the Law (224 patients), or because their age (444 patients) or limited prospects of release (884 patients) made sterilisation irrelevant or superfluous. This left 712 people, or about a third of the patients, liable to be sterilised, a fact which demonstrated to the asylum authorities 'the extent to which the asylums were catchment points for hereditary illnesses'.[81] At Kaufbeuren-Irsee, which housed a high number of schizophrenics, the radical steriliser Faltlhauser decided that 82.04% of his 1,409 patients were hereditarily ill in the sense of the Law, and accordingly he made 208 applications for sterilisation in the first year of the Law's operation.[82]

Of the 150 people sterilised at Eglfing-Haar in 1934, ninety-seven were men and fifty-three women. Of these, 108 were said to be suffering from schizophrenia, twenty-two from congenital feeblemindedness, seven from depression, nine from epilepsy, three from alcoholism and one from hereditary blindness. These proportions remained roughly constant over the following years. One hundred and twenty-six of them were under forty years of age, although twenty men and three women in the age range 41–60 were also sterilised, as was one male over sixty. Two thirds of the group had been in the asylum for less than a year, which meant that the people most vulnerable to sterilisation were those for whom prognoses were most favourable. Indeed, two thirds of those sterilised in 1934 had been discharged by 1935, about half of them within three months of the operation.[83] There was a similarly high discharge rate of sterilised patients at Eichberg, e.g. 78.6% of those operated upon in the course of 1938.[84] Proceedings were quickly systematised. New admissions to Eglfing-Haar were compulsorily categorised as 'E0' (no longer able to have children); 'E1' (early release anticipated, so expedite application for sterilisation); 'E2' (release not imminent, but the position on sterilisation to be regularly reviewed); and 'E?' (inconclusive findings).[85]

Because of these laws, doctors assumed a new range of extra- and intra-mural functions. Like most professionals, they carped at the increased workload while relishing the attendant reinforcement of their fragile sense of self-importance. Being nobodies, they needed this sort of external endorsement. This is not to make a crude 'anti-psychiatric' point, but rather just an observation about the nature of professionalisation in general. Eugenicists dreamed of being able to enmesh the population in a net whose knots were expanding local hereditary databanks. Some of these, such as those constructed by Astel or Kranz, covered entire regions.[86] From 1936 onwards, each asylum was allocated a catchment area within which specially chosen staff had to carry out a hereditary-biological survey of the families of people already designated 'hereditarily ill'. Although enthusiasts in some asylums (for example, Friedrich Panse in the Wittenauer Heilstätten) had been collating material of this sort since the late 1920s, the inauguration of state-sponsored hereditary databanks meant a further diminution of the number of medical personnel who actually had time to deal with patients.[87] Mindless bureaucracy marginalised medical practice.

In the last chapter we considered the expansion of outpatient care and its potentialities as an instrument of social control. This latter trend was accelerated under the National Socialists. The fight to eliminate hereditary illness was like 'the struggle against a Hydra': as soon as one person had been located more cropped up.[88] Discovering abnormal people outside the asylums was no longer left to chance, but became a matter of systematic investigation as care of individuals was superseded by care for collective racial hygiene.[89] At Kaufbeuren-Irsee, Hermann Pfannmüller, whom we have already encountered, was in charge of outpatient provision, clocking up about 21,000 kilometres a year as he toured the surrounding area in his Hanomag official limousine. In between his visits, Pfannmüller operated a eugenic advisory centre in Augsburg and gave talks on eugenics to National Socialist party formations. In line with the regime's view that 'defective people who are on the margins of the psychologically normal can never be the objects of medical attention', Pfannmüller thinned out his clientele by the simple expedient of consigning 'asocial drinkers, grumblers, refractory parasites and workshy psychopaths' to concentration camps.[90] As for the rest, district doctors and youth and welfare services referred cases to Pfannmüller's outpatient service, and then Pfannmüller set in motion their compulsory sterilisation. Mayors were enthusiastic exponents of these policies, not because they were fanatical National Socialists, but rather because they wished to prevent single mothers from burdening their communal budgets with illegitimate children.[91] Looked at closely, the amoral insidiousness of eugenic outpatient care almost beggars belief. Consider, for example, the case of a twenty-three-year-old woman who was sterilised because of her propensity to produce illegitimate children. The proceedings at the Hereditary Health Court in Kempten led Pfannmüller to believe that her family might contain further abnormal members:

In the course of a week's work I discovered in the clan that the father of the above-named woman was a feebleminded alcoholic, and that there were twenty-one further cases of hereditary degenerate feeblemindedness on the sidelines of the family. These were combined with speech difficulties and occasional instances of deafness which I recorded on card indexes. Ten cases had to be refereed immediately as being highly urgent, since the danger of reproduction appeared imminent.[92]

In order to disguise the real objectives of this sort of 'research' (for in Roman Catholic areas priests were advising schoolteachers not to report mentally deficient children), those involved recommended that projects be described in anodyne terms, as being research into psychopathy, or indeed simply a form of census.[93] In some areas, outpatient psychiatrists sought to coopt schoolteachers into the 'vital' task of systematically registering their pupils.[94] The teachers were in turn to encourage their pupils to reconstruct their own family trees in an attempt to involve these truly innocent victims in the eugenic sterilisation of their own families.[95] Schools, housing authorities and registry offices became watchposts in the fight against hereditary illness.[96]

So far we have been considering compulsory sterilisation largely in terms of numbers and categories. To discuss the subject solely in these terms is of course to slip into the dehumanised world of those responsible for these policies. How did sterilisation actually affect individuals?

The process of sterilising Alfred N. was set in motion in 1936 by the director of the asylum at Johannistal, and dealt with by the Hereditary Health Court at Krefeld. Alfred N. was thirty-five years old. After a chequered primary school education, he had become an apprentice furrier. He had acquired thirteen criminal convictions for (*inter alia*) theft, embezzlement, fraud and unauthorised assumption of authority. In November 1931 he was consigned by the police to the Johannistal asylum for psychiatric observation, on the grounds that he was a danger to the community. He began to express 'paranoid ideas', which consisted of feeling as if he was under observation by persons who took a dim view of him. He made 'preposterous' charges against those around him, suspecting them of unspecified plots, machinations and conspiracies against him. What Alfred called 'the competition' wanted to 'render him harmless'.[97] In December he was released on the grounds that he was an incurable psychopath, but not insane. Alfred was back in the asylum by June 1933, immediately following his release from a spell of imprisonment. Apparently a prison warder had said to him 'that people like him would be killed under the Third Reich, and that he would be given poisonous powder, mainly administered through the food'. This disquieting, and in the event prescient, intelligence had left Alfred in an agitated state. He was also 'thoroughly unreasonable, clearly silly, and periodically pronouncedly odd'. Not unreasonably, he thought that people were going to poison him. Alfred's work was irregular and unreliable. He felt the need to relay everything that he observed. Although it had become impossible to get through to him, he evidently wrote letters filled with religious meanderings. The Hereditary Health Court decided that Alfred was a paranoid schizophrenic and hence liable to be sterilised.[98] Following abortive appeals to the Higher Hereditary Health Court in Düsseldorf and to the Führer's Deputy, Alfred was sterilised in July 1937 at the municipal hospital in Wuppertal-Barmen.[99]

Anna V. was born in 1916 in the Ruhr, and was placed in an orphanage in Essen at the age of one. After a normal primary education, Anna's re-married mother decided to take her back home in 1933. She was taken into care shortly afterwards for consorting with boys and acts of petty theft. In 1936 she had trouble with the police because of gonorrhoea. In September 1937, at the age of twenty-one, Anna became a patient in the asylum at Hadamar. Within a month of her admission, the initial diagnosis being 'congenital feeblemindedness', the asylum applied to have her sterilised. She was 'sexually unrestrained, workshy and feebleminded'. On the basis of oral evidence, the Hereditary Health Court in Frankfurt am Main found Anna's intelligence 'adequate', and decided that she was not suffering from a hereditary illness, even if she had not been particularly successful in life.[100] Clearly not satisfied with this outcome, the asylum director attempted to overturn the verdict in December 1937. In a letter to the court dated 28 December 1937, he drew attention to the 'fact' that people who had passed through several institutions were old hands at theoretical intelligence testing, whose results therefore 'in no way corresponded with reality'. In a classic affirmation of the concept of 'moral

Plate 4. Anna V.

insanity', bolstered with a reference to the cogitations of Rüdin and Gütt on these questions, the director pointed out that 'more convincing proofs of the existence of congenital feeblemindedness are: the inability to earn a living through regular employment or to adapt to society; an uncritical approach to one's actions; weakness of will; the dulling of ethical sentiments; and gross defects of character'.[101] This line of argument paid off with the Higher Hereditary Health Court, which told its lower instance to rehearse the case again. Anna was put through another round of intelligence tests, in which she performed poorly, not on account of a deficit in her education, for it was a result 'which doubtless can be attributed to a weakness in her understanding'. Any consequences of the fact that Anna was pregnant at the time of the second round of testing were discounted, so that 'the noticeably unfavourable result of today's intelligence testing must to a considerable extent be regarded as the expression of an inherent intellectual defect'.[102] On 15 April 1938 Anna gave birth to a girl, who was put into care. Anna herself was sterilised in May 1938 at the asylum in Herborn.

Although there are a considerable number of studies of individual institutions, the dominant facts of compulsory sterilisation and 'euthanasia' have meant that the everyday lives of the patients during the 1930s have been neglected. In the absence of anything so colourful as autobiographies of the insane, what information we have on what Erving Goffman called the 'underlife' of public institutions has to be gleaned from interviews with former staff and patients, and from such written sources as the asylum annual reports and medical files, those heterogeneous gatherings of paper which fitfully shadowed the asylum careers of individuals.[103] The annual reports, as we have already repeatedly seen in this chapter, tell us a considerable amount about the formal life of asylums, although with the major proviso that they were for official public consumption. They therefore have about as much utility as, for example, detailed company reports. They are less eloquent about the patients themselves, unless the latter did serious injury to themselves or others. However, they do relay a considerable amount of global statistical information about the social origins and sicknesses of the patients, beginning with how they arrived in the asylums.

In 1933, for example, Eglfing-Haar admitted some five hundred people, discharging 395 in the course of that year. One of the latter was described as being 'cured', 292 as being simply 'better'. Some 369 of those newly admitted were from Munich, with far fewer people being transferred from other institutions in Bavaria or from Germany as a whole. The vast majority of new admissions had been referred from the university psychiatric clinic in Munich's Nussbaumstrasse, or from the psychiatric department of the hospital at Schwabing.[104] Responsibility for the person's initial entry into the psychiatric system was roughly divided between their own relatives (in 258 cases) and (in 217 cases) the authorities' use of statutory powers of committal to prevent them from endangering either themselves or others. Only one person had voluntarily requested admission to Eglfing-Haar that year.[105] In terms of age, the dominant group among these new admissions was those between thirty-one and forty-five (40.6%), with a further 23.6% between sixteen and thirty, and 25.6% between forty-five and sixty. Over half of these new admissions were unmarried. Artisans made up the single largest occupational group, although there were significant numbers of civil servants and academically trained professionals, small businessmen, and the unemployed. Workers and farmers were relatively under-represented. Among the patients as a whole, the dominant illness was schizophrenia, which accounted for 1,527 of the asylum's 2,325 patients. Trailing a considerable way behind this group were people suffering from manic depressive illnesses (142), alcoholism (68), epilepsy (118), progressive paralysis (109) and feeblemindedness (116).[106]

The reasons why families decided to put individual members in asylums were more or less straightforward. The combined impact of illness and straitened economic circumstances can be seen in the case of Hedwig S. The S. family hailed from a village called Giersdorf, near Wartha in central Silesia, about twenty kilometres from the Czechoslovak border. Josef S. came from a small village called Kamnitz near Glatz, and was a forestry worker of limited means, employed on the estate of the Graf Wollny. His wife Hedwig was from a similar background. The family (for they had two sons, Alfred and Josef, the latter being the source of this information) eked out a very modest living, sometimes bartering the wood they could collect on feast days for food. The children were automatically brought up in a very religious fashion, acting as altar boys in the imposing baroque church in Wartha. By way of reward, they received such luxuries as cocoa for breakfast.

In 1928, the twenty-nine-year-old Hedwig S. contracted meningitis, and was provisionally admitted for observation to a Roman Catholic psychiatric clinic at Leubus near Breslau, about 130 kilometres from the family home. This distance made visits costly and difficult. Because of the impact of the Depression upon the family's meagre resources, this initial spell in hospital developed into longterm institutionalisation. At Leubus, Hedwig S. performed modest amounts of work in the gardens and kitchens, up to her sudden transfer to an unknown destination in 1941, which in reality meant her death in the 'euthanasia' asylum at Sonnenstein of 'paralysis'.[107]

Less straightforward motives resulted in the committal of the dressmaker Klara S. Her own father connived at her committal to the asylum at Herborn, primarily in order to lay his hands on her inheritance, which he wanted to use to pay off his son's debts.[108] Covetousness was, and in some countries still is, a fairly routine motive for having members of the family institutionalised and rendered powerless.

The ways in which people were committed by the authorities were just as various. Fritz N. was a victim of the invasive agents of Nazi community care. After failing to complete a training in retail salesmanship, and abandoning the merchant navy, Fritz N. eventually signed up in the navy. His casual attitude to discipline and the navy's strict sartorial regulations

(a)

Plate 5. Emma Z. Obscure family tensions and moralising prejudices sometimes played a role in a person's permanent institutionalisation. This sequence of two photographs concerns Emma Z. Born into an affluent, dynastically conscious and deeply pious Swabian family, Emma Z. married a pastor in 1912. They had three children. Her husband and eldest child died within days of each other in the Asiatic influenza epidemic of 1918. Thereafter, Emma was increasingly thrown back on the charity of her parents and elder sisters, seen here in a family group portrait. Her efforts to eke out an independent existence in Mannheim – her sisters quietly subsumed her children into their own charitable foundations (whose motto was: 'children are a blessing, but whoever has them, must care for them') – resulted in an illegitimate daughter. Her eldest sister, who had already had Emma's brother put in an asylum, arranged for Emma's own admission to Weinsberg in 1932 on the grounds of what was called 'moral deficiency'. The initial

resulted in a period in a naval psychiatric ward and discharge from the service. At home, the erotic fixations which had plagued him since childhood took the unfortunate form of an obsession with a visiting Nazi community nursing sister. She reciprocated by arranging a call by an asylum psychiatrist, who committed Fritz N. on the grounds that he was 'a danger to the community'. He spent all but three of the years before 1945 in asylums, narrowly escaping death in the extermination centre at Obrawalde the year before the war ended.[109]

Lina C. was detained by an officer from the traffic police in April 1941 for a public order offence. She had attacked and insulted passers-by on the street in Niederlahnstein. A crowd had formed. The police called in a

(b)

diagnosis oscillated clumsily between 'psychopathy' and 'hereditary mental illness', the presence of her brother in the same asylum being 'useful' in this respect.

For the next eight years of her life, the 'Frau Pfarrer', as she was known, worked in the asylum. She is seen here in the second photograph, taking a rest during work in a vineyard. Although Emma's sister knew about the first mass transports from the Weinsberg asylum, she avoided removing Emma from the asylum by claiming that it was up to the authorities there to give her 'the nod' when to do so. On 4 June 1940 Emma and sixty-three other women were transported from Weinsberg to Grafeneck and gassed on arrival. On 22 June the family were notified of her death from 'acute heart failure' in the Sonnenstein asylum near Dresden. Her brother avoided the same fate because male transports were alphabetically organised, and 'Aktion T–4' stopped before the Community Patients' Transport Service had reached the letter Z in this asylum.

doctor, who administered a sedative and declared her to be 'a danger to the community'. Having been on the road for some time, Lina C. was in a very neglected state. The initial report following her committal to Eichberg noted 'she is physically neglected and unbelievably dirty. The dirt on her whole body is as thick as a finger[!]. Her clothes are unbelievably torn and filthy. She claps her hands above her head and screams continuously. Doesn't respond, and fails to react. Her face is blue and puffed up because of the constant raving and crying.'[110] After forcible baths designed to calm rather than cleanse her, Lina C. was placed in a ward. There, she said little, sat around on benches, 'and did no work'. The entries made on 'Form Number 1' were tantamount to a death sentence. Under the rubric 'main symptoms', the doctor wrote: 'noisy, swears, raves unbelievably, rips everything, is totally filthy, wanders about for days in the woods. Caused public disorder. Neglects herself. Now: negative, simpleminded, but quieter.' She did no work, and was said to be both a danger to the community and a longterm case.[111] Consequently, she died of 'heart failure' in June 1942.[112]

The third case illustrates the process of committal by the courts. Wilhelm B. was born in 1866 and had worked as a packager. In 1937 he had served a nine-month jail sentence for paedophile offences with young boys. In 1934 he had lured a fourteen-year-old to his home, ostensibly to see cigarette cards, in order to sexually assault him. In 1937 he had acted in a similar fashion with an eleven-year-old. Two years later, he had attempted to have sexual intercourse with somebody he picked up in a pub. In 1941 he was before the court in Wiesbaden for similar offences. An eighteen-year-old gardener had approached him for a light. Wilhelm B. had replied that although he had no matches on him, he would bring some to where the youth worked the following day. Having effected this unlikely rendezvous, Wilhelm B. offered the youth three cigarettes if he would accompany him into the woods to gather fuel. There, the accused had enquired whether the youth had had a girl, and 'whether he had whored around yet'. Thereupon, Wilhelm B. had begun to expose himself, until he was forced to interrupt his obscure pleasures because of a passing farmer. The court, which took into account both these previous offences and medical reports which spoke of senile dementia – Wilhelm B. was seventy-five at the time – sentenced him to four months' imprisonment for offences against Paragraph 175 of the Reich Criminal Code.[113] The reluctance of the local mayor to have a known, and recidivist, homosexual and paedophile around, and the absence of any relatives, ensured that Wilhelm B. was committed to an asylum on completion of his sentence. He died of 'heart failure' shortly afterwards.[114]

Many of the Bavarian cases of compulsory committal reveal political motives. Maria Z. had been a household tutor to the daughter of the Prince of Löwenstein. She fell in love with one of the Prince's huntsmen, who apparently was unaware of her. Maria Z. suspected that the huntsman was seducing her pupil. She began to behave bizarrely, turning up stark naked at one of the Prince's receptions. Maria Z. was first committed to Eglfing-Haar in 1916, on account of her rather novel explanation of the origins of the First World War. She thought that a painting of a nude in a Munich art gallery window was her pupil. The Löwensteins frequently entertained diplomats. Maria Z. imagined that the diplomats lusted after the daughter of the house. They fell out over her, and the First World War had resulted.

In 1917 she had attended the trial of a sex offender. By 1933 she was making rather unfortunate connections between this individual and the

German Führer in a letter to a court medical officer. Immorality, she wrote, was the root of all evil. The authorities were as mad as she was. They reasoned that anyone who could attribute the outbreak of war in 1914 to the charms of the daughter of the Prince of Löwenstein must be a 'pacifist', while 'whoever believes that the German nation is being governed by a sexual offender must necessarily be an opponent of the regime'. She was committed to Gabersee, with her release henceforth dependent upon the say-so of the Gestapo. In November 1940 they refused to contemplate her release, on the grounds that she was a 'fanatic pacifist' and that her freedom would 'signify an extraordinary threat to the security of the State'.[115]

In most asylums, such as Eichberg or Eglfing-Haar, patients were divided up amongst a number of different buildings and wards according to both gender and the seriousness of their condition. There were particular wards for patients who needed a high degree of attention; for those who were ill or who befouled themselves; for the agitated, semi-agitated and quiescent; and open wards, plus secure wards for those who were perceived as being dangerous.[116] Given the drastic economy measures which we considered earlier, a large part of the patients' waking hours – and probably hours of sleep – was probably taken up with the thought of food. Such information as we have regarding nutrition suggests scandalous insufficiency, a state of affairs which became life-threatening with the outbreak of war. At Eichberg, daily food consisted of the following: 'In the morning there was turnip on bread. We usually smeared that on the bread the night before so that it had time to sink in. There was also coffee in a tin mug, with no milk or sugar. Lunch was at noon. Turnips or swedes once more, cooked without any fat. Always the same thing. There were usually three potatoes, boiled in their skins. Once a week we had beetroot. At three o'clock we had coffee again, and bread with syrup.' Those who worked sometimes received the odd piece of sausage.[117]

Apart from visits and letters, both of which were at the whim of the authorities, there was little relief from the grinding monotony of life in the asylums. Periodically the authorities provided concerts, light entertainment or outings. In 1932, a doctor gave patients at Eglfing-Haar a talk and slideshow about his travel experiences. There were also theatrical performances, a concert of zither music, a performance of Haydn's *Creation* by the asylum choir and orchestra with soloists from Munich, and a visit from a conjuror. Normally, three dances were held each year to mark the Fasching carnival, May Day and Consecration Day.[118] In subsequent years there was a circus or performances by a ventriloquist as well as the usual Christmas festivities and services conducted by one of the resident chaplains.[119] The latter may well have played a bigger part in the patients' lives than the formal reports allow.

As in many 'total institutions', patients were subject to informal, but no less real, categorisation, according to whether they were clean or dirty, accommodating or refractory, hard working or idle and so forth. Privileges, such as less onerous jobs in the kitchens (with the potentialities for extra food), the writing or receipt of letters, visits, non-essential personal possessions, and outings depended upon these behavioural, but progressively more economistic, criteria, which eventually made capacity to work – and not just go through the motions – the arbiter of life and death. The acceptable forms of patient conduct can be gleaned from these entries regarding Wilhelm E., a former medical student who was a patient in Hadamar from 1921 onwards:

Since *1928* he has taken care of the asylum exits, runs errands, is usually the runner.

1933 occupies himself drawing or playing the zither, tends his pet monkey, takes it for walks.

1935 makes an entirely reasonable impression, despite minor eccentricities and tomfoolery. As before, responsible for errands, especially things for the pharmacy. Feels at ease, physically healthy, is proud when people listen to him playing the zither, for which he displays a certain talent.

1937 loyally performs his errands, trustworthy and unassuming. Values his skill in drawing and music very highly. Doesn't tolerate any criticism of this. Recently, typical manifestations of senility.

1939 performs his errands, and makes heavy weather of it, but very trustworthy. In his spare time he occupies himself by painting or composing poems. For several days has a feverish inflammation of the lower leg, and his spirits are very depressed; he believes he is going to die, and already feels death in his limbs, nonetheless he is very concerned about the state of his leg. Course of recovery seems good. His temperature has fallen.

1940 agitated from time to time, denounces the English, gets on badly with the patients on his ward, easily forgets things. No change in December 1940, continues to do the asylum's errands.[120]

In many respects, Wilhelm E. was a model patient. He was active, reliable, trustworthy, willing and did not require undue supervision. There were no difficulties in letting him out to run errands or to exercise his pet monkey. He was even capable of entertaining the staff. One could easily accommodate a short period of illness, the odd bout of depression and a few personal eccentricities, provided none of these things lasted too long. Had his bad leg meant he could no longer perform errands, or had his depression persisted, then one would not have rated Wilhelm E.'s chances in this asylum climate.

Patients who were less than accommodating were subjected to a variety of coercive practices, which ranged from open brutality to others which endeavoured to cloak sadism in a more or less therapeutic guise. At Eichberg, two patients who availed themselves of work outside the asylum to arrange assignations with members of the League of German Maidens were caught and confined, with the aid of covers which secured all but the person's head, in baths of lukewarm water, with reduced rations for the entire week they were restrained in this fashion. This was followed by periods in the 'bunker', a set of isolation cells, originally designed to house criminally dangerous lunatics.[121] They were damp, unheated and verminous.[122] These cells were soon employed to coerce recalcitrant patients in general. For example, a patient who absconded for three days was confined in the 'bunker' for eight days without food or water.[123]

In post-war trials, former patients repeatedly highlighted brutal and inhumane treatment by the medical and nursing staff. Patients were verbally abused ('Here, you can all see a whore and how she is going to the dogs!');[124] and punched or beaten with such implements as scrubbing brushes.[125] There was also a fine line between certain restraining techniques or therapies and straightforward abuse. These practices included prolonged confinement in the aforementioned lukewarm baths, and the 'Packsack' i.e. being bound inside wet sheets and blankets for long periods.[126] Although clinical shock therapy will be discussed in detail below, the *ad hoc* variety, i.e. four attendants lifting a patient with the intention of suddenly dropping him or her on the floor, deserves to be mentioned in this context.[127]

The annual reports from Eglfing-Haar regularly contained a section under the rubric 'special occurrences', which chronicled in some detail extreme cases of despair, i.e. those who fled, or mutilated or killed themselves. In 1933, two patients died by deliberately swallowing respectively the handle of a spoon and a ten-centimetre-long feather from a mattress. Suicide attempts included a schizophrenic who smashed a window and proceeded to slash his wrists on the broken glass.[128] The following year, a thirty-one-year-old 'Pfropfhebephrenic' who had been in the asylum for two and a half years walked into the path of a train. A twenty-five-year-old patient hanged himself in a wood. A forty-nine-year-old man hanged himself from a clothes hook in a bathroom; a fifty-six-year-old woman used the opportunity provided by a door to a veranda being left open at night to hang herself. Forty-eight patients attempted to escape.[129] Each year saw a regular number of suicide attempts, with patients attempting to hang themselves, jumping from windows and high buildings, or in a few cases setting themselves ablaze. These reports also often detailed physical attacks on staff and other patients, or attempts at self-mutilation. They never record attacks on patients committed by the staff.

In order to recapture something of the rhythm of the asylum routine as experienced by the people within them, we must turn to the information kept in their medical files. Most of these are so perfunctory as to be effectively useless. However, some are not. Beneath the constant surface noise of doctors and nurses scribbling down or typing up case notes and observations, we can occasionally hear the voices of individual patients, although, refracted as they are, they probably have as much authenticity as a scratchy recording of a famous operatic aria. Paul S. was born on 31 October 1913 at Niederrossbach, Kreis Westerburg. He died at 8.15 p.m. on 7 July 1941, allegedly of tuberculosis, in the Eichberg asylum, where he had been transferred that February.[130] The file which accompanied him from the asylum at Scheuern contained three photographs. In one with crimped edges, he stands naked, resting on crutches, for he was lame. He manages to look as dignified as these circumstances permit. Two smaller passport type photographs, taken in 1937, show him wearing a collar and tie, looking directly into the camera. Paul S. had been in the Krüppelheim at Bad Kreuznach from 1921 to October 1930, thereafter at Scheuern. He was diagnosed as being 'feebleminded (imbecility)'.[131] The causes were said to be hereditary. A sister of his father, who had died in 1924 in a coalmining accident, was deaf and dumb. A female cousin was also in Scheuern suffering from 'idiocy and epilepsy'. Non-hereditary causes of his 'imbecility', such as rickets, were merely mentioned in passing. On admission, Paul S. was crooked and could only stand unaided for a moment or two. Mobility depended upon two sticks, which enabled him to move slowly forward, dragging his feet in a circular movement along the ground. He spoke normally and his 'face betrayed no signs of a mental defect'. He knew why he was in the asylum: to learn a trade in its workshops. Although he read with difficulty, he did reasonably well in the intelligence tests he had to perform on admission to Scheuern: if '$x + 5 = 12, x = 7$'; he could distinguish between a lie and a mistake; and do a passable drawing of a house whose image he had been allowed to see for fifteen seconds, even if the windows gravitated to the corners below the roof.[132]

Four times a year, between 1930 and 1941, the asylum authorities formally noted down Paul S.'s progress. There were some successes, most notably in terms of his improved mobility. He was beginning to be able to negotiate steps with his sticks. He learned basketwork, which began with repairing chairs. Evidently mature for his years, he apparently preferred to talk with the staff rather than with patients of his own age. Judging from the number of references, they seem to have liked playing cards with him. He read the newspapers, and enjoyed discussing politics and current affairs such as the 1930 Reichstag elections. In the evenings he enjoyed games such as halma, nine men's morris and scat; or he would reminisce, as people in institutions tend to do, about such events in his pre-patient days as trying to join the brass band in Kreuznach. However, his major passion was football. So much so that he began to attribute his lameness to

Plate 6. Paul S.

an earlier playing-field mishap, which had 'done in his leg'. Although he could not play himself, he had become 'a fanatical supporter', always going on foot the half-hour journey to the sports ground in Nassau to support his favourite team. He read the sports pages avidly, and on Sunday evenings could scarcely contain his excitement at the results broadcast over the radio. 'He never says that he would like to play too, and never complains about his illness, which makes it impossible for him to play. He bears his condition well and is brave. He moves skilfully and surely, and can go up and down steps with one stick, using the ground, and sometimes taking two steps at a time. He can move quickly on level ground.' He was beginning to get picky about his food, and had become a heavy smoker, puffing away his tobacco allowance as soon as he got it; the small sums of money sent by his mother or sister in Berlin immediately went up in smoke. So far he had no interest in the opposite sex.

By 1935, Paul S. had lost his earlier interest in politics. He knew about rearmament – 'it doesn't affect me, since I cannot run' – and the names of the leading members of the government. As far as he was concerned, the main principles of the Third Reich were 'order, so that unemployment will cease, that everything will happen in moderation, that one will not have more than the other, and that people will be treated fairly'. Otherwise, politics 'had no worth'. In April of that year he allegedly applied to be sterilised, arguing that this would allow him to leave the asylum more frequently on extended home visits. This sounds as if he had been talked into giving his consent to the operation. Although 'sexually harmless', by 1937 he was beginning to take an interest in girls, reportedly discussing when no one appeared to be around – inevitably someone was – who was pretty, or which of his contemporaries had a 'treasure' of his own. Contact with his fami y took the form of letters – he did not trust himself to write the address – or the occasional visit home. Paul S. clearly wanted to spend more time there, and visits would end with him wanting to stay longer, a situation his family were not keen on encouraging. For a long time they did not answer his letters, but managed to send food parcels, a card game and some clothes for Christmas.

By the summer of 1938, following the resumption of home visits, Paul's mother had changed her mind. Paul was complaining about not being properly fed in the asylum and, even though she foresaw difficulties, she wanted him to live at home. Paul S.'s release depended upon their consenting to his sterilisation. This was decided upon by the Hereditary Health Court in Limburg on 21 July 1938, where (on the basis of two instances of illness in the family) Paul S. was deemed to be 'hereditarily ill'. The operation was carried out at the asylum in Herborn in September of that year. Afterwards, he 'preferred not to talk about the operation', although he apparently liked the food at Herborn, and regarded the operation itself 'as child's play, and not at all bad'. He was not discharged. By 1940, when many of the orderlies had been called up, Paul S. was effectively in charge of the basketwork section, with two younger trainees under his supervision. Practising his own brand of juvenile psychology, Paul S. was able to pacify the more difficult of his charges by rewarding him with twenty pfennigs from his own pocket money every time the boy behaved, for 'one had to know how to handle him'.[133] In January 1941, Paul S. developed an irritation in his throat and a rattling sound in his chest. With his condition deteriorating he was transferred, along with his Sunday suit, ten shirts, cap, gloves, belt, braces, watchchain, and 18.44RMS in cash, to the tuberculosis ward at Eichberg, where he died six months later.[134]

The medical records of two longterm schizophrenic patients bring us into the thought processes of people who were far less accessible or accommodating than Paul S. The files of both patients run into hundreds of sheets of paper, in the second case because Wilhelm D. seems to have been under some inner compulsion to cover even the backs of envelopes with words, drawings and sketches. Both sets of records illustrate the gradual slide from benign interest to incurability and thence to absolute medical neglect. They are about missed opportunities, loss, mental confusion, and the inherent boundaries of the psychiatric project.

Johanne B. was born in Hanover on 16 December 1885 and died on 28 May 1941 at Eichberg, allegedly of pneumonia and heart failure.[135] She was schizophrenic. Married to a railway-ticket collector since 1907, Johanne B. was the mother of five children, two of whom were deaf and dumb. After leaving school, where by her own account she was 'always one of the best pupils', she had worked as a domestic help, and then latterly in a jam factory. She had always been 'a cheerful person', sociable, never thinking about life too much, but 'taking it as it comes'. By her own account, her marriage was not particularly happy, since her husband had a propensity to drink the housekeeping money in the company of what she regarded as fairweather friends. She did not mind him having the odd glass of beer, 'but he didn't need to get drunk'. Her eldest son had left home after an altercation about money; her married daughter had left her to look after an illegitimate child. Her younger daughter had been put in the deaf and dumb school at Hildesheim, and her son was being confirmed. A lot was on her mind and 'all the burdens fell on her shoulders alone'. She clearly had many regrets about her marriage: 'if she did not have so many children she would have left her husband long ago'. Now she was too old. She had tried to train as a nurse, but 'that was a bit much for her'. Her parents had prevented her from pursuing this career.

In 1931 she was admitted for observation to the Langenhorn asylum, where she conceded that she had become 'a little nervous' and that she was hearing voices. She was experiencing delusional persecution. Voices were coming through the ceiling at home. The voices said: 'You old swine. You are crazy. You'll have to be sent to Langenhagen.' She was being burned with electric rays, which left her feeling hot and with a prickly sensation all over her body. A man called Seifert from a neighbouring village had been in her room, had touched her sexual parts, and had burned her face and legs with a lamp. Powerful chemical smells made it difficult to breathe. She had run away from home. The community nurse took her to Langenhagen where, diagnosed as suffering from chronic paranoia, she was committed to the closed asylum at Hildesheim.[136]

Over the ensuing years, the doctors at Hildesheim periodically tried to fathom her delusions, sometimes gently suggesting rational explanations for the voices. Beyond these intermittent interviews, there is no evidence of any form of treatment. The voices are omnipresent in what Johanne B. had to say. She countered any occasional doubts she might have had about their reality by referring the doctors to the accompanying phenomena of electric rays and burning sensations in her body. The following is a verbatim account of her sessions with the doctors. The voices, or rather Seifert, said: 'We are going to get you, we'll get you soon and then we'll burn you.' Sometimes the voices were gentle and sympathetic, at other times loud and hostile. When in desperation she tried to sleep elsewhere, the voices would follow, saying 'Ah, how nice, look in there, how nice and still she is.' They would wake her up with a tremendous noise in her ears, saying, 'What a pity she has woken up.' The voices were also getting at her husband, telling him, 'Herr B., you must do that with your wife.' She refused to accept that these voices were the product of her own imagination, because how would this account for the terrible heat she experienced in her sexual parts? 'Everything which she experienced at home was a fact, and she would not say it if this was not so.' She did eventually concede that she might have misheard conversations through an open window which she then misconstrued. She did not know who was responsible for the heat she experienced, 'but today one can do everything with electricity'. Sometimes at home, the walls had become so hot that she had burned her fingers when she touched them. At night she disturbed the other patients with her ravings, periodically threatening or actually assaulting them. One night she ripped a light from the ceiling under the involuntary influence of Seifert. The latter was giving her psychiatrist cigars, which infuriated her to the point where she smashed her hand through a window pane. Seifert spoke to her from a light bulb. Meanwhile, her husband had forgotten to write or to do anything to mark either her birthday or their silver wedding anniversary. She saw Seifert's baleful influence at work. He and her husband were 'as thick as thieves' ('der haltet mit dem Mann zusammen wie Pech und Schwefel'). Seifert was beginning to appear behind a cupboard in one of the rooms, for he had a key to open the doors of every asylum. She saw men wandering about at night, who had come for her. She swore at men who she thought were trying to sexually assault her, and felt as though she was being persecuted by other patients who passed by, or walked behind her, in the corridors. She was being impregnated in her sleep.[137]

At Hildesheim, where she remained until her transfer to Eichberg in 1941, she clung tenaciously to her main delusional preoccupations. In January 1933 the ubiquitous Seifert was still working on her heart with electrical power in order to make her sick.[138] Evil people kept tickling her sexual parts. She frequently argued with other patients, and at night sometimes got up to shout and swear from the window. Although she had periods of calm, and could be employed cleaning the doctor's house, sooner or later Seifert would return. (It transpired that Seifert was her husband's former superior and that she had been keen on him.) Cars were arriving which contained 'apparatuses' to work on her heart; sometimes the doctor was accused of being hand in glove with the 'dogs and murderers' tormenting her. Following an escape attempt in November 1936, she was confined in a secure ward, becoming calmer thereafter and settling down to sewing work.[139] Notes on her petered out in 1938, as if the doctors had given up, as if there was no more left to say. Shortly before her transfer in 1941 there is a final entry: 'Patient still works busily in the sewing room. Otherwise her condition is unchanged. A case of schizophrenia and congenital feeblemindedness. I myself had to look after two of the patient's children in the deaf and dumb school; both of them were also feebleminded.'[140] She had been written off. She was transferred to Eichberg in a group transport on 22 April 1941. The next entry said: 'Patient has worked assiduously for many years with periodic interruptions. Useful for all kinds of housework. She has brought seven children into the world, however they include the feebleminded and deaf and dumb!'[141] Six days later she was dead.

Wilhelm D. was born in Berlin on 22 April 1890 and died, allegedly of heart failure, at Eichberg on 20 October 1942. Most of his adult life passed in asylums, more than a decade of it being completely unrecorded. There is some compensation in the fact that he must have spent hundreds of hours covering pieces of paper with drawings and writings. The first signs of mental illness were detected by doctors in a naval sickbay at Kiel towards the end of 1914, during his military service.[142] Apparently he was sleeping badly, said little, and had the habit of kissing his comrades. Discharged from the navy, Wilhelm D. got a job ironing in a tailor's workshop. His employer reported in August 1916 that 'D. is an introvert. He makes an eccentric impression because he hardly speaks and works mindlessly.' He frequently requested sick notes. In August 1918, Wilhelm D. was admitted to the reserve sickbay of a military hospital in Berlin. He was sleeping badly and imagined that he was being followed on the streets. His wife complained that Wilhelm D. had become so violent that she sometimes had to flee with their child to her parents. In March 1918, he decided to go to America, making it as far as the home for seamen in Hamburg, where he worked on cargo ships in the harbour. He punched the doorkeeper at the seamen's home who asked him once too often for identification. This brought him to a cell in the Fuhlsbüttel prison, and thence to the psychiatric asylum at Langenhorn.[143]

At first he refused to speak, lying absolutely rigid with his hands folded over his chest, gazing fixedly at the ceiling. Occasionally he would get up to kneel, silently praying, by his bedside. He communicated with nods of the head, eventually establishing that he was a vegetarian. He wrote down his preferred fruit and vegetables. Further nods, escalating into a frenzy of eager affirmation, confirmed that God had instructed him to be a vegetarian; that he was the Lord's anointed; and – simulating a dagger being unsheathed with his hands – that he was both prophet and sword of the Lord.[144] In ominous anticipation of the hundreds of pages of drawings and letters he was to produce, Wilhelm D. began scratching figures on the walls. Otherwise, his only spoken words were directed to God. Other patients joined in his enthusiastic rendition of 'Await, my soul'. Another patient had invited Wilhelm D. to pray with him. They had both said 'Come, Lord Jesus, be our guest.' After several weeks of silence, he suddenly began to speak, asking when he would be discharged. 'He had long ago finished his sentence, he was not sick and there was no reason to

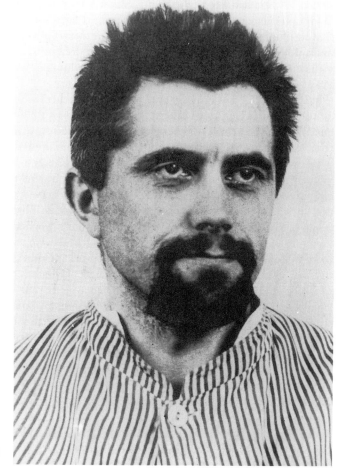

(a)

Plate 7. (a) Wilhelm D. (b) Drawings made by Wilhelm D.

keep him there so long. He conceded that he had been ill. He had not wanted to speak. "One can keep one's mouth shut if one wants to."'

The impression of reasoned outrage was rather quickly dispelled when he added that he had been 'hypnotised' and that he had seen flies which used their wings to communicate with him. He continued to demand his release ('my health is nobody else's concern and I am healthy according to my knowledge'); otherwise he spent his time singing and whistling from under the blankets, much to the annoyance of his fellow patients. When they complained, Wilhelm D. said, reasonably enough under the circumstances, that 'he had to amuse himself somehow'. Cryptic religious notes began to fill his patient file: 'The Lord Jesus is coming. Yes'; 'This is not

(b)

an iron staff'; 'I saw an angel come down from heaven, and he had a key to the abyss and a great chain in his hand'; 'I am the Son of God; what you do to one of my brethren, you do unto me'; 'it says in the Bible, an eye for an eye, a tooth for a tooth, my teeth have no nerves'.[144] Interviews with him were designed to put his thoughts gently back on to the strait and narrow. God's vegetarian injunctions were contradicted by the story of the Passover; attempts to propagate his eleventh and twelfth commandments were met with the fact that their content overlapped with that of the original ten. By February 1920, Wilhelm D. had taken to wandering around the wards with an improvised turban on his head, a lonely prophet awaiting the end of the world and the reincarnation of Christ.[145] He was occasionally violent towards both staff and other patients, and in March 1920 had to be put in an isolation ward. There he refashioned the bedlinen into a turban and cloak, proudly bestriding the room as the Holy Ghost.[146] Periodically he would punch an orderly in the face, or perform his bodily functions on the floor, bed or walls.

In 1921 his marriage was dissolved on the grounds that his insanity constituted a danger to his wife and the community. He wrote to probably non-existent relatives – only a sister seems ever to have communicated with him – and to an old flame, asking for copies of his birth certificate in order to be ennobled as 'Wilhelm von Europa Löwenburg', or for birthday surprises such as an English sportscoat, a travelling cap and new shoes. He complained that he was being held against his will and that he was being subjected day and night to murderous or sexual attacks. By 1925, Wilhelm D. had taken to tying up his testicles because 'something was running out', i.e. a fluid which was being poured in his ears. The doctors suggested that he might consider being sterilised. His family, he said, had been hypnotised for over three hundred years by Maximilian I of Bavaria, 'the old freemason King'.[147]

There are virtually no records from the asylum at Strecknitz regarding Wilhelm D. throughout the 1930s, beyond a few brief letters from his sister enquiring after his welfare. A letter dated 27 April 1940 to the welfare authorities in Hamburg explained that Wilhelm D. was in the final stages of schizophrenia with periods of hallucinatory excitement. He was 'asocial and a danger to himself of the highest degree'.[148] The only documentation from Eichberg concerning him was dated 20 October 1942, informing his sister of his death from heart failure. She was unable to attend his funeral.[149]

It would be misleading to conclude this account of mental health provision in the 1930s by suggesting total therapeutic dereliction. In the last chapter we saw the widespread adoption of occupational therapy along the lines essayed by Simon. Judging from the annual reports of asylums, by the mid 1930s the overwhelming majority of patients were engaged in virtually unpaid labour, a fact which totally contradicted the repeated claim that healthy 'national comrades' were having to shoulder the burden of maintaining unproductive 'ballast existences' in so-called luxury asylums. At Kaufbeuren-Irsee over 80% of patients did some form of work, in return for pocket money, sweets or smoking materials.[151] Virtually unpaid patient labour enabled the asylums to dispense with salaried clerks or telephonists; to operate very extensive agricultural enter-prises – Eglfing-Haar had 458,691 hectares under cultivation; and to sub-contract work – such as cigar manufacturing – from local industry.[152] As reports from Eglfing-Haar (where over 80% of patients worked) also show, occupational therapy saved outgoings on sedatives, for the physically tired tended not to be unruly patients.[153]

As we saw in the previous chapter, occupational therapy implicitly involved sifting the ablebodied and willing wheat from the 'therapy-resistant' chaff, and the application of the disciplines of productivity. For those fortunate enough to be selected for work, exhaustion was now going to spare them the slow vegetative existence which was the lot of those refractory to any form of treatment.[154] The idea of killing the 'incurable' began to be incorporated into the emerging therapeutic strategy. In a key article, published in 1935, Karl Knab contemplated the fate of those consigned to the Pflegeanstalten, i.e. asylums given over wholly to basic maintenance of the incurable:

We have before us in these [asylums] spiritual ruins, whose number is not insignificant, notwithstanding all our therapeutic endeavours, in addition to idiots on the lowest level, patient material which, as simply cost-occasioning ballast, should be eradicated by being killed in a painless fashion, which is justifiable in terms of the self-preservatory finance policy of a nation fighting for its very existence, without shaking the cultural foundations of its cultural values.[155]

This put in one, albeit rather convoluted, sentence precisely the strategy which was to be characteristic of the thinking of those psychiatrists involved in the 'euthanasia' programme.

We saw several times in the first part of this chapter that psychiatry was regarded with disdain by the men in positions of political power, and that its already poor public image suffered further from both the crude assaults of Nazi propaganda and widespread fears stemming from psychiatric collusion in the implementation of Nazi eugenic policies. People were literally terrified of being admitted to asylums. Much of the political, as distinct from popular, critique stemmed from the fact that psychiatric medicine appeared impotent in the face of mysterious forms of illness. This critique seems justified if one reads the sections in the asylum annual reports from the early 1930s dealing with what treatment was actually administered. Apart from massive faith in the merits of occupational therapy, treatment consisted of the administration of pyrifer and sufrogel for schizophrenia; cardiazol and opium for endogenous depression; and Wagner-Jauregg's malarial treatment of progressive paralysis. There was also frequent resort to those old stand-bys, drug-induced deep sleep, immersion therapy, isolation and immobilisation in straitjackets or damp sheets.[156]

In the mid 1930s these rather ineffectual methods were augmented by a range of new somatic therapies. Treatment of schizophrenics with large doses of insulin was pioneered and systematised by the Viennese psychiatrist Manfred Sakel (1900–1957).[157] Insulin-coma therapy involved starving the central nervous system of the glucose circulating in the blood, for it cannot metabolise substitutes even for short periods. Labour-intensive and very dangerous – death was averted by introducing glucose down a tube to stop a critical drop in the blood sugar level – insulin-coma therapy brought moments of lucidity to those who emerged from the coma.[158] Apparently, modern research has shown that the rate of remission achieved in treating schizophrenics in this fashion is identical to that obtained by putting them into deep sleep with barbiturates whose effects are then terminated with dextroamphetamine. In other words, insulin is not the specific therapeutic agent.[159] The relatively intense staff–patient ratio, with one nurse to between two and six patients, and the constant attention necessary for such a risky treatment, may also have encouraged patients to believe in the efficacy of what was being done to them.

In the eyes of its German devotees, the merits of insulin therapy were not exclusively medical. It reaffirmed the scientific status of psychiatry in the eyes of a sceptical government and public, thus indirectly raising the low professional self-esteem of psychiatrists. It silenced the doubting Thomases who saw in psychiatry merely the feeding and watering of incurable lunatics. It showed the wider world that mental asylums were hospitals.[160] No less important was the fact that at about 50RMs per two-month course of treatment, it was a good deal cheaper than longterm institutionalisation.[161] The authorities at Eglfing-Haar, where the treatment was employed in a major fashion, proudly drew attention to the fact that insulin shock therapy had halved the average duration of stay of twenty schizophrenic subjects: 'Even though only 10–20% more schizophrenics may be discharged or capable of working again, nonetheless this represents an economy measure which may well put into the shade all of the, sometimes highly dubious, economies which have hitherto been essayed in such areas as personnel or general expenditure.'[162]

Hans Roemer of Illenau was similarly enthusiastic about possible economies resulting from this type of somatic therapy:

According to the most recent statistics, on 31 December 1935 there were about 160,000 patients in approximately 256 public and private psychiatric asylums;

according to this writer's very cautious calculations, the general and purposeful adoption of this form of treatment would save about 10%, i.e. 16,000 psychiatric beds, which at a daily expenditure of 2RMS per patient would result in a saving of 10 to 12 million Reichsmarks.[163]

At Eglfing-Haar, the specially created insulin ward became an obligatory stopping-off point for psychiatrists attending conferences in Munich. Busloads of them braved wind and rain to take coffee and cake with patients in insulin-induced remission from their psychoses.[164] At Eglfing-Haar, insulin-coma therapy was directed at acute schizophrenics, the cases where prolonged and sustainable remission seemed most likely to result.[165] A course of treatment lasted between two and three months and involved anything between ten and sixty-six separate 'shocks', the mean being thirty-six.[166] These commenced at seven in the morning and took the form of intramuscular injections. Dosages depended upon people's tolerance of the substance: a 'zig-zag' pattern of low and high doses was sometimes used to induce susceptibility in certain cases.[167] Over the ensuing hours, the patient perspired, dribbled saliva, and went bright red in the face until lapsing into a coma. He or she then underwent spasms of about an hour's duration, and of an intensity which led the body to tense into an arc supported by the heels and back of the head, before returning to a more stable condition. People who underwent this treatment experienced extreme hunger (low dosages are used to treat anorexia nervosa); headaches; difficulties in moving; visual disturbances; disorientation; and an intense feeling of relief once the treatment was over.

Those described as being cured reported the sudden onset of a feeling of liberation from their illness during the treatment, a feeling only those who know the oppressive isolation of mental illness will appreciate. A young woman admitted to Eglfing-Haar in May 1936, and diagnosed as schizophrenic, was treated with insulin-coma therapy that November. At first she put up a great deal of resistance, making repeated bids for the doors, undressing, and covering herself with excrement. After a three-week course she became more clean and orderly, and took to sewing. After seven weeks she was put back in an open ward and was capable of rational conversation. Looking back she said 'I couldn't believe that I could have been so ill. Right in the middle of the cure I felt free again. Things got better so quickly; I can almost say, suddenly I felt well.' She was discharged on 24 January 1937.[168] That things could go drastically wrong can be illustrated simply by the fact that Braunmühl managed to kill two patients he was treating with insulin, and by the case of Karl H. at Eichberg, whose medical records include detailed descriptions of insulin-coma therapy.

Karl H. was a mathematics student at the University of Frankfurt who was admitted to the university psychiatric clinic for a month in 1931, and

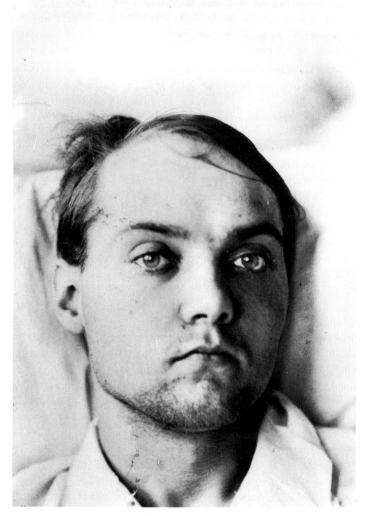

Plate 8. Karl H.

then again in March 1937, which ended in his committal to Weilmünster.
On the first occasion, he had become ill through a combination of overwork
and intellectual hubris, in the sense of venturing a thesis which assailed the
theories of Einstein. Karl's talents were not commensurate with the task;
as one of his professors put it, 'one cannot attack one of the old masters'.
Karl began to hear things, specifically someone saying in his ear, 'You are
the prodigal son.' He began to suffer persecution mania, acquiring sand to
throw in his pursuer's face, and a gun for a more final solution. He

imagined people were trying to steal his work. Resorting to self-help, he attempted to heal himself by smearing his body with fat, oils and zinc ointment, and by laying a talisman made out of tallow and a handkerchief on his stomach. He next tried to cut his wrists with scissors.[169]

During long sessions with him, psychiatrists noted that he could not remember his name; thought he studied geography; did not know where he was; and confessed apropos of Einstein: 'No, I never understood that. I've thought and dreamed of that, but I have never understood what Einstein was really all about.'[170] Pythagoras had also become a mystery; 'Oh dear, I don't know, it's gone entirely.' He was discharged, having been sterilised on 10 October 1936. According to his mother, Karl turned 'nasty' following the operation and had to be readmitted to the clinic. He had heard more voices and had eventually gone berserk, attacking his mother in the process. In the clinic, Karl cried for his mother and kept repeating 'I must die, I must die, now I am dying.' Each attempt to get him into the examining room had to be accompanied by force: 'No, I won't go in there, I want to go home.' Periodically hitting the locked door, he picked out words from the questions and repeated them. He thought the psychiatrist was God; that he was from Argentina; talked to himself in the third person; and urinated on the floor without even noticing.

In April 1937 the clinic began treating Karl with insulin. He was given between twenty and seventy units of insulin every day from 6 to 26 April. For the first four days his behaviour was erratic: he sprang out of bed and reclaimed a bed he had formerly occupied from another patient. He called out 'I am the Lord God. Adieu. Adieu, dear God, Adieu, Adieu.'[171] As the doses mounted Karl broke out in heavy perspiration or lapsed into extreme calm. By 19 April he wanted to get up, so increasing levels of force had to be used to keep him in bed. By the twenty-third the medical notes show his obvious distress: 'Adieu, I am going to die now, you have murdered me. Dear God, please help me. I want to get out of here.'[172] Three days later the treatment was hurriedly abandoned. Blood was coming out of Karl's eye sockets and from under his skin. This was a clinical novum. One of the doctors spotted a quick chance to extend his list of publications. And what had all this achieved? There was less of a tendency to run away and Karl had ceased his monotonous moaning. But, 'in essentials, there has certainly been no beneficial influence'.[173] He was committed to Weilmünster, where, frightened and helpless, he became virtually incommunicable. He contracted tuberculosis, and was taken, coughing and uttering his cryptic imprecations, to Eichberg, where Dr Mennecke and his colleague killed him on the day of his admission.[174]

Insulin shock therapy was augmented with Ladislaus von Meduna's cardiazol convulsive treatment, a somatic therapy based on the alleged biological antagonism between epilepsy and schizophrenia. Basically it involved injecting a cerebral stimulant, cardiazol, which was known to induce epileptic fits when given in toxic doses. Up to the point of losing consciousness, the patient experienced extreme anxiety, apparently analogous to the terror of being thrown off a high building, with a safety net being obtruded at the last minute to break the fall.[175] The seizures themselves were sometimes of a violence sufficient to cause fractures of the jaw or thigh.[176] What had begun as a treatment for acute schizophrenics soon became a way of disciplining the most disturbed and unruly patients, saving on sedatives and the stressful nursing duties of the disturbed wards.[177] In the late 1930s these techniques were finally augmented with Ugo Cerletti and Lucio Bini's electro-convulsive therapy, with Braunmühl of Eglfing travelling to Sondrio in northern Italy to learn the method at first hand. It was quick and easy to use, required no search for a suitable vein, and instantly rendered the subject unconscious.[178] It also induced headaches, memory loss and fear, as well as fractures if the correct procedures for positioning the patient were not followed.

The introduction of these new somatic therapies was accompanied by an avalanche of articles in the major psychiatric journals. Reading them one senses a renewed enthusiasm for the psychiatric project, a reaffirmation of the medical and scientific character of the discipline, and a chance to demonstrate that psychiatry could actually achieve something. Patients treated with these therapies also registered changes in spirit which must have seemed like a scientific miracle. A young woman was admitted to Eglfing-Haar in 1938 suffering from acute paranoia. At the time her thoughts were as follows:

I won't go to sleep tonight, I try to stay awake, because something terrible will happen. I was taken from the children's home [where she worked] under SA guard to Hamburg. I was also under SA guard in the Heckerschen home. But I still thought that something would happen to me. I was being persecuted. Someone said to me that I had murdered someone, 'indirectly murdered them'. Why am I being guarded? All the women say to me – I notice it – they say to me that I am a murderess. But I cannot confess to having killed someone when I haven't. Something awful must happen.

After seven or eight weeks' treatment with insulin and cardiazol she had undergone a complete change. Writing to her family she said:

My dear mother, dear grandmother! I wanted to wait a day to see whether the clicking together of my spirits will hopefully be long lasting. Now I can write to you once more as the Hilde of old! Imagine, mummy, Saturday evening in bed, it just happened following a conversation with the others. Naturally I am eating again, for not eating was just part of the persecution mania. You cannot imagine the feeling of being freed from every fear. One is born again, so to speak. Now I look forward to Sunday and to seeing you, dear mummy. It should have clicked together before, then you would have noticed something; but nonetheless, we should thank our lucky stars. How are you, then? I am so very happy.[179]

Paradoxically, these therapeutic successes, if that is in fact what they were, heightened psychiatric embarrassment vis-à-vis that proportion of patients for whom they could do nothing. Acute cases could be treated with occupational therapy, or with the range of new somatic treatments we have been considering. Any danger they represented to the hereditary health of race and nation could be dealt with by compulsory sterilisation. This still left the problem of the incurable and refractory, upon whom these therapies made no impact and who still cost money. Judging from a report by the director of Eglfing-Haar on 1 November 1939, this latter group were literally expendable:

[I] feel duty bound to highlight a genuine economy measure, which is capable of influencing the economic position of the asylum in a favourable fashion. Two groups of seriously defective, mentally disturbed people come under consideration: the totally idiotic, thoroughly asocial, absolutely dependent, chronic long-term patients who come close to idiocy, and whom we find in all age-groups and diagnostic categories of patient; and in addition, the criminally inclined, anti-social elements, the majority committed on grounds of public safety, who are increasingly silting up and burdening the asylum in ways which are intolerable. It is these patients who occasion high expenditure in terms of personnel, medical care, drugs, clothing etc.... Because they have lost all sense of individual responsibility for the struggle for existence, in the long term they represent a spatial and economic burden on the asylum, damaging the demands of those fit for life through the heavy expenditure which they occasion. Almost all of these patients are kept in asylums at public cost. The problem of whether to maintain this patient material under the most primitive conditions or to eradicate it has now become a subject for serious discussion once more.[180]

As we have seen time and time again, the incurable and refractory were being driven to the margins of the psychiatrists' field of vision. Selective therapeutic intensity was accompanied by an out-of-sight, out-of-mind attitude towards those patients for whom psychiatry could do nothing. Why not simply kill them? This developing paradigm within a psychiatry which was in any case permeated with eugenicist ideology dovetailed felicitously with the concern of an amoral and racist regime to throw overboard any 'ballast' in the context of harnessing national resources for war and of on-going racial purification. Not a few psychiatrists were comfortable with the idea of reconciling their emerging therapeutic paradigm with cold-blooded murder.

That was the way things were tending. Let us return finally to Professor Kleist's 1938 inspection tour of the asylums. After the war, Kleist revealed that he held Bernotat personally responsible. The latter was 'a little pen-pusher' who 'spoke only of idiots and life unworthy of life'. The 'entire tendency was to treat them badly. That was the spirit of the thing, from which the idea of killing them finally arose.' In his report on Herborn, Kleist noted the indiscriminate use of phrases such as 'an unproductive burden on the national community', and the conceptual lumping together of everyone in the asylums. Hadn't people like Bernotat heard of periods of remission between epileptic or schizophrenic attacks or of illnesses whose causes were exogenous, and were all patients to be written off as 'incurable'? Bernotat's economy measures were no savings at all. Arguing for more expenditure on active therapy and the proper care of the chronically sick, Kleist remarked, 'What I spend today, I save tomorrow and the day after tomorrow.' Apropos of chronic patients, he concluded: 'Those who cannot be saved have a right to a form of care which benignly maintains their existence, so long as there is no law for the destruction of life unworthy of life. Expenditure on these unfortunates should not fall below a tolerable minimum.'[181] Two years before the commencement of the 'euthanasia' programme, this rather interesting figure had identified the terrible logic which informed both the regime's economy measures and the thinking of many psychiatrists. How this fusion eventuated in mass murder will occupy the following chapters.

PART TWO

GODS IN WHITE COATS

CHAPTER 3

'WHEELS MUST ROLL FOR VICTORY!'
CHILDREN'S 'EUTHANASIA' AND
'AKTION T–4'

IN THE winter of 1938–1939, the parents of a malformed infant called Knauer petitioned Hitler in order to bring about its death. The child's grandmother had encouraged them to do so. This was probably not an isolated incident. In such a political climate, understandable human anxieties about severely disabled infants, terminal illness and severe incapacity were compounded by grass-roots ideological fanaticism. Requests for 'euthanasia' were also received from a middle-aged woman dying of cancer, and from a Labour Service official who had been blinded and severely injured after falling into a cement mixer.[1] Petitions to Hitler were dealt with by a sub-department of the Kanzlei des Führers (Chancellory of the Führer or KdF), an agency originally established to project Hitler as a leader who listened to the complaints and requests of plain Party members.[2] From 1934 onwards, the KdF was led by Reichsleiter Philipp Bouhler (1899–1945). He was a Munich-born Nazi 'old fighter' with literary pretensions, blessed with an attractive wife and the well-fed, instantly forgettable features of a thrusting middle manager of a self-satisfied assistant professor.[3] During the 1930s, the KdF retained its populist remit (branching out from 'Party comrades' to 'national comrades' in general), which it used to extend its influence into normative areas of government, such as pardons granted by the Ministry of Justice. It hired more personnel and spawned a series of Main Offices. Main Office II, under Oberdienstleiter Viktor Brack and his deputy Werner Blackenburg, dealt with affairs relating to Party and State; sub-department IIb, under Hans Hefelmann, was specifically responsible for handling petitions to Hitler.[4] According to Hefelmann, about two thousand petitions arrived each day.[5] The job of sub-department IIb was to settle ordinary people's problems with State or Party agencies in an informal and unbureaucratic way. That last quality, and the type of requests that flowed its way, ensured Bouhler's agency the leading role it played in the 'euthanasia' programme.

The exact origins of the 'euthanasia' programme are complex, there

(a)

Plate 9. The two senior figures responsible for organising the 'euthanasia' programme.
(a) Philipp Bouhler

being several versions of how it started. Depending on one's intellectual predilections, one can stress the importance of Hitler, ideology, or bureaucratic ambition. The doctor attending Hitler's retinue, Professor Karl Rudolf Brandt (who, having patched up Hitler's adjutant and niece after a car accident, was kept on hand to give medical attention after possible assassination attempts), testified at Nuremberg as to what happened to the Knauer child:[6]

BRANDT The father of a deformed child approached the Führer and asked that this child or this creature should be killed. Hitler turned this matter over to me and told me to go to Leipzig immediately – it was in Leipzig – to confirm the fact on

(b)

(b) Karl Brandt

the spot. It was a child which had been born blind, an idiot – at least it seemed to be an idiot – and it lacked one leg and part of an arm.

QUESTION Witness, you were speaking about the Leipzig affair, about this deformed child. What did Hitler order you to do?

BRANDT He ordered me to talk to the physicians who were looking after the child to find out whether the statements of the father were true. If they were correct, then I was to inform the physicians in his name that they could carry out euthanasia. The important thing was that the parents should not feel themselves incriminated at some later date as a result of this euthanasia – that the parents should not have the impression that they themselves were responsible for the death of this child. I was further ordered to state that if these physicians should become involved in some legal proceedings because of this measure, these proceedings would be quashed by order of Hitler. Martin Bormann was ordered at the time to inform Guertner, the Minister of Justice, accordingly about this case.

QUESTION What did the doctors who were involved say?

BRANDT The doctors were of the opinion that there was no justification for keeping such a child alive. It was pointed out that in maternity wards under certain circumstances it is quite natural for the doctors themselves to perform euthanasia in such a case without anything further being said about it. No precise instructions were given in that respect.

QUESTION Was this problem of deformities dealt with anywhere else?

BRANDT The problem of deformities was probably discussed before this Leipzig case. However, in the course of the summer it was worked on in a more concrete form, first of all by the Ministry of the Interior. In this case Dr Linden participated as a special consultant, probably as representative of Dr Conti – who became Reich Minister for Health after the death of his predecessor Wagner, and then afterwards State Secretary in the Ministry of the Interior.[7]

The object of this high-level solicitude had been brought to the University of Leipzig paediatric clinic, whose director was Professor Werner Catel. Recalling the course of events in 1962, Catel said he had discussed the case with the father, who, concerned about the effect the child was having on his wife's state of mind, had requested its admission to the clinic with a view to 'putting it to sleep'. Catel had then gone on holiday. When he returned, he was informed that one of his subordinates, a Dr Kohl, had given the child a lethal injection while the nurses were taking a coffee break.[8] Catel's memory then went strategically blank, until he recalled a strange series of events in the autumn of 1940, which, if nothing else, suggests he had a fertile imagination. A baby chimpanzee was born in the Leipzig zoo, whose mother died nine days after giving birth. Catel took the ape into his clinic, feeding it with human milk on a veranda. This profligacy with precious resources allegedly resulted in charges of being a 'parasite on the people', and the intervention of the senior mayor of Leipzig. The latter suggested to Catel that he might like to accept a post as an expert referee on the newly formed Reich Committee for the combating of serious congenital and hereditary illnesses. Having discussed the matter with an elderly academic mentor, Catel resolved to accept, in order to prevent 'euthanasia' falling into 'illegitimate and radical hands'.[9]

Both Brandt and Catel stressed the crucial importance of the Knauer case, not surprisingly given the element of explicit consensuality, and the implication that the relevant policies evolved *ad hoc*. The latter way of viewing these matters dovetails neatly with fashionable, and nowadays orthodox, 'structure-functionalist' accounts of Nazi policy-making, i.e. the view that Nazi exterminatory policies were contingent, local, and essentially short-termist in origin, if not in ambition.[10] This view of things conveniently overlooks some important elements in the story. First, Hans Heinrich Lammers, the head of the Reich Chancellory, recalled that Hitler had contemplated killing mental patients in 1933 when he was being advised on the Law for the Prevention of Hereditarily Diseased Progeny.[11] Secondly, Brandt recalled that in 1935 Hitler had told Wagner, the Reich Doctors' Leader,

> that if war should break out, he would take up the euthanasia question and implement it . . . because the Führer was of the opinion that such a problem would be easier and smoother to carry out in wartime, since the public resistance which one could expect from the churches would not play such a prominent role amidst the events of wartime as it otherwise would.[12]

Thirdly, Brandt recalled a meeting with Hitler at Obersalzberg shortly after the conclusion of the Polish campaign:

> I was called to him for some reason which I can no longer remember, and he told me that because of a document which he had received from Reichsleiter Bouhler, he wanted to bring about a definite solution in the euthanasia question. He gave me general directives on how he imagined it, and the fundamentals were that insane persons who were in such a condition that they could no longer take any conscious part in life were to be given relief through death. General instructions followed about petitions which he himself had received, and he told me to contact Bouhler himself about the matter. I did so by telephone on the same day, and I then informed Hitler about my conversation with Bouhler. . . . But this was not the cause of the Euthanasia Programme being started. In his book, *Mein Kampf,* Hitler had already referred to it in certain chapters, and the law for the 'prevention of the birth of children suffering from hereditary diseases' is a proof that Hitler had definitely concerned himself with such problems earlier.[13]

Brandt's account gives credit where credit was due. Bouhler seems to have drafted the practicalities of implementation, but Hitler gave the decision to go ahead, and had already established both the approximate timetable and what one might loosely call the moral-political framework. Those who dealt with incoming petitions in the KdF detected a pattern in how Hitler responded to 'euthanasia' requests; each decision he made reaffirmed them in the belief that this was what he wanted.[14] In other words, motives like the bureaucratic expansionism of the KdF are not mentioned, and hence have to be regarded as being quite secondary – except in the eyes of those who, like Lammers, were professionally exercised by questions of bureaucratic competence.[15] And even he, as we shall see, did not deny Hitler's crucial role in all of this. There is no reason to accord to bureaucratic expansionism the status of primary motive, certainly not to the neglect of the role of either Hitler or shared ideological conviction. The most salient fact, it should be stressed, is that we are dealing with a group of people who believed in the rectitude of what they did, even if they did not care to share their reasoning with the confused, traditionalist mass of humanity through some form of explicit legal sanction. As we shall see, they acted conspiratorially, deliberately and methodically to put their ideas into practice. The notion that these policies came about in an *ad hoc*, contingent or reactive fashion is preposterous. After the war, however, it was the standard line of defence.

Further sources throw doubt on the *ad hoc* nature of the administrative arrangements necessary to implement a 'euthanasia' programme. In 1936–1937, Artur Gütt had decided to create a 'Reich Hereditary Health Court' to act as a court of highest appeal in sterilisation cases. Although this court never materialised, a secret 'Reich Committee for Hereditary Health Questions' did. In order to emphasise its scientific character, this was shortly rechristened 'Reich Committee for the scientific registering of serious hereditary and congenital illnesses'.[16] The Reich Committee, which was based in the Chancellory of the Führer, where (logically enough) many grass-roots appeals would gravitate, drew upon a wide range of medical and psychiatric expertise. On several occasions between February and May 1939, these academics discussed 'euthanasia' with senior members of the KdF. In the summer of 1939 Hitler's physician, Theo Morell, spent much time assembling everything that had been written since the nineteenth century on the subject of euthanasia, with much of the material being relayed to him by the Reich Committee we have just encountered. Morell used this material for a memorandum concerning a possible law for 'the destruction of life unworthy of life'. The memorandum probably formed the basis of a talk he gave on this subject to Hitler.[17]

The draft law envisaged killing people suffering from serious congenital mental or physical 'malformation', because they required longterm care, aroused 'horror' in other people, and were situated on 'the lowest animal level'. The crucial question was whether to carry out these killings on the basis of a new public law, or surreptitiously by secret administrative decree. A careful reading of Ewald Meltzer's book, and in particular Meltzer's poll of parental opinion, led Morell to conclude that parents would prefer it if they were told that their child had succumbed to this or that illness. As for the *modus operandi*, legal guardians and official doctors could initiate proceedings, with asylum doctors being used purely as expert referees. A little further along, Morell decided that some form of compulsory registering of the congenitally ill might be preferable to formal initiation of killing procedures by official doctors. The method of killing, and the stage at which to inform relatives, had yet to be determined. The philosophical basis of these measures – with a typically Hitlerian admixture of banality, inhumanity, and bizarre 'historical' or 'natural' facts – consisted in rejecting notions of individual human rights originating, he claimed, with the French Revolution, and asserting collective values 'best compared with the economic concern of a businessman with the well-being of his enterprise' over the individualistic egoism of the 'bloated bourgeois'. Citing Ernst Mann, Morell drew attention to the counter-selective effects of modern welfare; citing Meltzer, he claimed there would be very little parental opposition. In past times, an extensive resort to capital punishment and epidemic disease had served to wipe out the deranged and delinquent. Selfconsciously returning to 'fear of excess', Morell noted that just as no one was ever executed nowadays by mistake, so no one – notwithstanding 'the romancings of Kaspar Hauser' – was being wrongly confined to a mental institution. The clincher in his line of argument was that:

5,000 idiots costing 2,000RMs each per annum = 100 million a year. With interest at 5% that corresponds to a capital reserve of 200 million. That should even mean something to those whose concept of figures has gone awry since the period of inflation. In addition one must separately take into account the release of domestic foodstuffs and the lessening of demand for certain imports.[18]

In addition to updating the crude collectivist materialism of Binding and Hoche to fit the economic circumstances of 1938–1939 rather than 1920, this memorandum began to address the grim practicalities of killing the mentally and physically handicapped. Some issues, such as how to institute killings, were actually resolved as Morell thought and wrote; others, such as method or when to notify relatives, were still open to discussion. In August, a Ministry of Justice commission on the reform of the criminal code sent the KdF a draft outline of what was ostensibly billed as a law sanctioning 'euthanasia'. Having proposed the decriminalisation of voluntary euthanasia, the lawyers blithely dovetailed this with the involuntary killing of psychiatric patients:

Clause 1. Whoever is suffering from an incurable or terminal illness which is a major burden to himself or others, can request mercy killing by a doctor, provided it is his express wish and has the approval of a specially empowered doctor.

Clause 2. The life of a person who because of incurable mental illness requires permanent institutionalisation and is not able to sustain an independent existence, may be prematurely terminated by medical measures in a painless and covert manner.[19]

On 18 August 1939, the Reich Committee introduced the compulsory registering of all 'malformed' newborn children, echoing both the language and the methods of Morell's memorandum. In return for a payment of 2RMs per case, doctors and midwives were obliged to report instances of idiocy and Down's Syndrome; microcephaly; hydrocephaly; physical deformities such as the absence of a limb or late development of the head or spinal column; and forms of spastic paralysis. The official doctors to whom they reported were in turn to forward the information to the Reich Committee at a Berlin box number (Nr 101), which happened to be the nearest to the KdF.[20] It should be noted that all of these measures predated by several months the cursory, and extra-legal, sanction eventually given them by Hitler.

The decision to kill these children was taken by three expert referees: Professor Catel, Hans Heinze of Brandenburg-Görden (an asylum some twenty minutes outside the town of the same name) and the paediatrician Ernst Wentzler. The son of a well-to-do leather manufacturer, Wentzler, author of a book entitled 'The Paediatric Hospital of the Future', and inventor of an incubator for prematurely born babies dubbed the *Wentzlersche Wärmewanne*, combined work at the Charité with an elite private practice. He treated Edda Goering for measles at Karinhall; he also treated the child of agricultural supremo Darré, and the children of Viktor Brack, whom we shall have repeated occasion to encounter.[21] Wentzler, testifying in 1963, claimed that he was suddenly visited by Brandt, who, outlining why Hitler had decided to pick up this particular 'red-hot iron', asked him to become an expert referee. A devotee of Binding and Hoche – he had read both editions of their tract – Wentzler rang Brandt back after a day or two to say that he would oblige.[22] The nature of the job was explained to the three assessors at a meeting in Berlin chaired by Viktor Brack. A week later, Wentzler received the first registered package of eighty to a hundred forms. He received more, virtually every other day, down to the end of the war. He was paid 240RM per month for the extra work.[23] In 1963 he recalled, 'I had the feeling that my activity was something positive, and that I had made a small contribution to human progress.'[24]

Hans Heinze was the son of a businessman and vice-mayor of Elsterberg in the Vogtland. Missing out on military service because of a stiff arm, Heinze joined the Red Cross, going on to study medicine at Leipzig. In 1934 he became director of the asylum at Potsdam, and in 1939 director of Görden, 'the most modern asylum in Brandenburg'.[25] Werner Catel, who at the time of his testimony in 1962 had just relinquished the chair of paediatric medicine at the University of Kiel(!), first became acquainted with severely handicapped children as an assistant at the paediatric clinic in Leipzig. An elderly nurse told him that his predecessor had tended to 'release' these 'mere existences' from a life 'below the mental level of an animal'. A reading of Binding and Hoche made him a convinced exponent of killing such children.[26] Clearly no fool, Catel claimed never to have taken the Hippocratic oath, pointing out that in any case the oath predated the Stoic concept of 'euthanasia'. He could not take Christian objections seriously, for had not the historian Ranke described the murder of 20,000 Huguenots, and hadn't a priest blessed the bomb dropped on Hiroshima?[27]

Without actually seeing the children concerned, these men scrutinised the registration forms, marking them with a ' + ' if they wanted the child to die, a ' − ' if it was to live, and a '?' in the (few) cases requiring further consideration. Thus they were utterly dependent upon the diagnoses of midwives and other doctors. Whoever received the forms last could also take account of the judgement of the two previous assessors. The Reich Committee then wrote to the relevant public health office, instructing them to arrange the child's admission to one of a number of paediatric clinics. This could involve compulsion, including pressure on the mother in the form of conscription for labour service. Initially, these clinics were located in Brandenburg-Görden, Leipzig, Niedermarsberg, Steinhof and Eglfing-Haar. In the course of the war, several more clinics were established: in Waldniel near Andernach, Ansbach, Berlin, Eichberg, Hamburg, Kalmenhof, Kaufbeuren, Hadamar, Grossschweidnitz, Loben, Lüneburg, Meseritz-Obrawalde, Schleswig, Schwerin, Stadtroda, Stuttgart, Uchtspringe and Vienna.[28] Since the larger population centres, such as Hamburg or Leipzig, often had two of these clinics, the total number was around thirty.

It is difficult to generalise about how these children (many of them were in fact teenagers or young adults) were pushed or pulled into the killing apparatus. Judging from photographs kept by the medical staff at Eglfing-Haar – and they clearly had an interest in recording only the most horrific cases – some of the children were born with very severe physical deformities, including missing limbs or gaps where facial organs should have been.[29] Their parents often had other young children, or lived in straitened economic circumstances, compounded by the absence of many of the fathers in the armed forces. The business of taking a sick child on a costly and fruitless round of visits to doctors and hospitals frequently seems to have worn down their patience. They had exhausted most of the options before they were promised specialist treatment for the child at the expense of the grand-sounding Reich Committee in its range of allegedly elite clinics.[30] Care was taken by the Reich Committee to distinguish their paediatric clinics from the asylums which frequently happened to share the same premises with them.[31] By 1941 asylums were the object of general, and justified, mistrust among the population, and it was therefore necessary to create an illusory distance between them and these clinics.[32]

The initiative to consign a child to one of these clinics sometimes came from the parents, some of whom, like the twenty-five-year-old mother of a blind and mentally handicapped four-year-old child, were already of the opinion that it would have been better if the child had died at birth.[33] The mother of four-year-old Klara E. was seven months pregnant, had four other healthy children, and could not cope with an 'idiot' toddler as well as tending the family farm in the absence of her soldier husband. The child could neither move nor speak, and hence regularly fouled herself. She died of 'pneumonia' two months after admission to the paediatric clinic in Kauf-beuren.[34] The mother of Christel F. was married to a senior official in the German Labour Front. Although this meant that she did not have to work, having to care for Christel, who would sit on a potty for hours and then foul herself, was 'making her very ill'. She took Christel to Eichberg, where she was shown a room full of playing children. Six weeks after her admission, Christel suddenly died.[35] Few parents were as explicit as the woman dis-cussed in a letter from the Public Health Office in Husum who had written to the Ministry of the Interior to have her two 'idiotic children' taken to the asylum at Schleswig 'in order to carry out euthanasia'.[36] In an unknown number of instances we are probably dealing with consensual killing.

Other parents were talked into parting with their child by their family doctor, or by public health or National Socialist People's Welfare nurses doing the round of family home visits or servicing mothers' advisory centres. National Socialist Germany was a paradise gained for an entire class of 'carers' and sundry health and welfare snoopers.[37] Maria H. gave birth to her third child, called Elsa, on 17 April 1939. Elsa's eyes never opened and her tongue protruded 'in a funny fashion'. The family doctor suggested that the child would receive better treatment in the paediatric clinic of Eglfing-Haar. The child was brought there in April 1941. Four weeks later the mother received in quick succession a letter and a telegram, the former saying that Elsa had bronchial pneumonia, the latter that she was dead.[38] Another family, with a lame child, had sought treatment for him in the university clinic at Tübingen. Upon his release, the authorities in the clinic recommended that the child be sent to Eglfing-Haar as being 'the best asylum in Germany'. This advice was emphatically endorsed by a woman from the Public Health Office in Biberach. The child was dead ten days after his arrival in the asylum.[39] Parental doubts were cleverly neutralised by the promise of specialist treatment, whose course might be highly risky and whose outcome was uncertain. In other words, everything possible would appear to have been done.[40]

Judging from extensive documentation from a number of post-war trials, conditions in the special paediatric clinics were far removed from the modernity touted by the Reich Committee and its many local agents. Chil-dren from Bavaria were concentrated in the paediatric block of Haar. Between November 1940 and May 1945, 332 children died there, either of deliberate starvation or through overdoses of a powerful sedative called Luminal.[41] Quantities of this (0.5 grammes for the under-tens) were mixed in with their food every morning and night.[42] After a few days the unconscious child would develop pneumonia, bronchitis and other fatal breathing irregularities. Sometimes they were also given lethal injections of morphium-scopolamin.

The precise number of deaths, published but not explained in the annual reports for 1941 and 1942, were:

November and December 1940: 5
1941: 34
1942: 62
1943: 100
1944: 100
January–May 1945: 31

Over half the people killed were aged between six and fifteen; they included two adults aged thirty-five and forty-five.[43]

Some of these children were designated 'E' cases by the Reich Committee, and hence were killed shortly on arrival. Others were dubbed 'B' cases, and hence were to be subject to further observation, after which the medical staff would ask the Reich Committee for permission to kill them.[44] The director, Pfannmüller, would write to the Committee, enclosing a report, and receive back the cryptic note 'nothing stands in the way of carrying this out'. Pfannmüller himself, whom we encountered frequently in the previous chapter, needed little encouragement. A convinced National Socialist, he was brutal and temperamental.[45] Words like 'drastic', 'impulsive' or 'manic' came readily to mind when witnesses had to recall him.[46] A former military judge recalled that during a lecture on racial hygiene, Pfannmüller had spoken of having visited a woman with a sickly newborn child. He left the child in an exposed place in order to bring about its death. He then subsequently announced to a state prosecutor what he had done, asking: 'What are you going to do about it?' The lawyer said he would prosecute him for murder, to which Pfannmüller, no doubt recalling his earlier experience with the alcoholic population of Augsburg, replied: 'Herr Staatsanwalt, before you can do that, you'll be in Dachau.'[47] Rude and abrasive, he was wont to say to patients, 'It would be better if you went somewhere else', i.e. to be gassed.[48] An admirer of Binding and Hoche, the latter of whom he had met, Pfannmüller regarded his victims as 'human husks'. He claimed to have letters from parents thanking him for having killed their handicapped children.[49]

Although Pfannmüller took an active part in killing the Reich Committee children, day-to-day running of the paediatric block was the responsibility of Dr Gustav Eidam and a small nursing staff. Pfannmüller's first choice, the existing paediatrician Dr Friedrich Hölzel, had used the opportunity of a rainy vacation to mull over Pfannmüller's offer to lead the killing operation. Human fellow feeling jostled fairly uneasily with an intellectual understanding of the 'necessity' of the 'measures' adopted by the Nazi state:

Schwarzsee bei Kitzbühel

28 August 1940

Dear Herr Direktor,

The heavy rains during the first part of my vacation had the advantage of affording me sufficient leisure for reflection, and I am very grateful to you for your great kindness and consideration in giving me this time to make up my mind. The new measures are so convincing that I thought I could let personal considerations go by the board. But it is one thing to approve of measures of the State with full conviction, and another to carry them out oneself in their final consequence. I am reminded of the difference which exists between a judge and an executioner. Therefore, despite all intellectual insight and goodwill on my part, I cannot escape the realisation that according to my personal nature I am not suitable for this task. Lively as my desire is in many cases to improve upon the natural course of things, it is equally repugnant to me to carry this out as a systematic policy after cold-blooded deliberation and according to objective scientific principles, and without any feeling towards the patient. What I have come to enjoy in working in the paediatric department is not the scientific interest, but the physician's desire, amidst our often fruitless labour, to help and at least to improve many of our cases here. The psychological evaluation, and the therapeutic and pedagogic influence, were always much closer to my heart than anatomical curiosities, no matter how interesting they were. And so it comes about that, although I am sure that I can preserve my full objectivity in giving expert advice, I still feel myself somehow emotionally bound to the children as their medical guardian, and I think that this emotional contact is not necessarily a weakness from the point of view of a National Socialist physician. However, it prevents me from combining this new duty with the ones I have hitherto carried out.

If this should oblige you to place the work in the paediatric department in other hands, it would certainly be a painful loss. But it seems better to me to recognise clearly beforehand that I am too weak for this task than to disappoint you later.

I know that your request to me was a mark of special trust, and I cannot repay that trust better than by being absolutely honest and open.

Heil Hitler!

Respectfully yours,

F. Hölzel[50]

Although Hölzel subsequently resigned in favour of Eidam, this was not before he had inducted several nurses into a task which included a built-in number of fatalities.[51] Eidam was a reluctant subordinate. He repeatedly requested a posting to the military, being brought back in line by Pfann-müller's threats and explosive temper. The nursing staff was led by a senior nurse, Emma D., who, together with her two younger colleagues, Emma L. and Maria S., was forced to swear an oath of loyalty, pledging eternal silence regarding what went on in the clinic, under pain of death.[52]

Initially, however, they swallowed the line that what they were doing was scientifically important, rationalising the high number of deaths as being merely what one might call collateral casualties. Although they sometimes requested transfers, and undoubtedly found the work disturbing, nonetheless they also regarded it as necessary to 'release' the 'regrettable creatures' in their care from their suffering.[53] Like many nurses who worked in these clinics, they received a 25RM-per-month supplementary payment, known pejoratively as 'Schmutzgeld'; the doctors sometimes received a 250RM Christmas bonus.[54] In some clinics (notoriously the Kalmenhof at Idstein), the tensions of the job were soothed by a visit to the wine cellars to mark every fiftieth killing with copious amounts of wine and cider.[55]

As the child being killed neared its end, the parents were informed that it was seriously ill, with notification of death normally going out before they had had time to visit what was often an inaccessible place. Somewhere like Eglfing-Haar was easy enough to reach if one lived in Munich (it is on the S-Bahn near the old Riem airport); but a journey to, say, Eltville, and then to Eichberg, perched on the slopes of the Rheingau, was another matter. In some asylums, the authorities simplified matters by prohibiting visits. Director Grossmann at the Kalmenhof in Idstein had a standard letter which fobbed off anxious parents with the injunction 'Wheels must roll for victory!' They were also told not to burden the administration with 'impossible' written requests.[56] Telegrams were sometimes used to lend this procedure an air of urgency; the cost was recouped through the subsequent funeral charges. Obviously, some parents were loath to part with their children, and requested up-to-date information regarding their progress. Margot E., born on 28 January 1941, was sent to Kaufbeuren on the advice of the district doctor and a nurse from the public health office in Leonberg.[57] The mother was told not to visit for the first five to six weeks, to help the child adjust to the new surroundings. After repeated letters, director Valentin Faltlhauser informed the mother that Margot was disturbed and cried constantly; then, on 3 November 1942, that she was saying the words 'mama' and 'papa' and had begun to play with things. The next paragraph paved the way for what was inevitably coming:

In sum, I cannot anticipate any favourable prospects for the future. Children who suffer from a disturbed development of the kind affecting your child always remain mentally retarded. In general, experience shows that 90% of these children fail to grow older because of their susceptibility to infectious diseases.

Rather testily, Faltlhauser concluded:

Unfortunately I am not in a position to give you a report every fourteen days. If you consider that we have 1,300 patients, then if we had to make a report every fourteen days for each one, we would have no time left over for medical activities.[58]

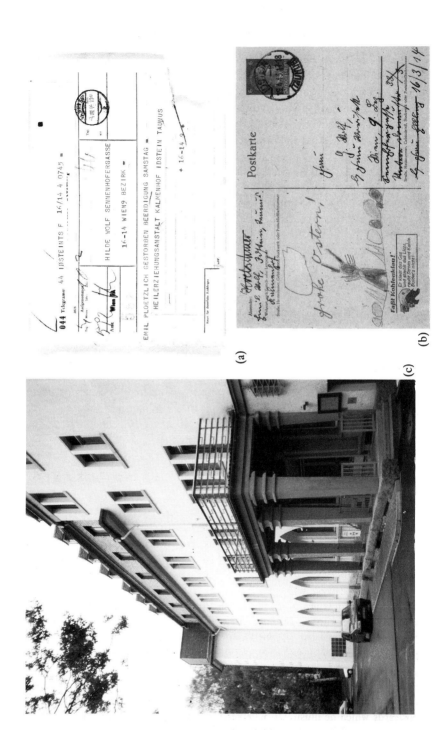

Five days later the child was dead.[59] Arriving at the asylum, the mother was given no cause of death, and noticed that the undernourished body of her daughter had been subjected to an autopsy.[60] The parents of four-year-old Friedrich S. were persuaded to consign their son to Eichberg because of severe cerebral cramps which ensued in the wake of meningitis. On 3 September the director of Eichberg wrote to the mother saying:

Your little son is well. It is a case of brain damage, the causes of which we are not able as yet to establish with any certainty, since we have had too short a time to observe him. If we are able to establish anything else, *or should your child become ill* [my italics], we will notify you immediately. You do not need to worry. We have recently commenced a course of medication.[61]

They visited the child there on his fourth birthday on 21 October 1941. He was malnourished and covered in bruises. The doctor forbade them to remove the boy on the grounds that they were still treating him. They were told to return in a month. After two weeks, the father wrote to the asylum. The answer sent on 14 November 1941 was that 'their little son Friedrich' was already dead.[62] Not surprisingly, some parents began to wonder how, for example, a child could be healthy when they visited him on Wednesday, and dead by Friday.[63] Parents who made scenes because their child had been the object of a crude autopsy, or who put two and two together when even the priests slunk away from the graveyard with shifty expressions on their faces, received scant satisfaction if they went to their local authorities to protest. The authorities themselves fared no better. In December 1941 the mayor of Oberjesingen wrote to Eichberg concerning rumours regarding the death of Ernst W. in the asylum. The director, Schmidt, replied on the 29th of that month, claiming that 'idiotic little children' frequently die of measles, and that the mother 'had behaved uncontrollably' when she had visited the asylum to take the boy home with her. He had refused to allow this on the grounds of possible infection, and advised the mayor to make her aware of the impossibility of the views she was currently expressing.[64]

Much of what has gone before has been concerned with doctors and parents. The altogether more taxing task now arises of recreating some of the circumstances of the victims. Since in many instances we are dealing with small children who could not talk, let alone write, we are largely dependent on how others, whether benign or malign, viewed them, and on what are inevitably indirect accounts. Anna Maria R. was born on 30 January 1935 in Cassel. She died of 'bronchial asthma and heart failure, a case of idiocy' at Eichberg on 27 June 1941. The relevant form described

Plate 10. (a) Telegram from the authorities at Idstein notifying a mother of the sudden death of her son. (b) The son, Emil W., regularly sent his mother postcards which he illustrated with seasonal scenes, such as this one depicting a child's view of Easter. (c) Photograph of the asylum.

Plate 11. Anna Maria R.

her 'job' as 'child'. She spent most of her life in institutions, first from 6 October 1937 at Hephata in Treysa (there is a photograph taken the day after her admission) and then from September 1938 in the asylum at Marburg. The on-going diagnosis was congenital 'feeblemindedness of the highest degree'. Her parents wrote and visited assiduously, sometimes – after the nine months' acclimatisation period had elapsed – taking Anna Maria (or Annemarie as they preferred to call her) home for a few days over Easter. Every time she got a cold, or broke a bone in a fall, they would write, being reassured that 'your dear Annemarie is in good health and order'. They sent clothing, chocolates and sweets; they wanted her hair cut in a particular way rather than the regulation style. Each time they received a considered and courteous answer. Both sides colluded in the language some people use when referring to small children. When she arrived in Hephata, Anna Maria was so weak that she could neither walk nor talk. By October 1937 the chief doctor was informing the parents that 'your dear Annemarie has adjusted to life here very well. She is always breezy and happy and shows no traces of homesickness. She is eating so well that she has gained 1 kg. I hope that your dear child will yet learn to speak.' They promised not to neglect anything that would contribute to her progress. She was then suddenly transferred in 1938 in a group transport to Marburg. The director there was more pessimistic about her future development:

Unchanged over the duration of this report. Dirty. Cannot stand. Very strong arms. Very good appetite, cries a great deal, particularly at night. Lies still in bed, moves her eyes when one approaches the bed, but shows no mimetic change, laughs a lot, but only says 'ah', otherwise nothing. Has not developed in any respect whatsoever. Unchanged, lies still in bed. Can only sit up.[65]

She died on the day she was transferred to Eichberg.

The paediatric clinic at Brandenburg-Görden was the jewel in the crown of the Reich Committee's thirty-odd clinics. This was where the doctors who were put in charge of other clinics learned the (rather elementary) task of murdering children with tablets and injections.[66] It was a regular hive of activity, with endless rounds of Binet-Simon and Rorschach tests, X-rays, and autopsies conducted on behalf of academics at a number of distinguished universities, who were barely capable of concealing their eagerness to lay hands on the jars of formaldehyde. Horst L., an hydrocephalic eleven-year-old, was admitted to Görden on 1 October 1942. He had been in various clinics and homes for half of his life, latterly in the Berlin Charité following a bout of diphtheria. The doctors there had 'arranged' his admission to Görden. The daily reports of the nursing staff describe a cheerful child who liked to tell stories and sang a lot. He was X-rayed and photographed in a series of positions. He described life at home:

HORST L. Mummy needs a helper, for she has so much to do in the kitchen, cooking, baking cakes, and therefore one needs ...
QUESTION Is she old or young?
HORST L. Young.
QUESTION Is she nice?
HORST L. Yes. She washes me in the morning, then gives me coffee, then she

always gets rid of the crumbs, and makes the bed. I always have to stay in bed at home.

QUESTION Do you know why?

HORST L. Because aunt H. cannot carry me anymore.

QUESTION [Why?]

HORST L. Yes, because I am too heavy.

His forester father's deer-hunting exploits were related in great detail, although the father tended not to talk with him much. He was clearly a mummy's boy. He recalled every detail about the family home, especially the gramophone and radio, which assumed vast importance in the life of someone perpetually confined to bed. Horst was particularly good on the entire programme schedule of Radio Breslau, being able to recall the closing message: 'We are now concluding today's broadcasts. We request our listeners to retune to the German Radio.' He was subjected to tests on 10, 25, 27 and 30 November and 3 December. These went on interminably, although Horst seems to have looked forward to them. Identifying pictures of spoons, ducks, shoes, apples, sailing ships, locomotives, wheelbarrows, buckets, cars, coffee mills, mushrooms, horses, cherries etc.; counting the fingers on his hands, the buttons on his pullover; putting two triangles together as a rectangle; rearranging wooden building bricks and geometric figures with sticks. Repeating sentences of a certain number of syllables: 'The dog fears the cat because it has sharp claws' became 'The dog feared the cat, but it has black claws'; 'The snail moves very slowly, but that is because it carries its home on its back' became 'The snail moves very slowly and takes its whole house ...' Repeating rows of numbers: '3681:3681', '93718:9...3, 718', '25084: 2504...298'. The war formed the basis of yet more questions. Questions like 'Why is there a war on?' or 'Why are they shooting?' brought the response: 'I will ask my mummy how long the war will last.' When his attention flagged during Rorschach tests – his vision was poor in both eyes – the doctor lost patience and held a stick in front of him by way of encouragement.

These rounds of questions, which would get on anyone's nerves – although children have an amazing capacity to tolerate such things – were occasionally broken by a pause. During one of these intervals, Horst chatted with a secretary:

HORST L. Miss D., I dreamed ... of dear God.

QUESTION What did you dream?

HORST L. He should make nice weather.

SECRETARY But it is very nice.

HORST L. Yes, but it isn't so simple! ... Everything passes.

QUESTION What is not so simple?

HORST L. Things aren't so easy in life ... I can't tell you why this is so. No I can't.

SECRETARY But things are going well for you?

HORST L. Miss D., things are better here than in . . . I know how things are, and at home too, my mummy has a lot to do. Perhaps I'll get a visitor tomorrow, perhaps aunt M. and H. will come. Perhaps aunt M. will bring something nice with her. Aunt M. came to the other ward, she brought me pears, beads and marbles, marbles made of glass. She didn't have any more, just a couple, with which Horst had already played, when he was small. Horst would prefer to be home, but now he has to stay here. I know that the sisters are nice here too. Yesterday sister L. said to me, as she carried me, 'Look Horst, you see, you are not so heavy, we can still carry you.' And sister L. was right. It is very nice here.

On 12 January 1943, Dr Schumacher, the consultant neurologist, dictated a letter about Horst to be sent to the Reich Committee. Horst's evident curiosity, happiness and imaginativeness were filtered out. He was now simply an eleven-and-a-half-year-old with the intelligence of a five-and-a-half-year-old. He would never improve, and would never perform 'socially valuable activities'. He recommended his 'treatment in line with the directive of the Ministry of the Interior'. Horst died on 5 March 1943 at ten o'clock. A suspiciously lengthy entry in his medical record on the same day attempts to fabricate a history of gradual decline. He had lost weight, stopped playing and talking to adults, and sat, staring vacantly into space. All of these things apparently happened in a day. The cause of death was given as 'bronchial pneumonia', but the autopsy revealed nothing wrong with his lungs. The skull, the report continued, 'is pronouncedly larger than the rest of the organism'.[67] That had not been Horst's problem.

This chapter began with the first tentative steps towards implementing a children's 'euthanasia' programme, and has advanced to a point – long after Hitler's alleged 'halt' order of August 1941 – somewhere in 1942–1943, at which the killing of children, adolescents and young adults had become routine and systematic. We have seen that this came about quite deliberately, as an act of moral and intellectual conviction on the part of a closely knit group of like-minded individuals. It is dogmatic, unimaginative and perverse to talk about choices made by mature, intelligent people in terms of the automatic functioning of bureaucratic machinery. As many as 6,000 children died, although many more were killed under the adult 'euthanasia' programme.[68] However, the killing of handicapped children was but one aspect of a broader strategy to decimate the asylum population in general, which in turn was but one aspect of the desire to kill all that was alien, imperfect or deviant.[69] The rest of this chapter will be concerned with what was codenamed 'Aktion T–4', i.e. the systematic murder of mainly adult patients.

Some time before July 1939, Hitler summoned State Secretary Leonardo Conti, Martin Bormann, and the head of the Reich Chancellory, Hans

Heinrich Lammers, instructing Conti to implement a 'euthanasia' programme. In 1947 Lammers recalled that Hitler had said that

he regarded it as right that the worthless lives of seriously ill mental patients should be got rid of. He took as examples the severe mental illnesses in which the patients could only be kept lying on sand or sawdust, because they perpetually dirtied themselves, cases in which these patients put their own excrement in their mouths as if it were food, and things similar. Continuing on from that, he said that he thought it right that the worthless lives of such creatures should be ended, and that this would result in certain savings in terms of hospitals, doctors and nursing staff.[70]

Word of this gathering was relayed to Hans Hefelmann by Wagner's press officer, Helmut Unger, himself the author of a key epistolary novel which advocated involuntary 'euthanasia'. Hefelmann told Brack, who then went hotfooted to Karl Brandt and Philipp Bouhler.[71] The latter, sensing a threat to a territory they were making their own, managed to edge Conti aside so as to keep the KdF in sole control of 'euthanasia' measures. Bouhler was apparently concerned that Bormann's cypher, Conti, would cast the net of victims too widely. He also wished to retain a centralised grip on killings which individual Gauleiters might carry out almost randomly.[72] According to Lammers, the young and ambitious Bouhler tried to make up for his lack of influence with Hitler by attempting to stray into Lammers's territory, sometimes diverting Reich Chancellory business in the direction of his own agency.[73] Hitler then told Bouhler and Brandt that 'he now wanted to carry out a particular solution to the question of euthanasia'.[74] To this end, he issued them with a laconic note of commission on his personal notepaper:

Reichleiter Bouhler and Dr med. Brandt are charged with responsibility to extend the powers of specific doctors in such a way that, after the most careful assessment of their condition, those suffering from illnesses deemed to be incurable may be granted a mercy death.[75]

Although this note bore the date 1 September, it was in fact written a month later and then backdated. According to Blankenburg's secretary, who typed the document, ten people – none of them doctors – discussed the brief text, the top copy of which went into Bouhler's safe.[76] This note did not have the force of law, for up to 26 April 1942, when the Reichstag accorded Hitler the right to issue laws himself, such proposals had to be publicly promulgated.[77] Let us be quite precise about this: even to be an official decree, the note ought to have been typed on paper headed 'Der Führer und Reichskanzler', and would have had to be countersigned by Hitler and Lammers, and then sealed with the great Reich seal and published in the Reich legal gazetteer.[78] None of these things was done. Nor did the note cover the creation of a covert, prerogative, bureaucratic apparatus designed to murder tens of thousands of psychiatric patients on a totally non-consensual basis. The note was thus a characteristic example of how Hitler could have his wishes indirectly interpreted as orders. In no sense did it lend what had happened, or was to happen, any legal sanction.

The first step in creating the means to carry out these policies was to beef up the three-man team of referees whom we have already encountered in the children's 'euthanasia' programme. Together with Herbert Linden of the Ministry of the Interior (the official responsible for state asylums), Bouhler and Brandt approached a number of seriously eminent academics and asylum directors. These included professors Maximian de Crinis, of Berlin; Carl Schneider, Heidelberg; Berthold Kihn, Jena; and Werner Heyde of Würzburg. In addition to Catel, Heinze and Wentzler, the core group also numbered the asylum directors Pfannmüller of Eglfing-Haar, Paul Nitsche of Sonnenstein near Pirna, and Bender of Berlin-Buch.

Werner Heyde was born at Forst in Lusatia in 1902. After attending school, he fought in the Freikorps in Estonia and then in Cottbus in the wake of the Kapp putsch. Between 1920 and 1925 Heyde studied medicine at Berlin, Freiburg, Marburg, Rostock and Würzburg, working in the docks, mines and a glass factory because his father had lost all he had through the inflation. After his studies, Heyde held a succession of grants and temporary assistant lectureships at Würzburg until he gained a full teaching appointment in 1932. In 1933 Heyde was asked to make a psychological assessment of the SS officer Theodor Eicke, whom Gauleiter Bürckel was trying to silence by committing him to a mental hospital. Heyde (wrongly) refused to describe Eicke as a psychopath, and hence made a favourable impression on Himmler. A follow-up meeting with the 'Reicharzt-SS', Grawitz, led to refereeing work in concentration camps. Professional criminals provided him 'with wonderful research material'.[79] In the mid 1930s Heyde came to the attention of the KdF in his capacity as an expert referee in sterilisation cases, as referee for the Gestapo, and through his two-days-a-week labours in the concentration camps. In late 1939 he became a full professor. Although most of the faculty wanted someone more famous – Heyde was too busy working for the SS to have written much – a couple of telephone calls from the Education Ministry and Philipp Bouhler settled the matter.[80]

Heyde was a member of the NSDAP from May 1933, and from 1936 a Hauptsturmführer in the SS. He was attracted to the SS because of its elitist image.[81] Until 1941, when Nitsche replaced him, Heyde was the senior referee and medical supremo of 'Aktion T-4'. He was replaced because the dark side of a successful life came to haunt him. As a fifteen-year-old he had been seduced by an older female friend of the family in a way which traumatised him. He had indulged his latent homosexual proclivities while in the Estonian Freikorps, practising mutual

(a)

Plate 12. Professor Werner Heyde. Photographs (a) during the period when he worked for 'T–4'; (b) a 'mugshot' taken while under American detention and (c) as the sports doctor, Dr Sawade, the assumed name he used between 1947 and his arrest and suicide in the early 1960s.

onanism with young soldiers. He had sought psychotherapy. In Würzburg he belonged to a circle of well-to-do homosexuals, sometimes seducing his own male students. This damaging information was on record with the SD; it made no difference that in 1927 Heyde had married. When Brack decided he had had enough of the professor's pretensions, he merely needed to dredge up this information to oust him.[82] Like many of his ilk, Heyde was tantalised by the trappings of power. It lent a spurious

(b)

respectability to a weak man prone to furtive activities. The KdF was the 'symbol of the state', radiating the power of the Führer and his accomplices towards this homosexual provincial university professor.[83]

Carl Schneider was born in 1891 at Gunbitz in Posen. His father gave up the business of running an undistinguished private school and went to America as a wandering musician. Later he came back broke, seeking support from his only child. He died in a home for the indigent. Schneider grew up with his mother, who ran a haberdashery in a small town called Pegau near Leipzig. As happens with many academics, his intelligence was his only means of social mobility. He won a scholarship to an elite boarding school, and then went on to study medicine at Würzburg. He spent the war working in military hospitals in Eastern Galicia and on the Western Front,

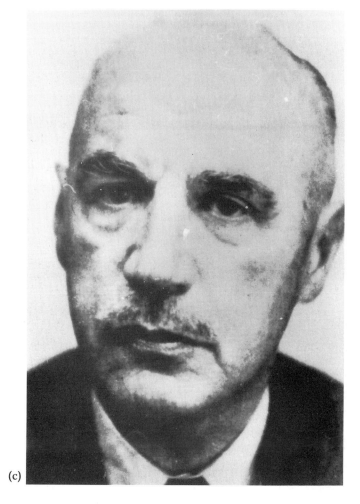

(c)

where he was wounded near Ypres in May 1915. The painter Max Beckmann served as an orderly in the same part of the front. Beckmann and his contemporary, Otto Dix, portrayed the horror of what they saw; Schneider took photographs which aestheticised the carnage in a manner reminiscent of the writer Ernst Jünger. He would later traduce Dix for his lurid portrayals of disabled veterans and demi-mondiste women of the Weimar period.

After the war, Schneider became an assistant at Leipzig under the eminent psychiatrist Oswald Bumke. When he married in 1920, Schneider left the university for the more secure post of a doctor in an asylum. He produced a stream of academic publications on schizophrenia, and in 1930 worked with Paul Nitsche devising the Hygiene exhibition in Dresden.[84]

Plate 13. Professor Carl Schneider

From 1930 to 1933 Schneider was chief doctor at Bethel, a Protestant asylum for epileptics and vagrants near Bielefeld. Joining the NSDAP in 1932, he moved a year later to the chair of psychiatry and neurology at Heidelberg. It was not a political appointment, although the vacancy had arisen because his predecessor had been sacked for insulting Goering and Hitler.[85] As leader of the university psychiatric clinic, Schneider was an enthusiastic exponent of Hermann Simon's individualised occupational therapy, while seeking to break down the barriers between asylums and the world beyond. In 1939, Schneider published a celebrated book, 'The Treatment and Prevention of Mental Illnesses', the first psychiatric textbook to be concerned with forms of treatment rather than diagnosis or nosological questions.[86] A Nazi Party member since 1932, Schneider was leader of the Racial Political Office in Baden. By the summer of 1940 he was working for the KdF. As we shall see, the quid pro quo for his refereeing activity was the chance to conduct autopsies on the victims.

Maximan Friedrich Alexander de Crinis (1889–1945) was the scion of an Austrian medical dynasty. Studying medicine at Graz and Innsbrück, he joined a nationalist duelling fraternity and was a pronounced opponent of Roman Catholicism. In 1914 he became an assistant at the University of Graz psychiatric clinic. There he was able to study battlefield psychiatric casualties at first hand, since Graz was near the Austro-Italian battle zone.[87] During the early and late 1920s, he was involved with the Styrian Heimatschutz, fighting marauding Slovenes and insurgent Communists; by most accounts he was also a 'fanatical antisemite'. In 1931 he moved yet further right by combining membership of the Styrian Heimatschutz with that of the NSDAP. Under Dollfuss's 'clerical fascist' dictatorship, de Crinis was eventually arrested in 1934 in connection with Nazi terrorist activity, i.e. the blowing up of a public telephone callbox. The Ministry of Education removed his right to teach in universities. He fled the country shortly before the July 1934 Nazi putsch against Dollfuss and worked treating the wounded among the survivors in refugee camps in Yugoslavia.[88] With suspicious rapidity, by July de Crinis had become professor of psychiatry at the university of Cologne, a vacancy created by the emigration of his Jewish predecessor. He produced a stream of publications on (*inter alia*) brain tumours, and a textbook on forensic psychiatry. In 1934, he became Führer of the Cologne university teaching association; two years later he joined the SS. In 1938 he succeeded Karl Bonhoeffer as both professor of psychiatry and neurology in Berlin and director of the psychiatric clinic at the prestigious Charité. The students and staff welcomed the replacement of the dour Bonhoeffer by this charming and gregarious Austrian Nazi. His laboratory assistants got to sail (and clean!) his boat, moored near his villa in Wannsee. With a bust of Hitler and swastika flags now adorning the clinic, de Crinis's inaugural lecture 'German Psychiatry' (!) unfurled the new intellectual message.[89] Extolling the virtues of the anatomical-pathological approach, de Crinis poured scorn on 'those un-German, racially alien, so-called expert colleagues who have been purveying their immoralities in Vienna and other German cities until quite recently', by which he meant Sigmund Freud. A host of roles devolved on the professor. He became a member of the steering committee of the Kaiser Wilhelm Institute for Neurological Research, expert advisor responsible for medicine in the Ministry of Education, and a leading military psychiatric advisor. Through his friend Walter Schellenberg of the SD, de Crinis had a bit-part, posing as an 'opposition leader' (!), in the entrapment of British Secret Service agents at Venlo. Clearly a game chap, Hitler awarded him the Iron Cross, first and second class, for his skill in skulduggery.[90] Like some of the sillier academics in other countries, he was evidently tantalised by the world of cloak and dagger. He was soon involved in the planning of a 'euthanasia' programme, and probably functioned along with Heyde as a senior assessor.[91]

Towards the end of July, these men – whose ideological fervour and utter lack of moral scruple should now be evident – met together with Bouhler in Berlin. Bouhler informed them that it was necessary to kill a proportion of psychiatric patients to make space for anticipated military casualties. The surplus nursing staff thus created could be used in military hospitals. Although foreign policy considerations dictated that no law could be made public, those present should rest assured that they would not be prosecuted for their actions. Apart from de Crinis, who said he was over-committed elsewhere, all those present agreed to participate. Afterwards, Conti presented them to Minister of the Interior Frick. The asylum directors slipped away to start the business of finding serviceable accomplices among the staff of their institutions.

After the rejection of such crude solutions as mass coach or train 'accidents',[92] the question of how to kill large numbers of people as efficiently as possible was resolved by the chemists employed by the Reich Criminal Police Office. Dr Albert Widmann, the acting head of the chemistry department, met an official of the KdF in the presence of his chief, SS-Gruppenführer Arthur Nebe. The conversation went as follows:

'Widmann, can the Criminal Technical Institute manufacture large quantities of poison?'
'For what? To kill people?'
'No.'
'To kill animals?'
'No.'
'What for, then?'
'To kill animals in human form: that means the mentally ill, whom one can no longer describe as human and for whom no recovery is in sight.'

Widmann agreed to work on the problem. The Criminal Technical Institute was to act as a front for acquiring toxic substances on behalf of the KdF; the Führer's name was never to be mentioned in this connection.[93] Having settled on carbon monoxide gas – Widmann had once had to reconstruct how two people had died of fume inhalation in a Berlin residence – Brack issued Widmann with a permit to acquire fifty cylinders from Mannesmann Steel, which were then filled with gas from I. G. Farben, the Ludwigshafen-based chemical conglomerate. The cylinders were refilled every two months. All of the invoices were made out to the Criminal Technical Institute.[94]

Plate 14. Grafeneck. This castle on the Swabian Alb near Munsingen, was expropriated from an ecclesiastical charitable organisation and then used to murder 9,839 people. It is currently used as a Samaritan Foundation home for the mentally handicapped.

With the means at hand, the KdF team set about the questions of 'Where?' and 'By whom?' The matter of where was resolved by despatching Linden – the most shadowy figure in the entire operation – to meet with the head of the Württemberg Health Service, Dr Egon Stähle, himself firmly of the opinion that 'one gives a mercy death to every domestic pet that cannot serve one any more'. Linden said he needed a small and isolated institution; Stähle came up with the Inner Mission's Samaritan foundation for cripples at Grafeneck, high up in the Swabian Alb. The two of them, exuding self-importance, paid it a flying visit. This Renaissance castle, within spitting distance of the world-famous stud farm at Marbach, had been bought by the Inner Mission in 1929.[95] It is still a home for mentally handicapped people, with elaborate workshops, livestock and a small line in eggs and rather good honey. Stähle and Linden hurried through, eyeing up the location, dimensions and bed capacity. It seemed ideal. Remote, but with road and rail links running alongside the densely wooded heights upon which the castle stood; surrounded with woods, meadows and a series of steep battlements from which to oversee access. Best of all, the patients could be relocated to the other Samaritan foundation at Obersontheim at Schwäbisch-Hall.[96] In the course of October, various visitors made the rather lonely journey to the asylum, which was confiscated from the Inner Mission on the twelfth of that month. They checked into the Gaststätte Marbach at the end of the valley, using false names, and answered any questions with the information that they were setting up a quarantine hospital in the former ducal-castle-cum-cripple-asylum. These incognito visitors included Brack, alias 'Jennerwein' (a famous eighteenth-century poacher), Gerhard Bohne, Werner Heyde and Reinhold Vorberg, alias 'Hintertal'. A few weeks later, a coachload of SS men from the Death's Head Division 'Brandenburg', dressed as civilians but carrying guns and their SS paybooks, arrived at Grafeneck, where, aided by fifteen local craftsmen, they began converting a home for cripples into an extermination centre. They installed offices; put up wooden and barbed-wire fences, signs warning people of the dangers of infectious diseases and a sentry box; and a few hundred metres from the castle installed a gas chamber and crematoria on the site now used to house chickens and farm machinery.[97]

While these preparations were happening at Grafeneck, the KdF was spawning a range of covert sub-bureaucracies. These included a Reich Working Party for Mental Asylums, under the lawyer Bohne, which was responsible for registering potential victims, dealing with their effects, and overseeing the registry offices which would fake their cause of death. The Community Foundation for the Care of Asylums, which officially employed the staff who carried out these killings, ran the buildings, acquired the gas, and recycled gold teeth and sold jewellery. And finally,

Plate 15. This villa at Tiergartenstrasse 4 was the operational centre for the 'euthanasia' programme, hence the codename 'Aktion т–4'. By using this anonymous suburban base, those responsible intended to mask the administrative connection with the KdF (Chancellery of the Führer), which was situated in the governmental heart of Berlin.

there was the Community Patients' Transport Service Ltd, or 'Gekrat', led by Brack's cousin Reinhold Vorberg and later by Brack's old skiing chum Hermann Schweninger, which took care of transporting patients to holding asylums and extermination centres. The name ensured its tax-exempt status. In April 1941 these agencies were augmented by a Central Accounting Office for Mental Asylums, under Hans-Joachim Becker (nicknamed 'Millions' from the abundance of his ill-gotten gains), which continued to collect the maintenance payments of people whose date of death they alone determined.[98]

On 1 December 1940, this assortment of bureaucrats, eminent professors, and failures at everything between business and film-making decided to move from the KdF into four rooms in the Columbus-Haus on Potsdamer Platz. In April they moved into a more gloomily imposing 'aryanised' villa at Tiergartenstrasse 4 in Charlottenberg, whence they derived the codename for the 'euthanasia' programme 'Aktion T-4'. It bore no identifying name plate. An untypically specific plaque on the ground opposite the entrance to where the Berlin Philharmonic is orchestra-in-residence marks the villa's former location.[99] The resort to eccentric locations, *noms de guerre*, and phoney company titles were an attempt to conceal the wires leading back to the KdF.

So far we have learned in some detail about the professors involved in the 'euthanasia' programme; we know far less about their bureaucratic superiors. Unfortunately, the major actors in these events later either committed suicide (Hitler, Bouhler) or were executed by the Allies (Brandt, Brack), so expeditiously that information is simply not available. War crimes trials dealt with offences against foreign nationals or 'humanity' (i.e. Jewish people), and the sort of procedures adopted – such as cross-examination – were designed to clarify forensic questions of guilt, rather than to probe motivational or personal issues in a way which West Germany handled more satisfactorily.

Viktor Brack was born at Haaren in 1904, the son of the doctor who treated Himmler's wife. An economist by training (an appropriate skill given the policies he implemented), Brack joined both the NSDAP and the SS in 1929. An occasional chauffeur for Himmler, by 1932 he was employed by Bouhler in Munich; they shared an interest in motor racing. He moved to Berlin two years later, and took over Main Office II of the KdF in 1936.[100] Alongside Brandt and Linden, Brack was clearly the man in charge of the 'euthanasia' programme, with Bouhler dealing with more high-level political issues. Employees in the Tiergartenstrasse recalled that when Brack showed up on the scene 'one had the impression that the Lord God had come in person'.[101] One of Brack's most senior subordinates, Dietrich Allers, recalled apropos of the relationship between Brack and the professors Heyde and Nitsche that 'In practice Brack was in charge,

Plate 16. Viktor Brack

because the professors, who from the outside appeared to be in control, merely carried out what Brack whispered in their ears. That didn't apply to medical matters, which they naturally enough decided themselves.'[102]

Judging from a vast body of subsequent testimony, most T-4 employees arrived through personal connections. Thus Hermann Schweninger, who began by leading transports of patients and ended up making films for the organisation, had known Brack since he was sixteen.[103] Likewise, Dietrich Allers owed his job to a chance encounter between his mother and his old SA comrade Werner Blankenburg, who assisted in getting Allers pulled out of military service.[104] Adolf Kaufmann joined his brother Reinhold;

Robert Lorent and Tillmann knew Brack from the old days; others, like Gerhard Bohne, had come to the attention of the KdF through their work as lawyers for other agencies.[105] A high proportion of these men were from the commercial sector; bank employees or salesmen, whose amorality and organisational acumen would keep things running smoothly, while turning in considerable profits. Hans-Joachim Becker was not nicknamed 'Millions' for nothing. Lawyers like Bohne were brought in once Brack and Bouhler had grasped that one could not simply make tens of thousands of people disappear without running the risk of exposure by a host of insurance, judicial, political or welfare agencies.[106]

Nepotism and personal contacts prevailed at every level. A telephonist was recruited by her sister, who was Tillmann's secretary.[107] Kurt M., who ran T–4's central card registry, was an old SA associate of Blankenburg's.[108] Kaufmann's wife ran the T–4 personnel rest home on the Attersee in Bavaria.[109] These men and women coldly and calculatingly organised the murder of thousands of people. It is no use describing them, as 'desk-bound murderers', somehow remote from murder, since even the secretaries shared their offices with jars of foul-smelling gold-filled teeth, listening to dictation which enumerated 'bridge with three teeth', 'a single tooth', and so on.[110] To bring this account down to the moral level at which those people operated, one should mention that all T–4 employees could avail themselves of cut-price dental work, which utilised gold recycled from the mouths of their victims.[111]

The men and women who operated at the sharp end were carefully selected for their proven brutality and ideological dedication. The lower echelons of T–4 included several individuals who would later pass from T–4 to the death camps of 'Aktion Reinhard' and on to the murder of Jews and partisans in Trieste. Josef Oberhauser, the elusive barman in Lanzmann's film *Shoah*, was an SS NCO who was recruited as a 'burner' for the crematoria in Grafeneck, Brandenburg and Bernburg.[112] One of Oberhauser's fellow recruits was the SS cook Kurt Franz (recently released from a thirty-year jail sentence), who would move up from being the cook in Buchenwald to commanding an extermination camp. Franz recalled that Brack showed their group a film about mental patients that was so shocking he could not look at it.[113] The former tram conductor Erich Bauer became a chauffeur for T–4, driving the doctors around Germany in a Fiat (nicknamed 'busy Lizzy'), moving onward and upward to a post at Sobibor.[114]

Those who were not centrally recruited were inducted at their future workplace. Those doing the recruiting did not mince words. A former butcher who belonged to the SS, and who felt queasy about grinding bones into oatflake-size pieces, recalled simply being handed a pair of asbestos gloves and told 'You'll get used to it.'[115] At Hartheim recruits encountered

Plate 17. Christian Wirth. This former Stuttgart detective worked in Bernburg, Brandenburg, Grafeneck, Hadamar and Hartheim before becoming commandant of Belzec and then inspector of the three 'Aktion Reinhard' death camps. He was assassinated by partisans while stationed in Trieste in 1944.

the ghoulish figure of Christian Wirth, a bull-like former Stuttgart detective, who would later be inspector of the 'Aktion Reinhard' death camps. Wirth announced:

Comrades, I've called you together here today in order to inform you about the present position in the castle and what is going to happen from now on. I have been assigned the task of running the castle from now on by the Reich Chancellory (*sic*). As the boss I am in charge of everything. We must build a crematorium here, in order to burn mental patients from Austria. Five doctors have been chosen who will examine the patients to establish what can or cannot be saved. What can't be saved goes into the crematorium and will be burned. Mental patients are a burden upon Germany and we only want healthy people. Mental patients are a burden upon the State. Certain men will be chosen to work in the crematorium. Above all else, the motto is silence or the death penalty. Whosoever fails to observe this silence will end up in a concentration camp or be shot.[116]

For these people, working for T-4 represented a modest form of social mobility, whereby butchers, cooks, policemen or tram-ticket collectors could, and did, become camp commandants. They were brutal and insensitive before they started: tough and hard-drinking working-class males, who could have a party around a corpse or weep drunkenly as they sang plangent songs about their homeland around the barracks stove in the extermination camps. They are very subtle liars, and their political fanaticism and low cunning become apparent only after long acquaintanceship with either them or the historical record.

Information about how T-4 selected doctors to turn on the gas valves – for apparently one needed to be highly educated at the tax payer's expense to do this – is sparse, but not impossible to tease out of the records. With his overview of the state asylums, Herbert Linden of the Ministry of the Interior was the primary culprit.[117] In Baden, for example, he asked Ludwig Sprauer, the head of the regional health authority, who obliged with the name of Dr Josef Schreck.[118] In Bavaria he approached Sprauer's equivalent, Professor Walter 'Bubi' Schultze, who recommended Pfannmüller.[119] Although he denied it, Werner Heyde also drew attention to suitable students, airing the subject with Aquilin Ullrich, who was taken to the Zuchthaus at Brandenburg and then offered the job of murdering people by Brack on the return journey.[120] Another talent scout was the SS 'Reicharzt' Grawitz, who endeavoured to recruit the former Buchenwald doctor Werner Kirchert.[121] Despite being offered double his current salary, and such inducements as extra alcohol, books and a radio, Kirchert refused to get involved – for Hefelmann's idea of mass train accidents seemed too radical – recommending instead his old student friend Horst Schumann.[122] None of these people were 'ordinary men'. They were carefully chosen because of the degree of political fanaticism they had evinced beforehand. That characteristic, as we shall see, extended right down the T-4 hierarchy.

The emergence of this covert bureaucracy, and the conversion of asylums such as Grafeneck, ran parallel with the definition of potential victims. On 9 September Conti wrote to all state governments requesting global figures on all extra-Prussian public and private asylums. (Information on Prussia was already to hand.) Each asylum then received further forms 'Meldebogen (Registration Form) 2', wanting more detailed overall information on area, budget, staffing levels etc., and 'Meldebogen 1', to be completed regarding every patient.[123] The purpose of these forms was given as 'economic planning'; the asylum directors and their staff had between three and ten weeks to register certain categories of patient. According to the accompanying notes, these were (1) people suffering from schizophrenia, epilepsy, senile dementia, therapy-resistant paralysis, feeblemindedness, encephalitis and Huntington's Chorea, who were incapable of anything other than merely mechanical work; (2) patients who had been in the asylums for more than five years; (3) the criminally insane, foreign nationals and 'racial aliens'.[124] Lest anyone had problems in defining 'those incapable of anything other than mechanical tasks', Linden clarified the matter by including all patient vegetable-peelers and cardboard-box makers. They were to register 'too many rather than too few'.[125] Some doctors suspected that something was amiss. The director of the provincial asylum at Göttingen, Professor Ewald, tried to diffuse anxieties among his staff by claiming that in wartime it could be assumed (with good reason) that patients likely to recover or capable of working would be better fed than the incurable, and that these forms were merely intended to help define these two categories.[126] Other asylum directors, who wished to retain capable patient-workers in the event that the forms were a form of labour conscription, made the fatal error of deliberately underestimating the patients' labour potential, in a political (and indeed psychiatric) context which had elevated work to the status of a cardinal virtue.[127] Few asylum administrators or doctors seem to have thought through the implications of questions regarding nationality, race or the number of visitors a patient received. Nor did they ponder what was going to be written in the box marked 'this space is to be left empty' in the bottom left-hand corner. The completed forms were sent back to the T–4 headquarters, where each was photocopied five times. Three of these copies were sent to expert referees.[128] We can follow these packets of forms in great detail in the case of Eglfing-Haar's Hermann Pfannmüller.

The packets came from Werner Heyde at the Reich Working Party. The following list gives the date, quantity and original asylum from which the forms came:

12 November	1940:	300 forms:	Dueren/Warstein
15 November	1940:	300 forms:	Hinsbeck/Johannistal
19 November	1940:	300 forms:	Neuss/Telgte
20 November	1940:	258 forms:	Arnsdorf/Ursberg/Idstein/Stadtroda
25 November	1940:	300 forms:	Lüneburg
28 November	1940:	300 forms:	Schleswig
9 April	1941:	11 forms:	Andernach
9 April	1941:	200 forms:	various asylums
16 April	1941:	200 forms:	Wiesengrund/Günzburg

16 April	1941:	200 forms:	Obrawalde/Lüneburg
23 April	1941:	200 forms:	Steinhof/Obrawalde
23 April	1941:	3 forms:	Zwiefalten/Andernach
29 April	1941:	21 forms:	various asylums
30 April	1941:	204 forms:	various asylums
3 May	1941:	217 forms:	various asylums
15 May	1941:	200 forms:	various asylums
29 May	1941:	200 forms:	various asylums.[129]

In a letter to his wife dated 22 April 1947, Pfannmüller claimed that in his refereeing capacity he 'was always assiduous, correct, never sloppy, well known and recognised as being capable and objective, careful and exact; I worked for others without thought of gain, solely in the interests of the patients in my care.'[130] As for the speed with which this diagnostic virtuoso swept through the three thousand-odd forms, it could be explained by his penchant for working every weekend and leaving a clear desk late at night. A prosecutor at Nuremberg, keen to expound the mysteries of the medical craft for a lay audience, established that Pfannmüller would have had to plough through hundreds of forms a day, at the rate of one every five minutes.[131] Pfannmüller's secretary recalled that he zipped through the forms 'ziemlich schnell'.[132] Although the record of 15,000 forms processed in a month was held by the stakhanovite, and aptly named, Dr Josef Schreck, Heyde and Brack regarded 3,500 as a reasonable norm. Rapidity paid, for the piecework rates were 100RMs for 500 forms per month; 200RMs for up to 2,000; 300RMs for 3,500; and a bonanza of 400RMs for over 3,500.[133] The forms marked with a ' + ', which meant that the person would be killed, were allegedly rechecked by the senior referee Heyde, and then converted into lists of names which were handed over to the Community Patients' Transport Service. It is now time to follow their coaches and trains to the asylums and extermination centres, but not before a crucial detour to north-eastern Germany and occupied Poland, where initially the 'psychopaths' of the SS did not concern themselves overmuch with the medicalised camouflage of mass murder.

CHAPTER 4

'THE PSYCHOPATHS' CLUB'

THE FIRST mass killing of psychiatric patients happened in north-eastern Germany and occupied Poland. Although these killings had little to do with T–4 – there being no attempt made to give a medical disguise to murder – it is necessary to discuss them because in 1941 these separate developments and the teams of experts involved came together to implement the 'Final Solution'. On 3 July 1939, SS-Brigadeführer Schäfer ordered the formation of a special SS guard unit, the Wachsturmbann Eimann, named after its leader SS-Sturmbannführer Kurt Eimann. Born in 1899, the latter was an unskilled labourer who joined the SS in 1932, reaching the rank of Sturmbannführer by the outbreak of war. It was another story of rapid social mobility, based in Eimann's case upon utter commitment and total ruthlessness.[1] The unit, consisting of four hundred troops with transport support, had among its initial tasks augmenting the regular police, transporting 'criminals', and 'protecting' Danzig while Germany attacked Poland. One of their first jobs was to execute the Polish postmen who surrendered after trying vainly to defend the Danzig main post office. (A cousin of Günter Grass's mother was one of those killed, hence the character Jan Bronski in *The Tin Drum*.)[2] Following the military defeat of Poland, approximately half the unit's strength was diverted to guard duties in the POW and concentration camps at Neufahrwasser, Stutthof and Grenzdorf. The remainder performed multifarious tasks, including the elimination of several thousand psychiatric patients.[3] In October 1939, Eimann was given 'the unpleasant task' of killing patients from several Pomeranian asylums, as part of a deal struck between Franz Schwede-Coburg, the president of the province, and the Reichsführer-SS Heinrich Himmler, who wanted the buildings for barracks and military casualty stations.[4] Originally, Schwede-Coburg was also thinking of using the empty buildings as hostels for ethnic German repatriates from the Baltic, one of several pointers to the fact that the 'euthanasia' programme may have been related to Nazi ethnic cleansing.[5] Eimann later said that in joining the SS he had said more or less 'in for a penny, in for a pound':

Plate 18. Kurt Eimann. An SS unit commanded by Eimann was responsible for shooting about three thousand psychiatric patients from Pomeranian asylums in order to create barracks space and hostels for ethnic German repatriates.

whatever the SS asked him to do, he could not refuse. Matters were that simple: one signed up ready for anything.[6]

The patients were taken by train from Stralsund, Lauenburg, Ücker-munde and Treptow to Danzig-Neustadt. Often drugged or in straitjackets and handcuffs, they were unloaded off the trains into lorries at nine or ten in the morning. Out in the woods near Piasznicz, each patient was led away by two SS men – chatting aimlessly about this and that – until he was out of sight of the rest, whereupon Eimann, who had ambled along behind, shot him in the back of the neck, into graves dug by a party of prisoners from Stutthof. The sound of gunfire was the signal for the next person to be taken out into the woods. Apparently some of the patients waiting to die thought the noise faintly amusing.[7] In the course of a day, all those involved – except the victims – exchanged roles in this macabre scenario, presumably in order to generate a sense of group complicity.[8] The lorries returned to the station at three in the afternoon, empty except for the patients' clothing. After several weeks of this it was time to do away with any potential witnesses, a procedure which was to become routine in the mass extermination camps established later. The prisoners from Stutthof, all men aged between twenty and thirty-five, who had dug the graves were taken for a ride by SS men drinking schnapps. They failed to notice that the contents of the bottle they themselves were offered had been tampered with. Once asleep, they too were shot into a ditch. Everything was covered over with sand, soil and clutches of undergrowth.[9] Although no one knows exactly how many patients this unit killed, their own report in January 1941 speaks of over three thousand.[10] For this Eimann eventually received a four-year jail sentence.

In East Prussia, 1,558 asylum patients from Allenberg, Kortau and Tapiau were killed, on the orders of Higher SS- and Police Leader SS-Gruppenführer Wilhelm Koppe, by a special SS unit under Herbert Lange based at Soldau.[11] These killings took place between 21 May and 8 June 1940.[12] Forty patients at a time were loaded on to lorries – including one adorned with the name of a firm 'Kaisers-Kaffee-Geschäft' – and killed with toxic gas released from a cylinder in the cab. Dr Hans Renfranz, who witnessed these men in operation, beating up mental patients or forcing local Jews to make suits for them, noted that they had liberal recourse to alcohol, while hardly bothering to conceal from the patients (or anyone else) that they were going to kill them. Accurately enough, Renfranz and his wife referred to Lange and his men as 'the psychopaths' club', in other words men who revelled in destruction.[13] These killings were carried out on the understanding that the Sonderkommando Lange's seventeen-day out-of-area spell in East Prussia would be covered by a premium of 10RMs per patient killed, payable by the Higher SS- and Police Leader of Königsberg Friedrich Wilhelm Rediess. We know about this simply because Rediess and his successor, Sporrenberg, were late payers, and hence charge and counter-charge went back and forth to Gruppenführer Wolff of Himmler's personal staff.[14] Wolff apparently then telephoned Viktor Brack, with the possible consequence that the T–4 financial bureaucracy, which disposed of big bank deposits, eventually paid Lange.[15] After all, they were all in the same line of business. Although this book is emphatically not a history of the Holocaust, it is important to note that Lange's unit, augmented after a spell in Berlin, moved next from Posen to Chelmno (in early December 1941) in order to run Kulmhof, the first mass extermination camp used in the 'Final Solution of the Jewish Question'.[16] There they murdered about 145,000 people. The killings at Soldau had shown how this magnitude of destruction could be possible.

Between 1939 and 1944, German authorities – for civilian asylum personnel were involved – killed 12,850 Polish psychiatric patients.[17] There are several accounts by Polish asylum staff of what was done to their patients. The asylum at Owinka in Poznan province was large (1,100 patients) and venerable, having celebrated its centenary in 1938. It was occupied by thirty members of the SS-Totenkopf Standarte under an officer called Sache. Described as being 'loud and vulgar' – after all, they were members of the 'master race' – these uniformed delinquents destroyed the chapel and burned two thousand rare books in the asylum library. Their attitude to the patients was, 'It won't be long before you'll all be put against a wall and shot.' Ethnic German civilians eventually arrived and perfunctorily 'refereed' the patients. The first to go were the criminally insane, who were loaded on to lorries with their hands tied behind their backs. The SS guards had rifles and spades. When they returned with the empty lorries (with a fifty-kilometre round trip registered on the mileometer) the spades were dirty and sometimes flecked with blood. They explained the former by saying that they had had to dig the wheels out of mud. They did not account for the blood. Not surprisingly, the remaining patients experienced extreme terror, since they soon realised what was happening. Drugs had to be used to neutralise any resistance. By November, when the children had been taken away, the asylum was empty.[18] About 900 patients had been murdered.[19]

These events in Poland ran parallel with preparations for an adult 'euthanasia' programme in the Reich. The expertise acquired in both of these separate actions would eventually be brought to bear on annihilating the Jewish population of occupied Europe. The level of personal and technical interchange quickened. At Christmas 1939, Viktor Brack summoned SS-Oberscharführer August Becker (known as 'Red' Becker because of his hair colour, and to distinguish him from the 'Millions' whom we have already encountered), of the Reich Main Security Office to the KdF (Chancellory of the Führer). The meeting was arranged by Reichsführer-SS Heinrich Himmler, whose menacing presence was never very far away from the events we are considering, even if (like Hitler) he thought it expedient to stay at several removes from the events we have been considering.[20] Brack explained to Becker that an adult 'euthanasia programme' was about to commence, whose purpose was 'the extermination of all idiots and mental patients'. The chemist Widmann had found a suitable method, namely carbon monoxide gas. Having joined the staff of the KdF, Becker, who was a professional chemist, spent some time with Widmann killing mice and rats. In mid-January, Becker went to BASF in Ludwigshafen to collect gas cylinders, which he then ferried to the former Zuchthaus, or hard labour prison, at Brandenburg near Berlin. A sizeable party had gathered, including Widmann, Brack, Brandt, Heyde, Nitsche, the bull-like policeman Wirth (who ran the administration at Hartheim), and the asylum doctors Irmfried Eberl (Brandenburg) and Horst Schumann (Grafeneck). Wirth, Eberl and Schumann were to figure prominently in 'Aktion Reinhard' and at Auschwitz. Fifteen to twenty naked men were put in a purpose-built gas chamber constructed by engineers from the Reich Main Security Office, where after a minute or two –

Plate 19. The former hard labour penitentiary at Brandenburg where the first experiments in gassing patients were carried out. Subsequently, 9,722 people were murdered there.

according to Becker – they 'tipped over or lay on benches'. Widmann spent part of the time – which suggests that Becker rather than he carried out the gassings – administering lethal injections of curare and scopolamin to eight further patients – who, not dying rapidly enough, were then also gassed. According to Heyde, these killings were carried out by Brandt and Conti, to symbolise the involvement of the highest medical authorities.[21]

This training session, which was obviously being used to resolve differences of opinion regarding the comparability of gas and lethal injections, was then repeated, with Dr Eberl taking control of the gas valve. Becker, describing himself accurately enough as a 'Gasfachmann', had to help Eberl when things went slightly wrong with pressures. By way of conclusion, Brack informed the assembled company that henceforth 'this action will only be carried out by doctors, according to the motto that the needle only belongs in the doctor's hand'.[22] Apparently one needed two university degrees to turn a valve clockwise. It is almost otiose to note that none of the participants in these activities ever expressed an iota of concern for the victims, or even disgust regarding what most people would find inhuman, sordid and emotionally upsetting. In the following weeks, Becker travelled to Grafeneck, Hartheim (where Wirth was responsible for inducting Dr Renno) and Sonnenstein near Pirna, delivering gas cylinders and demonstrating how to operate the equipment.[23]

While the T–4 personnel were practising how to murder thousands of people, the circle of those who knew what was taking place widened. This is an important subject, since thousands of people, even including those literally out of sight and mind, do not simply fall off the face of the earth without a lot of others noticing. In modern societies we are all, sane or insane, thoroughly enmeshed in bureaucracies.

Most importantly, it was necessary to find accomplices in the various regional governments, for outside Prussia the asylums came under the administrative aegis of their health departments, rather than the Ministry of the Interior. It was not difficult to light upon fanatics operating among these senior functionaries. In the previous chapter we encountered Fritz Bernotat, harsh lord of all the asylums he surveyed, from his office in the expropriated provincial parliament building in Wiesbaden. Given his reported views, he would experience no difficulties in decimating the psychiatric population. In Württemberg, the head of the health service was Dr Egon Stähle, the director of health services in the Baden Ministry of the Interior and a sometime NSDAP Reichstag deputy.[24] We have already seen (p. 121 above) how Linden visited Stähle in the autumn of 1939 in order to find a suitable site for killing mental patients. Stähle in turn inducted his subordinate Otto Mauthe, the official directly responsible for asylums, into what was happening. Every decree regarding, for example, the prohibition of patient discharges, obliging tardy asylum directors to complete Registration Form (Meldebogen) 1, or ordering the transfer of patients to other asylums was issued by these two men.[25] Hence they were the first and last court of appeal, so to speak, for those asylum directors (and relatives) who wished to rescue individual patients.[26] In Upper Bavaria, dealings between T–4 and the asylums were conducted by Professor Walter 'Bubi' Schultze, the senior medical official in the Bavarian Ministry of the Interior, situated in one of those elegantly Italianate pastel-coloured buildings near Munich's Ludwigsstrasse. A graduate of Munich's august Maximilian University, Schultze had abandoned a career as a surgeon because of a war wound. A member of the NSDAP since 1928, he became head of the health department in the Bavarian Ministry of the Interior in 1933 and an honorary professor at the university a year later.[27] Schultze's attitude towards the mentally ill was apparent in a speech he delivered while opening a second state medical academy in 1933. He strongly objected to the 'beefing up of the physically and mentally hopeless and valueless', and extolled the exterminatory virtues of concentration camps in the battle against the unfit and deviant.[28] In 1936 he had discussed the idea of killing the incurably mentally ill and 'idiotic' children with a circle of friends including Gerhard Wagner and Walter Gross, respectively the Reich Doctors' Leader and Head of the Racial-Political Office of the NSDAP.[29]

It would be misleading to imagine that all public health administrators were as keen to murder the asylum population in their regions as Bernotat, Stähle or 'Bubi' Schultze. The overall national picture is more nuanced, with some administrators being seriously exercised by either the legality or the morality of what they were being asked to do. In two areas of Germany, namely the Rhineland and Hanover, the authorities seem to have made an effort to minimise either the impact of, or their own involvement in, the 'euthanasia' programme. In Hanover, the desk officer for asylums was the lawyer Dr George Andreae. He had overall control of the asylums at Wunsdorf, Hildesheim, Göttingen, Lüneburg and Osnabrück. He was an NSDAP member from May 1933 and a convinced Christian. In the summer of 1940 Andreae met with the asylum directors under his aegis to discuss 'Registration Form 1'. They were unhappy about the rapidity of the procedure, especially since many doctors would be on holiday. Andreae then discussed the matter with Dr Ludwig Gessner, the head of the provincial administration. Gessner had heard rumours of what was afoot in Germany, and, more to the point, knew about the shootings and gassings in Pomerania. Gessner then went to Berlin, where Hefelmann of the KdF put him in the picture. Both Hefelmann and Linden failed to convince him of the legality of what was occurring. Back in Hanover, Gessner instructed Andreae to draw up a memorandum to the Reich Minister of the Interior, whose purpose was to ensure the omission of Hanover from the 'euthanasia' programme. Andreae contacted Professor Gottfried Ewald of Göttingen, the only academic to have refused to take part in the refereeing of patients. Andreae was also contacted by Professor Walter Creutz, his opposite number in the Rhineland, who was unhappy about the legal basis of the whole enterprise, although that did not stop him participating in it. When the transport lists arrived, Andreae went to Heyde in Berlin, primed with the argument that Reich authorities had no business interfering in a field which came under the ambit of the provincial administration. Heyde tried to trump this by producing a copy of Hitler's authorisation to Brandt and Bouhler, insisting too on the overriding authority of the Reich Defence Commissars to authorise transfers of patients. Gessner and Andreae capitulated in the face of arguments from military necessity. The latter told the asylum directors to comply with orders; the former stayed away from the meeting to evade personal responsibility. Andreae stayed at his post, hoping to use exemptions to minimise the damage, and aware that if he resigned he would be replaced by 'a more robust National Socialist'. Andreae drew up the transfer orders; Gessner left them lying around for days before signing them. In the event, 1,669 patients were transferred from Hanover's asylums. An unknown proportion were murdered.[30]

Andreae's equivalent in the Rhineland was Professor Walter Creutz

(1889–1971). Upon learning of the 'euthanasia' programme while in the army, Creutz sent a memorandum to Heinz Haake, the head of the provincial administration in the Rhineland. Since ethical objections would have cut little ice with Haake, who had been the first NSDAP Gauleiter in the province, Creutz stressed the inadequacies inherent in the ways patients were refereed, the likelihood of mass hostility towards asylums, patient panic, the inflationary potentialities latent in the entire programme, and finally, the precarious legal basis upon which the doctors involved were operating. These arguments seem to have worked, in the sense that Haake resisted every attempt by T–4 to establish a killing centre in the Rhineland. It took a visit from the T–4 top brass, Heyde, Vorberg and Tillmann, the first again equipped with a copy of Hitler's letter of commission to Brandt and Bouhler, to persuade Haake to allow them to use Andernach and Galkhausen as holding or transit asylums for Rhenish patients en route to Hadamar. Haake's deputy, Wilhelm Kitz, refused to have any involvement in these measures; the director of Galkhausen, Georg Beyerhaus, apparently died of a heart attack on the platform at Düsseldorf station after learning what was in store for his institution. Creutz, who stayed in his post, and enjoined others to do likewise – allegedly to minimise the impact of the 'euthanasia' programme – nonetheless still despatched about one thousand people to the two transit asylums, and thence to Hadamar.[31]

It is time now to move from these administrative heights to the asylums whence patients were spirited into the 'euthanasia' programme. Again, the range of response was as broad as the variety of types of institution. The arrival of 'Registration Form 1' was the first formal encounter between the authorities involved in carrying out 'Aktion T–4' and Germany's hundreds of private, religious and state asylums. At Schussenried, the senior doctor thought it was a statistical exercise.[32] More in keeping with the drift of contemporary psychiatric thinking, Dr Josef Wrede of Rottenmünster thought that the authorities were planning to hive off chronic patients to cheaper facilities in 'Pflegeanstalten', where they would receive care but no actual treatment.[33] Johannes Recktenwald of Andernach similarly thought that the forms were part of an economy drive.[34] Dr Gebhard Ritter, the senior doctor at Liebenau, became suspicious about the purpose of the exercise when he noticed the question concerning how many visitors patients received. He recalled: 'I feared that something lay behind the form.'[35] Delays, deliberate incompetence, or extreme pedantry in filling out the forms provided no potential escape route.[36] A few asylum directors refused to fill in the forms once they knew what their purpose was.[37] This did not help matters, since T–4 simply despatched roving teams of assessors who worked more expeditiously and capriciously. Teams of doctors and secretaries drove around in 'Busy Lizzy', leaving the actual business of

Plate 20. Roving teams of T–4 assessors were despatched to the asylums to ensure that the work of registering patients to be murdered was carried out efficiently and expeditiously. This photograph shows Dr and Frau Steinmeyer posing on either side of Eva Mennecke and their driver, Erich Bauer, who himself subsequently worked in the 'Aktion Reinhard' death camps.

refereeing to young assistants and students while they went sight-seeing. The staff at Schönbrunn, who were forewarned by the chaplain of Neuendettelsau who arrived in tears, described a visitation from the men in Berlin as being like the 'spreading of a burial shroud over the asylum'.[38]

As their patients began to be transferred elsewhere, the individual asylum authorities either suspected or heard rumours – usually from relatives of the dead or on the medical grapevine – that the transferees were being killed. The responses to this intelligence were as varied as the asylums themselves. Active resistance was rare; passive resistance in the form of damage limitation or procrastination quite common. The trouble with the latter, as we shall see, was that one was playing the game on the other side's terms by accepting work as the criteria for exemption. Of course, that came naturally to most psychiatrists, since they themselves had elevated work to a therapeutic first principle long before the 'euthanasia' programme had started. Some asylums, such as Attl, Schönbrunn and Ursberg, did their best to falsify or hide patient records, or to reclassify state-funded patients as private payers.[39] In some places, such as Schweinspoint, the occasional patient would temporarily flee the asylum when the buses arrived, hiding under a bridge until they had departed.[40] The odd enterprising individual evaded certain death in this fashion; the majority did not.

The Christophsbad private establishment in Göppingen near Stuttgart was used by the Stuttgart authorities to house the overspill from state mental asylums in Württemberg. The cost was split between the local welfare offices and the Ministry of the Interior in Stuttgart. Some 265 of these state patients were the first to be 'retrieved' between 17 April and 14 October 1940 from the Christophsbad by asylums in the state sector. This threatened financial ruination for the asylum. Having learned that a large number of these people were dead, the medical authorities at the clinic decided to visit Mauthe, the asylum supremo in the Stuttgart Ministry of the Interior, to find out what was happening. They were told not to listen to 'rumours and fairytales', and that the spreading of rumours was a serious criminal offence. The authorities in Stuttgart then asked the clinic to register the private patients. Dr John took it upon himself to visit several industrial firms in the area, arranging for them to employ even seriously ill patients. He was a sort of psychiatric Schindler. When the clinic was subsequently visited by a Dr Schmalenbach of the Ministry of the Interior, they were able to claim that 80% of their patients were working. When he insisted that some patients had nonetheless to be transferred, they asked him point blank whether he meant to a state asylum or directly to wherever they were to be exterminated. The asylum authorities wrote to the Minister of the Interior in Württemberg, enclosing references from the firms employing the patients, in order to show that 'the value of the lives [of the patients] was proved by their achievements'.[41] Twenty-eight patients were transferred to the state asylum at Weinsberg on 27 March 1941. In November, another roving commission arrived. The asylum doctors persuaded them that the forty-seven patients under threat were in fact valuable workers.[42] If one had the requisite moral properties, and persisted enough in the face of arbitrary authority, one could sometimes achieve modest dividends.

The T–4 personnel were reliant on the complicity of the asylum authorities, for how else could they have hundreds of sick people ready to travel on the Gekrat transports? In Hessen, for example, the directors of Haina, Marburg and Merxhausen met together in Cassel on 23 April 1941 to expedite the removal of their own patients to the transit asylums at Eichberg and Herborn en route to the extermination facility at Hadamar.[43] At all stages in the process, a certain amount of plea bargaining was possible over individual cases. After all, everyone seems to have acknowledged the crudity of the initial criteria for selection. At every stage, senior asylum staff – who were advised by senior nurses – were allowed the semblance of decision-making – without, of course, being able to alter the overall objective one iota. Every person saved would be replaced by someone who was lost. Haggling would satisfy many uneasy consciences; later it could be reinterpreted as 'resistance'.

In some asylums, such as Mariaberg in Württemberg, the Protestant asylum authorities seem to have gone systematically through the lists of transferees, working out each individual's capacity for work in percentage terms. These new lists then became the basis of hurried negotiations with the regional authorities who relayed T–4's transfer orders. They were simply carrying out their own form of selection, introducing precision into T–4's randomly incompetent 'variegated throwing together of everything, loyal and willing workers in together with those needing constant care and epileptics'.[44] In other words, except in cases where race was the criterion, the dominant therapeutic trend dovetailed easily with the crude materialism which underpinned the 'euthanasia' programme. A psychiatry which construed the goal of full recovery in terms of reemployment outside the asylums had few lines of defence against policies which made work the criterion for being alive or dead. Work (and race) was the sum total of identity. Thus 'protests', if one can call them that, were couched in precisely the same language as that of the regime itself. In August 1940, the asylum authorities at Markgröningen were told to prepare ninety-one named patients for transfer. Since twelve were either dead or had been released, that left seventy-nine patients. On 2 September, the asylum director wrote to the welfare authorities in Stuttgart asking that several patients be removed from the list. They included:

Running number 8: Ernst D., born 22.1.1883 in Stuttgart, cared for on an open ward. Allowed to go out on Sundays; holidays alone in Stuttgart. *As asylum gardener he saves this asylum the cost of having to employ someone. D. is a good worker and indispensable to this asylum.*

Running number 16: Gustav F., born 15.1.1870 in Vaihingen, cared for on an open ward, reveals not the slightest evidence of illness. *He works the whole year as an assiduous and punctual agricultural labourer, and he can be occupied where no supervision is necessary* (my italics).[45]

When the Community Patients' Transport Service arrived, the asylum's economic administrator Scholder began the business of negotiating further exemptions. He said that some of those on the list were valuable workers; the transport leader cynically suggested he try the labour office for replacements. Scholder wanted eleven patients reprieved; the transport leader insisted on taking seventy-five away with him. The eleven were exempted, but eight substitutes had to take their places. One patient who knew what was going to happen to him had to be dragged out of the building.[46]

Since what leeway there was by way of exemptions was tightly controlled, asylum doctors were reduced to haggling over individuals, or, more dangerously, simply releasing people from the asylum back into the community. This was dangerous because the regional authorities imposed an effective ban on discharges and the unlicensed transfer of patients.[47] Dr Hugo Götz of Schussenried was told he could exempt 10% of those to be transferred. He duly held back a patient whose job it was to show visitors the baroque library, and the son of a senior officer whose family was likely to cause trouble. It also proved possible to release a schizophrenic woman into the custody of her son, notwithstanding the fact that her husband expressly would not have her.[48] For attempts to discharge patients into the safekeeping of their families often ran aground on their unwillingness to have them. Director Adolf Nell of Hephata recalled that 'it was not always simple to deal with the parents of patients. We frequently encountered an absence of feeling regarding taking these patients home again.'[49] The authorities at Mariaberg tried to release Otto G. into the custody of his brother. On 2 December 1940 the brother replied. His wife had a weak heart; a son was in the army; two soldiers were billeted in the house; the seventy-nine-year-old mother-in-law was half blind; a nephew from Cologne had just been to stay with his three children; two children were coming to stay at home; visitors said they were coming from the north. No, there was no room at the inn. Of course, he was not trying to slide out of his responsibilities, and the asylum could 'rest assured that Otto would never be forgotten'. It would soon be Christmas, and Otto would be getting a little something. As things turned out, Otto did not have much use for Christmas presents, since he was transferred to Grafeneck on 13 December and died on arrival.[50]

Neither private nor religious asylums faced the regime from a position of strength. Private institutions, like the Christophsbad asylum considered earlier, faced economic ruin because the majority of their patients were being paid for by the state. Those who ran ecclesiastical institutions felt impotent in the face of a regime which was at the height of its power both in Germany and in Europe, and threatened by one which could easily secularise and sequester their charitable foundations.[51] At the asylum of Scheuern, rather dedicated lay or clerical Protestant philanthropists had been shoved aside by political appointees to the steering committee. The asylum owed too much money to the health authorities in Wiesbaden to be able to stand up to them.[52] What bargaining power did a small group of religious in, say, the Schweinspoint charitable institution for men near Donauworth have against a regime that for years had been handing out chocolate to the patients so as to induce them to make allegations of sexual impropriety against the brothers who tended them?[53] And given the totally covert nature of T–4, whose door were they supposed to knock on?[54]

Even though their institutions were part of ramified networks of Christian charity, these pious souls could often feel individually isolated, let down by the heads of their organisations. Nonetheless some asylum personnel did refuse to cooperate. Ludwig Schlaich, the director of Stetten, which was part of the Inner Mission network, received an order to prepare ninety-two patients for transfer in October 1940. With a characteristically ambivalent type of reasoning, Schlaich felt that the initial selection had been done under false pretences, and that the eighty-year-old deputy asylum doctor who had filled out the forms had been totally incompetent. Protests along these lines meant the arrival of a doctor from Berlin who proceeded to referee all 199 other patients in a few hours. The transport party duly arrived to take away ninety-two patients. By-passing Minister President Stähle, Schlaich telephoned Linden in Berlin to register a further protest. This did not affect the position regarding the ninety-two transferees. Schlaich refused point blank to help the transport leader identify the ninety-two patients. One of the arguments he used was that many of the patients had heard what was happening from earlier transport personnel, who made snide remarks such as 'Where they're going they won't need clothing or food any more', or that there would soon be seventy-five fewer 'silly clots' (*Dackel*) in the world. Although the director persisted in refusing to cooperate, a female assistant doctor eventually helped identify the victims. Eight patients managed to hide themselves. Pitiful scenes took place among those who had to go. They cried, begged not to go, and tried to defend themselves. One man asked everyone for forgiveness, told the senior sister that they would see one another in heaven, and screamed at the transport personnel 'Our blood cries out for revenge.' Others cried: 'I just want to live, I just want to live.'[55] Patients transferred from Merxhausen in Hessen apparently called out from the train at Sand station: 'All the best, we won't be back ever again; we are all going to be killed.'[56] At the Elisabeth Foundation at Lauingen in Swabia, the asylum priest held a service of general absolution the night before the first transport. A patient ran down the choir screaming 'we are all going to be killed'.[57] At Sigmaringen, a patient who evaded one of the transports interrupted the lunchtime meal with the intelligence, 'Where they've all gone to, they'll all be poisoned and burned.'[58]

Although the first patients to be transferred may have believed the story that they were being taken on an outing, with some of those transferred first from Stetten acting out courtly farewells and kissing hands while others felt aggrieved not to be going too, people destined for subsequent transports were often under no illusions about their ultimate destination. Consider a letter dated 1 October 1940 from Helene M. to her father:

Dearest, beloved father!
Unfortunately it cannot be otherwise. Today I must write these words of farewell as I leave this earthly life for an eternal home. This will cause you and yours much, much heartache. But think that I must die as a martyr, and that this is not

happening without the will of my heavenly redeemer, for whom I have longed for many years. Father, good father, I do not want to part from you without asking you and all my dear brothers and sisters once more for forgiveness, for all that I have failed you in throughout my whole life. May the dear Lord God accept my illness and this sacrifice as a penance for this.

Best of fathers, don't hold anything against your child, who loved you so very profoundly; always think that I am going to heaven, where we will all be reunited together with God and our deceased dear ones. Dear father, I am going with firm resolve and trust in God, never doubting in his good deeds, which he tests us with, but which unfortunately we do not comprehend when we are here. We will reap our reward on judgement day. Decreed by God! Please, tell this to my dear brothers and sisters. I won't lament, but shall be happy. I send you this little picture by way of a memento, your child will be meeting the saints in this way too.

I embrace you in undying love and with the firm promise I made when we last said our goodbyes, that I will persevere with fortitude.
Your child Helene.
On 2 October 1940. Please pray a lot for the peace of my soul. See you again, good father, in heaven.

This was the second of two letters which Helene, an epileptic, had managed to smuggle out of the asylum. Since the first spoke of patients being transferred and killed, her brother (the father, a retired doctor, had a weak heart) had gone to the Stuttgart health authorities to establish what was happening. He was reassured that if there were such steps being taken(!), epileptics would not be affected. The father visited the asylum and was advised to contact the authorities in the interests of having his daughter struck off the transfer list. He succeeded, but a little too late. A letter confirming that Helene should not be transferred arrived shortly after a letter informing the family of her death in Brandenburg because of 'breathing problems'.[59]

Although many accounts stress that relatives were appalled to learn that family members were being transferred and killed, this response was not universal. Dr Paul Morstatt of Schussenried recalled that while some relatives were deeply affected, others were 'indifferent', regarding the person's death as the workings of 'destiny'. Others welcomed the death of people with whom they had no human contact, or were relieved at no longer having to make maintenance payments.[60] Some, like a man whose brother died of 'influenza complicated by meningitis' in either Grafeneck or Hartheim, were clearly aware of what was being done; but he was merely exercised that the home asylum, Mariaberg, had not put him in the picture: 'I would have been agreeable to these proceedings, however, they should have sought my agreement beforehand.'[61]

Before the autumn of 1940, the buses and trains used to transport the patients went direct to the first generation of so-called 'Reich Asylums', i.e. Brandenburg, Grafeneck, Hartheim near Linz and Sonnenstein near Dresden. These killing centres were augmented, and partially superseded, by Bernburg and Hadamar. The dates between which these centres functioned as mass extermination centres were as follows:

Brandenburg on the Havel	January 1940–September 1940
Grafeneck, near Munsingen	January 1940–December 1940
Hartheim, near Linz	January 1940–1944
Sonnenstein, near Dresden	April 1940–August 1943
Bernburg, near Halle	November 1940–April 1943
Hadamar, near Limburg	January 1941–August 1941

Over seventy thousand people were killed in these asylums. Each of them was responsible for killing patients from a particular catchment area. For example, Hadamar, where mass killings commenced in January 1941, was used to murder patients from Hesse-Nassau, Hanover, Hessen, Westphalia, the Rhineland and, once it superseded Grafeneck, Baden-Württemberg.[62] To disguise exactly where patients were being taken, as well as to control the 'inflow' into the killing process, each of these six asylums spawned a ring of holding or transit centres, i.e. asylums where the victims could be held in closer proximity to where they were to be killed. Thus, patients coming in from the Rhineland would be held at Andernach or Galkhausen; those from Baden at Wiesloch; from Württemberg at Weinsberg; and from Hessen itself or further afield, say Göttingen or Lüneburg, at Eichberg, Herborn, Idstein, Scheuern or Weilmünster.[63] This enabled T–4 to minimise any inconvenience to themselves by precisely staggering transport, killing and cremation. As with the satellite camps orbiting the concentration camps, or the Soviet Gulag Archipelago, we are dealing with a broad and densely detailed chart of a sea of human degradation, albeit in a society which in purely geographical terms, had no Arctic or Siberian wastelands at its disposal in which to murder people discreetly.

The Community Patients' Transport Service initially used red postal buses, with the windows painted over with blue,[64] since this enabled them to avail themselves of a nationwide network of repair depots should any vehicle break down. Later these buses were painted camouflage grey, the colour eyewitnesses mainly remember them by. Let us follow them on their way, as recalled by an orderly at Hadamar who was part of the transport personnel:

From 21 January 1941 I accompanied ten transports of patients from various asylums to Hadamar. We drove to Weilmünster, Scheuren near Katzenellnbogen, Eichberg in the area around Weinsberg, and to Kalkhausen near Cologne. Normally we drove in three buses, which had originally been used by the Reichspost; later we used buses which were painted grey, which must have come from Berlin. These buses had seating room only, there were no places to lie down. They did not

Plate 21. Community Patients' Transport Service buses parked in the forecourt outside the main administrative building at Eichberg in the Rheingau. Although trains were often used to transport patients, there post buses were favoured because they would not attract much notice in rural areas, and because they could be repaired in a nationwide network of garages.

have lavatories. I don't know any more how many seats they had. A transport consisting of three buses contained about sixty to seventy patients; sometimes it could have been as many as eighty. We did not make any stops on the journey to let the patients stretch their legs. The journeys were never very long. The longest journey I made was with the transport from Weinsberg. There was no stopping on that trip either. I assume that the patients were given something to eat in the asylum they were taken from. They had no provisions for the journey. There was a nurse and orderly on every bus. The transport leader drove ahead in a car ... When we reached the asylum concerned, the patients were already ready to travel. The asylum personnel led the patients up to the buses. We then took over. We helped those who could not board the buses on their own. The other patients climbed aboard on their own.[65]

Today, Hadamar is a small, isolated town nestling amidst rolling hills just north of the episcopal see of Limburg. It has the feel of a German version of Alfriston or one of those enlarged villages which doze in the Sussex Downs. The odd commuter train ambles through the level crossing; otherwise it is rather still. Wayside shrines discreetly signal rural Roman Catholicism. The asylum, which is on a slope perched over the town centre, consists of a group of nineteenth-century buildings, next to the remaining parts of a seventeenth-century priory. The latter gave the entire site the name 'Mönchberg'. There are some modern additions, including a secure section, replete with armoured doors and security cameras, for delinquents. A steep set of steps takes one up to the cemetery area, whence there is a good view of the town below. It is still used as a mental hospital, with a mix of long-stay patients, some of whom watch nervously to ensure that visitors actually re-emerge from its cellars, and young delinquents and drug addicts, whose ghetto-blasters and trainers would not be out of place in some decaying urban nightmare such as Hackney or the Bronx.

The asylum was established in 1906 in buildings which had been used since 1886 as a workhouse. In 1920 an extra wing was added to house sixty young female 'psychopaths', many of them fourteen- to twenty-four-year-old prostitutes from the Frankfurt area. Seven years later, the asylum acquired a farm at nearby Schnepfenhausen, where, as was customary, selected patients could enjoy the benefits of unpaid occupational therapy in the interests of the asylum's domestic economy.[66] By 1930, Hadamar housed about 320 patients, with a further 229 scattered about in paid family care. Most of the patients were from disadvantaged backgrounds: unskilled men and women, fewer than 10% of whom had progressed beyond elementary education.[67] From the autumn of 1939, most of Hadamar's patients were transferred to other asylums in the region, except for a contingent which continued to service the asylum's economic needs from the farm at Schnepfenhausen. Hadamar was to be used as a military hospital for German soldiers and wounded Polish prisoners. On 1 November 1940 administrative responsibility for the asylum passed from the regional health authorities in Wiesbaden to the Berlin-based Community Foundation for the Care of Asylums.

Hadamar had several things in its favour as an extermination centre. Most of the staff and patients had already been removed to make way for a military hospital. The asylum lay amidst a ring of other institutions which could be used as staging posts. The transport connections were good, both to the autobahn network and by rail from Hadamar's small station. Secrecy was evidently not a high priority. The asylum is overlooked by hills, and a road winds through the town directly underneath the main entrance. Hadamar, unlike many other asylums such as Eichberg, did not have its grounds surrounded by a high wall.

Following the leasing of the asylum to what in reality was the T-4 apparatus, the Community Foundation – a front organisation for T-4 – despatched craftsmen and fitters whose job was to convert the cellars below the right wing of the asylum into a gas chamber and crematorium. Bernotat's brother-in-law, Fritz Scherwing, was one of the fitters. The job offer was made in the hunting lodge Bernotat kept in the woods up above the asylum at Weilmünster. He received detailed plans for the project from Kaufmann of T–4. Scherwing the fitter set about cutting and assembling pipes. To be very precise, for there are people who have difficulties with reality: in the second room that one enters from the cellar steps, he and his colleagues attached a row of showerheads to the ceiling, and fixed a three-quarters to one-inch gas pipe 75cm off the floor. They drilled fifty to sixty 4mm holes into the pipe, hiding it beneath benches, and installed airtight doors and a ventilator.[68] The pipe was connected to gas cylinders stationed in a recess outside what was to all appearances a shower-room. These gas chambers were so convincing that sometimes victims walked in carrying soap and facecloths.[69] A reinforced glass aperture would enable anyone in the alcove to observe this room. A lot of people did, out of mere voyeuristic compulsion. Miniature railtracks facilitated hauling corpses along the long corridor to a pair of crematoria.

Twenty-five staff from the original personnel or from other asylums in the vicinity were kept on at Hadamar. This is important to note, since the killings were not necessarily carried out by a specially selected cadre of murderers. These staff members included the asylum's administrative supremo, Alfons Klein. The rest were nurses and orderlies; cooks; a gardener; a carpenter; and a gatekeeper. This group was in turn augmented by more practised murderers, notably Drs Ernst Baumhardt and Günther Hennecke, transferred from Grafeneck or direct from Berlin. There were some tensions between the locals and the so-called 'Berliners' or 'Foundation' personnel (the latter were thought to have taken the place over), but one should not imagine that this had much impact on the functioning of the extermination programme. Eventually between seventy-five and a hundred people worked in the asylum. The main divisions of labour were seven people in a transport section; about twenty-five people actually to carry out mass killings and to dispose of the bodies; an administrative staff of twenty or so, whose job was to fake causes of death and to issue death certificates and perfunctory letters of condolences to relatives; and finally, an economy section which serviced the day-to-day needs of the personnel.[70]

Since this book is concerned with mass murder, it is necessary to be very specific about the actual crime. We cannot comprehend what people suffered, for on this the record is necessarily silent; but there is testimony in abundance about the terrible physicality of murder. Those involved agree that this was literally, if not metaphorically, 'dirty work', notwithstanding the sanitised procedures described in Nazi propaganda films. On arrival at Hadamar, either from the station or further afield, the buses drove into a row of wooden garages, recently rediscovered on a nearby farm serving as a tractor shed. The patients disembarked and were taken, via a specially constructed wooden corridor attached to the side of the

(a)

(b)

(c)

building, into a large room on the ground floor. There, they were undressed and given military overcoats to cover themselves. An administrative official checked each person's identity, and a doctor looked them up and down in order to match the person's age and physical condition with a plausible cause of death. The doctor had a list of sixty-one causes of death, complete with all the likely symptoms and forms of treatment. The patients were then weighed and photographed, for a collection of pictures of mental patients. Anyone causing any trouble during the inevitable periods of delay was quietened down with an injection. Each patient was stamped with a number and given a cardboard number with which to retrieve his or her clothing. Some were also marked with chalk or ink crosses on the back. The transport personnel escorted the patients to the entrance to the cellars, where two orderlies then took over. This division of labour served to maintain the psychological fiction that only a handful of evil characters down below were actually involved in killing.

The patients descended a dozen or so steps in batches of sixty at a time, and were then shut into the gas chamber. A doctor stationed in the alcove outside turned on the valve, and gas streamed in through the pipe installed by Scherwing. So far from it being a 'gentle death', the victims experienced extreme terror, as well as the symptoms of carbon monoxide poisoning. After an hour, all was quiet. The ventilators extracted residual fumes, and the 'burners' or 'disinfectors' (to give them their preferred *nom de guerre*) moved in to disentangle the bodies. Those who had been marked beforehand as being of potential scientific interest were separated out and taken to a nearby autopsy room. Their brains would go to the university clinics in Frankfurt or Würzburg. All of the corpses were trundled along the corridor and, after gold teeth had been wrenched out, burned in the two crematoria. The ashes were either discarded or distributed among urns. Care was taken not to put too much ash in an urn notionally containing the remains of a child.[71] Bones were crushed in a mill or with mallets on wooden tables.

Eyewitnesses living in the town recalled that shortly after the arrival of each transport, a thick dark cloud of smoke would be emitted from the asylum chimneys.[72] If you went to Hadamar, you found out what was happening. Fritz Neumann, a young doctor at a hospital in Bonn, went there to learn for himself. He went into the local inn, from which one had a

---

Plate 22. (a) The main administrative building of the asylum at Hadamar. (b) Patients were escorted into the cellars running beneath the building and (c) gassed in this room, which was disguised as a shower room. A pipe hidden by benches ran around the walls, through which carbon monoxide gas was released by a doctor stationed in an adjacent alcove. Rechristened a 'psychiatric clinic', Hadamar is still a psychiatric hospital.

clear view of the asylum. The innkeeper refused to answer any questions. When Neumann persisted, she said that it was right that 'idiots' were being killed to spare 'healthy national comrades' unnecessary sacrifices. She objected to the appalling smell of burning corpses. Neumann's remonstrations were met by the lady picking up the telephone to summon personnel from the asylum, many of whom were regular customers.[73]

After each cremation session, the ashes were gathered together, quantities of them being randomly packed into urns. If the family of the victim wished to have the ashes, they were sent from the address 'Crematorium II Wiesbaden'; if they did not, the urns were sent to a cemetery near the family's place of residence. The former priory building housed the administrative staff, many of them young women, but also including the former criminal policemen Christian Wirth and Gottlieb Hering, both future commandants of Belzec, and in Wirth's case, future inspector of Belzec, Sobibor and Treblinka.[74] These bureaucrats faked death certificates, wrote standardised letters of condolence and tied up loose financial ends which included continuing to draw payments for the maintenance of patients who were long since dead. They had a map on the wall, the better to ensure that the asylum was not reporting a suspiciously high number of deaths to small places. With the aid of coloured pins, representing a given month, they could stagger the bad news, or – to simplify things – send the information to one of the registry offices in another extermination centre, so that a person killed in Hadamar would be registered as having died in Bernburg or Sonnenstein.[75]

As we saw above, the doctors had a list of sixty-one likely causes of death which they matched with the age, sex and physical condition of the patients before they gassed them. In each case the etiology, symptoms, treatment and possible complications were precisely recorded. Each example concluded with the merits and demerits of using it as a cause of death:

Meningitis
Abscesses on the brain are relatively rare as such and require a long period to develop, so that this illness can only be considered by us in a few very exceptional cases. It is useful if any of the symptoms are already evident, such as a discharge of pus from the ears, nose or sinuses. . . . Every age-group can be affected by this illness.

Pneumonia
Pneumonia is an ideal cause of death for our action, because the population at large always regards it as a critical illness which means therefore that its life-endangering character will be plausible. . . . Pneumonia can occur in every age-group and in both sexes. In the case of young and fit individuals, one simply has to calculate a somewhat longer duration than in the case of elderly and frail patients.

Strokes

This cause of death is especially suitable in the case of older people, of at least forty or more years of age; in the case of young people it is so rare that one should not choose it. As a cause of death it is particularly suitable because it is so sudden, has no particular contributory symptoms, and results in the patient dying a relatively painless death. This cause of death always seems reasonable to relatives, and they like to believe in it. It is also always credible that the patient has died without any prior symptoms.[76]

A few key items of cryptic correspondence kept relatives several steps behind the actual whereabouts of the patient. They were told about the original transfer after it had happened, and of the person's arrival in one of the transit asylums after he or she was in fact already dead, for usually the patients were killed on the same day they were transferred. This method served to confuse relatives, whose enquiries always had to be written, since visits had to be arranged eight days in advance. That gave the asylum time to get off a letter announcing the patient's death before the relatives turned up. Unexpected visitors were turned away by armed personnel, or told to get lost by the asylum administrator.

Relatives received the following letter of condolence, customised with the odd detail, such as the ring mentioned here, but all essentially telling the same story:

Landes- Heil- und Pflegeanstalt
Hadamar

25 March 1941

Dear Frau U.,

On 13 March 1941 your husband Ernst U. was transferred to our asylum, in accordance with a ministerial decree issued on the instructions of the Reich Defence Commissar. This measure took place in the context of the current military situation.

We regret to have to inform you that the patient died suddenly and unexpectedly of acute meningitis on 24 March 1941.

Since your husband suffered from a grave and incurable mental illness, you must regard his death as a form of deliverance.

Since our asylum is merely to be regarded as a transit asylum, a stay here being partly for the purpose of establishing whether any of the patients are carrying infectious diseases (which experience teaches us is often the case with mental patients), the health police responsible for the prevention of contagious diseases ordered the immediate cremation of the body. Your consent is superfluous in cases like this.

If you would like to inter the urn with the remains in a cemetery or family burial plot near your home, then please let us have proof of the acquisition or possession of the burial place within fourteen days. We will then send the urn free of charge to the cemetery concerned. Otherwise we will bury the urn elsewhere.

The clothes of the deceased had to be disinfected for the reasons given earlier. They were badly damaged during disinfection. When you have given us proof of being the legitimate heir we will be happy to send you the clothes and effects, the latter consisting of a wedding ring. If we do not receive proof of inheritance within fourteen days, we will give the clothing to the poor and needy patients in the asylum.

We ask you to inform other relatives of the patient since we possess no other addresses.

We enclose two death certificates which you should keep safe for presentation to the authorities.

Heil Hitler

Dr Fleck [the alias used by Dr Hennecke]

Enclosures:
2 death certificates[77]

Having described the methods used to kill and deceive, it is time to become more closely acquainted with the immediate perpetrators. There is a photograph of Dr Bodo Gorgass, taken in 1946 shortly after his arrest. Judging from his many layers of clothing it must have been cold. He is unshaven, and his rather intense face is pinched with strain. He looks a worried man, and had reason to be. Born in Leipzig in 1909, the son of a senior railway inspector, Gorgass studied medicine in his home town, deciding to specialise in psychiatry. Perhaps this choice was influenced by the fact that both of his parents and a sister needed to be treated for depression. Obviously, the question of 'euthanasia' cropped up from time to time during his medical training. He saw no moral difference between assisting someone in chronic pain to die peacefully, and the involuntary killing of mental patients for whom 'release from this life signifies an act of mercy'.[78]

Speaking in 1947 from his vast fund of practical experience in killing over one thousand people, Gorgass noted that mentally ill people were a financial and psychological burden on their relatives. Since the latter were too emotionally involved, the state should make the decision to kill for them.[79] In 1936, Gorgass went to work at Eichberg alongside the infamous Mennecke; two years later, aged twenty-nine, he moved to the post of chief doctor at the Kalmenhof in Idstein. One might attribute this to his membership of the SA (1933) and NSDAP (1937), were it not for the suspicion that Gorgass was just one of those competent young men who rise up hierarchies because their fundamental mediocrity and lack of personality make them few enemies. He had also studied at Leipzig, which had a reputation as a centre of excellence in paediatrics.[80]

In December 1939 Gorgass was conscripted, taking part in the invasion of France the following summer. In April 1941 he was put into the category of reserved occupation. He reported back to Bernotat in Wiesbaden,

Plate 23. Dr Bodo Gorgass

who despatched him to Viktor Brack at the KdF in Berlin.[81] Appearing in his smart SA uniform 'in one of the most important buildings in Germany', Gorgass was told by Brack that he was one of the 'particularly trusted' doctors chosen for the task of killing mental patients. Gorgass claimed to have been rendered virtually speechless.[82] He was given no time to mull the matter over, being told simply to report to a Dr Lohnauer in Hartheim near Linz. At Hartheim, Lohnauer stressed that the victims would only be people with whom 'all therapeutic possibilities had been exhausted, those in the terminal stages of illness, for whom there was no more treatment'.[83] Lohnauer then recited the roll of distinguished figures involved in the programme: Heyde, Nitsche, Schneider and so forth. This 'naturally reassured' Gorgass. Indeed, Nitsche apparently turned up personally in Hartheim to stress the scrupulousness of T–4's procedures and the scope for Gorgass to revise diagnoses. Gorgass spent four or five weeks at Hartheim, peering through the little window into the gas chamber where two or three transports of patients a week were murdered.[84] 'The death', he said, 'was a peaceful one. It is simply going to sleep in the true sense of the word. The people grew weary, lost all sense of the outside world, and went to sleep.'[85]

Having been inducted this far, Gorgass was sent to Sonnenstein for a day or two, where he was given direct experience in using the gassing equipment. At Hadamar, Berner made him swear an oath of secrecy, and reminded him that he was now like an officer ordering soldiers into certain death. The moral threshold at which Gorgass baulked had in the meantime lowered from killing mental patients in general to the odd 'extreme unpleasantness' he underwent when, for example, he realised one day that he was about to gas a pregnant woman. After attempts to persuade Mennecke to readmit her to Eichberg, Gorgass carried out an order from Berlin to kill her by instructing one of his orderlies to administer a lethal injection.[86]

In Hadamar, as elsewhere, doctors were the highest echelon of those directly or indirectly involved in mass murder. A massive amount of work has been done regarding their motives – some base, others 'idealistic' – and on the psychological processes which enable apparently ordinary people to become habitually unreflective killers.[87] There is no magic formula to explain this last question, which, as we have seen in the case of Gorgass, involved attitudes and impressions casually acquired during medical training; social insecurity and impressionability when confronted by big names in grand places (i.e. the usual accompaniments of petty-bourgeois academic ambition); and finally an infinite capacity for self-pity, unaccompanied by any awareness of the suffering one was inflicting on others. I rather doubt whether men such as Gorgass spent the day as two different people in the manner posited by some psychiatrists who write about these matters.[88]

Regrettably, psychological accounts of the perpetrators tend not to bother with mere nurses and orderlies. At Hadamar, as we have seen, the nursing staff consisted of practised hands brought in from Grafeneck, and a residual number of personnel left over from Hadamar itself or transferred in from the neighbouring asylums of Herborn or Weilmünster. The women were mostly between thirty-five and thirty-eight years old, unmarried, and of petty-bourgeois origin. The so-called 'Berlin sisters', i.e. the women from Grafeneck, tended to have a higher incidence of membership of the NSDAP than their Hessian equivalents. The male orderlies tended to be older (the average age being forty-one), children of the Kaiserreich whose modest aspirations had been crushed by the instability of the Weimar Republic. They were of working-class origin: gardeners, lorry-drivers, plumbers and the like, with years of unemployment behind them. Many of them had belonged to the NSDAP or its various formations before the 'seizure of power', that being regarded as the equivalent of a meal ticket in those *déclassé* circles.[89]

Paul R., whom we encountered in the previous chapter, was trained as a nursing orderly at Weilmünster. He was an early recruit to the Party, and regularly attended its Nuremberg rallies to gawp at Goebbels and the others. In 1940 he served briefly as a soldier in Poland, before being sent back to Weilmünster that October. In July 1941 he was ordered to Hadamar. He worked as one of the transport personnel, helping the patients undress and escorting them to the cellar entrance. Later he was to administer lethal injections to at least twenty patients, and acted as the asylum grave-digger for many more. Now (1993) a stocky, ruddy-faced man in his eighties, Paul R. is a diabetic. A widower, he lives in a small village not far from Hadamar, next door to a son with whom he has strained relations. As in most small German towns and villages, life is arranged in a dense network of associations. The members periodically exercise their local brand of Teutonic exuberance in the Gaststätte. Paul R. is honorary president of the pigeon-fanciers' society in W., and a respected senior citizen. As with many elderly people, the past looms larger in his memory than the present, which seems filled with trips to the doctor or athletics and football on the television. Despite these twentieth-century intrusions, Paul is a countryman at heart. He watches deer from a hide, savours home-made *wurst*, and can talk for hours about the robber bands which plagued the vicinity in the sixteenth or seventeenth centuries. He is precise about time, enjoys the odd schnapps, and feels bitter about being turfed out of the Hadamar inn (mentioned earlier), lest he embarrass anyone, by the same owner who was quite happy to serve the T-4 personnel when they sat there drinking and discussing a day's murder.[90] He talks quite animatedly about the past in his capacity as living witness; he visibly shudders when the conversation turns to his own role in killing people.

During the 'Aktion T-4' period, Paul R. lived and slept in a large room in the main building, which was partitioned into sleeping cubicles. The common canteen was usually full. He had every fourth Sunday off to visit his wife and children; otherwise he was permanently resident at Hadamar during this phase of the killing programme. He acted as one of the escorts on the transport buses, and was directly responsible for undressing the victims, reassuring them that 'they were going for a bath'.[91] On one occasion he said to the doctor concerned that he wished to see a gassing

Plate 24. Paul R. at home together with Josef S. Paul R. worked as an orderly at Hadamar during 'Aktion T–4', subsequently receiving a four-year jail sentence for his part in killing 10,072 people. Josef S.'s mother was murdered at Sonnenstein during the T–4 programme. A retired Mannheim policeman, Josef S. has developed a cautious dialogue with Paul R. to discover the facts about the Nazi 'euthanasia' programme. They met while Paul R. was giving evidence at the trial of one of the doctors accused of 'euthanasia' killings.

(this sort of ghoulish curiosity seems to have been common), and peered through a small aperture set in the wall as 'about thirty' people were killed.[92] The only time when he was forced to confront the humanity of the people he was helping to kill seems to have been when a patient in the line turned out to be the son of a farmer who had employed Paul R. a decade before. They exchanged a few words before the young man was led away. It was not politic to do anything.

Unlike what happened at other extermination centres, where alcohol flowed liberally and the staff went for 'R & R' sessions to the lakes of Upper Bavaria, life for the staff of Hadamar was all drill, sport and exhortatory singing, punctuated by sessions in the local pub. Because he happened to be on leave that day, Paul R. missed the notorious celebrations which attended the murder of the ten-thousandth victim, merely receiving a bottle of beer left over from this macabre bacchanalia the next day. During the festivities an encephalitic corpse lay on the table as

Plate 25. Pauline K.

Gottlieb Hering, masquerading as a priest, conducted a blasphemous ceremony for the amusement of the carousing company.[93]

Eventually, in 1943, Paul R. grew weary of humping decaying corpses up the hill for a 'lousy 40 marks' (an experience that gave him bad dreams at night), and told the administrator Klein, 'do your own shit job yourself'.[94]

Paul R.'s reasons for doing what he did were straightforward. At his trial he said that he was told by the doctor who inducted him at Hadamar: 'this is a Führer order, and we must carry out the orders of the Führer'.[95] During his nursing training at Weilmünster, it had been impressed upon him that he was to carry out the orders of the doctors unconditionally.[96] Other nursing staff said that they respected and treasured the 'gods in white coats' who gave them their orders. This type of pass-the-parcel with

(a)

(b)

Plate 26. (a) The exterior and gas chamber at Bernburg (b) Hartheim near Linz (c) Sonnenstein near Dresden.

(c)

responsibility was the sort of thing one said on trial. Recently, Paul R. reflected more freely on the climate of the times. He said he had been told that the victims were 'life unworthy of life', and that the costs they occasioned could be better spent building houses for families 'rich in children', and that 'there were patients who had been in asylums for thirty or forty years', 'which cost so many thousands, that is what they said'.[97] We have encountered these arguments many times before; by 1941 they had been internalised by this Hessian peasant.

In contrast to Paul R., Pauline K. was one of the 'Foundation' personnel, that is she came to Hadamar from Grafeneck. She was born in 1900 in the Ukraine, into a large ethnic German family which had migrated from the Black Forest to Odessa. They had fled the Bolsheviks, washing up in diminished circumstances on a small farm in Westphalia.[98] The farm was sold in 1934, and the father went to work on the railways. Unlike many of her T–4 colleagues, Pauline K. was on the way down rather than up when she gave up sewing for a career in nursing. She worked for various confessional and private institutions in Duisburg before switching to the state sector, with a job at the asylum Berlin-Buch. She joined the NSDAP in 1937, becoming an NS-Womanhood official two years later, activities she combined with singing in a Protestant church choir. She was summoned to the Columbushaus headquarters of T–4 in December 1939. Blankenburg explained that they were looking for experienced nurses to carry out a 'euthanasia' programme. She was given a few minutes to think the offer over, which meant she could have refused. None of those present said no, and 'none of us had moral reservations'. Unlike others who claimed to have done this work by accident or under compulsion, she admitted: 'It was absolutely voluntary for those at this gathering to agree to participate.'[99] What she saw at Grafeneck was a shock, and she was not happy about the deception involved in the entire programme. The relentless, routinised killings got on her nerves. But after fifteen years' experience of psychiatric nursing, Pauline K. was also convinced that the lives of the patients meant nothing to them, and that death was a form of deliverance.[100] Although we will meet her again in the next chapter, it is necessary to pursue Pauline K.'s career briefly here. After Grafeneck, this fluent Russian speaker spent some time in a field hospital near Minsk, along with Paul R. and many of their T–4 colleagues. What they were doing there, so close to seriously wounded German soldiers, remains an open question. She then returned to Weilmünster, was sent to Bernburg, and finally in 1942 resurfaced in Hadamar, where as deputy senior nurse she instructed others to kill and administered lethal doses of sedatives. She had a knack of reassuring relatives in a friendly fashion regarding the health of people she had just killed. In 1944 she was transferred to Kaufbeuren-Irsee for the last intensified spasm of mass murder. In 1948 she was jailed for three years and one month, being paroled a year later.[101]

The three individuals we have encountered, namely Gorgass, Paul R. and Pauline K., were typical of the people who carried out mass murder. Together with their equivalents in the other extermination centres, and guided by the staff of the T–4 headquarters, these rather ordinary people were responsible for tens of thousands of murders. Between January and August 1941, 10,072 people were murdered in the gas chamber at Hadamar. Another four thousand would be killed there by other means during the next three years, in ways we shall be considering in a later chapter. At Grafeneck, 9,839 people were murdered between January and December 1940. At Bernburg, 9,722 people were gassed between February and September 1940. At Sonnenstein, 13,720 people were gassed from June 1940 to August 1941. And 18,269 people died at Hartheim near Linz between May 1940 and August 1941.[102] In total, 70,273 people were killed in the course of 'Aktion T–4'.

We know this because of a series of statistical tables discovered by the Allies in a steel filing cabinet at Hartheim in June 1945. These gave the monthly 'kill-rate' for four asylums designated B, C, D, E, statistics also shown in the form of coloured lines on a graph.[103] Drawn up by T–4, these tables precisely calculated the longterm economic consequences of 'disinfecting' 70,273 people. The global sum saved, assuming an average patient life expectancy of ten years, would be 885,439,800RMs by 1 September 1951.[104] Tables, charts and graphs established the quantities and money equivalents saved on such foodstuffs as eggs, marmalade and potatoes. For example, assuming that each patient murdered would have consumed

700g of marmalade per month, their deaths would save 5,902,920kg, and therefore, with a kilo of marmalade costing 1,20RMs, there would be a net saving over ten years of 7,083,504RMs.[105] Savings on cheese totalled 1,054,080RMs, on bread 20,857,026RMs, on meat 36,429,588RMs, and so forth. There was no talk here of how psychiatry might be 'modernised' or 'reformed' in consequence.

CHAPTER 5

'GENTLEMEN'S AGREEMENTS'?
RESPONSES TO THE 'EUTHANASIA'
PROGRAMME

THE 'EUTHANASIA' programme involved mass murder by stealth. The villa from which 'Aktion T-4' was organised bore no identifying name plate.[1] Even the secretaries who worked there knew that the organisation and its subsidiaries were a front to conceal the connection with the KdF (Chancellory of the Führer).[2] Secrecy especially exercised Reichsleiter Bouhler.[3] Immense pains were taken to keep T-4's operations covert. As we shall see in this chapter, whenever a gap appeared which the T-4 people had not anticipated they rushed to close it. This was especially true of the wider legal repercussions of murdering asylum inmates.

It is difficult to describe how information filtered out. People living near the extermination centres regularly saw the transports arriving, and had their homes and streets polluted by noxious smells shortly afterwards. At first, the staff in the extermination centres had to do their drinking in the canteens. At Grafeneck, excess led to prohibition, and that resulted in a demonstration, a strike of sorts by the 'burners'. A staff choir was probably not a satisfactory compensation. Eventually, works outings were organised to the generously stocked canteens of concentration camps, where one could drink, fill one's face, sing and weep alongside more practised (and homesick) murderers. Sometimes T-4 men and women were allowed out for recreation, to inns like the one midway between Grafeneck and the stud farm at Marbach where they tended to talk in their cups at their *Stammtisch*. That was also what happened at Hadamar. Being crude individuals with a heavy sense of humour, these working-class chaps and their female escorts tended to make extravagant claims about numbers, or jokes about the improving quality of the local topsoil.[4] Local businesses in Hadamar, Pirna or Munsingen benefited from increased sales of everything from milk to books and stockings. One person visited the shops to purchase for all the rest – driving on, in the case of Grafeneck, to Tübingen or Stuttgart to post off the urns or ashes. Clearly on good terms with the shopkeepers, he also did their errands in the cities.

Not surprisingly, what was going on in these asylums soon became widely known, to the point where workers repairing the track that runs directly below the asylum at Grafeneck removed their hats and stood in silence whenever a train carrying patients passed through. The staff of asylums from which patients were transferred also began to suffer through association. When some orderlies from Weissenau attempted to buy cherries from a stall, the woman in charge told them 'You lot aren't having any of my cherries, go somewhere else! We're not selling you anything if you treat our neighbours like that, simply taking them away to be shot!'[5] Sometimes the blatancy of what was being done resulted in popular outrage. In early 1941, a group of buses, under the direction of a Professor from Erlangen, pulled up in the market square of Absberg. Instead of driving into the courtyard of the Ottilienheim, the transport personnel began loading about a hundred feebleminded patients into the buses, in full view of the townspeople. The patients resisted, and had to be loaded on with physical force. The asylum priest had raised the temperature in this very Catholic area by taking the patients to confession and communion in the town church the night before their enforced departure. A crowd of weeping people gathered, including some members of the National Socialist party, who vented their hostility towards a state which was in such a deleterious condition that it was having to kill the handicapped to fund its war effort.[6]

Sometimes, the sheer volume of killings set off suspicions. An official in the Rhineland began to receive packages of duplicate death certificates for entry into his records. Though no one had told him about the 'euthanasia' programme, he said that it was as clear as if 'the sparrows were whistling from the rooftops that the patients were not dying of natural causes'. He opened up a secret record of these cases.[7] Some people made contact with friends in high places. Else von Löwis of Menar wrote to the wife of Walter Buch, the senior judge in the NSDAP. She said it was perfectly plain what was happening at Grafneck, 'an open secret', and that the victims were not incurably benighted idiots. The quicker a law was passed the better. Plain people were being only temporarily appeased by the convenient fiction that the Führer did not know what was happening.[8] Buch got off a letter to his 'dear Party comrade Himmler'. In his life (he wrote), he had been privileged to know three tall and striking Nordic goddesses: Karin Goering, Else von Löwis and her sister, the father of the latter two being the former Baden Minister of Justice. When they and their brothers stood up – they were all between 1.80m and 1.90m tall – everyone else seemed to shrink. With 'fathomless trust in my Reichs-führer–SS', Buch relayed the intelligence from Else, whom he said was an ardent supporter of the Party. There were things that men had to do today on behalf of the eternal life of the nation, things which women shuddered at. (He clearly did not move in the same circles as Pauline K. at Grafeneck.) Therefore, these things needed to be kept more secret than seemed to be the case. Himmler let Buch into the secret – the Führer had instigated everything – and stressed that the SS only had minimal involvement. He was going to recommend that Grafeneck be shut down.[9] SS internal security experts sent detailed reports to their superiors concerning how the 'euthanasia' programme was playing havoc with popular morale, to the point of weakening trust in Hitler. People were afraid that these measures would be extended to encompass the elderly, invalids, or mentally disturbed soldiers. Workers past their prime would be discarded like 'burdensome ballast'. They were angry that while the regime made capital out of an RAF attack which allegedly hit the Bethel asylum at Bielefeld (on the night when no British bombers were in the vicinity), hundreds of patients were being taken away from other asylums and killed. There followed a grim catalogue of individual cases. One concerned the son of a former State Secretary in the Ministry of Defence, who had won the Iron Cross in World War One, had been in an asylum as a private patient since 1928, and had died in August 1940 in Hartheim of 'blood-poisoning'.[10] His mother wrote an impassioned letter to the Ministry of the Interior in Stuttgart, furious that she had not been consulted about the transfer of her son (whose maintenance costs she paid), to an asylum (Grafeneck) where there was apparently risk of contagious diseases. Regardless 'of the way he met his death' in Hartheim, the mother hoped her letter would spare other parents her suffering.[11]

Nearer the nerve, relatives noticed major administrative errors. In one case, a family received an urn putatively containing the ashes of a son whom they had removed from an asylum some weeks previously.[12] Another received two urns when only one person was in an asylum; hairpins cropped up in the ashes of males; people died of acute appendicitis who had had that organ removed years earlier.[13] Even relatives who were convinced Nazis, and who for years had wished this to happen to relatives in asylums, did not like either the deception or the illegality that was involved. Two sisters died within two days of each other in Sonnenstein. Their surviving sister noted that they had very different illnesses and were separated by a nine-year age gap. 'No one was going to tell her that this was coincidental.' She had often wished that they were both dead(!), but she could not believe that her secret wishes would be fulfilled in two days. She did not object to their deaths, just to the fact that she was being lied to, and that there was no legal basis. She would keep quiet if she was told what had really happened.[14] Dr Schumann wrote to Heyde: ironically, the two had died of natural causes! Blankenburg informed Linden, who contacted the local Party Chief of Staff Heinrich Sellmer to establish whether the woman was politically reliable. They eventually told her what had happened.[15]

Plate 27. Death notices from a Lübeck newspaper dated 22 October 1941. Next to announcements of combat fatalities is a notice (bottom right, indicated with an arrow) concerning the 'sudden and unexpected' death of a fifty-seven-year-old woman, whose 'silent' (in the sense of 'hushed-up') burial had already taken place at the Eichberg asylum.

Families who wished to make an issue of how their relatives had died sometimes placed insinuating death notices in the local newspapers. One is shown in plate 27; the *Frankische Zeitung* ran another which read 'torn from us by a tragic fate'.[16] Grotesquely, one or two put their faith in appeals to the highest authority, petitioning Hitler via the KdF and prefacing pleas for the lives of their own children with birthday greetings to him.[17] Others braved the vagaries of wartime transport, and a bureaucracy bent on lying to them, in the interests of finding out exactly what had happened to their relatives. Elsbeth R.'s mother allegedly died of a heart attack in Hartheim in July 1940. Her daughter, who lived in Berlin, went to Linz, on to Alkhoven and then by foot to the castle. A policeman at the door summoned his superior (Wirth?), who told her to see a doctor at the asylum of Niederharth. The latter, a man in his thirties, was unable to say where her mother had been cremated. She remarked sarcastically that there could not be that many crematoria in the area. He promised to send information to her in Berlin, which of course never happened. The crematorium staff in Steyr said that they had come across many similar cases, and that wherever people were being cremated, it was not in their facilities. She eventually went to a Berlin lawyer to institute legal proceedings; he advised her that this would result in her consignment to a concentration camp. She abandoned her struggle.[18]

As is usual, middle-class professionals were able to assert their rights more effectively than others. They were not so easy to brush off, knew people, and were articulate and disputatious. Dr Wilhelm F. had an elderly schizophrenic uncle in the Philippshospital at Goddelau, for whom he was the legal guardian. When the uncle was suddenly transferred to Weilmünster, Dr F. immediately telephoned both institutions. The staff at Weilmünster said his uncle was well. Since Dr F. suspected that patients were being killed, he went to Weilmünster and demanded to speak with the doctor in charge. He told the doctor that he knew what was going on, and that he would press charges of unlawful killing. The doctor agreed that patients were indeed being killed, but said that this was legal. There then ensued a long discussion about the nature of law in the Third Reich. His interlocutor claimed that there were laws which were not published; Dr F. argued that publication was an inherent feature of any law, and that he would bring charges of murder. Four weeks later his uncle was returned to Goddelau.[19]

Popular anxieties gradually fused with the fact that half of the victims in the 'euthanasia' programme originated from ecclesiastical institutions. The Protestant Inner Mission alone had 512 asylums and homes with beds for over 35,125 people.[20] As we saw in Chapter 1, some of those who ran this network of institutions, notably Hans Harmsen, had begun to subscribe to the new hereditary biological tidings, whereby an absolute and axiomatic concern for the poor and weak was supplanted by a more mundane preoccupation with such relative abstractions as cost or national biological wellbeing, with all the moral slippage that that necessarily entailed. One of the few leading figures in the Inner Mission not to be tantalised by these glad tidings was Pastor Gerhard Braune of Lobetal.

From May to June 1940, Braune – who had himself received an order to transfer twenty-five feebleminded girls in his charge at Lobetal – visited government ministries and the high command of the Armed Forces, to probe deeper into what was happening. He enlisted the support of the immensely influential Pastor Friedrich von Bodelschwingh (1877–1946) of the world-famous Bethel establishment at Bielefeld. Having eventually found the right address, Braune and Bodelschwingh were received by Brack and Linden. The latter began by simply denying the existence of any such measures, moving on to threats when the two clerics confronted them with unassailable evidence. Having run into a brick wall, the two – now joined by the eminent surgeon Sauerbruch – turned to Minister of Justice Gürtner. Still amazingly trusting in the power of Caesar, Braune decided to gather up the reports he had received concerning the 'euthanasia' programme into a formal memorandum, which he sent to Hitler.[21] He said that the events he described could not be coincidental, but were rather an attempt to save money and to 'breed up' the German nation. Countering the former argument, Braune said that killing one patient per thousand people could make no difference whatsoever to the wartime economy, and that asylums had already made thousands of beds freely available for military casualties. The inviolability of human life was one of the foundation stones of the rule of law. Braune then proceeded to give chapter and verse on the *modus operandi* of the 'euthanasia' programme. He concluded with the warning: 'Videant consules, ne quid detrimenti res publica capiat!' – 'Let the leading men in the state take care that it comes to no harm!'[22] Fourteen days later, Braune was told that Hitler had seen his memorandum, but that he could do nothing to stop the killings beyond ensuring that they were carried out more carefully. On 12 August Braune was arrested by agents from the Reich Main Security Office and kept for three months in 'protective custody'.[23]

A handful of more senior clerics decided to follow Braune in protesting privately to the authorities. As they were members of the old establishment, this was their preferred *modus operandi*. On 19 July 1940, the Protestant bishop Theophil Wurm of Württemberg wrote to Minister of the Interior Frick. Like Braune he built his case upon intelligence he had received from members of the laity whose relatives had been murdered. Unlike Braune, he appeared to go some of the way towards understanding the regime's position. There were embarrassing references to the military victory over France and to the 'positive Christianity' mentioned in clause 24 of the Nazi Party programme. He felt that these measures must be emanating from atheistic circles connected with the SS journal *Schwarze Korps*, bent upon decoupling ethics from Christian belief.[24] As far as he knew, Hitler still stood by positive Christianity, which was based upon pity towards suffering 'national comrades'. Worse was to follow. Having once served as a priest in a state asylum, the bishop could 'naturally' understand how people could arrive at the view that it would be better to put an end to 'such existences'. The mass mortality of patients during the First World War was 'a natural result of the war' and an act of God. In a pathetic appeal to the preservation of social order, Wurm said that if the state abandoned the doctrine of the sanctity of human life, youth would soon follow, leading to a general brutalisation of society. Either the National Socialist state acknowledged the limits set by God, or it would preside over a total collapse of public morals.[25] In several further letters. Wurm still subscribed to the fiction that the 'euthanasia' programme represented some sort of derailment of a once-pure National Socialism, or that it was being carried out without the knowledge of Hitler.

Braune's associate, Bodelschwingh of Bethel, was an equally ambivalent figure. A supporter of eugenic sterilisation in the late 1920s, he was opposed to 'euthanasia'. It would undermine popular trust in asylums, and the bureaucracy needed to carry it out would cost three times the sums such a policy would save state and nation.[26] Initially, he enjoined his staff at Bethel not to render any assistance to the T–4 programme by, for example, refusing to carry out the registration of patients. Karsten Jaspersen, chief doctor of Bethel-Sarepta, who as it happened was a Nazi 'old fighter', distinguished himself by hurriedly re-writing patients' medical records to save those categories most endangered, and indeed tipped off colleagues at other asylums and in university psychiatric clinics – as well as Bishop Galen, whose response we shall shortly encounter.

Bodelschwingh, as mentioned earlier, found it risible that the regime expected him to condemn an alleged RAF mishit on Bethel when that regime was itself organising the mass removal of his charges. The word 'mass' seems to have been the sticking point. For in a letter to Minister of the Interior Frick dated 28 September 1940, Bodelschwingh began to modify his absolute opposition to the 'euthanasia' programme. He began by stating that it was 'truly not our intention to make difficulties for state authorities'. He had much understanding for the 'hard necessities of war'. From Pastor Constantin Frick, the president of the Central Committee of the Inner Mission, he had heard that changes were being made in the programme's *modus operandi* so that it would henceforth only affect 'patients no longer capable of any human contact'.[27] He would not allow his staff to be involved in these measures, but they would not obstruct representatives of the state or refuse access to medical records.

Pastor Frick seems to have removed the ground from under the feet of the directorate of Bethel. In secret negotiations with Reich Health Leader Conti, Frick consented to completing the registration forms, on condition that the 'euthanasia' programme would proceed more circumspectly. As we shall see, senior members of the Roman Catholic Church also seem to have gone native in discussions with the authorities. To be charitable, this lack of a unified front seems to have led Bodelschwingh to permit the state to send teams of referees to his asylums. More difficult to explain was his decision to order his own doctors to categorise patients according to their ability to work, in other words do the job of selection for the authorities. The criteria were developed by Dr Gerhard Schorsch; they covered seven categories of patients ranging from 'vegetative existences' up to 'very good performance'.[28] A large and high-powered T–4 team arrived, including Professors Brandt, Heinze, Heyde, Kihn and Pohlisch as well as the ubiquitous Viktor Brack. The latter reassured Schorsch that 'he was not a criminal'. Since Bodelschwingh was handled with kid gloves by the 'Berlin gentlemen', he attempted to use the opportunity to introduce delays and safety checks into the procedures. 'Aktion T-4' stopped before the efficacy of Bodelschwingh's brand of decentralised opposition through apparent accommodation could be tested.[29]

In most societies, the sane and the insane are enmeshed in some sort of legal system. It may concern itself fitfully enough with the latter's human rights; but it is usually always on guard in matters of inheritance, or when a person is deemed irresponsible for his or her actions, or a threat to other people. In the case we are concerned with, the normative legal apparatus quickly discovered that incursions were being made into its territory by prerogative agencies.

The Ministry of Justice was the first port of call for those members of the judiciary or legal profession who wanted to know what was happening. On 8 July 1940 Minister Gürtner received an urgent report from the Brandenburg provincial judge Lothar Kreyssig. Born in 1898, Kreyssig had fought in the First World War, winning the Iron Cross for bravery. His superiors regarded him as 'an open, honourable character; very conscious of his responsibilities and conscientious; manfully represents his views against anyone.' As we shall see, he had iron determination, unreflective confidence, and a degree of moral and religious conviction which meant that he was not intimidated by anyone. This was not some ambitious petty-bourgeois professor whom one could impress with uniforms and titles, or corrupt through what Heyde called 'the nimbus of power', but rather a man of conviction, integrity and moral substance. Kreyssig was a member of the Confessioning Church, and first came to the attention of the Nazi authorities in Saxony, where he began his career, by walking out during the unveiling of a portrait of Hitler and murmuring 'Heil Hitler' once (rather than shouting it the requisite thrice) at a reception. In 1937 he purchased a small estate some thirteen kilometres from Brandenburg, whence he requested a transfer. He wanted to raise his three young sons near the soil, and away from urban chaos. He was already considering retirement.[30] In 1939 he was in trouble again, this time for obstructing the sermon of an adherent of the German Christians (a sect which fused Lutheranism with extreme nationalism), in favour of a pastor from the Confessional persuasion. His military call-up papers arrived before the matter could escalate.

Deconscripted because of his age and possession of a farm, Kreyssig soon lighted upon the fact that patients from the asylum of Brandenburg-Görden were being transferred and murdered. These included persons who, as wards of court, were his formal responsibility. On about 8 July 1940 Kreyssig addressed a protest to Minister Gürtner deploring what were wholly illegal killings. Friends and acquaintances with wards of court had been supplying him with information. To this he added his religious and philosophical objections to ideas (he cited Binding and Hoche) and policies which arbitrarily and illegally interfered in God's secret design.[31] A few days after receiving Kreyssig's report, Gürtner had an audience in his Berlin-Grünewald home with Pastor Braune, Bodelschwingh and the eminent surgeon Sauerbruch. According to Braune, Gürtner was appalled by the scale of what they described, commenting: 'It is a fateful day when reliable people inform the Reich Minister of Justice that "people are being murdered on a regular basis in your state, and you know nothing about it?"' He began to recollect that several months before Bouhler and Conti had sounded out his general views on involuntary euthanasia.[32] This was probably disingenuous, since members of T-4 recalled discussions with officials from the Ministry of Justice before the war, i.e. before the killings started.[33] It was the scale rather than the existence of such measures which probably startled Gürtner.

On 12 July 1940, he received similar intelligence, and a request to begin an investigation by the Gestapo(!), from the Stuttgart state prosecutor general. Noting the number of transfers from Illenau and Rottweil, the state prosecutor general was concerned that the populace would lose faith in the judicial authorities should they fail to stop policies which, rumour had it, were about to encompass the elderly.[34] The state prosecutor general in Graz was similarly exercised by the resultant loss of popular esteem affecting the entire legal profession. More pragmatically, many lawyers in several parts of Germany began to ask awkward questions about matters of inheritance and wardships, or regarding the fate of people temporarily committed for psychiatric observation under paragraph 42b of the Criminal Code.[35] They also wondered what they should do when people required them under the law to institute proceedings regarding deaths in suspicious circumstances, or whether they should deal with those who discussed the 'euthanasia' programme – which officially was not happening – under laws designed to prevent the spreading of 'malicious rumours'. In the latter case, the Ministry of Justice suggested it would be better to let sleeping dogs lie rather than to risk a rehearsal by the accused (even *in camera*) of what was officially not happening. Although T-4 was to benefit from all of these queries – by relaying the information, the Ministry of Justice helped close loopholes in the operation(!) – it is clear that the entire legal edifice was thrown into acute embarrassment, with nobody at the top quite sure how far to inform subordinate officials.

As for Kreyssig, he was summoned to Berlin for a face-to-face encounter with State Secretary Roland Freisler. The latter was in his sane mode. Freisler said he had been in contact with the KdF, which had assured him that they were following instructions from Hitler. When Kreyssig asked to see this in writing, Freisler told him that 'the will of the Führer creates law', and that he was working on providing these policies with a legal basis.[36] Kreyssig refused to be satisfied, and said that he would prevent asylums in his area surrendering their patients. A further meeting about six weeks later forced Freisler to reveal a little more about T–4, and to mention that Bouhler was the official responsible. Again, Kreyssig refused to be fobbed off, threatening this time to bring charges of murder against those responsible. Freisler seemed to perk up on hearing this (he had no love of Bouhler), helpfully suggesting that the judge go to the state prosecutor in nearby Potsdam. The latter took no notes and responded inconclusively. Kreyssig went to the asylum at Brandenburg-Görden and summoned the personnel to inform them that the 'euthanasia' programme was illegal, the result of a misunderstanding of Hitler's intentions. It would either be called off entirely or given legal sanction. He also mentioned major differences of opinion between Bouhler and Freisler.[37]

In late August he wrote to the directors of asylums in his jurisdiction, warning them of the legal consequences should they venture to transfer any patient subject to his authority. This earned him a further summons to the Ministry of Justice, where he was confronted by Gürtner. Gürtner showed him a copy of Hitler's 1939 note commissioning Brandt and Bouhler; Kreyssig spotted that the signature was a facsimile and refused to accept its legality. There was no mention of Freisler or of retrospective legislation. Clearly exasperated, Gürtner concluded the meeting, telling Kreyssig he could say nothing further.[38] He added that Kreyssig would be compulsorily retired, which happened that December.[39] Kreyssig was one of the few people to survive these events with any residual integrity.

Anxieties regarding the illegality of the T–4 programme were shared by some of those involved in implementing it. This particularly applied to the doctors who turned on the gas taps.[40] Separate draft laws were essayed by Lammers and by a team consisting of Brack, Hefelmann, Heinze, Heyde, Linden and Wentzler. Secretaries who worked in the KdF recalled typing the same text hundreds of times.[41] One should also mention the law drafted earlier by Theo Morell, discussed at the beginning of this chapter.[42] An unwanted interloper into those proceedings was the SD and Security Police chief Heydrich – the Nazi St Just – whose apparatchiks wanted a comprehensive 'Law for the Killing of Unfit Life and the Asocial'.[43] In July 1940 an agreed text of the draft law was sent to about thirty persons, including T–4 doctors and professors, referees, members of the Reich Main Security Office and key officials in the regional health administrations. The only surviving responses are those of Dr Irmfried Eberl of Brandenburg, but we know that everyone who saw the draft was enthusiastic about it. Eberl elevated work, including work done in one's earlier life, to the status of sole criterion for 'euthanasia', insisting upon the inclusion of those patients who just ran along beside agricultural work parties, not to speak of all criminals and sufferers from senile dementia.[44]

He also advocated the total conflation of voluntary and involuntary 'euthanasia' for both the mentally ill and the terminally suffering. Eberl thought that a published commentary upon the draft law, along the lines of Gütt, Rüdin and Rüttke on sterilisation, might iron out any difficulties with the host of authorities who would be involved in these measures.[45]

Further revised drafts of the law did the rounds, culminating in a conference in the autumn of 1940 which was attended by most of the T-4 professors and referees, Heydrich, and regional health administrators such as Schultze, Sprauer and Stähle. The young medical gas-killers were represented by Eberl, Renno, Schumann and Ullrich; the older hands by Faltlhauser and Pfannmüller. The question of what to call the law seems to have been worth several minutes' discussion; votes were taken on such issues as whether to have a lower age limit of twenty or twenty-five, with provision for more mature eighteen-year-olds.[46] In the event, the law never went beyond a final draft. Hitler killed the project on the grounds that it would fuel enemy propaganda. Some suspect that the real reason why the law never materialised was that the pedantic scrupulosity of its provisions would have slowed the momentum of the Nazi killing programme by substituting expertise, precision and normative processes for procedures hitherto based on the broad, arbitrary approach.[47]

While the draft law came to nothing, the Ministry of Justice was still stuck with the problem of what to say to lawyers, judges and prosecutors who raised the issue. Gürtner's successor, Schlegelberger, approached Bouhler in March, receiving a portfolio of material on the 'euthanasia' programme from Brack. In other words, T-4 and the Ministry of Justice were going to cooperate with each other; henceforth any complaints and protests sent to the Ministry would effectively be used to iron out mistakes in the 'euthanasia' programme. The Ministry of Justice in turn began the potentially delicate business of informing its subordinate officials on a need-to-know basis. In late April 1941, Schlegelberger invited the state prosecutors general and the presidents of the regional higher courts to a meeting in Berlin to hear talks 'regarding a question which is particularly important for the judiciary': talks which said all and nothing. After they had stood in silence for a minute to commemorate the deceased Gürtner, Schlegelberger treated them to the sort of circumlocutory mutually congratulatory oracular flatulence which is usual on such occasions. Half an hour of this eloquent rubbish set the scene for the guest expert speakers: Viktor Brack and Werner Heyde.[48] Brack, appearing in SS uniform, read the draft law to the judges, mentioning *en passant* that the time was not right for it to be passed and promulgated. This minor contradiction did not matter, since (according to Schlegelberger, who organised the meeting) none of the judges and lawyers was concerned about the legality of the 'euthanasia' programme.[49] He then gave them chapter and verse on the programme, albeit including a number of safety checks which in reality were rarely utilised. Photographs of mental patients were handed around, glanced at and then passed on.[50] Heyde blinded them with science about such matters as how to forge a cause of death.[51] There was no discussion. Having heard an economist (of doubtful political standing) detail the organisation of murder, and an obscure professor freely admit to having the courage to kill people himself, the 'close-knit family' of Germany's legal finest left in silence. Word passed discreetly to the lesser echelons of the judiciary. Henceforth, any difficulties would pass on upward into the yawning moral void of Schlegelberger's Ministry.

The KdF's discussions with the lawyers were fitfully accompanied by equally secret talks with those other professional guardians of morals in the Roman Catholic church. This is a complex subject, where apologias or anti-clericalism often cloud people's judgement. Key pieces of evidence have gone missing. Many of those involved were probably lying (at the time and later), or indeed believed their interlocutors to be inherently duplicitous. Regardless of any courageous steps on the part of individual clerics, the crucial point to bear in mind is that public protests by a few senior Roman Catholic (or Protestant) clerics began in August 1941, by which time T–4 had murdered over 70,000 people. Half, and I repeat half, of these victims were patients in ecclesiastical or private institutions. Concentration upon a few heroic individuals tends to distract from this long period of public silence. It also means that less attention is paid to a series of crucial behind-the-scenes negotiations.

As was the case with the Protestant Church, intelligence regarding the 'euthanasia' programme filtered from the laity via the priesthood to the Roman Catholic episcopate. Being members of Germany's residual establishment, the bishops used classic establishment methods to register their concern or disapproval. They gathered together the information they had to hand, and wrote confidentially, sometimes relaying detailed memoranda, to what they regarded as the appropriate, legally constituted authorities. Being networkers, they tended to concentrate upon men like Gürtner who were also Roman Catholics. Thus Archbishop Gröber of Freiburg wrote to the Badenese Minister of the Interior on 1 June 1940, and to Lammers in the Reich Chancellory two months later.[52] This was a forlorn endeavour, since the agencies carrying out the 'euthanasia' programme were covert and the programme itself illegal.

On 22 August 1940 the Fulda Episcopal Synod decided to register a protest with the government. Specifically, they wanted the latter to stop what they were doing, and – this was a rather crucial 'and' – to consider the wishes of parents and relatives; and to exempt their charitable foundations from participation in the 'euthanasia' programme.[53] They also deputed bishop Heinrich Wienken, since 1937 the leading light of the Caritas

Association, to register their concerns in person at the highest level. Wienken was invited for talks in the Ministry of the Interior. There he was met by Linden, who was joined later by Hans Hefelmann. We have Wienken's recollection of what was said, and indeed Hefelmann's own by no means unproblematic account from roughly the‿ same period in 1960. According to Wienken, his interlocutors switched from general pleasantries to a long justification of killing 'lives unworthy of life'. They stressed the cost factor, pointing out that human and material resources were needed for the care of wounded soldiers. They claimed, no doubt with Meltzer's poll in mind, that nurses and relatives largely consented to these policies. Wienken responded by quoting the Fifth Commandment, demanding that the programme be halted. He warned them that the Church would make public protests. Wienken was evidently taken seriously, for he was recalled to the Ministry a few days later to be told that the programme would be terminated.

Hefelmann talked about the same negotiations in ten of the many interrogation sessions he had with prosecutors and police between 1960 and 1964. It should be said at the outset that he was trying to present himself as small fry – despite claiming authorship of the Madagascar Plan to resettle Jews on that island – denying any involvement in the adult 'euthanasia' programme. What he said has therefore to be treated with extreme caution.

However, it is necessary first to set these talks in a slightly wider context. In Chapter 1 we saw that some sections of both churches approved compulsory sterilisation. One of those who did so was the Catholic professor of moral theology Joseph Mayer (1886–1967). In 1966 Albert Hartl, a former Catholic priest, who through connections with Himmler joined the SD in 1934, claimed that before the commencement of the 'euthanasia' programme, he had been ordered to sound out the position of the Catholic Church regarding such a policy. Not being a theologian, Hartl approached first a priest who was a cousin of Himmler (too crude), and then Mayer, who eventually supplied a hundred-page Jesuitical paper – which has never been rediscovered – rehearsing both sides of the argument, without coming to a firm conclusion.[54] Hartl picked Mayer because of his earlier accommodating stance on sterilisation, and because he occasionally relayed ecclesiastical tittle-tattle to the agency Hartl worked for. Hartl relayed the paper to Hitler, who (Hartl claimed) followed up his suggestion of informing Cardinal Bertram, Bishop Wienken, Bishop Berning and the papal nuncio Cesare Orsenigo of what they were planning.[55] He contacted a priest who worked in the Ministry of Churches; Bouhler allegedly informed the bishops. In her account of these matters, Gitta Sereny concluded that the Church had foreknowledge of the 'euthanasia' programme, and tacitly sanctioned it.[56]

Before we leap to the same conclusion, a number of points need to be made. Mayer spoke with no special authority, and as a known SD informer was regarded with some scepticism in more exalted ecclesiastical circles.[57] Hartl was a renegade priest whose job within the SD was to monitor his former brethren. He claims he was able to duck out of leading one of the Einsatzgruppen in Russia – a task he was given because he was a known 'weakling' – but he crops up fitfully alongside such people as Blöbel, who took him to the ravine at Babi Yar outside Kiev, proudly announcing 'My Jews are lying in there.'[58] Hartl is really not the most reliable witness regarding the thoughts and strategies of cardinals and bishops.

Mayer's paper did, however, perform one vital function. When Linden and Hefelmann had their sessions with Wienken in 1940, it meant that Linden was well primed to counter the bishop's moral and theological objections.[59] Careful reading of Hefelmann's accounts of the meetings suggest that he and Linden were trying to fix up a 'gentlemen's agreement'. They would agree to tighten up T-4's operational procedures by (for example) introducing longer periods of observation in the special paediatric clinics, if the Church would desist from its protestations.[60] Apparently Wienken agreed, saying 'Yes, these are very careful measures.'[61] On 30 January 1961, Hefelmann said that Wienken agreed to 'tolerate' the 'euthanasia' programme within redrawn parameters.[62] Again, it is vital to set these talks in a fuller context. As is clear from correspondence between Wienken and Cardinal Faulhaber of Munich, the former was coming to be regarded as a soft touch when it came to dealings with T-4 officials. He was becoming fixated upon such details as exemptions for sick priests from the 'euthanasia' programme(!), measures which 'could lead to the conclusion that the Church had come to an arrangement regarding the application of these measures to other persons'.[63] Not for the first time, negotiations with mass murderers were becoming too cosy, at the expense of moral first principles. In a letter to Wienken dated 18 November 1940, Faulhaber made mincemeat of the arguments which a priest had relayed to him on behalf of Wienken. Judging from Faulhaber's reply, Wienken was beginning to sound like the men from T-4, as 're-skilled' in theology by Joseph Mayer. Faulhaber reckoned that it was a pretty pass when 'Englishmen and the Middle Ages' – he meant Thomas More – were being cited to justify policy. Referring obliquely to Meltzer and the issue of alleged consensuality, Faulhaber noted that there would always be people who went in for the 'Chinese-heathen custom' of exposing female infants. He explicitly told Wienken that it was not a matter of exempting this or that category of victim, but rather that 'domestic national comrades were being cleared out of the way to create space for foreign national comrades'.[64] According to Hefelmann, the talks collapsed because Hitler would not allow Minister of Interior Frick to put the more circumspect procedures in writing as the bishop wanted.

Specifically, Hitler thought that while the German Catholic hierarchy might remain silent, they might well use the Italian or Spanish churches to ventilate indirect protests.[65] The other side of the story is probably that the Catholic hierarchy had begun to distance themselves sharply, à la Faulhaber, from their own representative. In this they were bolstered by an unequivocal condemnation of 'euthanasia' by the Holy See dated 2 December 1940.[66] Pius XII nonetheless thought it less 'provocative' to substitute the word 'killing' for 'murder'.

Few Roman Catholic clerics ventured a public confrontation with these policies. One of those who did was the bishop of Münster, Clemens August Graf von Galen (1878–1946). Galen came from an aristocratic Catholic family in Oldenburg, whose ancestral home was the idyllic moated castle at Dinklage. This background probably inclined him to take the longer view of such short-term phenomena as liberalism, socialism and Nazism. He attended an Austrian Jesuit school in Feldkirch, whose roll-call was prefaced by the abbreviations which prefixed the many princes, marquises, counts and barons among its pupils. From there he passed on to a Jesuit neo-Thomist training at the University of Innsbrück. Although his mentality was clannish, snobbish and thoroughly illiberal, Galen's first posting was to a parish in Berlin. Specifically, he was in charge of a Catholic home for wandering journeymen, the general idea being to keep the young and itinerant lower classes away from louche pubs, doss-houses and hostels.[67] Transferred to Münster as a priest in 1929, he became a bishop in 1933. His Easter message in 1934 was the first blast against a regime he equated with neo-paganism, and saw as an assault upon the lay Catholic organisations he cherished.[68] He publicly objected to meetings in Münster at which the Nazis' chief 'neo-pagan' mouthpiece Alfred Rosenberg, would be speaking. Hostile articles and cartoons of him began to appear in the *Völkische Beobachter* and *Das schwarze Korps*. This did not stop him protesting against the dissolution of Catholic labour and youth associations in the following years.

Reading his successive attacks on National Socialist policy (and for him the latter element in the Party's name was no fiction), one can see that it was not just neo-paganism which exercised him. Judging by an address he gave in 1937, Galen had a thorough-going contempt for the way people he regarded as social upstarts and foreigners were dictating to people like himself what constituted quintessential German characteristics. He did not need lessons on this subject from people who hailed from 'Riga, Reval or Cairo or even Chile', by which sarcastic flourish he meant (*inter aliis*) Rosenberg, Hess and Darré.[69]

In July 1941 the local Gestapo's decision to eject Jesuits from property they occupied in Münster led Galen to preach a sermon in the Lamberti-kirche, denouncing a state which routinely crushed opponents in Gestapo

Plate 28. Bishop Clemens August Graf von Galen (1878–1946). Galen's sermon of 3 August 1941 constituted the most comprehensive and damning indictment of the 'euthanasia' programme. Copies of his sermon were leafletted over Germany by the RAF.

cellars and concentration camps. This may have been the reason why he now decided to make public the intelligence he had received regarding the 'euthanasia' programme since 25 July 1940.[70] When he had first contemplated doing so, in August 1940, Cardinal Bertram had counselled against it because of the wide-ranging possible consequences. A direct attack on the order which had trained him propelled Galen to act.

On 3 August 1941 the tall, bear-like Galen clambered up to the pulpit in a crowded Lambertikirche. In a long sermon, in which he invoked a God rumbling overhead Mars-like, Galen detailed what he knew regarding the killing of patients, including registration, transfers and the deception of relatives. Articulating no doubt widespread anxieties regarding the inflationary potentialities latent in the 'euthanasia' programme, Galen continued:

> If you establish and apply the principle that you can kill 'unproductive' human beings, then woe betide us all when we become old and frail! If one is allowed to kill unproductive people, then woe betide the invalids who have used up, sacrificed and lost their health and strength in the productive process. If one is allowed forcibly to remove one's unproductive fellow human beings, then woe betide loyal soldiers who return to the homeland seriously disabled, as cripples, as invalids . . . Woe to mankind, woe to our German nation, if God's holy commandment 'Thou shalt not kill!', which God proclaimed on Mount Sinai amidst thunder and lightning, which God our Creator inscribed in the conscience of mankind from the very beginning, is not only broken, but if this transgression is actually tolerated, and permitted to go unpublished.[71]

It was his legal obligation, he said, to institute charges of murder against those responsible. He had heard nothing since he had done so.

This sermon was then repeated in diocesan churches in the form of a pastoral message. The responses of the Nazi authorities suggest they had been stung by it. Their low gangster mentality came quickly to the surface. Gauleiter Meyer thought Galen should be arrested and sent to a concentration camp. Walter Tiessler, of the Ministry of Propaganda, suggested executing him, a sentence Bormann thought equally appropriate.[72] Against his instincts, Hitler decided to postpone a final reckoning for the duration, possibly because Goebbels had warned that radical measures would mean that Westphalia would be lost to the Nazis. In his characteristic Chicago gangster mode, Hitler said:

> I am quite sure that a man like the Bishop von Galen knows that after the war I shall extract retribution down to the last farthing. And that if he does not succeed in the meanwhile in getting himself transferred to the Collegium Germanicum in Rome, he may rest assured that in the balancing of our accounts no 't' will remain uncrossed, no 'i' left undotted.[73]

Nothing was done to Galen, despite the fact that the RAF leafletted copies of his sermon over Germany. Those priests or ordinary people who disseminated or discussed his sermon lost their jobs, were sent to concentration camps, or were executed. In Hadamar, a young woman, Paula S.,

Plate 29. Paula S. served six months in Ravensbrück concentration camp for possessing a copy of Galen's sermon condemning the 'euthanasia' programme.

commuted daily to work in nearby Limburg. On the platform she had seen patients arriving, and had noted the noxious smoke which emanated from the asylum chimney a hour or so later. At work, two colleagues whose father had died suddenly while a worker-patient at Schnepfenhausen, asked whether it was true that people were being killed in the asylum. She said that it was, and mentioned that she had a copy of Galen's sermon. She was denounced and arrested. The copy of the sermon was discovered in a search of her home. After four weeks in solitary confinement in Frankfurt, Paula S. was sent to the women's concentration camp at Ravensbrück.

There was no trial. Today, she still cannot describe what she experienced during her six months in the camp. When she was released, she discovered that she had lost her job, and that people in Hadamar avoided her.[74]

Many people imagine that Hitler decided to 'halt' – not 'stop' – the programme of mass gassing as a result of Galen's sermon. Certainly this alleged connection figures more prominently in the literature than the negotiations of Heinrich Wienken, or the long official silence with which the two churches regarded the 'euthanasia' programme. Indeed, much later Wienken claimed he had visited Galen to tell him that thanks to his own secret labours, the sermon had already been rendered superfluous.[75] Hitler certainly orally told Brandt to 'halt' the programme, with Brandt then telephoning Bouhler to pass on the instructions to Brack.[76] This did not apply to the 'children's euthanasia', which was extended to adolescents. Hefelmann recalled that Brack had passed on Hitler's 'temporary' halt order. Hefelmann had enquired whether this covered the children's 'euthanasia' programme. Brandt checked with Hitler. The latter said 'no', it did not.[77] Two equally pressing reasons may account for why the T–4 programme, if not the T–4 organisation, was halted. Firstly, by the summer of 1941 they had slightly exceeded their initial target figure of killing one chronic patient per thousand inhabitants of Germany. Secondly, in the summer of 1941 Viktor Brack was already exercising his mind on behalf of the Reichsführer-SS regarding how one might compulsorily sterilise large numbers of Jewish people in order to preserve their labour potential.[78] By the autumn, T–4 personnel were en route to Riga and Lublin, the former to construct gassing vans, the latter on loan to Odilo Globocnik, the organiser of 'Aktion Reinhard'. They were going there to deal with the millions of Jewish people deemed to lack labour value. The 'euthanasia' programme was not halted because of some local difficulties with a handful of bishops, but because its team of practised murderers were needed to carry out the infinitely vaster enormity in the East that the regime's leaders were actively considering.

PART THREE

'EUTHANASIA' AND RACIAL WARFARE

CHAPTER 6

SELLING MURDER: THE KILLING FILMS
OF THE THIRD REICH

THE MAKERS of the documentary film *Erbkrank* 'Hereditarily Ill, (1936) intended to criminalise, degrade and dehumanise the mentally and physically handicapped so as to justify compulsorily sterilising them. The film was made under the aegis of the Racial and Political Office of the National Socialist Party. Shown as part of the film's credits, the Racial and Political Office's emblem of two horses' heads facing outwards suggests fitness and fine breeding, oddly out of place in what follows in the ensuing twenty minutes. The officials appear fitfully in the film themselves: confident-looking, well-fed men in their thirties and forties, clean shaven and well groomed, wearing white doctors' coats. Although not the primary object of the film's attention, these men merit careful consideration, like the 'blank' spaces between figures in a painting or the pauses in a piece of music; for, after all, they orchestrated everything one sees in the film. They prowl in white coats and shiny boots behind nurses leading a ragged row of severely handicapped children up to and past the camera. They beckon patients towards the cameraman, or hold them there by means of a conversation we cannot hear, for *Erbkrank* is silent. They give patients an encouraging prod or shake to make them move, smile, or talk. They support others with spinal problems, the better to demonstrate helpless immobility, to show that if the patients move, they will fall – this being achieved with a matter-of-fact brutality common to medical training films in Germany at the time. These men are like stage hands or prompters in a theatre, manipulating the *mise-en-scène*.

Some patients join in this orchestration. A girl of eight or nine props up her younger sister's head for the camera. She even manages a fleeting, selfconscious smile. We know they are sisters, because the caption tells the viewer what it costs the state to keep them both alive. The patients seem shy rather than resentful of the camera. Maybe the arrival of the film crew was a big event in their lives, bringing fresh, unfamiliar faces and new activities to the familiar and routinised world of the asylum? When talking, they blink nervously, or keep their eyes focussed on the ground. Men doff or remove their caps and hats, for they are in the presence of authority. A few of the children act up for the camera. The blind, and the one lying in bed with atrophied legs, don't. Someone is telling the latter to move limbs which have long since ceased to move. The effort creases their faces with pain.

Watching this film one has to resist not just a sense of disgust towards its makers, but also against the sameness engendered by shaven heads, or (in the case of women) amateur and rudimentary haircuts; and by drab clothing – no collars on men's shirts, food spills on jackets and coats, cheap floral print dresses and shapeless cardigans, wooden clogs and scuffed shoes. Even if this film were not in black and white, there would be little or no colour in the people. This film is of a place where the very people are monochromatic. And there was somebody who selected and filmed these images: a man called Herbert Gerdes, from the Racial and Political Office. He jotted down basic symptoms and the duration of the person's institutionalisation, to be multiplied by the food and clothing bill to establish that individual's particular 'burden' upon the 'national community'. It was probably a trying day. The disturbed do not oblige by standing still or walking into view on cue. Gerdes probably rounded off a long day with location shots: wide views of imposing nineteenth-century buildings and panoramic sweeps of the surrounding landscape, a world of colour and smell – wasted, the film claimed, on the asylum's monochromatic inmates. Later, Gerdes carefully edited the film footage and interspersed additional material and captions. He made editorial decisions, deciding where to apply razor and cement, with all the enthusiasm of an amateur. The additional footage was of grimy 'normal' children playing tag in grim urban Hinterhöfe, with white washing billowing against a massed grey brick background. A grinning SA man is there as a representative of salvation. Then comes yet more film of the world of work, of digging and ploughing: in other words, a world not just different from, but expressly superior to, the 'feeding' (never 'eating') and 'playing' (with balls of wool or clocks) world of the asylum patients. The captions are a simple affair of white paint on black card, rather less artfully effective than the headlines on tabloid newspapers. Thicker brush strokes, underlining, and exclamation marks supply any required emphasis. They are given a sort of lurid shimmer whenever a word like 'Lustmord' is used to describe the activities of a sexual offender; for the film effortlessly blends prisons with psychiatric institutions, playing to existing prejudices. The captions become rhetorically strident as the film moves towards its inevitable conclusion. 'Should it go on like this?' 'No, No, NO, NEVER!' is the response.[1]

Let's get the tone and the line of argumentation through the captions of a film Hitler liked so much that he personally commissioned a more elaborate sound sequel:

Erbkrank

Away from the bustle of everyday life in an alluring landscape lies ... An asylum for the incurably mentally ill.

What casualness and frivolity have destroyed, what thoughtlessness and lack of conscience have handed down, is protected and cared for here.

Many of the mad have to be spoon-fed, or even fed artificially. Only a small proportion of the mentally ill can be trained to do productive tasks.

The majority are oblivious of their surroundings and of the passage of time.

Hereditary dropsy.

Hereditary schizophrenia.

Idiots are kept alive through medical science and the sacrifices of the nursing staff – idiots who for the entire duration of their lives cannot be taught to speak or to make themselves understood.

Special protective clothing prevents many of the patients from harming either their surroundings or themselves.

Hereditarily deaf and dumb and mentally ill.

Two brothers, both sexual offenders, with deformed hands.

The younger of them committed a SEXUAL MURDER.

Robber murderer who has evaded punishment up to now because of 'diminished responsibility'.

A large number of mental patients reach old age because of a nutritious diet and a healthy environment.

In the natural world, in the divinely ordained struggle for existence, they would have become extinct at the start.

A senseless play in their day's labour.

Against all the laws of nature, the unhealthy are cared for disproportionately, while the healthy are neglected.

Old men and women become indigent after a lifetime's productive hard work.

Young people cannot find any work and go to pot. Hereditarily healthy families have to live in badly lit and run-down slums.

Many mental patients produce children before they have been committed to an asylum, and in this way they pass on their suffering to their descendants.

Hereditarily ill father of three children.

This feebleminded woman has produced five illegitimate children.

The completely idiotic hereditarily ill father of three feebleminded children.

The sins of the fathers have been surreptitiously visited upon their children.

Themselves innocently wrecked in mind and body ... a burden to themselves and to others!

Chained to a bed for a lifetime.

Idiotic negro bastard from the Rhineland. Just as physical characteristics are passed on, so too are mental traits. What has been inherited from one's forefathers is passed on further to one's offspring.

GRAPHIC: Grandfather a sexual offender – both parents dissolute – seven of the ten children are still alive, and already four of them are in institutions.

Three brothers and sisters of this clan.

Feebleminded girl with a mentally ill mother. Grandfather weak nerves, father mentally ill and a feebleminded brother.

Up to now this clan has cost the state 62,300RMs.

Mother and son, both twenty-six years in institutions. Cost to date 29,016RMs.

Epileptic brother and sister. Cost to date 20,900RMs.

Two brothers; a third brother is an alcoholic and workshy – together, twenty-eight years in institutions. Cost to date 30,880RMs.

In many instances several members of an hereditarily ill clan are maintained in the same institution.

Four feebleminded brothers and sisters, together institutionalised for seventy-four years. Grandfather and father were disorderly and alcoholic. Cost to date 86,000RMs. The mother has produced ten children.

Expenditure on the mentally ill amounts to 1.2 thousand million RMs p.a. The administration of the Reich, federal states and communal government costs only 713 million RMs.

The institutionalisation of the chronically ill costs 112 million RMs p.a.

Identical twins, both stunted and retarded. Cost to date 10,200RMs.

Mother and daughter.

Two sisters.

Two brothers.

Mother and son.

Two sisters.

Identical twins, feebleminded, father a fraudster, mother a nervous alcoholic.

Acute case. Feebleminded brother and sister. Cost to date 13,800RMs. Parents: workshy vagrants.

Frequently cases of hereditary mental illness are accompanied by physical handicaps.

Idiotic deaf and dumb girl – there are four further deaf and dumb cases in her clan.

Feebleminded and deaf and dumb. Grandparents both deaf and dumb.

Brother and sisters, deaf and dumb and feebleminded. Cost to date 10,700RMs.

Mad and blind.

Mentally ill and lame. Chained to a bed for life.

Denial of the laws of nature and a false attitude towards Christianity means that criminals go unpunished. Rather, they are maintained in an institution provided one can establish diminished responsibility.

Thirty-seven-year-old fraudster.

Sexual offender.

Aided and abetted by his sister, this 'mental patient' committed the dastardly murder of his brother-in-law.

This twenty-eight-year-old murderer comes from a notorious criminal clan. Three siblings are also criminals.

Notorious criminal from a flawed clan, previous convictions for pimping and sexual offences, multiple robberies and sexual murders, institutionalised in an asylum for the last twenty-nine years.

Feebleminded thirty-year-old, with twelve previous convictions for theft and embezzlement.

This frequently convicted alcoholic has been in institutions for twenty-eight years. While on parole he committed a murder and an attempted murder.

Forty-four-year-old epileptic, multiple sex murders.

Foreign violent criminal.
Not every physically or mentally handicapped person is hereditarily ill ...
but all – even the apparently healthy – members of a hereditarily ill clan can be the
carriers of diseased hereditary properties.
The majority of their descendants end up in asylums or prisons.
Illegitimate idiot in institutions for the last twenty-two years. Cost to date
24,200RMS.
The sums which have hitherto been expended upon the insane, who are incapable
of a real life, would have provided the start-up housing capital for forty thousand
poor families, rich in children.
One leaves healthy families in semi-derelict housing and dank courtyards; but one
constructs palaces for the insane, who are totally oblivious to their surroundings.
Can we burden the coming generation with such an inheritance?
The prevention of hereditarily ill progeny is a moral imperative. It signifies
practical love for one's neighbour and the highest respect for the God-given laws
of nature.
The farmer who prevents weeds taking over promotes what is valuable.
Should things go on like this?
Should yet more distress be produced through casualness and irresponsibility?
No, NO, NEVER!
And for this reason we are carrying out the sterilisation of the hereditarily ill.
Their suffering must not be perpetuated in the bodies of their children.
Otherwise our great nation and its culture will be destroyed.[2]

The Racial and Political Office made five 16mm silent films, including
Erbkrank. These were *Sünden der Väter* ('Sins of the Fathers, 1935); *Abseits
vom Wege* ('Off the Path', 1935); *Erbkrank* (1936); *Alles Leben ist Kampf*
('All Life is a Struggle', 1937); and *Was du ererbt* ('What You Have
Inherited', date unknown). These films built upon, and adapted, the
propaganda techniques used in the handful of psychiatric films produced
in the 1920s. The latter were designed to justify institutional psychiatry to
a public alienated by the wartime starvation of patients and the therapeutic
abuse of shell-shocked soldiers.[3] The Nazis followed these films' emphasis
upon aesthetically attractive asylum settings and the alleged quality of
psychiatric treatment. Their own unique contribution was a filmic version
of techniques already pioneered in journals such as *Neues Volk* and *Volk
und Rasse*. The stark contrasting of a racial paradigm with its opposite; an
army of the unfit marginalising healthy 'national comrades'; the village
idiot or simian 'creatures' burdening the broad, honest-to-God shoulders
of the 'German' worker; slovenly, dipsomaniac females engendering
columns of drunks, murderers, prostitutes and vagrants from their well-
worn loins.[4] Still photographs and graphics were followed by slides, which
in turn were superseded by films of ever-increasing sophistication,
employing sound, interviews, cameo scenes, graphics, montage techniques, music and so forth. The mounting complexity of these films meant

ꞕier trägſt Du mit

Ein Erbkranker koſtet bis zur Erreichung des
60. Lebensjahres im
Durchſchnitt 50.000 RM.

(a)

the involvement of commercial film studios and the relevant department of
the Reich Propaganda Ministry.

'Victim of the Past' (*Opfer der Vergangenheit*) was a sound film produced
on Hitler's orders as a coproduction by the Racial Political Office and the
Reich Propaganda Ministry. Altogether a more professional and polished
piece of work than its exemplar *Erbkrank*, 'Victim' was made between
February and June 1936.[5] It was publicly premiered in Berlin in March
1937 and, following Hitler's intercession, shown on a compulsory basis in
all German cinemas thereafter. It is a more artful version of its prototype,
confidently mapping out the Social Darwinian cosmos.

The film begins with shots of lowering clouds, mountains, stormy seas
and fast-flowing rivers. Lumberjacks, ferrymen and labourers are shown

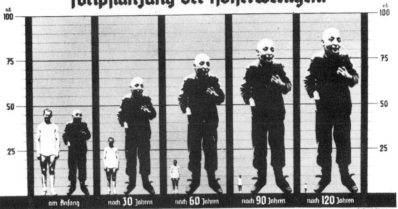

Qualitativer Bevölkerungsabstieg bei zu schwacher Fortpflanzung der höherwertigen.

So wird es kommen, wenn Minderwertige 4 Kinder und höherwertige 2 Kinder haben.

(b)

Plate 30. (a) 'You are bearing this too', informing the 'German worker' that a hereditarily ill person costs 50,000 RMs to maintain until he or she has reached the age of sixty; and (b) qualitative demographic decline due to a failure to reproduce on the part of the more 'valuable' sections of the population. After 120 years, the more 'valuable' would be hopelessly outnumbered by the 'unfit'. This type of fear-mongering regarding demographic and racial terrors, and appeals to base material self-interest, were taken over in subsequent propaganda films.

battling against the hostile elements to the accompaniment of a sub-Wagnerian musical score, which shifts from the darkly swirling to the lightly stirring. The film moves in the space of a few seconds from clouds, waves and the sweaty torsos of labourers, via a wild deer in a clearing, to the courtyard of a 'luxury', 'palatial' psychiatric asylum. The commentary smoothes these inherently ridiculous transitions:

All living things on this earth are engaged in a permanent struggle with the forces of nature. Only mankind subordinates the elements to his own ends and purposes. Wherever fate puts us, whatever station we must occupy, only the strong will prevail in the end. Everything in the natural world that is weak for life will ineluctably be destroyed. In the last few decades, mankind has sinned terribly against the law of natural selection. We haven't just maintained life unworthy of life; we have even allowed it to multiply. The descendants of these sick people look like this!

· 189 ·

Drawing upon the propaganda of the Weimar psychiatric lobby, the film placed far greater emphasis upon therapy than was the case with its exemplar:

A modern psychiatric asylum is not a prison. The buildings are usually situated in large, sunny gardens. Non-acute and harmless patients are kept occupied working in the fields and gardens, naturally under the constant supervision of trained warders. They are even entrusted with tools, naturally after prolonged observation. Every day the patients are escorted into the fresh, sunny air of the asylum grounds. Excitable patients are allowed to let off steam quietly in the open air. The patient cannot do any harm, since he is constantly observed by an orderly who can intervene at any given moment ... Twice a day the asylum doctor convinces himself of the wellbeing of his charges. There is one orderly for every five patients, and one doctor for every two hundred patients. Many of these patients will live to an old age because of this care and attention, which needs strong, healthy people to administer it. Their longevity costs thousands and thousands from the nation's resources. Healthy people have to perform arduous, often disgusting tasks, to ease the lives of these innocent victims wherever it is possible.[6]

'Victim' utilises the then unusual techniques of direct interviews to convey the inner mental confusion of the patients and to demonstrate the practice of institutional psychiatry. All of the patients are shown talking to doctors in pleasant outdoor settings. The patients' interlocutors are either brusquely aggressive or knowingly insinuating. A chubby, dark-haired woman is used to illustrate how 'even in illness a patient reveals her race through speech and gesture', i.e. she is Jewish. Talking half to the camera, half to the doctor perched behind her shoulder, the woman not unnaturally weaves about, answering the doctor's questions in a semi-joking manner, culminating in her 'Very interesting, these are private matters, why don't you tell me something about *your* life?' Every reference – to a Dr Marx, to Frankfurt am Main – and every gesture – hands on hips, head cocked back – is designed to convey 'Jewish' facetiousness. This theme is picked up and generalised a little later: 'The Jewish race is particularly heavily represented among the insane, and provision is made for their care too. Healthy German national comrades have to work to feed and clean up after them. Anyone who visits one of the larger asylums can establish this fact.'[7]

Borrowing liberally from the visual repertory of *Volk und Rasse*, the film directly contrasts healthy 'Aryan' nursing personnel with patients with physical abnormalities:

It is shocking to see a young healthy nurse next to such a pitiful creature. Nursing entails a degree of self-overcoming which should be regarded as almost heroic. Only totally healthy, fit girls are trained to be nurses. Twice a day the students in a state nursing school do sport to increase their powers of resistance for this difficult work, being ideologically and academically trained as assistants to the medical professionals.[8]

Doctors, described as 'the guardians of national hereditary health', are shown in their preventive role, through cameo scenes showing one of them advising a young couple about their genetic suitability. A general chat about the responsibilities of marriage leads on to the question of responsibilities to the hereditary collective:

DOCTOR Therefore it is important to have one's physical constitution and hereditary health tested, so that one may discover whether the hereditary disposition of one's forebears is worth passing on.
BRIDE Yes, that's why I've come to see you with my fiancé.
DOCTOR You see, in cases like this, the doctor is not just a healer, but a friend, an advisor, who will protect you and will prevent you making a mistake, even an unconscious one.
BRIDE Herr Doktor, you have a wonderful profession!
DOCTOR Yes. Do you think so?
BRIDE Yes.
DOCTOR Well, now we understand one another. Now let's take a look at your file.[9]

Any sceptical tittering among the audience about this absurd exchange is first encouraged, and then firmly countered, by the figure of 'the man from yesterday', an elderly reprobate who dismisses such counselling as being superfluous. His confident air towards the woman's fiancé in the waiting room is suddenly superseded by self-doubt once he is alone with the doctor.

A prurient interest is generated among the audience through commentary lines such as 'the German people hardly knows the full extent of this misery', or visual techniques which include filming through the spyholes on the doors of cells in secure wards or the bars of psychiatric prisons. Yet further scenes of human suffering prepare the way for the film's final message:

In future these poor creatures will no longer live alongside our healthy children. Sterilisation is a simple surgical operation. It is a humane method designed to spare the nation endless misery. The innocent should never suffer on account of the sins of the past. However, every honest and proud person will understand if we prevent these sins from becoming an endless chain. In the last seventy years our population has increased by 50%, while over the same period the number of hereditarily ill has risen by 450%. If this development continues, in fifty years there would be one hereditarily ill person for every four healthy people. An endless column of horror would march into the nation. Limitless despair would come upon a valuable population which would march towards its doom with giant steps. The Law for the Prevention of Hereditarily Diseased Progeny is not interference in divine law, but rather the restoration of a natural order which mankind has disrupted because of a false sense of humanity.[10]

So as not to leave audiences too depressed by these issues, the film ends with a rousing overview of a strong and healthy national community, showing the Hitler Youth and League of German Maidens, athletes and gymnasts, the various branches of the armed forces, the SS, and a beaming Hitler amidst his people at the 1936 Nuremberg Party rally.

Which common techniques and themes can be discerned in these hereditary health propaganda films of the 1930s? Most obviously, these films promote a crudely Social Darwinian view of life as a perpetual struggle for survival amidst a hostile natural environment. Apart from waves pounding rocks under lowering skies, several of these films introduce natural history footage of animals hunting or destroying one another. In the documentary film *Das Erbe* ('The Inheritance'), a young laboratory assistant joins a group of scientists viewing natural history footage accompanied by this commentary:

Nature carries out its merciless selection among these animals. The sick bird falls victim to the cat. The weak hare is caught by its pursuer. Even animals of the same species have their battles, in which the weaker falls victim to the stronger. Some female birds instinctively eliminate their poorly developed offspring.[11]

Eventually, even the *ingénue* female assistant grasps the point, exclaiming, as the professorial penny drops, 'So animals too pursue proper racial policy?' The inclusion of professors and doctors was obviously designed to lend these bleak tidings an air of authority and irrefutable scientific logic. Lest audiences confuse the professors with cinema's ubiquitous 'mad scientists', the scripts and treatments invariably characterise them as omniscient men of the world, straight of eye and firm of hand.[12]

The films' claims to scientific objectivity were in turn supported by appeals to resentment and common prejudice. We have already seen how the filmmakers contrasted conditions in supposedly luxury asylums with the squalid circumstances of many ordinary Germans. The films constantly detail the longterm cost of caring for patients, stressing how these sums might be better expended on housing projects for the socially disadvantaged – these arguments being designed to strike a chord among the nation's lower orders.[13] On a less overtly materialist plane, some of these films stress instead the squandering of youthful energy and idealism on the part of the nursing staff in asylums.

But how do these films achieve their primary objectives, namely degradation of the sick and the undermining of normal human sympathies among the viewers? As we saw earlier, patients were shown making a mess of their food and moving or speaking in abnormal ways. The filmmakers accentuated abnormalities by their choice of camera angle or lighting, using light from below, for example, to enhance facial deformities.[14] In addition to these obvious techniques, unexplained shifts in context were employed to erode instinctive sympathies with the disturbed or distressed. For example, people suffering from physical disabilities were visually

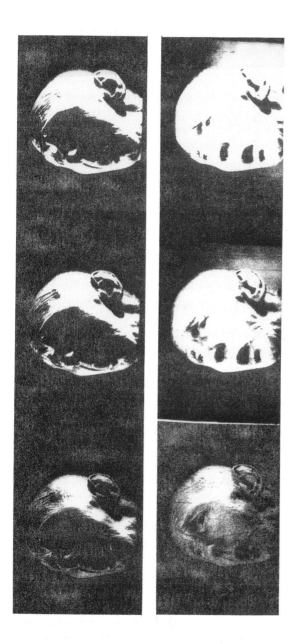

Plate 31. Sequence illustrating lighting techniques used in Nazi propaganda films. This sequence is from unedited footage. In the final version, the more 'normal' images would have been cut out.

aggregated together with the insane, who in turn were then visually elided with common criminals. The walls between asylum and prison become suggestively transparent. Popular resentment towards an allegedly liberal legal and penal system (everyday fare nowadays in rightwing US election broadcasts) is then fanned by suggesting that criminal offenders are effectively evading punishment: psychiatrists having declared that offenders acted with diminished responsibility, many of them are inevitably being let loose, on day release or parole, to commit yet more heinous offences.[15] Again inevitably, sex offenders, robbers and murderers figure prominently among the ranks of these criminals. Quite what these characters have to do with blind or handicapped children is naturally left undeveloped. All of these disconnected categories of people are subsumed under the rubric 'hereditarily ill' without any further explanation.

Most insidiously, these films deny the sick their human attributes and systematically seek to subvert received moral precepts. Apart from the ubiquitous epithet 'Erbkrank', the captions and commentaries in these films refer to the people being shown as 'beings', 'creatures', 'existences', 'idiots', 'life unworthy of life', 'travesties of human form and spirit', etc., etc. In some of these films they are explicitly situated a considerable way below the level occupied by animals, who are invariably depicted with greater affection and sensitivity – particularly if, as is the case with pedigree hunting dogs or racehorses, they are being used to illustrate the merits of selective breeding.[16]

Affection for thoroughbred animals was one thing; doting on domestic pets become child surrogates for single women quite another. The film 'What you have inherited' (*Was du ererbt*) includes a bizarre diatribe against female dog-owners, accusing them of wrongly diverting their procreative instincts towards the four-legged habitués of poodle parlours. The captions sternly admonish these urban sophisticates: 'An exaggerated love for an animal is degenerate. It doesn't raise the animal, but rather degrades the human being!'[17] In one or two of these films people are explicitly equated with animals, notably in *Erbkrank*, where a shaven-headed youth is shown eating handfuls of grass.

Human individuality is further disputed by a remorseless collectivism which reduces the person to a mere link in hereditary chains, valuable only in terms of the genetic properties he or she inherits and transmits to the future. The future is conceived purely in terms of the collective's capacity to wage war effectively against other nations. The deindividualised insane are wiped out of the picture by the deindividualised collective ranks of military and Nazi formations. Marriage and procreation are also deindividualised (and de-eroticised), becoming instead a duty to the all-important national community. Denial of the humanity of the people shown in these films would not be effective if the audience were allowed to retain its received moral norms and pre-Nazi values. Insidiously, the films appropriate the language of mercy, morality and religion in order to subvert them the more effectively. Mankind is shown 'sinning' against the 'law of natural selection', for welfarism is deemed counter-selective. Sterilisation becomes a 'moral command' and practical 'love for one's neighbour'. Christian teachings have been hitherto 'misunderstood'; scientific intervention is designed merely to 'restore' the laws of the Creator. The alleged 'natural' order must take precedence over a 'false sense of humanity'. Liberalism is regarded as a recent and temporary aberration. Hedonism, and a casual approach to procreation are comprehensively damned by these latterday puritans. At the very least, these conceptual sleights of hand would have sown some degree of moral confusion among the audience, opening up a few chinks in conventional morality alongside the (no doubt more successful) appeal to widely held prejudice. The constant emphasis upon 'natural laws' and hereditarian biology also served to propagate a certain passivity and helplessness in the face of problems which seemed to permit only a 'final' solution. An audience consisting of members of the Nazi Women's organisation came away horrified by what they had seen in *Erbkrank*, but also convinced that 'nothing could be done to alleviate it' through individual, as opposed to state, initiative.[18] These films did not need to make audiences into active apostles of compulsory sterilisation; they merely needed to render most people angry, impotent, and morally confused in the face of a 'problem' whose proportions were deliberately magnified so as to be beyond individual comprehension or resolution. Of course, there is no way of knowing how successful these films were in achieving this shorter-range goal, for evidence to the effect that audiences left these films with 'horrified' expressions on their faces is, to say the least, highly ambiguous. But just as it is important not to overestimate the effects of propaganda, so it is important not to underestimate its capacity for creating a moral void, as distinct from merely reinforcing the prejudices of a minority of its audience.

These documentary films were used by the organisers of the 'euthanasia' programme to induct their subordinates into the process of mass killing. The building worker Kurt Franz recalled that prior to his deployment at Hadamar, he had had to watch a film showing psychiatric patients 'who could scarcely be described as human'. This film was so shocking that he 'had to avert his gaze'.[19] Another recruit, Hermann Schweninger, was also shown a film, which seemed like 'an accumulation of fantasies'. Schweninger was a veteran of the Freikorps Epp who subsequently eked out a living in the lower echelons of the film industry and then as a travel guide and lorry driver. Brack, who had befriended Schweninger on a skiing holiday, recruited the latter as a front man for the Community Patients' Transport Service, with the assurance that he would be able to make

films.[20] These were to include a final account of the 'euthanasia' programme; propaganda designed to justify it; and lastly, scientific documentary films. For the time being, he was sent to the south-west to run the
transport of patients to the Grafeneck extermination centre. This experience was enough to convince him of the rectitude of the politics he was
helping to implement. Recalled to Berlin in the autumn of 1940, Schweninger was commissioned by Nitsche to visit several asylums in order to film
material to be used in documentaries for which Nitsche had already
mapped out a provisional treatment.[21]

The treatment was part psychiatric self-justification, part propaganda
designed to allay popular disquiet by showing the scrupulousness of the
T-4 selection process. The first part of the projected film was intended to
convey the costs of caring for the mentally ill, in a fashion already familiar
from the earlier RPA documentaries. A map would show the number of
asylums in the Reich, with a ground plan being used to convey the sheer
scale of one psychiatric institution. The asylums actually shown were
selected because of their aesthetic impact: 'Shots of particularly beautiful,
architecturally and aesthetically valuable asylums, for example Sonnenstein, Hubertusburg (beautiful, imposing castle site), Werneck near
Würzburg (castle probably by Balthaser Neumann), Leubus in Silesia.'[22]
Statistics showing the proliferation of asylums since 1880 were to be
accompanied by the number of patients and the scale of medical provision.
The second section of the treatment was designed to convey the extent of
human suffering within these institutions. Not just the suffering of
schizophrenics, idiots, epileptics, or patients in a state of paralysis –
though the treatment specifies several examples of these and other conditions – but also scenes showing the 'mental burden' which these patients
'imposed' upon their visiting relatives. Nitsche's third section emphasised
prevention – sterilisation and marriage counselling – and active therapy,
consisting of before-and-after scenes of patients being treated with drugs
or psychotherapy. This shaft of psychiatric light was then enveloped in the
Goyaesque gloom of 'the incurable and life-unworthy' to whom the final
section of the film was to be devoted. The film was to show the percentages
of longterm patients, including the small number of the latter deemed to
be capable of work. It would then dilate upon the expenditure in terms of
money and manpower devoted to the care of these 'Ballastnaturen'. These
scenes paved the way for a detailed look at the processes of selection from
the completion of registration forms in the asylums – i.e. establishing the
patient's 'social worth' – to the central selection procedures used at T-4.
The film would conclude by showing the 'course of the action'.[23]

Nitsche corresponded with his colleague Heyde regarding the statistical
material to be used in the film. Regional governments were to supply
information regarding the area taken up by asylums or the costs of building

work to extend them. In conversation with Nitsche, Professor Carl Schneider recalled existing film, dealing with psychiatric patients, which might have an exemplary function for these current projects. Hans Hefelmann sent memos to Heyde, drawing his attention, *inter alia*, to 'the asylum for idiots in Kramsach in the Tyrol which houses 70 idiotic children who would provide particularly exemplary film material'.[24] Nitsche gave Schweninger copious instructions, requiring him to film children next to adults, or retarded patients against a background of landscaped gardens.

Armed with treatment and tips, Schweninger and a producer lent by the Tobis Film group set off on a tour of twenty or thirty asylums to find suitable locations. Apart from the (in the event) elusive search for 'luxury' asylums, the itinerary seems to have been plagued by impromptu excursions brought on by sudden intelligence of yet more appalling cases of human suffering. On the actual shoot, Schweninger, Stoppler and their crew had to hurry to the asylum concerned to film the subjects before they disappeared into the gas chambers. It is known for certain that on 1 and 2 November 1940 they were filming in the paediatric ward at Eglfing-Haar and then at the psychiatric section of the Kaiser Wilhelm Institute in Munich.[25] Over a considerable period, Schweninger shot about ten thousand metres of material, much of it with sound, which could then be edited into various filmic formats.

The main projects which resulted from this material were the educational film 'Existence without Life' (*Dasein ohne Leben*) and the scientific documentary 'Mentally Ill'. Both films dealt explicitly with the theme of medicalised murder, with one of them cold-bloodedly detailing the actual process of selection and killing. 'Existence without Life' was probably completed in the course of 1941, as it was shown, along with the raw material Schweninger had shot, grouped now along rough thematic lines, to a select audience on 10 March 1942.[26] Until recently, all of this material was known only in the form of various draft treatments, the films themselves having vanished. Eight of the twenty-three rolls of film Schweninger shot for these films, complete with soundtracks, were discovered in 1989–1990 by the author in Potsdam.[27]

The script for 'Existence without Life' survives in two separate versions, one rather fragmentary, with further written suggestions for alterations by Nitsche. The first version consists appropriately enough, of a lecture by a Professor Kämpfer to an audience of students, although the script is quick to point out that the lecture deals with a 'question of humanity which concerns us all'. The Professor, described in the script as having 'intelligent, kind eyes' as opposed to being 'an alienated bookworm', begins with a *tour d'horizon* of the history and practice of institutional psychiatry. Montage techniques are used to conjure forth

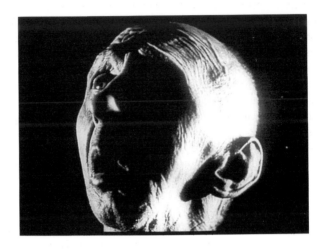

Plate 32. One of the interview subjects filmed by T–4. Direct sound interviews were relatively unusual at this time. In this sequence, the subject is interviewed while wearing a straitjacket. First employed in *Opfer der Vergangenheit*, these interviews were designed to denigrate mental patients.

'demonically mad faces' about whom the Professor pronounces: 'An existence without life. These are the realisation of today's highly developed psychiatry.' A brief history of the discipline ensues, ranging fluently from eighteenth-century madhouses to the achievements of Emil Kraepelin (1856–1926), one of the founding fathers of psychiatric nosology. The audience is constantly bombarded with statistics concerning the sheer extent of contemporary psychiatric provision, with occasional asides to emphasise its utter futility: 'How well-intentioned: the sick are supposed to enjoy the first rays of Spring sunshine! [The scene shifts from the park at Werneck to the ward for disturbed women at Lohr.] But the behaviour of these retarded or disturbed women reveals no rapport with their surroundings.'[28]

The Professor moves on to the beneficial effects achieved in some cases by occupational or more direct forms of therapy: gardening and potato-peeling for some, insulin and electrocardiazol shocks for others. While the attention of two of the students is temporarily diverted by a reproduction of a Goya madhouse interior hanging on the lecture theatre wall, the Professor returns to the subject of the high percentage of patients catego-rised as 'incurable'. Interviews with a selection of these 'unfortunates' are used to convey the extent of their inner madness. The interviewees included a woman 'with the taste of a murdered head', who appears in the raw film material discovered in Potsdam, where she is seen explaining her delusion of seeing and then tasting her own murdered head. Borrowing freely from some of the themes explored in the earlier RPA documentaries, the Professor dwells upon the 'greatness of spirit' evinced by nursing staff who voluntarily 'bury themselves alive in such houses of pain'. Inevitably, it is 'unnatural and intolerable in terms of a higher morality that entire generations of young fit people grow old in caring for the incurably mad and idiots'. What is the point, the Professor asks, of keeping such 'creatures' alive? Freely wearing his emotions on his sleeve, the Professor says how 'heartrending' it is to see brain-damaged and handicapped children, posing the question 'What shall become of these innocent victims?' to which he, inevitably, has the only answer. A 'merciful destiny' is invoked to 'liberate' these 'pitiful creatures' from their 'existence without life'. Appealing to 'humanity', the Professor invokes the Law for the Prevention of Hereditarily Diseased Progeny, before finally passing on to his personalised peroration. In the eventuality that he should ever find himself in the condition of the people shown in the film, the Professor would 'rather die', indeed, 'I would thank whoever would help me to die.' Every healthy person, indeed every incurable patient and idiot, would agree with him. With his words accompanied by a musical furioso, the Professor – by now enlarged so that his eyes and forehead fill the screen – bursts into a passionately self-righteous exterminatory frenzy:

Isn't it the duty of those concerned to help the incapable – and that means total idiots and incurable mental patients – to their right?
Is that not a sacred command of charity?
Deliver those you can't heal!
The Director of a large mental institution asked this question of the parents of all his incurable charges.
73% answered 'Yes'.
A mother wrote: 'Don't ask, do it!' [this citation literally burning on the screen].[29]

The second version of 'Existence without Life' is a less elaborate rewrite of the early parts of another script which is no longer extant. Beginning with a bucolic sunrise, the film moves swiftly through woods, along viaducts and autobahns to a factory where the audience would have seen people at work. The commentary ominously intones: 'The destiny of the individual is merely a small, insignificant destiny. The nation's destiny remains decisive.' Passing from office workers to a sculptor's studio, the script dwells upon health and sickness, the latter leading into the chilling thought: 'The sick are human beings in exile. They deserve our pity. They deserve even more. They deserve mercy. Nature was always more ruthless than civilised mankind, because it operates according to ineluctable laws! It decrees that the weak are subordinate to the strong, that everything weak or sick is eradicated and exterminated! That is a sacred command.

And this command has always existed.' Shots of 'degenerate' modern art dissolve into images of psychiatric patients shown in ever closer focus. The sick, we are told, stand 'outside the community', pitiable beings who deserve our care, 'if it is possible to help them'.[30]

Nitsche's corrections are the third and final written source for 'Existence without Life'. Practising the neurologists' version of having one's cake and eating it, Nitsche attempted to perform the delicate task of writing up the therapeutic value of modern psychiatry while simultaneously stressing the fact of incurability. He was also keen to spell out that the sick were both a burden upon, and a danger to, the community. Modern psychiatry, he claimed, was able to pacify difficult patients with occupational therapy, while insulin and electroshock treatment were achieving results in cases where the illness had been detected in its early stages. Without bothering with facts, figures or percentages, Nitsche remarked that 'admittedly, these new forms of cure fail in many cases'. The asylums were filling with incurable cases, whose symptoms were merely being suppressed by lavish medical attention. It was a thankless labour of Sisyphus. The rest of Nitsche's suggested improvements dwelt upon the causes of certain categories of mental illness.[31]

The second projected documentary film, for which Schweninger and Nitsche were responsible, was the scientific film 'Mentally Ill', for which Schweninger's treatment of 25 October 1942 survives in two versions, one for a lay and one for an academic audience. Twenty-three rolls of film were available to cut into this form, with four reserve rolls, two of which were interviews with professors in Heidelberg (Schneider) and Munich (Nitsche himself). 'Mentally Ill' begins with a history of insanity, culminating with the achievements of contemporary psychiatry. In keeping with all the examples we have been considering, the film stresses the cost of psychiatric care (with the aid of graphics), and the problem of incurability. Schweninger attempts to emulate Nitsche's delicate balancing act between extolling the achievements of modern therapy and wishing to eradicate 'hopeless cases':

It is totally impossible to do anything about brain damage or to eradicate hereditarily determined illness. However, in many cases, especially when the patient receives specialist medical treatment at an early stage, it is possible to alleviate some of the symptoms of the illness. These scenes, taken before, during and after treatment, show how powerful the effects of treatment can be. Many of them can return to life outside and can resume their former occupations. However, most of the patients are incurable and must remain in asylums for the rest of their lives.[32]

This argument is given a further fatalistic twist:

Incurably mentally ill! The most terrible fate that can befall a person, because they can neither recover nor die! They must remain in their hopeless condition, passing away the decades, frequently on account of so-called care, in an existence which medical provision frequently prolongs. They have to vegetate in an existence which no longer has anything in common with the purpose and value of human life.[33]

The cards of the new morality are displayed openly on the table in an explicit attack on received precepts:

Yes, they must! Because the exaggerated concern for humanity evinced during the last two hundred years, coupled with a religion which is alienated from reality, have given rise to medical ethics, still current today, which make it the task and duty of the doctor to preserve the life of every person under all circumstances and in all cases, even when that life has long since forfeited the purpose and character of human life.[34]

This text was accompanied by Schweninger's repertoire of women imagining consuming their own murdered heads, etc., as well as close-focussed images of encephalitic children or adults suffering from Down's Syndrome. These images were used to provide an 'irrefutable' case for the measures adopted by the National Socialist state, i.e. T–4. A highly sanitised version of these measures, which repeatedly stressed their fail-safe scientific character, went as follows:

[Montage and graphics to show registration and refereeing.]
Thus an organisation has been created, which for the first time in Germany will carry out the central registration of every mental patient in an asylum.
A commission of specialist doctors, acting as referees, will examine the history and previous diagnoses of the patients to establish the incurability of those who are to be delivered through death in the course of these measures.
Dubious or doubtful cases will be further assessed by senior referees.
[Shots of Grafeneck and Hartheim.]
Those patients whose incurability has been established beyond any doubt will be taken to specially converted asylums.
[Arrival and unloading of patients.]
[Doctor goes through ward.]
In these special asylums the patients will be carefully re-examined by the asylum doctor, who will also examine their case history and previous diagnoses in order to prevent all possibility of a mistake or biased decision by the referees.
[Investigatory commission.]
And so the day of deliverance for the patient arrives. Once more the personal and medical details of the patient are checked and established under the supervision of the asylum doctor.
[Photograph.]
Photographs of the patient are taken for archival purposes.
[Gas chamber.]
[Intercut to turning on of valve, gasometer, observation by a doctor.]
In a hermetically sealed room the patient is exposed to the effects of carbon monoxide gas.

The gas which streams in is totally odourless and initially robs the patient of his powers of judgement and then of consciousness.
Without pain or struggle, and totally unnoticed by the patient, the deliverance of death takes effect.
[Before and after.]
The tortured face and distorted inhuman form of the unfortunate suffering from incurable mental illness is smoothed into repose through the peace of a gentle death which finally brings the salvation of deliverance![35]

The reality that this 'text' envisaged was described by Schweninger in October 1970:

During a gassing in Sonnenstein I had the only opportunity of filming through an observation window. The patients were led into a room which looked like a large bathroom. The doctor closed the doors and opened the valve ... It looked as though the patients slowly went to sleep. Many of them sank down and several collapsed. It did not last long. I believe that once shots were done of a patient being gassed in bed. As far as I can remember it was a particularly bad case.[36]

Rumbling opposition to the actual 'euthanasia' programme led to an intensified interest in feature rather than documentary films. The *pièce justificative* which preambled the treatment for one such feature film explained:

We were given the task of writing a script for a film about euthanasia, about the extinguishing of unworthy life. Because of the circumstances of the time, we became convinced that it was necessary to avoid everything which seemed like deliberate propaganda, but also everything which hostile opinion could construe as a threat emanating directly from the state. In our film we have let the dictates of the heart speak in the belief that this will pave the way for the dictates of the law.[37]

These feature films therefore had two purposes: to prepare the ground for anticipated changes in the law on 'mercy killing', and to envelop the fact of the state murdering the mentally and physically ill on a mass basis in a cloud of sentimentality about individual ethical dilemmas. The object was not, as Viktor Brack would later claim, to stimulate a debate about Nazi policy, but rather to divert popular disquiet into a discussion of the actions of characters in what amounted to soap operas. Three detailed treatments of this type are extant, all probably written by the ubiquitous Hermann Schweninger.

The first, entitled 'Three People' (*Drei Menschen*), has as its epigraph Nietzsche's dictum 'What causes more suffering in the world than the stupidity of the compassionate?' The storyline, set in Thuringia or Swabia in 1931 and 1932, concerns a psychiatrist, Dr Hans Gontard, who is in love with an actress, Maria Hansen. Their conventionally platonic relationship is disturbed with the arrival of Gontard's childhood friend, the dynamic and successful actor Michael Haas, who comes to town to play Romeo opposite Maria's Juliet. Michael sets about converting what has become a three-way friendship into a two-way love affair between himself and Maria. Michael makes his move on Maria during a bathing expedition by deliberately mislaying Gontard's swimming trunks so that the hapless psychiatrist is forced to remain beachbound looking for them. Maria returns from bathing preferring Michael's favourite music – the second movement of Beethoven's Fifth Symphony – to Gontard's – the first movement. Having quickly conquered Maria, Michael secures a longterm contract in the town. The lovelorn psychiatrist meanwhile seeks consolation in the company of his superior, Professor Nitsche(!), a 'master of life'. It transpires that Nitsche once treated Michael's father, an industrialist who committed suicide, in whom he diagnosed degenerative schizophrenia. Nitsche introduces Gontard to the Haas family's medical records, recalling that 'something wasn't quite right either' in the case of Michael's grandfather. The genetic horror story is completed with the intelligence that an uncle of Michael's had produced a feebleminded child. Therefore, Michael must be 'severely hereditarily burdened, even though he may make a totally healthy impression on the exterior and enjoy great success in his profession'. Gontard confronts Michael with this information just when the actor arrives to announce his intention of marrying Maria, helpfully suggesting that Michael devote himself to art rather than thoughts of reproduction. Michael not unnaturally suspects nefarious motives. He dismisses the evidence of the medical records as a product of 'doctor's fantasies', of a madness engendered by regular professional communion with the insane. 'Destiny.' the script tells us, 'takes its course.'

Despite his having designated Michael a walking genetic disaster area, the couple eventually make Gontard godfather of their first child. Michael and Maria depart on a prolonged theatrical tour. Upon their return they are gradually forced to accept that their eight-month-old baby is devoid of any normal human reactions. Gontard is on hand to confirm Michael's worst fears about the health of his son, suggesting that the actor give it another four months to be certain about the provisional diagnosis. During that period, Michael tries ever more desperate stratagems to elicit any reaction from the child. He dresses up as a clown, jumping up and down in front of the cot, with his maniacal laughter ringing through the house. Nitsche confirms Gontard's diagnosis: the child is irremediably subnormal. A pall descends on the marital home, with the oppressive silence of the nursery pervading everywhere. Encouraged by an aunt to discount the verdict of the psychiatrists, Michael uses the opportunity provided by the coming of Christmas to try once again to stimulate his child. The couple try singing carols; Michael dangles the Star of Bethlehem in front of his son's eyes. Realising that this is having no effect, Michael seizes the Christmas tree, holds it high above his head, and then throws it – the candles have set the tree aflame – across the room. In yet another interview with Nitsche, Michael asks the professor to put an end to his son. Nitsche refuses 'because to me, being a doctor means helping'. Michael counters this by asking:

'And who are you helping with your compassion, with the mercy of your asylum . . .? Are you helping the incurably ill . . .? Are you helping the parents, the relatives?' Looking out of the window he observes: 'Nature helps itself.' Turning back towards the room he concludes: 'But we humans use science to prolong suffering, where we could use science to bring deliverance.'[38]

Touching on one of the key themes of the treatment, Nitsche coolly comments: 'The dictates of emotion may be on your side, Herr Haas, but the law isn't.'

Michael and Maria continue their professional careers, seemingly typecast as Romeo and Juliet. During a performance of the play, Michael slips out of the theatre between scenes, driving in costume to the family home. There he kills his son. He returns to the theatre to complete his performance in the play. Upon returning home, Maria finds Gontard playing Beethoven on the piano. The three sit around the fire, where Michael dementedly soliloquises upon the characteristics of that element, until he eventually confesses to his act of murder. The scene shifts frenetically between the fireside and flashbacks to Nitsche gravely explaining the hereditary history of the Haas family. Finally, Michael says 'I have killed our child.' Michael makes his exit through the deserted town, with the pale moonlight bringing an unfamiliar calm to his face, 'accompanied and led on his arduous way by the earthily portentous beats of Beethoven'.

Assuming that it was not intended as a farce, much is wrong with 'Three People'. The main character, Michael, is clearly mentally unbalanced, unable to bear being the father of a subnormal child. Dressing up as a clown, hurling Christmas trees, and leaving an entire theatre in the lurch while he drives off to commit a murder are the actions of a maniac. The incident with the bathing trunks, and the way in which he uses the play as an alibi, also suggest a certain degree of low cunning. If Michael is an unsatisfactory protagonist for the ideas of 'euthanasia' (why did he not just put the child in a home or asylum, and why does he run away if he believes so strongly in the legitimacy of his own actions?), the psychiatric duo are not much better. Gontard is lacklustre and embittered, and derives too much obvious satisfaction from Nitsche's damning collective diagnosis of the Haas dynasty. Together, the two are a thoroughly unappetising pair, with their knowing laughs virtually reducing them to the status of pantomime villains. Worst of all, the two doctors assume an essentially passive role in the final 'tragedy', leaving it to a deranged actor to take the decisive action. Maria Hansen is merely colourless, a puppet passed around between Gontard and Michael. Scenes that are supposed to be high drama are profoundly farcical, with any (limited) dramatic interest being derived from Shakespeare or Beethoven. The seasons and time pass interminably, with the aid of lavish meteorological effects or that old standby, the desk calendar.

Schweninger's second effort was entitled 'The Foreman'.[39] An industrious foreman has high aspirations for his eldest son. The latter has a terrible accident resulting in permanent brain damage. The doctors agree that death would have been the preferred outcome. The father's health, productivity and sanity begin to suffer as he agonises about whether to put his son in an asylum. He decides to do this. A visit to the asylum convinces him that it would be better if the son died. (This was probably the cue for the interjection of documentary footage of patients in asylums.) The doctor there acknowledges the justice of this, but feels bound by the dictates of an (outmoded) legal code. The foreman's workmates favour 'mercy killing', denouncing laws which are 'alien to life and nature'. The foreman removes the son from the asylum and kills him. He surrenders himself to the authorities. His wife is horrified by his actions and decides to divorce him. The factory 'leader' hires a famous lawyer, who uses the case to lobby for a new law sanctioning 'euthanasia'. An indulgent panel of judges decides that 'it is impossible today to condemn the killing of such unfortunate creatures as murder, when tomorrow it might be permitted, indeed even ordered, in some other form by a new law'. The foreman receives the minimum statutory penalty of two months' imprisonment, and is reconciled with his wife, who finally acknowledges his 'noble motives'. The foreman is promoted.

Considerably shorter than 'Three People', this treatment had other merits over its predecessor. A terrible accident was altogether more accessible as a stimulus for debate than the dubious and possibly *parti pris* diagnosis of hereditary illness deployed in 'Three People'. The protagonist in 'The Foreman' was also more plausible as a figure with whom audiences could identify than Michael Haas had been in 'Three People'. Opponents of 'euthanasia' could also (temporarily) identify with the mother, at least up to the point when she undergoes a conversion. A final courtroom drama was a good way of rehearsing the ethical and legal arguments. Despite these promising aspects, the characters were hopelessly one-dimensional, and the film would have lacked the (slight) elements of romance fitfully present in its predecessor. Wolfgang Liebeneiner, the director already chosen to make a feature film about 'euthanasia', found ways of not making 'The Foreman'.

By this time, Schweninger had been directed towards Helmuth Unger's novel 'Vocation and Conscience', first published in 1936. Unger, an ophthalmologist by profession, was the author of fifty books on great scientists, plays and novels. He had been active in the 'euthanasia' pro-gramme since 1939 as an assessor.[40] His feet were already through the door into the film world, since in 1939 Tobis Films had used his book on Robert Koch as the basis for their eponymous biopic. Schweninger took Unger's successful epistolary novel and began turning it into a film treatment entitled 'I Accuse' *Ich klage an.*[41] The main difference between the treatment and its prototype was simply that Schweninger dropped the epistolary format and introduced a married couple to hang the action on.

'I Accuse' was to be set in and around a landed estate in Brandenburg owned by Baron and Baroness von Passow. Baroness Lena seeks out Professor Terstegen, the chief physician in the local hospital, in order to get strychnine to put down her old, blind and lame hunting dog, Caesar. The scene is observed by one of Terstegen's subordinates. The Professor argues that a bullet would be a more honourable end for such a faithful companion; Lena accordingly shoots old Caesar. She is assisted in this task by the old fisherman Wollanke, who not unnaturally enquires:

WOLLANKE Why didn't the lord and master do it himself? This isn't a job for a woman!
LENA Ah, Wollanke, he has no love for animals, and he has long forgotten the service the dog did for him.
WOLLANKE (softly) He has forgotten many other things too.
LENA What do you mean?
WOLLANKE I only mean that her ladyship has not been happy herself for a long while.
LENA When one loves a man one wants to be everything to him, but he doesn't need me. He almost doesn't notice me any more. The dog and perhaps I have become useless items.
WOLLANKE I didn't wish to upset her ladyship.
LENA No, Wollanke, you haven't.[42]

These intimations that all is not well in the Passow marriage are confirmed by scenes dominated by the Baron's boorish and drunken behaviour. The Baron is eventually thrown from a horse while riding to hounds. Terstegen is brought in to treat the unconscious Baron. He predicts that the patient will either die after a couple of days or, worse, remain alive:

'insensate like a beast. No, much worse. It is hell. Daily, hourly, no every minute … He will be only a wreck of a human being. He won't recognise you, his surroundings, his friends, nor have any pleasure in being alive. He may well see things with his eyes, but he will not recognise them. He may still hear things, but he will not understand these noises. If you want my opinion, I'd rather be dead than live like that, as a burden upon others, especially those whom I love most. He will require permanent attention, but will never be able to express his gratitude for it. It is a life so meaningless that one would regard the deliverance of death as a gift and as an act of grace.'[43]

Pondering this awful fate, the Baroness suddenly recalls one of the Baron's moments of lucidity, in which she believes she discerned his desire to die:

'And if you knew him, you would know that a man like this can never lie there vegetating. He cannot be a cripple, either physically or mentally. He was never a weakling, and only weaklings beg heaven for mercy. He only had one desire: call me a doctor who has the courage to give me a drug so that I can die painlessly in my sleep.'

Terstegen resolves to 'help' the Baron. Rather confusingly, the (comatose) Baron then rallies round a final time to inform his wife that he hates her and that he has never expressed a desire for her assistance in dying. This angry exchange is overheard by a servant. The Baron passes away. In order to preempt charges likely to ensue from the sickbed conversations now doing the rounds among the village gossips, Terstegen informs his assistant Lang that he is going to bring charges against himself: 'I will accuse myself! I accuse!' He even obliges the (sympathetic) public prosecutor by surrendering a dossier which reveals that he has acted in the same way in dozens of other cases: 'Certainly I have contravened the letter of the law. But in my view there is something higher than the letter of the law. There are moral imperatives to which one is more duty bound than the stipulations of lawyers.'

With the ethics of the case occupying the habitués of the *Stammtisch* at the village inn, old Wollanke the fisherman (become folk philosopher) is wheeled out once more to put the crudely Social Darwinist view:

'I've never really considered whether one ought or ought not to allow people to die. But what must be right for an animal must be right for a human being. In the natural world, in which I've lived for seventy years now, there is a remorseless law. Everything that is weak is overwhelmed and destroyed by the strong. Everything weak dies and everything strong stays alive.'[44]

The case eventually comes to trial, with the issues being rehearsed again and again both in Terstegen's cell with his lawyer and on the bench of jurors, although some of the latter would prefer a case of murder or robbery, 'since with that one at least knows where one is at'. During the trial every conceivable argument is used to justify 'mercy killing'. Other places – Illinois, Denmark, Great Britain – have introduced or debated the problem of 'euthanasia'. The public prosecutor produces Terstegen's dossier, and a juror's interest is suddenly aroused: 'This is a real mass murderer. I would never have believed it.' Terstegen's career in killing began, it transpires, as a result of his failure to 'help' his cancer-ridden mother. Flashbacks are used to sketch in Terstegen's humble working-class origins and the selflessness of his mother, who skimped and saved to

put him through university. His punctilious adherence to ethical convention meant that his mother died in terrible pain. His next encounter with
'euthanasia' occurred in wartime France, where an old schoolfriend,
Thom, arrives shot to pieces in Terstegen's field hospital. After remi-
niscing about games of cops and robbers and Red Indians and Trappers,
Terstegen resolves to put Thom out of his misery:

THOM (laughing) [!] Can I sleep now?
TERSTEGEN Yes, comrade.
THOM Did we save our position?
TERSTEGEN We even took prisoners.
THOM You must write that to Hilde.
TERSTEGEN Yes.
THOM And love from me! Write that everything is well.[45]

Terstegen's ever more fanatical account of his practice of 'euthanasia'
begins to take hold of the onlookers in the courtroom. The latter becomes a
forum for the adumbration of an idea which has assumed human form.
The possibility that the professor might occasionally make a mistake – a
thought tentatively raised by the presiding judge – is dismissed with the
platitude 'to err is human, and doctors are human too'. The business about
Lena von Passow requesting strychnine is shown to be based upon a
misunderstanding – it was for the dog Caesar, not her husband – and Lena
confirms that she relayed the Baron's request to die to the professor.
Terstegen explains away the Baron's sudden change of heart by putting it
down to the soothing effects of his (fatal) dose of morphia. The issues
raised by the trial are rehearsed by the jurors, who decide to acquit the
professor. After the trial, Lena von Passow visits Terstegen. Despite his
acquittal, the professor is dissatisfied with the outcome: 'I would have
liked to have fought the struggle for the legitimisation of mercy killing to
the end. Perhaps a younger man will do it now, someone even more
dedicated to doing so. When he wins, he will have achieved something
worthwhile, because everything is good that serves the wellbeing of
humanity. Do you understand me?' The film treatment ends with hawks
circling above old Wollanke as he fishes against a backdrop of spruce trees
in the twilight. Any symbolic connection between the hawks and Terstegen was no doubt unintentional
    Like its predecessors, this treatment was unusable. The poor state of the
Passows' marriage would lead any audience to suspect foul play. Terstegen, who in the treatment confesses to having killed four or five people,
but who in the book notches up a final tally of fifty, nonetheless seems
rather quick to resort to bullets and morphia. The public prosecutor is
virtually on Terstegen's side, and the character of the latter's assistant,
Lang, is not developed as a vehicle for arguments against 'euthanasia'. The

Plate 33. Wolfgang Liebeneiner. The star director who made 'I Accuse'. The close interest T–4 had in 'I Accuse' was reflected in the fact that Viktor Brack inserted certain key scenes, while Philipp Bouhler visited the set to check the crucial jury scenes where the arguments for 'euthanasia' were rehearsed by a panel of 'ordinary' people.

Baron's desire to die is relayed secondhand, while his subsequent plea to live seems more in keeping with his drunken hedonism. Like its predecessors, 'I Accuse' is boring and manifestly the work of someone quite devoid of any dramatic sensibility.

Nonetheless, these treatments supplied certain ideas and themes which merely required a more skilful touch than Schweninger and his academic accomplices possessed. The KdF decided to call in a professional, the up-and-coming Tobis director Wolfgang Liebeneiner. Liebeneiner read Unger's material – presumably as rewritten by Schweninger – and decided he could do little with it. Viktor Brack agreed, and suggested that both of them get together with Hefelmann and the real Professor Nitsche to discuss the whole issue of 'euthanasia'. Liebeneiner spent a night with an eminent neurologist in order to find an illness appropriate to the film's weighty moral concerns.[46] Simultaneously, Harald Bratt, the chief dramatist at Tobis, came up with a concise storyline which went as follows:

> Two doctors love a woman. She marries one of them. As she falls ill with multiple sclerosis, she asks one of them to kill her. He turns her down. Thereupon she asks the other, who does her bidding. A trial results, in which the case is discussed.

This outline was worked up into a script by the writers Georg Fraser and Eberhard Frowein, and then reworked by Brack and Liebeneiner, the latter almost Wagnerian in his desire to eradicate anyone else's authorship of his *Gesamtkunstwerk*. The result was the film 'I Accuse', which he began to direct on 21 March 1941.[47] Filming lasted about two months. The substance of the film was described in the *Illustrierte Filmkurier*:

> Professor Heyt and his young wife Hanna lead a happily married life. The Professor has worked his way up from humble origins to the position of a scientist, which has permitted him to have a more comfortable lifestyle. A party held to mark the Professor's appointment as head of a world-famous research institute further reinforces the couple's happiness. During a musical recital, Hanna is suddenly forced to stop playing the piano because her left hand stops functioning. As the paralysis continues during the following days, Professor Heyt calls in their friend Dr Lang to examine Hanna. With the aid of an ophthalmoscope, Dr Lang diagnoses multiple sclerosis, an illness which results ineluctably in decline and death. The condition of the young woman visibly deteriorates. Professor Heyt regards finding the cause of the disease as his greatest challenge. His work results in other, important scientific discoveries, but he does not find a means of saving Hanna. It seems to be the end for the young woman. She suffers indescribable pain and is beyond help. The Professor resorts to desperate measures. The soothing drink which he gives her results in her death. 'Oh Thomas, if only that was death!' she says, and he answers in a voice which encompasses all his love, but also total responsibility: 'Yes, Hanna, it is death!' Profound gratitude radiates from her eyes as she passes away. Serious accusations are made against the Professor; these result in a trial on charges of death on demand. His friend Dr Lang, who initially condemns his deed and is hostile towards him, becomes Professor Heyt's supporter because of scenes of indescribable misery he has to witness in a mental institution. The court and the jurors endeavour to engineer an acquittal. Up to then Professor Heyt had remained silent. But now he accuses, as he sees that the charges against him are about to be dropped. Following his fiery speech, Professor Heyt asks for the verdict.[48]

'I Accuse' was powerfully lit, with smooth and graceful camera-work. It has a memorable and moving score by Norbert Schultze, one of the leading popular composers of the day. Both the major players and the character actors who did the minor parts were well known to German cinemagoers: Paul Hartmann, Matthias Wiemann, Heidemarie Hatheyer, Charlotte Thiele, Albert Florath and so forth. Hartmann quickly establishes Heyt as the embodiment of dedication and integrity – with appropriate demonstrations of tenderness to his flibbertigibbet wife – while Wiemann makes Lang into a conscientious and sympathetic physician, going about Christlike amongst the humble and suffering. Having said this, none of the main players invests the material with the electric screen presence and understated skill of Ingrid Bergman or Spencer Tracy – whom one could imagine in similar roles: but the cast of 'I Accuse' put what lesser talent they possessed into their performances. Despite the high drama of the storyline, the end effect is curiously cold and unmoving, even if one knows nothing of the film's background and ulterior agenda.

The film is essentially a fusion of such popular genres as triangular love story, medical drama and courtroom drama.[49] These carry the minimal argument for voluntary 'euthanasia'. Several elements have simply been taken over from the three treatments developed by Schweninger. The three-way love affair is a reworking of Gontard, Maria and Michael Haas in 'Three People'. Heyt is a drastically toned down copy of Terstegen; Lang a built-up version of Terstegen's assistant. The trial and jury scenes are directly borrowed from the treatment based on Unger's book.

'I Accuse' begins by showing the Heyts in full enjoyment of a bourgeois professional idyll: he has been promoted and his friends and colleagues have come to celebrate. A few markers are laid down to suggest that all is not well with Hanna. At first Hanna thinks she is pregnant. In one of the few genuinely dramatic moments in the film she visits Lang, who gradually realises that the object of his concealed affections is suffering from multiple sclerosis. This, we are told, is tantamount to 'a death sentence'. The film follows Hanna's physical and spiritual decline. A formerly vivacious young woman gradually becomes bed- or chair-bound, unable to perform such simple tasks as buttering a piece of bread. Strain and dark shadows begin to show in her face. Scenes of Hanna's physical decline are interspersed with others showing Heyt's desperate, round-the-clock quest for a cure. Nothing results. However, the scenes in the laboratory provide an opportunity to reincarnate old Caesar, the blind hunting hound in the first version of the story, in the form of an experimental mouse. Heyt and his team deliberately paralyse a mouse in the interests of replicating Hanna's illness. A young laboratory assistant takes pity on the mouse, 'releasing' it from its suffering with a drug overdose. This scene, with its implication that what one can do for a mouse one can do for a person, cuts

Plate 34. Dr Lang (Wiemann) consoling a distressed Hanna Heyt (Hatheyer) in a scene from 'I Accuse'. Hanna's vivid descriptions of the terrifying terminal condition she wishes to preempt through 'mercy killing' corresponded precisely with the sort of language used by the Nazis to denigrate the disabled and mentally ill. The apparently liberal idea of determining one's own fate was thus deliberately confused with involuntary medicalised killing. Lang's conventional objections to 'euthanasia' gradually undergo a sea-change as the film progresses. A sub-plot, involving the fate of a mentally handicapped child whose life he has once saved, is used to effect his change of mind, and to confuse Hanna Heyt's wish to die with the idea of involuntary killing of the mentally handicapped.

away to Hanna's sickroom. (The mouse episode was inserted by Viktor Brack.) Hanna, by this time, is firmly prophesying her own imminent loss of human attributes: she is about to cease being 'a person any more – just a lump of flesh, torture for Thomas'. Lang, to whom this furious outburst is addressed, is adamant that he will not kill her. She addresses the same plea to her husband, by now anticipating being 'deaf, blind and idiotic': 'Promise me, Thomas, that you will deliver me before that happens.' Heyt reaches a dead end in his laboratory simultaneously with the onset of his wife's acute and distressing respiratory problems. With Lang playing moodily downstairs on the piano, Heyt overdoses his wife. In a scene which lasts some three minutes, Hanna expresses her relief that it is all over, and they both affirm their undying love. Glistening tears and white sheets are accompanied by Lang's mournful tune. The mood shifts abruptly as Lang bursts in and accuses his friend of murder.

The remainder of the film oscillates between a courtroom, where Heyt is on trial, and Lang's handling of the case of Trude Günther, a child whose life he once saved, but who has become 'blind', deaf and idiotic', in other words exhibiting every condition anticipated by the deceased Hanna. The parents, who once thanked Lang for saving their child's life, are now thoroughly embittered: 'Yes indeed, you've healed her wonderfully, doctor. Instead of allowing such a poor creature to die peacefully.' Lang goes to visit Trude in an institution. Evidently Liebeneiner overruled Brack's desire to include shots of an actual patient, opting instead for a fifteen-second freeze on the door to the paediatric ward, and the look of horror on Lang's face as he comes through it, as a way of explaining Lang's Pauline conversion to 'euthanasia'. Lang returns to the court, resolved to speak on Heyt's behalf.

Back in court, the judges and jurors are hearing the evidence of various witnesses. Insinuations of base motives at work are crushed through careful examination of Hanna's brother and the Heyt's servant, and the judge's repeated references to Heyt's unimpeachable human and professional virtues. Heyt's love for his wife is recalled by his patron and superior Professor Schluter, who also ventures a few forthright criticisms of existing law; and even a pastor is wheeled out to condone Hanna's desire to die and her husband's fulfilment of it. The jury scenes, which were shot before anything else, and in which Reichsleiter Bouhler took a keen interest, were designed to lay out an apparently broad range of views on the ethical issues in question. Although a simple Christian and an invalid are included to fleetingly put the contrary view, or in the latter case to express some well-founded popular anxieties, a consensus emerges that existing law has to be reformed. The consensus is articulated not by the rather coldly academic schoolteacher Schönbrunn – who actually maps out T-4's *modus operandi* – but by the apparently plain-speaking retired major Doring, who voices virtually all of the prejudices to which Nazi propaganda had hitherto pandered. In the script, the scene is as follows:

HUMMEL THE PHARMACIST But it was a good deed, simply intended to make the poor woman's end less painful!
SCHÖNBRUNN THE TEACHER Euthanasia, as it was called in antiquity.
ROLFS THE MASTER FITTER Eu- thana-
SCHÖNBRUNN -sia -sia, from thanathos – 'death' in Greek . . . You see, gentlemen: the ancient Greeks and Romans permitted it.
DR SCHEU I don't regard it as a case of grievous bodily harm since his intentions were obviously otherwise.
KNEWELS You would acquit him?
SCHEU Yes, unconditionally!

KNEWELS I don't know. The case has thrown up so much dust; a lot more doctors might decide to kill their patients.

ZIERNICKE THE FARMER That would be a terrible sin.

SCHÖNBRUNN Gentlemen, if you ask me, Professor Heyt must be acquitted because he is an example to every doctor. I know I am touching on a sensitive issue, but at the same time it is a very inflexible point in our current moral and social view.

HUMMEL I don't know . . . if one simply allows this sort of thing – will people still go to see their doctors?

SCHÖNBRUNN 'Simply allows?' One must . . .

ROLFS Now look, what if I – and I've been drawing an invalidity pension all my life – what if I go off sick one day, then they might simply do away with me?

SCHÖNBRUNN For God's sake! . . . The most important precondition would always be that the patient wished it!

ROLFS Many of them will, for a moment or two.

HUMMEL When one of them is mentally ill, they sometimes want it.

SCHÖNBRUNN Yes: if someone is deranged, or depressed or for one reason or another has no will of his own, then the state must assume responsibility! It must establish a commission consisting of doctors and lawyers, with a proper legal character. One should no longer have to stand by watching thousands of people who in earlier times would have died a gentle death, but who nowadays have to endure the most awful suffering simply because the doctors know how to prolong their poor lives artificially.

ZIENICKE God wills it. He sends suffering so that people will follow His cross, thus achieving eternal bliss.

MAJOR DORING My dear Herr Zienicke . . . With all due respect to your Christian beliefs . . . and I am not entirely free of them myself – but I'd rather not hold our dear Lord responsible for such terrible things.

REHEFELD THE GAMEKEEPER Gentlemen, when we foresters have shot an animal and it continues to be in pain, then we give it the *coup de grâce*, and whoever doesn't do this is regarded as a rogue and not as an honourable countryman.

ROLFS But those are animals!

REHEFELD No, no, leave it out! Humans are sometimes like wounded animals.

GRIEBELMEYER THE PRESIDING JUDGE Gentlemen, what you say is of extraordinary interest to a lawyer, but things are not as simple as all that. If one goes along with our teacher [Schönbrunn] to the effect that one removes the right to die from the individual and transfers it to the state – which is the case in all other questions of life and death – then one will naturally have to promulgate new laws for these 'medical courts' or what you will.

SCHÖNBRUNN The ancient Romans had these laws – but that was an heroic age.

DR SCHEU Five German states had these laws in the last century.

MAJOR DORING In many respects, our forefathers were more rational than we are. Don't get me wrong, gentlemen, but when one deploys hundreds of thousands of doctors, nurses and orderlies, and sets up massive buildings containing laboratories and drugs and God knows what, simply in order to keep a few pitiful creatures alive who are either too crazy to get anything from life, or dangerous to the community, or just like animals – and this at a time when one has insufficient manpower, room or money to keep the healthy in health or to give proper care to mothers of newborn babies – that is simply the most hare-brained nonsense! The state has the primary duty of caring for those who are the state – namely for those who work. And as far as those are concerned who want to die, because although once healthy they can no longer endure things, it is my view that the state which can command us to die should also afford us the right to die ... I am an old soldier and know what I am talking about.

SCHÖNBRUNN As the poet Lessing said: 'Should someone be able to deny the freedom to die which the gods have granted us in each and every one of life's situations?

KNEWELS Where did Lessing say that?

SCHÖNBRUNN In *Philotas*.

GRIEBELMEYER Gentlemen, what old Lessing said in his poetic licence is naturally nowadays not legally binding; our laws are otherwise – for the time being at least.

MAJOR DORING Naturally as jurors we will judge in accordance with the law. But forgive me if I say that the laws are not there to prevent people from doing what is honourable and right, and if they have this effect, then they must be changed.[50]

Lang arrives in court to testify on behalf of his friend. Before he can get into his stride, Heyt breaks his silence and rises to speak:

'Here I stand, Karl Thomas Heyt, and I confess that I delivered my wife, who was incurably ill, in accordance with her wishes. Here I stand, the accused, and now I accuse.

'I accuse the proponents of outmoded beliefs and antiquated laws. This is not just about myself, but about the hundreds of thousands of those who suffer without hope, whose lives we unnaturally prolong, and whose suffering we unnaturally increase ... and it is about those millions of healthy people, who cannot be protected against illness because everything that is needed to do so has to be employed keeping beings alive whose death would be a deliverance for them and liberation from a burden for the rest of humanity ... and now, Gentlemen Judges and Jurors, please deliver your verdict!'[51]

What distinguishes 'I Accuse' from both the earlier documentary films and the feature film treatments? What are its salient features? What do we know of its impact upon its vast mass audience? Unlike the earlier documentaries, 'I Accuse' is almost devoid of any references to its immediate political context. There are no references to National Socialism, and no columns of behelmeted SS men. Apart from the fact that the judges have Nazi emblems on their robes, and that the jury chamber is adorned with a modest bust of Hitler, the film could just have well been set in the 1950s as in the 1930s. Perhaps it is the film's very ordinariness – it has the feel of any competent melodrama – that makes it so insidious. On one level, it is just *Twelve Angry Men* minus Henry Fonda and the talent of Sidney

Lumet. In contrast to the early Racial Political Office (RPA) documentaries, there are no direct attempts to depersonalise the sick, except through the mouths of the sick themselves or their relatives. A terrible individual tragedy leads to the general advocacy of death on demand, followed by an equally open-ended call for the sanctioning of 'euthanasia'. By a series of insidious transitions, desire to terminate the suffering of Hanna Heyt has mushroomed into a call to do away with 'hundreds of thousands' of 'beings' who represent an alleged drain on overall medical resources. This is the thrust of the parallel being drawn in the film between Hanna and the handicapped child Trude in the subsidiary plot. In other words, two separate questions are being deliberately conflated – i.e. those of voluntary and involuntary euthanasia. We see Hanna ask to die; Trude's fate is to be sealed by her parents. (Obviously, the mouse is just killed.) Hanna's death is served up as a form of 'deliverance' or 'release' from terrible suffering: she simply goes quietly to sleep. At the point of death, she reassumes something approaching her former radiance. Killing the mouse or Hanna is almost a means of restoring a lost perfection. Death becomes an aesthetic event. In fact, like all its exemplars and variants, 'I Accuse' is about an incapacity to tolerate disease and imperfection, or to accommodate and value anyone outside a narrowly defined norm based upon racial purity, physical fitness, social conformism and productive performance.

As far as the film's reception was concerned, there were slaps on the back for all concerned. Liebeneiner became chief of production at Ufa (the Nazi film industry holding company) and was granted the title of professor. He also received the massive sum of 30,000RMs from a slush fund controlled by Goebbels. The film picked up an award at the Venice Biennale. Apart from a docile press, primed to omit the word 'euthanasia' from reviews, the film clearly enjoyed immense popularity; by January 1945 it had been seen by 15.3 million people. In Berlin it ran for fifty-one days at the Capitol; 40,000 flocked to the Mannheim Alhambra within a space of three weeks; 275,000 people saw 'I Accuse' in Munich.[52]

Audience figures are not the same as audience responses. That the film was very popular is evident from a report dated 15 January 1942:

All the reports to hand indicate that the film 'I Accuse' has aroused great interest in all areas of the Reich. In general it can be stated that, with the help of extensive word-of-mouth publicity, the film has been favourably received and discussed. Characteristic of the interest this film has provoked among the population is the fact that in many towns which had not yet seen it the film was being described – even by unsophisticated people – as one which simply had to be seen. The performances were generally enthusiastically received, and the film's content has actively stimulated people to think about it and has provoked lively discussion.[53]

Reports from the Party leadership in certain regions agreed that the film had made a deep impression, sparking off considerable debate. The

Gauleitung of East Hanover reported on 10 January 1942 that people had almost unanimously endorsed the film's message, and that 'if a law concerning this issue were to be introduced, by far the larger part of the population would immediately understand why this was so, especially since it is known among the population that corresponding measures have already been carried out'. However, the report also noted that the film's effect had been almost instantaneously and comprehensively nullified by Galen's sermon.[54] A subsidiary report, from the SD in Lüneburg, was rather more analytical. Young people in particular seemed to favour euthanasia in cases of chronic illness. A civil servant thought that such measures would release productive forces, tied down in care for the sick, to the benefit of the wider community.[55] Most people thought the film was propaganda designed to pave the way for a change in the law; 'unsophisticated people had no reservations about this'. A lawyer thought it impossible to devise a procedure which would be free of error or abuse. Educated middle-class women were deemed to be infected by an outmoded liberalism based upon respect for individual rights, or by religious sentiment. These virtues were discarded in the report as the 'educational remnants of an earlier age'. Doctors in Lüneburg were also hostile towards the film. A young doctor was of the opinion that it was a doctor's duty to keep people alive; in his case, however, it was solely so that he and his colleagues could better understand the causes of fatal diseases: employing the example of Robert Koch, he remarked, 'Killing these patients will mean the cessation of science.'[56] Apparently one did not need to be so scrupulous in the case of longterm psychiatric patients.

In Carinthia, people were observed leaving the cinemas in a preoccupied silence. Their immediate reaction was to agree with the film's arguments. Significantly – and this shows the difficulties in using this kind of evidence – further meditation and a little contrary reasoning led people to change their initial opinions. Intellectuals and doctors were again said to be hostile towards the film; the 'broad masses' agreed with it. The hostility of sections of the Roman Catholic Church was reflected in a pastoral letter from the bishop Konrad of Passau appended to a report from the Party leadership in the Bavarian Ostmark. The bishop made an explicit connection between the film and the 'reprehensible efforts' actually to implement 'euthanasia' which he had recently heard rumours of. He felt duty bound to spell out Christian moral teaching, as well as the universal conviction of civilised peoples, regarding the sanctity of human life. Man could take life if directly attacked, in war, or by the state's monopolistic device of capital punishment, but 'There are no further exceptions and there never can be any.' No earthly power had the right to alter the Fifth Commandment. Killing the incurably sick was murder in terms of paragraph 211 of the Criminal Code; consensual killing was an offence under paragraph 216, carrying a minimum three years of imprisonment. These were the laws of the land. In the light of these facts, the bishop enjoined his flock not to be deceived by the counterfeit sentimentality currently doing the rounds on the cinema screens.

A detailed SD round-up of these local reports, produced in January 1942, gave a detailed breakdown of audience responses according to age, confessional allegiance, social class and profession.[57] Although it echoed the general trends observed at a local level, some significant differences had crept in, particularly regarding the views of medical practitioners. Apparently, most of the population accepted 'in principle, though with reservations' the film's argument that 'people suffering from serious diseases for which there is no cure should be allowed a quick death sanctioned by law'. Although many religious-minded people agreed with this alleged consensus – which, it should be stressed, was not extended to the film's subsidiary message – 'the attitude of the Church, both Catholic and Protestant, is almost total rejection'. Priests had admonished their flocks not to see the film 'on the grounds that it is an inflammatory film directed against the Catholic Church or a state propaganda film designed to justify the killing of people suffering from hereditary illness'. However, even in these circles the film had occasioned a conflict of opinion between those who rejected the film outright for advocating 'murder', and others who were prepared to accept voluntary 'euthanasia' provided it was consensually and correctly administered. Reported comments on the film suggest that people regarded it as a riposte from the state to the accusations made by Bishop Galen. Others were concerned about the inflationary and socially discriminatory potential of any form of state-sanctioned 'euthanasia': 'as soon as laws like this are introduced it will be easy for the government to have anyone they consider undesirable declared incurable by a commission, for any reason at all, and eliminate them'. Protestant clergy were prepared to accord Caesar more latitude than their Roman Catholic counterparts: 'to take the responsibility and to ensure that loving kindness is extended to those incurables who are suffering'.

Medical and legal opinion was also divided. Younger doctors, particularly those devoid of religious beliefs, were generally in favour. Older practitioners drew attention to problems of diagnosis, to the powers of recovery of apparently incurable patients, and to the erratic judgement and mood swings evident among seriously ill or elderly people. Confusing the film with the T-4 assessors, some doctors felt that the institution of commissions of doctors, each of whom would examine every patient, would put these doctors under an immense psychological burden. Apparently many doctors thought that matters would be best served by being left as they were; i.e. that individual doctors would informally assist people to die without suffering, in the light of their own professional judgement.

Lawyers were concerned to put current medical practice on a firm legal footing, although they acknowledged that, given the immense variety of individual cases, this would be a labour of Sisyphus. Only the working class was said to be favourably inclined towards the film; and that largely because of the pragmatic consideration that they were least able to cover the costs of prolonged medical attention.

If opposition to the film was a minority response, the majority who allegedly approved the film's message nonetheless had major reservations. Diagnoses of incurability were to be made by a medical commission acting in consort with the family doctor. 'Euthanasia' had to be voluntary, or in the case of 'a feebleminded mental patient' – a category of person not mentioned in the film(!) – based upon the express consent of relatives. People were adamant that these decisions should never be taken by an individual, and that only doctors should have the right to administer euthanasia. The report concluded: 'To sum up, from the wealth of material to hand it emerges that in general the practice of euthanasia is approved, when decided by a committee of several doctors with the agreement of the incurable patient and his relatives.'[58]

The reactions of Germans suffering from multiple sclerosis were neither solicited nor recorded.

CHAPTER 7

EVIL EMPIRES: FROM 'AKTION 14F13' TO TRIESTE

THE PERSONAL and operational contacts between the SS and T–4 were multiple, even though the SS leadership chose to keep a low profile regarding the 'euthanasia' programme. Sometimes, however, the SS chiefs broke cover. When the mood in the population around Grafeneck turned sour, it was Himmler who wrote to Brack telling him to suspend operations in that extermination centre. He suggested that Brack organise the screening of films about hereditary illness, of the sort discussed in the previous chapter, to quell popular anxieties.[1] In early 1941 the Reichsführer-SS began to call in old favours. Specifically, he approached Bouhler regarding the use of T–4's gassing facilities to dispose of 'ballast existences' in the first and second generation of concentration camps.[2] The latter lacked installations for mass murder, as distinct from the quotidian round of individual torture and execution. The results of this arrangement became known as 'Aktion 14f13', named after the abbreviation used for the Inspectorate of Concentration Camps followed by the code used to describe the death of a 'sick' inmate. Other codes included '14f5', meaning 'shot while trying to escape', '14f6' for suicide, and '14f7' for a natural death.[3]

The SS authorities in the camps made a preliminary selection of 'sick' inmates, including many people who simply got on their nerves. As became paradigmatic in the 'Final Solution' as a whole, the victims were deceived and lulled into a false sense of security by the device of keeping a small window of hope ajar. At Mauthausen, ailing prisoners were encouraged to register for transfer to a 'recovery home' at Dachau.[4] In Auschwitz, which had yet to be given over to mass extermination, they were told that they were being relocated to a 'rest home' called Sonnenstein.[5] These 'sick' prisoners were then refereed (or better, 'selected') by roving commissions of T–4 doctors. As a direct result of this, fifteen to twenty thousand prisoners died in the gas chambers of Bernburg, Hartheim and Sonnenstein.[6]

From April 1941, the following T–4 doctors and professors were involved in this programme of selection: Werner Heyde, Paul Nitsche, Friedrich Mennecke, Horst Schumann, Kurt Schmalenbach, Otto Hebold, Rudolf Lonhauer, Robert Müller, Theodor Steinmeyer, Gerhard Wischer, Viktor Ratka and Hans-Bodo Gorgass.[7] They began in Sachsenhausen and moved on to Buchenwald, Auschwitz and Mauthausen. The first group of 2,500 victims in this initial sweep came from the ranks of the 'asocial'. It is important to stress the non-medical criteria being used by the doctors. This can be demonstrated by the fact that after the victims were killed, other prisoners working in the camp medical offices at Buchenwald were handed a medical dictionary and told to pick out a cause of death for the certificates they had to complete on their dead comrades.[8]

From September 1941, by which time 'Aktion T–4' had come to a temporary halt, the commissions of doctors visited Dachau, Mauthausen, Ravensbrück, Buchenwald, Flossenburg and Neuengamme, where they selected over twelve thousand victims.[9] By this time, they were not looking merely for 'asocial' or 'sick' inmates, but also for criminals, Jews and political prisoners, presumably in order to make full use of T–4's by now surplus gassing capacity. This extended operation kept the organisation ticking over. Again, it should be emphasised that doctors were using wholly non-medical selective criteria, based upon a person's race, way of life, or political persuasion, not to speak of such non-psychiatric criteria as whether the person was myopic or had an artificial limb. This was not a novel experience for them. One of the criteria used to register and exterminate patients under 'Aktion T–4' was 'race': membership of the Jewish 'race' made all other medical criteria superfluous.[10]

We know a considerable amount about the 'Aktion 14f13' selection tours, because Mennecke was in the habit of writing virtually every day to his wife Eva whenever the two were temporarily parted. Over the years, he wrote over two thousand letters. His wife, who doubled as his laboratory assistant and secretary, was a mere surface on to which Mennecke could project the detailed impressions he wished to record for posterity. He was living in 'the greatest of times', and believed in the adage 'Whoever writes remains!'[11] The son of a Social Democrat stone-cutter, Mennecke had had to postpone his medical ambitions because of the inflation, working in the commercial sector until he could resume his medical studies in 1927/1928. He joined the National Socialist Party and SS in 1932, qualifying as a doctor two years later. Clearly no great intellect, he had to sit the final exams twice, and had to make a dozen applications before he was taken on for practical training in gynaecological surgery, a field he dropped in favour of psychiatry. As we saw in Chapter 2, Mennecke was eventually taken on as an assistant doctor at Eichberg in the Rheingau, moving up to become director of the asylum in January 1939.[12] The man he was first foisted upon and then supplanted as director, Dr Wilhelm Hinsen, recalled

(a)

(b)

Plate 35. (a) Friedrich Mennecke (b) Friedrich and Eva Mennecke.

his initial impressions of Mennecke. At first, Mennecke seemed mature (he was merely older than the usual junior doctors) and not unsympathetic. Gradually, Hinsen realised that he was dealing with someone whose knowledge was 'broad rather than deep', and who had major problems in the sensitivity department.[13]

The Mennecke marital letters, all dashed off in his bold, extrovert handwriting, consist of exchanges of cloying infantilisms ('Mein liebstes Puttli-Muttilein'; 'Mein liebstes Herzli-Putt'; 'Liebste Mutti'; 'Liebes Evchen'; 'Mein liebstes Muuuu-Puttilein' being among the less embarrassing) signed off with a piratical 'Ahoichen'. In Eva Mennecke's eyes, her husband was 'Pa'; he definitely wore the trousers. Clearly dependent upon his wife-cum-audience, Mennecke could not wash, shit or shave in the morning without relaying these facts of quotidian existence to his partner. Nor could he pass over exactly what he had to eat or drink each day, the food in the officers' mess at Buchenwald being a typical bargain: 'soup, boiled beef, red cabbage, boiled potatoes, apple compote, and all for 1.50RM!'[14] He was also something of an amateur wine buff.

Since this man was so thoroughly appalling – bullying, garrulousness and gluttony being the lesser vices that come to mind – we will confine our discussion of him to one day in his hectic schedule. Ensconced at the 'Hotel Elephant' in Weimar, the doctor rose at 7 a.m. ('Bim-bim-bim: 7 o'clock! Got up! A right good morning to you, mummikins! Kissy-wissies! You're dozing still, am I right? Now I'm off – to shave! Ahoy! 7.30 a.m. Ready, I've had a shit too . . . and now off to the new day. I'll write again tonight. Kissykins! Ahoy!')[15] Returning after a long day at 7.50 p.m.: 'Home again, my little mouseykins! The first working day at Buchenwald is over.' In the intervening hours, he had met the camp top brass (being an ambitious son of the working classes, Mennecke was radar-sensitive to other people's uniforms, medals and titles), and had worked his way through forms concerning the life or death of what he was pleased to call 'portions of Aryans'. After lunch, he moved on to 'examining' (his inverted commas) 105 'Pats', or patients, moving on to 1,200 Jews, in whose case he just scribbled down the grounds for arrest in the space marked 'diagnosis'. At five he and his colleague Schmalenbach broke for supper, a cold platter of cervelat sausage, bread and butter, and coffee. Then his SS friends gave him a lift back to Weimar, where he skipped a visit to a comedy in the theatre, preferring to attend to ironing and running repairs to his suits. He read and listened to the radio in his room, pondering future work in Ravensbrück and Gross-Rosen. Tired now, he signed off: 'So, my dearest mummykins, now you'll receive sooooooooo many lovely kisses again, and be embraced so strongly in anticipation of your coming, you eensy-teensy mouse – from your loyal Pa.'[16] One has to read this several times to remind oneself that in the course of the day Mennecke had been despatching

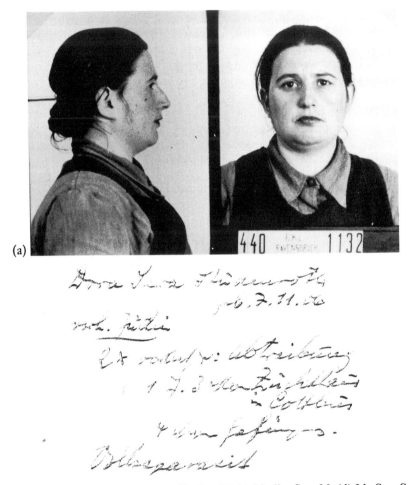

Plate 36. (a) Dora Sara S. (b) Emilie Sara H. (c) Marlies Sara M. (d) Ida Sara S. (e) Felizia Sara N. In the course of 'Aktion 14f13', the 'euthanasia' programme was extended to encompass 'sick' concentration camp inmates. These camp 'mugshots' have Mennecke's original diagnoses scrawled on the reverse side. The diagnoses did not reflect medical or psychiatric criteria, but rather racial and social prejudices.

people to a gas chamber, and that his wife was about to join him to marvel at his efficiency and general importance. This was not atypical, since Professor Nitsche took his wife and daughter with him to Dachau.[17] These men did not live 'double' existences, allegedly split between 'work' and peaceful domesticity; they spilled the 'work' into their private lives, or – puffed up with their own importance – brought their families into their workplace.

Mennecke kept his wife abreast of how the work was going, regularly giving the 'numbers' achieved by himself and his three colleagues. The process of selection became a form of competition. Thus on 29 November 1941, he reported that Schmalenbach had 'done' eighty-nine; himself 470; and Dr Müller 403.[18] He had another 1,038 to go. Although he distanced himself from his human material through numbers or abbreviations such as 'pats' or 'Portions', Mennecke gave vent to his considerable battery of prejudices in the notes he scribbled on the backs of camp identity photographs of his victims. The euphemisms (or 'denials' as psychologists call them) were alternatives, not substitutes, for several deep-seated hatreds. One should note that all of the following people bore the compulsory 'Jewish' name of Sara. They included:

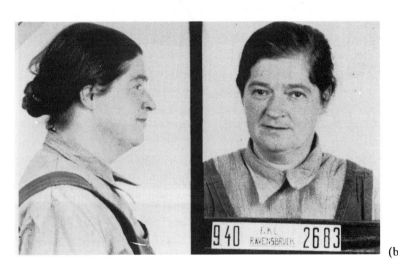

(b)

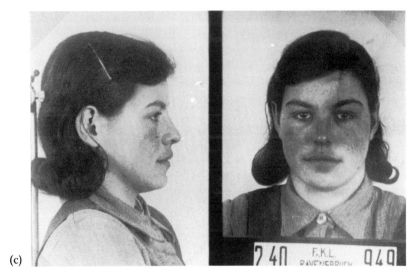

Dora Sara S. married Jewess. Twice convicted for abortion. Four years in prison. Parasite on the nation.

Emilie Sara H. Regular miscegenation. In the camp: unbelievably insolent.

Marlies Sara M. Unmarried Jewish servant in Göttingen. Continual miscegenation with German soldiers (was a school pupil in England). In the camp: punished many times for insolence and laziness.

Ida Sara S. Divorced Jewess. Continuous miscegenation with married German men.

Felizia Sara N. Homeless Jewish whore who hangs around combat troops. Repeated sexual diseases. Previous convictions: Special Court Kattowitz for prostitution.[19]

In so far as they actually bothered to examine any of the prisoners (as we have seen, Mennecke sometimes relied upon their criminal records), this

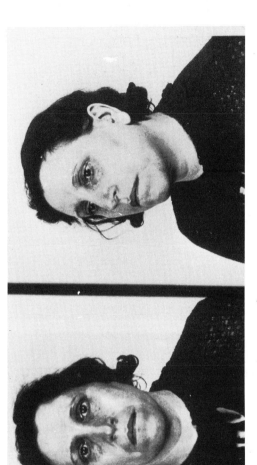

(d)

took the form of casting an eye over hundreds of men and women who were simply marched past them. Those who failed the criteria being used – which had nothing to do with Mennecke's psychiatric background – were separated out to be killed, in clear anticipation of the 'selections' on the ramps of the death camps.

We can follow these procedures through the eyes of many former concentration camp inmates who were fortunate enough not to participate directly in these selections. They watched and stored away what they saw for posterity. Karl K. was a prisoner in Dachau between October 1937 and August 1944. In the autumn of 1941 he was told to move some records from the political department to Block 29. The prisoners to whom these records referred were then paraded past four men in civilian clothes seated in Block 29, who asked them a few perfunctory questions. The spokesman of this group told those prisoners who were separated to the left side of the room that they would be sent to a camp with better general conditions. The spokesman was Werner Heyde, the rest of the party T–4 doctors. Sometime afterwards, the prisoners were transferred; their personal possessions came back to the camp a little later.[20] Former prisoner Hans H. remembered Mennecke and his colleagues sitting behind some tables after the evening roll call. Prisoners who were sick or unfit for work were told to register so that they might be taken to a sanatorium. Some two to three hundred inmates did. Since this was too few, the doctors and the SS made some further selections among the *Muselmänner*, i.e. inmates in a dire physical condition. After ten days, seven hundred of these inmates were loaded on to lorries, a process which was repeated eight days later with a further 650 inmates. Their clothes came back to the camp. Hans H. read a death notice in a newspaper regarding a friend of his who had voluntarily registered with the doctors because of a hand injury.[21]

Prisoners who realised what was afoot on such occasions advised people wearing glasses, or with armbands which proclaimed partial sightedness, to take them off, and to march past the doctors in an upright and confident fashion.[22] Others regarded it as very ominous that those prisoners who were being transported were ordered to leave behind artificial limbs, spectacles and trusses.[23] While the T–4 doctors had an interest in extending the categories of victims – with Dr Eberl of Bernburg contracting the burning of corpses issuing from a satellite camp of Buchenwald – the central SS authority which controlled the camps was interested in restricting their remit in order to exploit even the sick prisoners' labour value. In a circular to all camp commandants dated 27 April 1943, the SS Economic and Administrative Main Office said:

The Reichsführer-SS and Chief of the German Police has decreed that in future only insane prisoners can be selected for Aktion 14f13 by the medical commissions appointed for this purpose.

All other prisoners unfit for work (persons suffering from tuberculosis, bedridden invalids, etc.) are definitely to be excluded from this action. Bedridden prisoners are to be given suitable work which can be performed in bed.

The order of the Reichsführer-SS must be strictly observed in the future. Requests for gasoline for this purpose will therefore be discontinued.[24]

These selections in the concentration camps ran concurrently with the German invasion of the Soviet Union, which was waged as a racial war *à outrance*. As is well known, the various invading army groups were accompanied by 'task forces' or *Einsatzgruppen*, consisting of the SS, SD, Gestapo, and various kinds of policemen under the Higher SS and Police Leaders, whose task was to murder the politically and racially undesirable – which principally meant Jewish people, since the Nazis equated Jewishness with Bolshevism. The regular reports of these units frequently appended the intelligence that they had also murdered the 'asocial', i.e. gypsies and mental patients. Soviet sources detail the *modus operandi*. Einsatzgruppe A, consisting of over a thousand men, operated in the former Baltic states and the Ukraine. They either poisoned, starved or shot the inhabitants of psychiatric asylums. Einsatzgruppe B, operating to the south around Smolensk, used a variety of techniques to destroy the patients in the Lotoschinsk Psychiatric Clinic. They gassed some of the patients and poisoned others. Some were starved, others left outside to die of exposure, or to be hunted down by members of the unit mounted on horseback. About seven hundred patients were killed.[25] These methods were carried out face to face, and hence not without deleterious psychological consequences for some of the men involved. Chronic alcoholism and nervous exhaustion sometimes resulted. When in August 1941 Himmler personally witnessed the shooting of a hundred prisoners in a Minsk prison, he instructed Einsatzgruppe B's commander, Arthur Nebe, to develop less brutalising methods.[26] Nebe summoned experts from the Criminal Technical Institute, including Albert Widmann, who drove to Russia in trucks laden with explosives and gassing equipment. Arriving in Minsk on the Saturday evening, they set off on Sunday morning to a wood outside the town where there were two wooden bunkers. They packed 250kg of explosives into them, wiring the detonators to an electric plunger. About twenty mental patients who had been brought along for this purpose were then locked into the bunkers. The first attempt to blow them up was not successful, so Nebe and his team added another 100kg of explosives, picking up the wounded and disorientated victims from the first botched attempt and putting them back in the bunkers. The second attempt 'succeeded' too well, in the sense that Jewish captives had to spend most of the next day retrieving parts of human bodies from the surrounding trees and undergrowth.

Journeying on to the Mogilew asylum, Nebe and his men attached a pipe to the exhaust of a car, which they then connected to a pipe leading into a bricked-up laboratory in the asylum. A few patients were shut into the room, and the driver Bauer turned on the car engine. Having checked that this was not working quickly enough, Nebe decided to exchange the car for the group's lorry with its more powerful engine. This killed the patients in eight minutes. Nebe probably telephoned Himmler to report on the comparabilities of the two methods.[27]

Along with Einsatzgruppen C and D, the other two units continued to murder psychiatric patients throughout 1941 and until late 1942. The final technical refinement consisted of mobile gassing vans using bottled gas released from the cabin, and then the vehicle's exhaust fumes recycled into the van's container. Each of these refinements was treated as a mere technical problem, deliberately divorced from the 'product's' actual use. Parallel with the mass murder of Soviet Jewry, these units systematically swept the asylums, leaving nothing in their wake except destruction. They worked quickly and with deadly efficiency, regarding themselves as gardeners destroying greenfly on roses, or harsh colonial conquerors come to obliterate lesser races. Unfortunately this last side of things tends to be underplayed in many of the scholarly accounts which ponder the theoretical origins of this reversion to barbarism.[28] No one knows the exact number of victims among the patients, but judging from the Soviet sources, they probably numbered about ten thousand people.

At about the same time as Herbert Lange and his team were settling into Kulmhof, with three gassing vans supplied by Viktor Brack, a subordinate of Reich Commissar Hinrich Lohse in the Baltic was also making arrangements with Brack for the supply of expert personnel (the chemist Kallmeyer) and the 'Brack remedy', i.e. gassing apparatus.[29] According to Brack, by 1941 it was 'an open secret' that Germany's rulers intended to exterminate the whole Jewish population of Germany and the occupied territories.[30] With the agreement of Eichmann, camps established at Riga and Minsk were to undergo a change of purpose, from housing Soviet prisoners to murdering Jewish people from the Reich who were deemed incapable of working. That winter, a further party of between twenty and thirty T-4 personnel from Hadamar, Hartheim and Sonnenstein slipped away to Minsk on another 'top secret' mission. Brack led them in person.[31] They went to Berlin and exchanged their SS uniforms and paybooks for clothing issued by the Organisation Todt.[32]

That winter was particularly harsh in Russia, and frozen railway tracks meant it was necessary to ferry wounded or frozen soldiers from the front at Smolensk to rear area hospitals in Minsk.[33] Buses were brought by T-4 for that purpose. The doctors who went to Minsk included Eberl, Schmalenbach, Schumann and Ullrich, the nurses and orderlies Pauline K. and Paul R. No one knows exactly why they were chosen for this mission, although there is indirect evidence that Pauline K. admitted having given wounded soldiers lethal injections.[34] The fact that all of the survivors of this mission tend to brush over it rather quickly raises the suspicion that they were involved in the ultimate taboo, namely the murder of wounded soldiers on their own side. Why else would Brack have been in charge, and the mission designated 'top secret'? Why else use precisely this group of people?

While Lange's unit began murdering 145,000 Jewish people at Kulmhof, building work commenced on the first of three extermination camps in eastern Poland. These were Belzec, Sobibor and Treblinka, the camps used to kill the inhabitants of the Polish ghettos. Operations in these camps were codenamed 'Aktion Reinhardt', hence they were individually designated by the numbers R1, R2 and R3.[35]

Quite modest in scale – they would be easier to obliterate once operations were over – these camps consisted of barracks for the SS and Ukrainian guards, huts for small groups of working prisoners, including e.g. the *Goldjuden*, and a funnel-like walkway which led straight into the gas chambers. Their sole purpose was to kill as many people as quickly and smoothly as possible. Operational command lay in the hands of SS-Brigadeführer Odilo Globocnik, a former bricklayer foreman, at Lublin. Globocnik apparently outlined the nature of the work to future commanders like Franz Stangl while sitting on a bench in the park surrounding his headquarters. On 'a beautiful spring day', the two of them pored over the plans of the Sobibor extermination camp.[36]

The ninety-two former T–4 personnel whom Brack, on Bouhler's orders, 'lent' to Globocnik for the purpose of killing Jews on an industrialised basis were commanded by Christian Wirth, the Stuttgart detective we have already repeatedly encountered at Hartheim. Wirth was known as 'a beast' even by the 'burners' at Hartheim.[37] Those who were not SS members already received a crash training course in that organisation's essential ethos at Trawnicki. The T–4 staff continued to be on that organisation's payroll, and regular courier vans from Berlin kept colleagues in the East supplied with cigarettes and alcohol.[38] The entire operation was self-financing, in the sense that Wirth arranged for the valuables of Jewish people killed to be sent back to T–4 in Berlin.[39] Suitcases filled with valuables were taken there by T–4 couriers. The SS were not entirely happy about this.[40]

The group seconded to Globocnik from T–4 consisted of hardened psychopaths. 'Ordinary' psychopaths perhaps, but psychopaths nonetheless. These men were not gradually brutalised. Like Rudolf Hoess at Auschwitz, they had records of brutality right from the outset, although (unlike Hoess) they were often ex-policemen rather than former convicted murderers. More germanely, they were also experts in camouflage and deliberate deception. Like Brack, Globocnik wanted the work done as covertly and rapidly as possible, lest some day 'one gets stuck right in the middle of it'.[41]

The dense connections between T–4 and the 'Final Solution' can be easily demonstrated. Josef Oberhauser, an SS NCO, had already worked in Grafeneck, Brandenburg and Bernburg before being selected for Belzec.[42] Mennecke's driver, Erich Bauer, was given a brand-new Walther automatic by Allers before departing from the Charlottenburg station for Lublin and on to Sobibor.[43] Brack's driver, Lorenz Hackenholt, another T–4 veteran, arrived in Belzec to operate a tank diesel engine connected to a gas chamber, christening the latter 'the Hackenholt Foundation' in a typically perverse attempt to make light of the work through black humour. Franz Stangl, from Hartheim, went to take over the construction and running of Sobibor. When he moved on to command Treblinka he was replaced by another ex-Hartheim colleague, Franz Reichleitner; at Treblinka, Stangl succeeded the first commandant, Dr Irmfried Eberl, the doctor from Bernburg.[44] Stangl was brought in at Treblinka to put a stop to such practices as having naked Jewesses dancing on tables for the delectation of Eberl and his men. Stangl was rather puritanical about such sordid excesses, which to his mind got in the way of the main business of killing trainloads of people within an hour of disembarkation.

The estimated numbers of people killed in these three camps are:

Belzec (March–December 1942) 550,000 men, women and children
Sobibor (April–June 1942 and October 1942–October 1943) 200,000 men, women and children
Treblinka (July 1942–October 1943) 750,000 men, women and children[45]

After more than one and a half million people had been killed in these three camps (other former T–4 personnel such as Dr Horst Schumann were as active in Auschwitz), the final balance sheet represented massive material profit from an ocean of human loss. The end accounts for 'Aktion Reinhard', drawn up in December 1943, totted up millions of items of foreign currency ranging from US dollars to dinars, ducats, kroner, Peruvian pounds and złoty; 15,883 gold or diamond rings (market value 23,824,500RMS); over nine thousand ladies' watches; 29,391 pairs of spectacles; 627 pairs of sunglasses; 41 silver cigarette cases; opera glasses; powder puffs; 230 thermometers; and 6,943 alarm clocks needing repair. Time had stopped for the clocks as well as their owners. No one would be needing the opera glasses, powder puffs or sunglasses either. There were 1,901 waggon loads of clothing, towels and bedding, valued at 26,000,000RMs, requiring shipment. All of these things had once belonged to people, who had been denuded of such possessions (not to speak of items of more sentimental value) and killed, alone or with their entire families, in the dark of vast gas chambers. German officials who loitered about outside said that the screaming was 'just like in the synagogues'. A total of 100,047,983RMs was transferred to the Reichsbank, the Ministry for the Economy, and the SS Main Administrative and Economic Office.[46] The 'resettlement' was described as having been 'dealt with and concluded'. Following a visit by Himmler to Lublin on 12 February 1943, several of the T–4/Aktion Reinhard men were promoted, including Wirth, Hering, Reichleitner, Stangl and Oberhauser.[47] In this inverted world, psychopaths could make a career out of mass murder.

In the autumn of 1943, many of the T–4 killers who had serviced 'Aktion Reinhard' were sent southwards to Istria on the Dalmatian coast to run a holding centre for Italian Jews en route to death in Auschwitz, and to kill Italian or Yugoslav partisans, which in practice meant anyone allegedly vaguely connected with them. Since this final spasm of destruction on the Dalmatian coast is less well known than 'Aktion Reinhard', I shall be treating it here in some detail.

The ubiquitous Odilo Globocnik and Christian Wirth were in charge of those fifty or so 'Aktion Reinhard' veterans (Franz, Gley, Hackenholt, Lambert, Oberhauser, Stangl, Unverhau etc.) who were sent to the Dalmatian coastal area. Using the same codenames as they had employed in Poland, Wirth's team set up three camps: R1 in a suburb of Trieste called San Saba; R2 in Fiume; and R3 in Udine. According to Dietrich Allers, who succeeded Wirth in 1944 after the latter was ambushed and killed by Italian partisans, the job consisted of building bunker networks and guarding stretches of railway.[48] Gitta Sereny surprisingly goes along with Stangl's innocuous account of what the 'Aktion Reinhard' men were doing in Italy, by simply relaying his story that they were engaged in 'anti-partisan combat'.[49] Actually, there was more to it than that, namely torturing and killing about 5,000 Italians and Yugoslavs. The men from T–4 set up shop in a former rice warehouse called the Risiera. They had a gassing van with them, and Erwin Lambert – whom we last encountered drilling holes in gas pipes at Hadamar – was brought southwards to build a wood-fired crematorium capable of taking up to a dozen corpses.

The group's tasks included expediting the deportation of Italian Jews, killing Jewish mental patients from asylums in Trieste and Venice, and interrogating and executing people loosely described as 'partisans'.[50] The 'partisans' they tortured included a woman who had been caught writing anti-German graffiti on a wall after she had seen German troops shoot three young girls, and the mothers, sisters, or wives of putative resistance

Plate 37. T–4 personnel in Trieste. As veterans of both the 'euthanasia' programme and the death camps in Poland, T–4 personnel were sent to the Dalmatian coast to kill Jewish people and alleged partisans in a disused rice warehouse. Lorenz Hackenholt (with Iron Cross Second Class), in whose honour the gas chambers at Belzec were called the 'Hackenholt Foundation', is seen here being congratulated and presented with a potplant by his comrades after his recent award of the decoration. Erwin Lambert, who constructed the gas chambers used in 'Aktion T–4' and elsewhere, is on the left in the front row.

members. The 'Risiera' was a multi-purpose centre for storing stolen goods, prison, secret court, deportation centre and place of torture and execution. The victims scratched the salient facts of their lives on the cell walls. The following concerns a family, whose last surviving member recorded the removal of her husband and children:

Imprisoned on 21 September 1944 – Venice. Husband: Aldo S. born on 19 December 1894, deported 12 October. Wife: Giannina S., born 24 May 1896. Children: Ugo S., born 6 January 1925; Paolo S., born 24 May 1927; Elena S., born 30 March 1930.
May God protect my family – THE MOTHER.

Ugo, Paolo and Elena taken to Germany, 11 January 1945 – THE MOTHER.
6 January 1945, Ugo's birthday – THE MOTHER.
May God protect my children and my husband, I am afraid – GIANNINA BORGIGNON S.[51]

The woman concerned was the 'Aryan' wife of an Italian Jew. Released by the Security Police because of her racial unimpeachability, she had made

Plate 38. Hans Dietrich Allers in Trieste. Allers replaced Brack as administrative chief of T-4.

the mistake of requesting the return of the 30,000 lire which they had taken from her.[52]

In the Risiera, death came in the night, muffled with music blaring out of loudspeakers. It came in the form of a Ukrainian guard wielding a club, or strangling the victims with his powerful hands. If the victim was small enough, he or she was stamped to death. The stench of burning bodies polluted the surrounding city. Those killed at the Risiera included a mentally ill Jewish man who was deemed unfit to be sent to Auschwitz, presumably lest he upset the smooth flow of deportations; two prisoners who had the misfortune to share a cell with two others who escaped during an air raid; five Jews who were wrongly held to have hidden five gold coins in a lavatory; a man who failed to turn up for work with the Organisation Todt; and so on.[53] As we shall see in the final chapter, the men responsible for these murders quietly melted away into the ranks of German soldiers heading homeward, or went on the run to distant destinations. First, however, we must turn to the various continuations of the 'euthanasia' programme, notwithstanding Hitler's order for the partial cessation of mass gassings.

CHAPTER 8

'MEDIEVAL' OR MODERN? 'EUTHANASIA'
PROGRAMMES 1941–1945

THE HALTING of mass gassings of the mentally and physically handicapped did not stop 'euthanasia' killings. Henceforth, an extended range of
state asylums was involved, including some of the six asylums employed
hitherto for gassing patients. They all used lethal medication and deliberate starvation to murder people. Since T–4 still continued to referee and
transfer patients, and indeed supplied the large quantities of sedatives used
to overdose them, we can continue to speak of centrally planned murders,
albeit carried out on a more decentralised basis than in the original 'Aktion
T–4'. The 'children's euthanasia' programme also continued until the end
of the war.[1]

It is important to stress that these methods of killing were being
considered years before they were eventually introduced. These policies
did not materialise out of thin air in response to unforeseeable wartime
circumstances; they were entertained long in advance, by people who were
very conscious of past precedents and of what they were doing. There was
nothing *ad hoc* or 'reactive' about this. Memories of what had happened in
asylums during the First World War were fresh in the minds of those who
wished to pursue a policy of deliberate starvation after 1939. Director
Pfannmüller of Eglfing-Haar told a meeting of his doctors in September
1939 that during the First World War, bedridden patients had been
adequately fed, while those who worked had died of malnutrition. The
National Socialist government would be bound to introduce measures to
obviate similar 'errors'. Patients would have to be examined to establish
whether they were capable of recovery, or whether they had no further
'social utility'.[2]

On 1 November 1939, Pfannmüller produced a detailed memorandum
on economy measures in the asylums, in response to a cost–cutting report
from the Bavarian government auditors. Peeved at the ignorance of
laymen, Pfannmüller decided to make drastic economy recommendations
of his own, which would accommodate questions of cost to his own
aberrant therapeutic criteria. Naturally, it was the 'self-evident' duty of

any National Socialist asylum director to 'screw down' the cost of maintaining his charges. The asylum was silting up with 'asocial', old or sick patients who required high levels of care and expenditure on sedatives.[3] Given the increased number of patients (2,692 in January 1937; 3,005 in November 1939), it was becoming impossible to offload the chronically sick and geriatric on to charitable institutions in the area in the fashion recommended by the ignorant auditors. As a 'non-confessional and convinced National Socialist asylum director' – he recommended *en passant* that in future all correspondence should be addressed to 'the Director' and not to a more oligarchic 'directorate' – Pfannmüller put forward his own peculiar economy measures. It was time to 'draw the final consequences in terms of eradication, with respect to the medical care of lives unworthy of life'.[4] Two groups would be affected: 'the totally idiotic, thoroughly asocial, absolutely dependent, chronic cases' and 'criminally inclined, anti-social elements' in protective custody who were 'burdening and filling up' the asylums.[5] Discussions were taking place as to whether to keep these people 'under the most primitive conditions' or whether to 'eradicate them'. He reckoned that 35% of his patients (1,000 people) fell within these two categories. He found it incomprehensible that young, fit men were dying at the Front while 'living corpses' were being maintained in the asylums.[6] As we have seen, the initial strategy was indeed to 'eradicate' certain categories of patient by way of 'Aktion T–4'.

We can see how Pfannmüller dealt with the 'asocial' through the case of Walter D. The latter was a professional criminal, consigned to Stadelheim prison for fraud and extortion. He had seventeen previous convictions. In May 1940, the senior public prosecutor in Munich organised Walter D.'s transfer from Stadelheim to Eglfing-Haar. (He had escaped from Stadelheim in August 1939, and the director of the prison refused to have him back.)[7] Pfannmüller took in Walter D., but then quickly changed his mind, after D. escaped again. Pfannmüller was in charge of an asylum, not a maximum security prison. He was not transferring patients elsewhere to create bedspace for 'scoundrels' and 'notorious criminals' like Walter D. The latter was capable of organising revolts and mutinies among the mad; he should be kept in an institution where there would be ruthless resort to firearms should he try to escape. Pfannmüller was clearly anxious about Walter D., who had written to him while at large, threatening to murder him. Had the authorities forgotten that when last apprehended, D. had been in possession of a revolver? Almost as an afterthought, Pfannmüller mentioned that there was 'a special Reich agency whose name I am not allowed to mention' which was 'in complete agreement with him regarding the case of D'.[8] He meant T–4.

Following the partial cessation of mass gassings, 'eradication' was achieved through the 'most primitive conditions' which Pfannmüller spoke of in his riposte to the auditors. On 17 November 1942, the directors of Bavarian asylums gathered for a conference in the Ministry of the Interior, chaired by Walter 'Bubi' Schultze. The latter explained that since centrally organised mass gassings had ceased, it was time 'for the asylums to do something themselves'.[9] The subject for discussion was whether the asylum directors would be prepared to introduce a 'special diet' for certain categories of patient. The lead in the discussion was taken by Pfannmüller and Valentin Faltlhauser of Kaufbeuren-Irsee. This was not surprising, since both men were already using 'special diets' in their asylums. Faltl-hauser had introduced the 'E-Kost' at Irsee in August and at Kaufbeuren in October 1942, in other words before the Munich conference.[10] Indeed, Pfannmüller went about openly bragging to the other conference partici-pants that 'he had once snatched a piece of bread from a nurse which she had wanted to give to a patient'.[11]

In his contribution, Faltlhauser recommended two alternative diets, one for those who worked and one for those who did not. The latter were to receive no bread, fats, meat or carbohydrates, but rather vegetables boiled in water. This meant 50–100 grammes of turnips a day. According to one participant at the conference, Faltlhauser explained that he had initially been an opponent of 'euthanasia', but had changed his mind: 'Since the abandonment of the transfer transports, one could continue the matter by gradually starving the patients. Those patients who were incapable of working, or hopeless cases, would be given a fat-free diet, consisting for example of vegetables cooked in water. The effect would be the slow onset of death after a period of about three months.'[12] Faltlhauser brought along a pair of sample weekly menus from Kaufbeuren-Irsee to demonstrate the sort of diet he had in mind. One of these is reproduced as plate 39; it consists of nothing more than cabbage, root vegetables and potatoes.[13]

On the insistence of those attending the conference, on 30 November 1942 Walter 'Bubi' Schultze wrote to the chiefs of the various regional governments announcing the introduction of drastic differential diets in the asylums:

With regard to wartime food supplies and the state of health of those asylum patients who work, we can no longer justify the fact that all inmates of asylums are receiving the same rations, without regard on the one hand to whether they perform productive labour or are in therapy, or on the other hand to whether they are simply being kept in the asylum without performing any labour worthy of the name.

It is therefore decreed, with immediate effect, that those inmates of asylums who do productive work or who are receiving therapy, and in addition, children capable of being educated, war casualties, and those suffering from geriatric psychoses, shall be better fed – in both a quantitative and qualitative respect – than the remaining inmates.

Wochentage		VI. Woche (v.15.11.-21.11.1942)	VII. Woche (v.22.11.-28.11.42)	VIII. Woche (v.29.11.-5.12.1942)	IX. Woche (vom 6.-12.12.1942)	X. Woche (v.12.-19.12.1942)
Sonntag	Mittag	Blaukraut	Blaukraut	Blaukraut	Blaukraut	Blaukraut
	Abend	Kartoffel	Kartoffel	Kartoffel	Blaukraut	Blaukraut
Monntag	Mittag	Weisskraut	Weisskraut	Weisskraut	Weisskraut	Weisskraut
	Abend	Weisskraut	Weisskraut	Kartoffel	Weisskraut	Weisskraut
Dienstag	Mittag	gelbe Rüben	gelbe Rüben	Blaukraut	gelbe Rüben	Dotschen
	Abend	Kartoffel	Kartoffel	Kartoffel	gelbe Rüben	Kartoffel
Mittwoch	Mittag	Blaukraut	Blaukraut	Weisskraut	Weisskraut	Weisskraut
	Abend	Blaukraut	Blaukraut	Kartoffel	Weisskraut	Weisskraut
Donnerstag	Mittag	Blaukraut	Blaukraut	Blaukraut	Blaukraut	Blaukraut
	Abend	Kartoffel	Kartoffel	Kartoffel	Salzkartoffel	Salzkartoffel
Freitag	Mittag	Weisskraut	Weisskraut	Salzkartoffel	Weisskraut	Weisskraut
	Abend	Weisskraut	Weisskraut	Kartoffel	Weisskraut	Kartoffel
Samstag	Mittag	gelbe Rüben	gelbe Rüben	gelbe Rüben	gelbe Rüben	Dotschen
	Abend	Kartoffel	Kartoffel	Kartoffel	Kartoffelpürree	Kartoffelpürree

Plate 39. Weekly menus for the special diet given to patients at Kaufbeuren-Irsee in late 1942 with the express intention of killing them. Minute quantities of root vegetables were boiled in a fatless liquid. Patients in a weakened condition were then more easily killed with relatively small amounts of sedatives. This technique economised on pharmaceuticals.

Reference is made to the conference of asylum directors which took place in the Ministry of the Interior on 17 November 1942. The asylum directors must immediately bring about the relevant measures.[14]

At Eglfing-Haar, patients subject to these 'special diets' (a term so redolent of 'special treatment' in the concentration camps) were grouped in two houses: numbers 22 and 25. These came to be known as the 'hunger houses'.[15] The starvation diets were ruthlessly enforced. Pfannmüller visited the kitchens at Eglfing-Haar three or four times a week, tasting the 'food' for illicit protein supplements, while insisting on the regular weighing of those patients affected. He was rarely circumlocutory about what he was doing, announcing to one of the orderlies: 'We'll keep them without fats or proteins and then they'll die of their own accord.'[16] Individual members of the nursing and auxiliary staff – notably the cook – did their best to subvert Pfannmüller's strategy. At the weighing sessions Pfannmüller, demanding to know why certain patients were not lighter, would receive the intelligence that they had stored a lot of water in their bodies.[17] The cook would politely dispute Pfannmüller's capacity to distinguish between fat and fat-free gruel, or wait for him to depart before adding more nourishing items to the cooking pots. The patients subject to this diet resorted to such survival strategies as mentally rehearsing recipes once savoured, or imagining the contents of foodstores and delicatessens. Whenever the priest visited these two houses, he was confronted by rows of patients who shouted 'Herr Pfarrer, just a bit of bread.' They were all suffering from malnutrition.[18] Between 1943 and 1945, 429 patients died in these two 'hunger houses'.[19]

At Kaufbeuren-Irsee, Valentin Faltlhauser instituted a 'basic diet' of the sort contained in the weekly 'menus' discussed above. Meetings were held in the asylum to establish different diets for several categories of patient. Those who worked on the asylum farms, commencing at 4 a.m., would be fed twice a day, with an additional ration of bread. There followed the 'normal diet', and then the 'basic diet' or 'E-Kost'.[20] The latter was given to all patients who were selected for house MII at Irsee.[21] According to the priest who had to conduct burial ceremonies, the rapidly rising death rate led the asylum authorities to prohibit the ringing of church bells, lest this alert people in the vicinity of the asylum to the suspicious number of deaths in the asylum.[22] He was burying up to six or seven people each afternoon.[23]

Deliberate starvation based upon differential diets was practised in asylums throughout the length and breadth of Germany. Hadamar began receiving transports of patients again in August 1942. Of the 4,817 patients transferred there from various parts of Germany between August 1942 and March 1945, 4,422 died. A maximum of about five hundred patients were in the asylum at any one time, including two hundred or so worker-patients at Schnepfenhausen. According to eyewitnesses, because of over-crowding new arrivals were often left lying on straw sacks on the floor.[24] On arrival, patients were immediately categorised by gender or capacity to work. Those who worked ate; those who did not work were given stinging-nettle soup three times a week and died.[25] Some patients wrote desperate postcards to their relatives begging for extra food. When the relatives complained to Wahlmann, he cynically and patronisingly explained that mental patients lived 'monotonous' lives, and hence lacked subjects other than food to write about. Feeling perpetually hungry was inherent to their condition even in normal times; the relatives should show more under-standing for the need to feed 'soldiers and productive national comrades'.[26] When the provincial authorities in the Rhineland queried why so many patients transferred from Hoven to Hadamar were reported dead, Wahl-mann blamed this on the poor 'patient material' they had supplied him with. He could not reconcile his National Socialist views with 'prolonging the lives of individuals who had totally fallen out of human society' through any form of medical attention.[27]

(a)

(b)

(c)

Plate 40. Three views of the asylum at Eichberg. (a) The main administrative building, (b) one of the buildings housing patients which are staggered along the road winding through the asylum, and (c) a longer view, showing the pavilion-style asylum running above vineyards in the foreground.

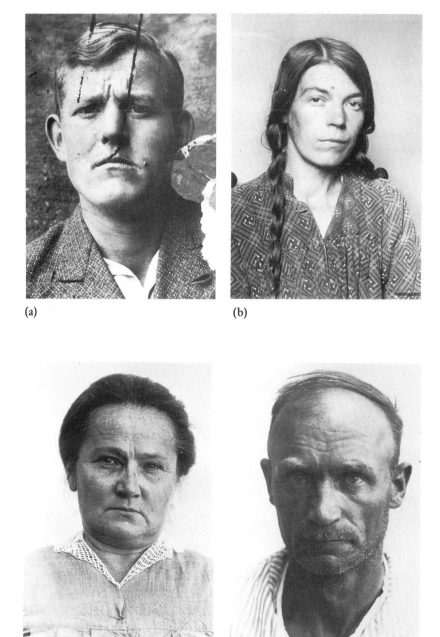

(a)   (b)

(c)   (d)

Plate 41. Four patients killed at Eichberg during the second phase of the 'euthanasia' programme.

Some of those accused after the war of organising deliberate starvation tried to exculpate themselves by pointing to wartime food shortages. Faltlhauser tried this line of defence at his trial. It cut little ice. The case of Eichberg, where Mennecke and Schmidt also introduced a 'B-Kost' starvation diet, shows that the wartime shortages were non-existent. Eichberg lies in one of the most fertile regions of Germany: the slopes along the Rhine near places like Rüdesheim are bursting with vineyards and agricultural produce. In the period under consideration, the asylum had extensive vineyards, and also ran a substantial farm at Wachholderhof. Yet even patients who paid for their own maintenance in the asylum were reduced to writing desperate letters to the doctors begging for more food. They received thin soup and potatoes twice a day, with boiled spinach once a week as a special treat.[28]

The reasons why patients were starved to death amidst abundance were firstly that Mennecke and Schmidt wanted this to be so, and secondly that Bernotat was diverting the asylum's considerable agricultural and viticultural surpluses to what he regarded as more deserving causes. This meant that livestock were sent to a National Socialist welfare home at Hofheim, the Gau rest home at Schlangenbad, the League of German Maidens' school at Tiefenthal, and a sanatorium at Mammolshöhe. The wine went to Bernotat's own staff in Wiesbaden.[29] Quantities of food were also diverted from the asylum to an SS military casualty station.[30] Exactly the same story was evident at the Kalmenhof psychiatric reformatory in Idstein, whose thousand-acre estate in the suburb of Gassenbach should have been generating surpluses. And indeed it was, except for the fact that vast quantities of meat, milk and butter were systematically diverted from the trainees to Bernotat, Director Grossmann and his staff. Thus, between August 1941 and February 1943 the trainees received less than 20,000 demi-litres of milk instead of the 37,997 demi-litres which should have been allocated to them. Over the same period 1,674,4 kilograms of meat and forty-seven hundredweight of butter and margarine also went 'absent' each year.[31]

Nor did the doctors who presided over mass starvation stint themselves. In the summer of 1942, Mennecke went on a psychiatric refresher course at Heidelberg.[32] He spent several days administering electro-shocks and hobnobbing with Carl Schneider, with whom he cut a deal to supply brains to the latter's clinic following a 'recommencement' of 'euthanasia' killings. Schneider was also 'very interested' in Mennecke's experiences in the concentration camps, hinting at collaborative projects in the future.[33] Mennecke's nights were passed drinking wine and 'marvelling' at the scholarliness of Schneider's books. During the day he obsequiously trailed along in the professorial wake, sometimes being allowed to accompany Schneider on a stroll along Heidelberg's many hills, dressed in his white doctor's outfit. They seem an odd couple: Schneider smoothly handsome and not unlike John F. Kennedy; Mennecke overweight and physically rather repulsive.

Writing to his wife, Mennecke made various observations about his colleagues (carefully recording every minor social courtesy shown him by the 'great' man), including *inter alia* the fact that Gorgass was in the habit of raiding the storerooms at Idstein in search of 'large quantities of meat'.[34] In the gluttony stakes, this was definitely a case of the kettle calling the pot black. Let us pick up his pantophagous trail that summer. On 16 June Mennecke tucked into a lunch 'naturally' consisting of meat: to be precise, 'two thick slices of boiled ham, peas and carrots, green salad, boiled potatoes and barley soup'. Not forgetting cheese and cherries.[35] As for the breakfasts, they were so generous that Mennecke had to abandon his efforts to guzzle through them. On 30 June he had 'the usual quantity of butter, bread, two rolls, and a portion of cheese. I kept some of the cheese and the two rolls for tonight, since it was too much for me.' And so on to lunch, 'a perfect bouillon with home-made noodles, three Heine's Halb-städter sausages (one to be polished off tonight), vegetables, potatoes and green salad'.[36] At home in Eichberg, Eva Mennecke was not going wanting either. On 1 July she lunched with a friend. The meal consisted of soup, schnitzel, peas, boiled potatoes and strawberries with sugar. Indeed, she had to lie down on the couch to digest this blow-out before starting on the coffee.[37]

Starving people to death was a relatively slow process. Matters were accelerated by giving them lethal quantities of sedatives mixed in food and drink, or by lethal injections. Doctors inspected arriving transports, stalked the wards, held conferences with the senior nurses and orderlies with the express purpose of selecting victims. Every day at Hadamar, Dr Adolf Wahlmann held a small conference at 9 a.m. with his senior staff, who came armed with their own notes and observations regarding potential victims. It was there that Wahlmann took the decision to kill a patient – in so far as they were not designated for destruction on arrival by T–4, which was the fate of most of those who were transferred there. He then issued the appropriate instructions to the senior nurse or orderly, who relayed the order to their subordinates in the form of a slip of paper with a name on it.[38] Each ward had a medicine cabinet, kept well supplied by Bernotat or from T–4 in Berlin.[39] The nursing staff and orderlies, including Pauline K. and Paul R., mixed eight to ten tablets of sedatives such as Luminal, Veronal or Trianol into bedtime drinks, the usual effect of which was that the patient had ceased to breathe by daybreak. If the person was still alive, he or she was given a lethal injection of 1–2cc of morphium scopolamine.[40]

So far, it has been suggested that the people killed in this second phase of 'euthanasia' were those deemed incapable of working. As a broad generalisation, that certainly holds true. But, of course, it is far too mechanistic. Even those who laboured on the farms or in the kitchens could fall ill, cease working productively, attempt to escape, talk too much, or just get on the staff's nerves through impertinence or minor acts of delinquency. Any of these things could be tantamount to signing one's own death warrant in an institutional climate where bullies ruled. No one was safe in the presence of the carers.

The last point applied to people like a fifteen-year-old boy of 'gypsy' ancestry called L. who was killed at Kaufbeuren. L. was himself a little bully and a thief, but many of the staff seem to have felt rather affectionately towards him, organising his transfer to a work party to save his life.[41] When L. stole again, despite a severe reprimand, Faltlhauser gave the order to kill him. This proved difficult. Clearly what we call 'streetwise', L. knew what was happening in the asylum; on one occasion he gave an orderly he liked a photograph of himself inscribed 'in memory'. He said he was not going to live much longer.[42] L. refused to drink coffee which he detected had been laced with Luminal. However, it was noted that he was anxious about typhus in the paediatric department. His anxiety opened up other avenues of opportunity. Faltlhauser decided to delegate the job to the ubiquitous Pauline K. (i.e. to a professional murderess, brought in to Kaufbeuren for this sole purpose). She came upon L. at one in the morning, informing him that he was to be inoculated against typhus. She gave him two injections. During the night, his face turned purple and he groaned heavily. Foam and powder were evident around his mouth. Although he had hitherto been in rude good health, L. died before the following morning. One day he was working and acting the fool; the next he was dead.[43]

At Hadamar, Alfred S. worked on the estate at Schnepfenhausen. In October 1942 the medical reports noted that he was 'unpleasant', and that 'he often told stories about the asylum in the town'. On 2 December he was restricted to the asylum, for again he had been talking too much. Three days later he was dead. The same fate befell anyone who complained about the conditions in the asylum.[44] Sometimes the nursing staff just wanted to lay hands upon a watch, a nice suit or a good pair of shoes belonging to a patient, who was then killed to satisfy their cupidity.[45]

Patients who tried to escape were treated correctly, up to the point where they began talking to outsiders about life and death in Hadamar. This normally resulted in their dying of 'pneumonia' shortly afterwards. Selmar S. was eighteen years old at the time of these entries in his patient records:

31 August 1942 has been employed in a work party for a few days. Transferred today to the [Schnepfenhausen] estate.

9 September 1942 industrious and very skilful. Ran away today. Was in Hundsangen. Detained by the police. 8 days in bed.
17 September 1942 working again on the estate.
24 January 1943 still working as before on the estate. No complaints about his behaviour.
9 June 1943 has been working for a long time in the carpentry shop ... and is very reliable. Ran away in May or April, but was rapidly recaptured. Ran away again today. Received 20 Marks and ration cards from a female employee. Did not return from visiting the town.
20 June 1943 picked up yesterday in Neudorf near Wiesbaden; today unchanged. Threatens to escape again, and says he will tell things about the asylum. He told the police various things about the asylum. Stays in bed.
30 June 1943 ill with pneumonia. Died of pneumonia today.[46]

At the Kalmenhof in Idstein, where adolescent boys were beaten with an oxhide whip, or smashed in the mouth with soup ladles, or made to do five hundred kneejerks for minor infractions (the house regulations specifically banned any form of corporal punishment), anyone who stole or disobeyed orders was killed. This applied to those who inconvenienced the staff by persistent bed-wetting.[47]

People confined in asylums on the grounds of diminished criminal responsibility under paragraph 42b of the 1933–1934 'Law against Dangerous Habitual Criminals and Measures for their Securing and Improvement', were also among the victims of the first and second phases of the 'euthanasia' programme, as is proved by the presence of a category for the 'criminally insane' on Registration Form 1. Although National Socialist propaganda films always dilated upon murderers and rapists, the run of 42b inmates in Hadamar consisted of petty thieves (bicycle thieves, handbag snatchers, etc.); abortionists, homosexuals and perverts (a man who put his hand up a woman's skirt); and various types of political offender.[48]

Both the type of person killed and the degree of continued T–4 involvement can be demonstrated in the case of a few petty criminals who became patients at Eichberg. Friedrich K. was born in 1907 in Mannheim. He had been deaf and dumb since a bout of measles when he was three or four.[49] He had been in an institution for the deaf and dumb from 1915 to 1923. He had wanted to be a car mechanic, but had only managed to find odd jobs, punctuated by long periods of unemployment. From 1928 onwards he worked in a Mannheim foundry, and then as an auxiliary worker in Frankfurt, walking out of the job there without giving notice in March 1942. He was arrested in a Heidelberg tourist hostel. The lack of notice resulted in a four-month spell in a Wiesbaden prison. His past began to catch up on him, and bureaucracies exchanged data on his life. He had eleven previous convictions, for theft, breach of contract, begging and deception.[50] Efforts by the Frankfurt criminal police to send him to a concentration camp were rejected by their headquarters in Berlin on the grounds that the camps did not cater for the deaf and dumb. Instead, K. was sent to Mennecke at Eichberg, naturally without any form of due process.[51]

Mennecke's interviews with him were conducted in writing, since Friedrich K.'s efforts to speak were incomprehensible and his lip reading skills inadequate. He was asked a number of fatuous questions about Bismarck, Luther and Goethe, none of whom he could identify; but he went on to give a reasonable enough account of why he had walked out of his job, namely because he objected to being paid seventy-six pfennigs an hour. Life since 1930 had been hard on him, because he 'lacked experience and was deaf and dumb'. He was desperate to work, and promised to be 'another, better man in future'. He wanted to go home, find a job and get married. But, of course, he had no future. Though Mennecke described K. as 'willing, orderly, good, industrious and calm', the 'diagnosis' read 'deaf and dumb, slightly debilitated, asocial psychopath'. Shortly after this interview, Mennecke departed on his trip to Heidelberg. Despite the nights spent attacking 'two huge Bratwurst, each weighing 200 grammes, roast potatoes, and cabbage', Mennecke found time to destroy Friedrich K. He asked his wife Eva to verify that Dr Schmidt had sent off a letter regarding Friedrich K. to Berlin.[52] On 15 July 1942, Dr Schmidt relayed the 'diagnosis' to the Reich Committee (i.e. T–4) in Berlin, unhelpfully adding that there were no prospects of recovery.[53] He wanted 'permission to act'. Schmidt obviously received it, since on 29 September 1942 he wrote to Friedrich K.'s uncle, informing him that his nephew had 'been delivered from his incurable suffering' the day before.[54] The cause of death was 'pneumonia and heart failure; deaf and dumb psychopath'.[55] It was probably the latter rather than the former that killed him.

Another petty criminal who had a 'gentle death' in Eichberg was a Polish woman called Marianna D. Unmarried with four children, Marianna D. had come to 'the old Reich' to find work. In July 1941, her eldest son, Zygmunt, decided to help himself to some clocks and an ironing press from a shop owned by Jews who had been 'resettled'. There was no morality at the bottom of the heap. His mother hid the stolen goods under the floorboards. Her German fellow lodger had said that one could take things from Jews with impunity. This was a mistake, since their property belonged to the state. She received a four-month sentence for aiding and abetting. In prison, she went mad. When she was transferred to Eichberg, Mennecke tested her intelligence. Hindenburg was 'a Russian'; Pilsudski 'one of those who had a bit to say in Poland, an Emperor?' Her attempts to be witty in her broken German were a serious mistake. Asked what the difference was between a mirror and window, she replied: 'that's obvious, you must know yourself what a mirror is'. Gradually her initially confident front collapsed, and she confessed to being afraid. In May, the case notes described her spitting and shouting; she kept making herself sick because she thought she was being poisoned. She probably was. On 13 June 1942, Mennecke informed her sister that Marianna D. had died the day before, the cause of death being 'heart failure-schizophrenia'.[56]

Of course, T–4 did not confine its attentions merely to people notionally designated 'habitual criminals' or 'the criminally insane'. Other paragraphs (namely 42c and 42d) of the Law against Dangerous Habitual Criminals(!) were designed to put drunks and vagrants in drying-out clinics or one of the twenty-six Reich workhouses. The occupants of dosshouses and hostels had largely vanished into the concentration camps during the SS's 1938 'Action Workshy in the Reich'.[57] If one goes to Dachau, one can see photographs of them engaged in such purposeful activities as dragging around a massive roller to which they were harnessed.

Shortly after Christmas 1941, a high-powered team descended like carrion birds on the Rummelsburg workhouse in Berlin. Paul Nitsche hand-picked the visitors.[58] It was a galaxy of Nazi experts on various aspects of the 'asocial' question: Linden, Heinze and Hefelmann representing the Ministry of the Interior and T–4; Professor Heinrich Wilhelm Kranz, one of the leading lights of research on the 'asocial' from Giessen; and Dr Robert Ritter, the foremost expert on 'gypsies' and 'criminal biologist' in the Criminal Police headquarters.[59] This team demonstrates the high levels of cooperation which prevailed in the implementation of Nazi racial policy. There was someone present to identify each potential category of victim, be they 'asocial', criminal, mad or 'racially alien'. Commencing from different starting points, they all converged on the inmates of one workhouse. Using a new form for the registration of 'community aliens', the racial experts carried out the selections, with the T–4 men on hand to size up their future victims. The referees agreed unanimously to kill 314 of the inmates, but could not agree on a further 765.[60] For reasons which probably had to do with the war effort and mounting competition from the SS, T–4 failed to get its hands on these people. In line with the strategy of 'extermination through labour', the Rummelsburger inmates were sent to a satellite camp of Sachsenhausen instead.[61]

Many of the murders described in the preceding pages were carried out by women. These included doctors such as Mathilde Weber, who presided over a special paediatric ward at the Kalmenhof, but also literally hundreds of nurses. In the second phase, the victims were not total strangers whom one loaded and unloaded from a bus, to be gassed within the hour by a Gorgass or Ullrich in the cellars, but – for a time at least – patients with whom one could build some sort of relationship. True, one was not helping to treat them for anything – that was rarely the case anyway – but one went about keeping the place running. Killing in this phase was not done *en masse* and remotely, but by nurses who consciously handed their individual victims drinks laced with drugs, or administered lethal injections.

There is no major psychological mystery about why these 'carers' became killers, once one has jettisoned the powerful received stereotypes one has about medical professionals in general. If one surveys their life histories, one finds that these people were often bitter, frustrated, disillusioned, tired, underpaid and undervalued. To this one should add the usual problems of patriarchal power structures, naturally including those in which the doctor-patriarchs were in fact matriarchs.

Most of these women had been nurses for a long time, and were hence in some respects inured to other people's suffering. A degree of desensitising was probably an inevitable part of the job, particularly if one was not very sensitive in the first place. It was no doubt frustrating dealing with people who were sometimes difficult or dirty. In the nature of things, some psychiatric patients had difficulty following basic instructions, or problems in expressing themselves in a non-aggressive or coherent fashion. Beds were wetted, and excrement smeared or thrown around. This clashed unhappily with a profession which fetishised cleanliness and order from day one of basic training. These were also essential values in wider society. The patient-victims thus became the aggressors. Tempers quickly frayed on both sides of the fence, as is evident from the frequent reports of brutality, particularly when patients were being bathed and hence most physically vulnerable. Because of budget cuts and deliberate overcrowding, conditions in the asylums had deteriorated since the mid 1930s, with patients coming physically to resemble the regime's propaganda stereotypes. To this can be added the fact that an unknown number of relatives said to the nursing staff that they wished the patients were dead. Many of them internalised and generalised the message.

Many of the women discussed here were not hardened killers, although some undoubtedly were. In some cases, the tasks they performed clearly grated on their received moral or religious principles, although never to the point of making them walk out or stop. It is important to remember that it was possible to refuse to carry out these policies; the only sanctions that existed concerned breaking the code of secrecy. It was also possible to become ill or pregnant, or to insist on (not just request) a transfer. The women considered below did none of these things.

Irmgard Huber was born in 1901 as one of ten children. After elementary school she worked as a domestic servant, before training as a psychiatric nurse at Gabersee. Having qualified, she left the state sector with the intention of finding a marriage partner. Having failed in her quest, she applied for a job at Hadamar in 1932, returning to state employment because she was anxious about provision for her old age. In 1934 she began a forlorn love affair with one of the office personnel, the eight-years-younger Alfons Klein. The latter was separated from his wife and down on his luck; Huber soon travelled 'the short distance from pity to love', helping the ponce-like Klein with regular handouts from her pay packet. They do not look like a well-matched pair. Klein was lean, tall and reptilian; Huber greying, squat and dumpy. In 1940, she was one of the Hadamar staff retained in the asylum to help implement 'Aktion T–4'. Klein moved up to be chief administrator, divorcing his wife in order to marry another woman, alas not called Huber. Working in the kitchens, and keeping herself apart from the 'Berlin' personnel, Huber maintained the psychological fiction that she had nothing to do with the murders in the asylum cellars. In the second phase of 'euthanasia' killings, she was promoted to the post of acting senior nurse. This was surprising, since there were other, better-qualified candidates for the job. Her superiors calculated that her unrequited love for Klein, and hence her total obedience, would be more powerful than her religious faith.

Although she 'suffered' because of what was happening in Hadamar, and knew 'that one should not kill', Huber nonetheless became a functioning cog in the machinery of extermination. She said that she could not sleep at night. She asked Bernotat and Klein for a transfer; the former said that he could not get a replacement, and that she should think of the soldiers at the front.[62] She used various strategies of denial and evasion to distance herself from what she was doing, namely attending Wahlmann's morning conferences and passing on his instructions to kill patients to her subordinates. Wahlmann made the key decisions; the strange 'Berlin' sisters carried out the dirty work. She gave toys to children, and food to starving 'foreign workers'. She arranged for the latter to celebrate Mass if they were Roman Catholics.[63] The local priest testified that she was desperate to leave the asylum.[64] In her own eyes, she was thus a passive vessel, simply relaying instructions from the doctor to her subordinates. A few instances of individual charity cancelled out routine inhumanity.

Irmgard Huber's older colleague, Margarete Borkowski, worked in Hadamar from 1924 until 1939 re-educating juvenile 'psychopaths'; she then moved to Herborn. There she saw patients being transferred to Hadamar, regarding this as 'completely wrong'.[65] She then worked at the Kalmenhof in Idstein between July 1941 and January 1942, moving on to Weilmünster and then back to Hadamar in January 1943. She worked in a children's ward where killings were carried out by Berlin sisters under the aegis of senior nurse Käthe Hakbarth. On the latter's days off, or when she was on night duty, Borkowski had to carry out killings herself. She found the business of overdosing 'about fifty' children 'terrible', but it was an order and she could do nothing against it. Complaining to her superior, she was satisfied by the answer that the victims had been carefully selected. Her comments on specific victims, including a group of children of 'mixed race', include several expressions of pity, on account of the fact that they were dressed in rags, wore shoes with no soles, were starving; or were intelligent, well-behaved, never coming to one's attention; happy even despite their miserable circumstances. But each comment ends with the observation 'he or she was killed too'.[66]

A younger woman, Lydia T., arrived in Hadamar in 1941, returning there in early 1942 after the Organisation Todt operation in Minsk. She spent the time until August cleaning the deserted wards in readiness for the first wave of second-phase transports. Klein eventually got around to telling her, 'Now it's time you started working.' A senior nurse handed her a list of names, telling her to give the patients concerned eight to ten tablets. If they did not die shortly afterwards, she was then told to give them a lethal injection. Like her colleagues, she found the work disturbing, and told Klein she wanted to stop. He apparently responded 'You lazy cow, if you do, you'll be next.'[67]

At Eglfing-Haar, three women were responsible for day-to-day killings in the paediatric ward. Between November 1940 and May 1945 they killed 332 children. Before commencing work in the clinic, the three had to sign a statement promising to obey all instructions and swearing total secrecy on pain of death. This last point was entirely fictional, since the women were volunteers, and there is no recorded instance of any person being punished for refusing to carry out such killings.[68] (Though the women admittedly did not know this at the time.) Every day they rose at 5 a.m. to begin administering Luminal two hours later. Pfannmüller told them which child to kill. The senior nurse, Emma D., passed on the instruction and the sedatives to her subordinates, Emma L. and Maria S. The under-tens received two doses of Luminal a day; older children up to three.[69] All three women were convinced that killing these children was the correct thing to do. The children were 'pitiful forms, which one could only describe as creatures'.[70] Killing them was an act of deliverance, sparing them suffering in later life. Nonetheless, the women clearly felt uncomfortable about what they were doing. Emma D. felt horrified every time she had to kill one of the children, and repeatedly requested a transfer to other duties. She felt guilty about the bonuses and supplementary payments she received for working in the clinic. The asylum chaplain reported that for religious reasons she wanted to cease working in the clinic, but that she was terrified of Pfannmüller, who was at the time 'an important personage', well connected with the KdF (Chancellory of the Führer).[71]

Finally, we can come back to Pauline K., who, as we saw in Part II, worked successively in Grafeneck, Hadamar, Bernburg and Kaufbeuren-

Irsee. In 1944, Faltlhauser asked the Ministry of the Interior for personnel who would be able to carry out 'euthanasia'. Many of his own nursing staff were members of a religious order, and were hence regarded as unsuitable. (This did not prevent them living and working cheek by jowl with murderers.) The staff at T-4, ever-present in the shadows, sent him Pauline K., who had actually been to Kaufbeuren before, on one of the Community Patients' Transport Service buses to take patients from there to Grafeneck.[72] The two of them met in Faltlhauser's office several times a week. On the first occasion Faltlhauser told her which patients to kill, asking whether she could do the job alone. She said that she could, having done so at Hadamar.[73]

Pauline K. was in charge of her own ward with between forty-five and fifty beds. In the course of forty-eight weeks, 256 women and a few men died there. A graph drawn after the war shows the deathrate rising sharply after her arrival, only falling off when she went away on holiday. This evidence was corroborated by Sister Gualberta, who testified that K. went on holiday for four weeks in September 1944, there being almost no deaths during her absence.[74] Things picked up quickly when she returned. Many of those she killed died simply because they were foreigners, or had scabies. Nurses who deputised for Pauline K. at night left patients healthy at daybreak and returned the same evening to find them critically ill, with traces of powder smeared around their mouths or the odd mislaid tablet resting below the collars. Asked what had happened, Pauline K. speculated that they must have had a weak heart or lungs.[75] Some of the religious nursing sisters made a habit of hiding patients lest Faltlhauser transfer them to Pauline K.'s ward.[76] They knew that she was very dangerous.

We do not know whether particularly complex psychological processes helped Pauline K. as she travelled from one asylum to another, cold-bloodedly killing patients practically every day for four years. Her own explanations after the event, as she gave evidence with her eyes closed at Faltlhauser's trial, were matter-of-fact and unreflective. There were few signs of remorse, although she did mention the odd attempt to transfer to other duties. Why should she have bothered to reveal much about her state of mind? She received a three-and-a-quarter-year jail sentence in 1948, for an 'unknown' number of murders, and was released on parole a year later. One of her few flashes of self-knowledge was to mention that her religious beliefs jostled uneasily in her mind with the 'laws of nature', laws she was quite prepared to help along whenever necessary.

Her former landlady in Irsee shed more light on the inner life of a mass murderess than Pauline K. herself. Apparently Pauline K. would turn 'white as chalk' whenever there was a thunderstorm. Her landlady took a perverse delight whenever this otherwise confident and friendly woman was reduced to a cowering wreck. Although Pauline K. never ventured a word about what she was doing in the asylum, the storms seem to have triggered memories of her winter in Russia. Perhaps this reminder of human vulnerability to elemental forces stirred some vestiges of guilt. She said she regretted having given German soldiers lethal injections in military hospitals. Asked why she had done this, she said that it had paid well. Apparently the victims were not badly wounded, but mad.[77]

The second phase of 'euthanasia' killings was not confined to German psychiatric patients. As is well known, Germany relied upon millions of forced 'foreign workers' for the functioning of its agrarian and industrial economy. By 1944, one in five workers in Germany was a foreigner: either volunteers, prisoners of war, or just young people kidnapped off the streets, and from churches, trains and cinemas. Their presence meant (*inter alia*) that the regime would not have to mobilise as many women as its democratic opponents; and that ordinary German workers could move up into supervisory positions. They were a pool of virtually unpaid labour which could be housed on site; for whom there were no safety regulations, Sundays off or overtime payments; who could literally be told when they could eat or visit the lavatory; and whom one could send to special 'works disciplinary camps' run by the SS if they slacked off or caused any trouble. This usually resulted in a spell in hospital.

These foreign forced labourers received differential treatment according to their 'racial' origin, with 'eastern workers' somewhere very near the bottom rung of the racial hierarchy. Many of these people fell desperately ill, or (for many of them were young women) simply became pregnant. Since they were in Germany solely for their labour, before 1943 the regime immediately repatriated anyone who was pregnant, fell sick or had a mental breakdown. The repatriates were gathered together in special camps: in the case of Hessen, these were located at Kelsterbach, Friedewald and Pfaffenwald.[78] Thereafter, the course of the war, demands upon transport networks and the damage repatriation was doing to the voluntary recruitment of labour led to a different policy.[79] Women deemed 'racially' undesirable were encouraged to have abortions; if it was too late for this, their infants were killed by starvation and lethal injection. At Kelsterbach alone, sixty-eight children under three died between 1943 and 1945.[80]

The problem of adult foreign psychiatric patients was resolved in the following way. In each region, an asylum was designated which would receive those foreign forced workers whom doctors employed by the labour offices decided would not recover within the six-week period they were allowed. There were eleven 'collection centres', including Hadamar and Kaufbeuren. The selection, transfer and 'maintenance' costs of patients despatched to these centres were defrayed by the Central Accounting Office for Asylums in Linz, or in other words by Hans-Joachim 'Millionen' Becker's department of T–4 in Berlin. The involve-

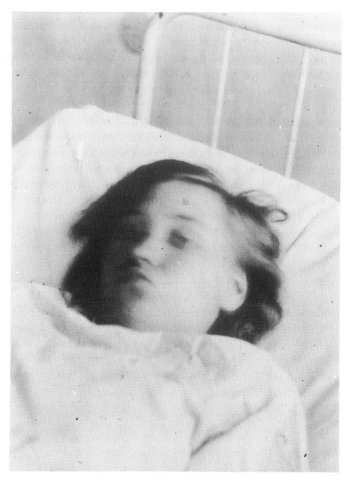

Plate 42. An 'eastern' worker who was murdered at Eichberg asylum.

ment of T–4 signified that the foreign forced workers faced two alternatives: death or recovery.

Even those who travel in times of peace to civilised countries know that being ill away from home is a worrying experience. When we are ill, most of us atavistically prefer going to ground, in our own bed, comforted by the familiar. Going mad in a hostile country whose language one does not know, where one has no friends or relatives, and where one is officially regarded as subhuman and hence totally expendable, is fortunately something few of us have ever experienced.

Sick foreign forced workers arriving at Eichberg often came wearing nothing but ragged, dirty, lice-ridden clothes which had to be incinerated immediately.[81] Their possessions consisted of nothing more than the clothes they were wearing.[82] In the asylum they lay silent in bed; stood in corners unable to speak; or shouted and raved in Russian.[83] They were unable to speak German, and hence there was no way of knowing anything about their medical history, beyond what one could glean from pointing or nodding. Attempts to get them to write something down failed, since they were sometimes illiterate.[84] Clinically depressed or 'schizophrenic', they lay in a catatonic stupor, or in some cases raved to a point where they died. As this was Eichberg, the cause of death given should naturally be treated like treacherous sands, for it is more probable that they were murdered. Every one of the cases concerned resulted in the person's death at Eichberg within a month or two of admission. Writing to the Labour Office in Frankfurt am Main regarding a Russian woman, Dr Walter Schmidt made it brutally clear why this happened:

The above-named is a mentally ill Russian female who is no longer capable of deployment in Germany. Nor can we anticipate that she will be capable of working again in the foreseeable future; she is lying here simply as burden upon our authorities.[85]

By 10 July 1943 she was no longer a 'burden' on anybody.[86]

At the first Hadamar Trial, which was solely concerned with crimes against four hundred foreign nationals, Margarete Borkowski described the arrival of a 'shipment' of Russians and Poles in late July or early August 1944. She was being questioned by Leon Jaworski, the judge advocate (and later Watergate special prosecutor; for further details about his career see p. 269 below). Jaworski had seen Hadamar's tenebrously bleak rooms, with their empty iron beds, rendered cold to the touch by wind whistling through paneless windows. Carefully controlling a high degree of pent-up fury, he clinically made each of the accused recount every stage of the killing process:

JAWORSKI Were you on duty at the Institution at the time the shipment arrived?
BORKOWSKI Yes, I was on night duty which began at 7 o'clock. The shipment arrived round about 10 o'clock.
JAWORSKI Had any preparations been made in the ward in which you worked to receive these laborers?
BORKOWSKI The small rooms in the back were cleared before I arrived on duty.
JAWORSKI Did you see any people brought upstairs to occupy these rooms?
BORKOWSKI Yes.
JAWORSKI Men, women, or children?
BORKOWSKI About fourteen or fifteen women and two children.
JAWORSKI Did you see the Chief Nurse Huber on that occasion?
BORKOWSKI Yes; she walked to and fro and saw that everything was all right.
JAWORSKI After these women reached these rooms, what if anything was done with them?

BORKOWSKI They were partly undressed; some of them undressed themselves, but otherwise we helped them to get undressed and then we put them to bed.

JAWORSKI About what were the ages of the two children?

BORKOWSKI Between one and four years old.

JAWORSKI What was done with the little children?

BORKOWSKI The children also were injected.

JAWORSKI Before that occurred, were the little children put to bed, too, as the grown-up folks were?

BORKOWSKI Yes.

JAWORSKI Did you see Alfons Klein on that occasion?

BORKOWSKI Yes.

JAWORSKI What was he doing?

BORKOWSKI He just walked through the ward to see whether everything was all right or not.

JAWORSKI And did you see Philipp Blum on that occasion?

BORKOWSKI Yes; at first he just walked around in the ward.

JAWORSKI What was his purpose in walking around?

BORKOWSKI He just walked through.

JAWORSKI Now, after these women and the two little children were put to bed, did anyone else come into their room?

BORKOWSKI Yes, Heinrich Ruoff.

JAWORSKI Did he carry any equipment when he walked in?

BORKOWSKI Yes, a syringe.

JAWORSKI Did you hear him say anything to the occupants of those bedrooms as he walked in?

BORKOWSKI Herr Ruoff talked very nicely to them and told them that they would receive a vaccination against infectious diseases.

JAWORSKI Did you see Heinrich Ruoff give this so-called immunization?

BORKOWSKI No.

JAWORSKI Did the patients survive that immunization?

BORKOWSKI No.

JAWORSKI What happened to those women and children and the two little children?

BORKOWSKI They were injected, and then they slowly fell asleep.

JAWORSKI Into eternal sleep?

BORKOWSKI Yes.[87]

Sick foreign labourers were but one of the groups of people killed in the second phase of the 'euthanasia' programme. At Hadamar, victims included soldiers who had been discharged on psychiatric grounds, and five young foreign volunteers (from Hungary, Holland, Spain and Yugoslavia) in the Waffen-SS who had deserted or gone insane.[88]

Worsening Allied air raids on Germany's cities necessarily entailed local, regional and central planning for the eventuality of mass catastrophes. In March 1941, cities such as Hamburg began transferring the occupants of asylums, infirmaries and old people's homes to outlying institutions where care was often minimal.[89] These measures were a panic reaction to unforeseen circumstances. They inevitably triggered off further movements lower down the institutional hierarchy, in line with the notion of weakest to the wall. Their relationship to the 'euthanasia' programme is complex and not undisputed, and stems primarily from one significant appointment.

In July 1942, Hitler designated Professor Karl Brandt – one of the original architects of the 'euthanasia' programme – Plenipotentiary for the Health and Sanitation System. The post involved coordinating the needs of the civil and military health sectors. One of the obvious concerns was emergency bedspace in the event that urban hospitals were destroyed by bombing. Although 'Aktion T–4' had decimated the longterm psychiatric population, it had also resulted in the alienation of tens of thousands of psychiatric beds for other uses. Statistics drawn up in January 1942 revealed that 93,521 psychiatric beds had been redirected: 31,058 beds were lost to military casualty stations; 6,348 to the National Socialist welfare organisation; 8,577 as hostels for repatriates; 7,170 to the SS; 650 to Adolf Hitler Schools and so forth.[90] Together with Linden, Brandt developed a system whereby psychiatric asylums would continue to function, with the patients keeping the beds warm, and the staff occupied and in reserved occupations. Catastrophes in the cities resulted in the removal of people in asylums and various kinds of home to asylums in non-endangered areas. When these in turn filled up, the patients deemed most expendable were sent to Hadamar or Meseritz-Obrawalde and killed.[91] To recapitulate the cycle: the bombs rained down, hospitals went up in flames, and psychiatric patients deemed non-essential to asylum economies were despatched to their deaths. It was a sort of chain reaction, with death for the most expendable elements being built into the calculation. For example, in the week beginning 24 July 1943, the Allies carried out 'Operation Gomorrah' against Hamburg, which resulted in the deaths of about 44,000 people and the destruction of virtually all of the city's hospitals. Between 22 June and 7 August, 349 mentally ill women were transported from Hamburg to Hadamar. Around 20% of them had gone mad during the firestorm which devastated the city, and had hence been sent to the asylum at Langenhorn.

One of them was Minna H. Born in 1894, she had moved to Hamburg in 1920, marrying a widower with three children of his own, to which they added another two. As a railwayman, Minna H.'s husband was able to find a flat for the family in a housing cooperative in the Dennerstrasse. Like the family concerned, many of the occupants of the flats were supporters of the SPD or Communists. In the mid 1930s, the flats began to receive Jewish families, many of them victims of racially motivated, enforced downward social mobility. After 'Reichkristallnacht', a Jewish family moved into the

Plate 43. Minna H.

same block. The H.s befriended them, although this was dangerous. Minna H. had a developed sense of justice. When the Jewish family was forced to emigrate, the H.s arranged for their neighbours to dispose of their remaining furniture. This resulted in interrogation by the Gestapo, and Minna H.'s depressive state which resulted in periods in the clinic at Hamburg-Eppendorf and Langenhorn. In 1943 she returned to Langenhorn. She was terrified out of her wits by air raids and refused to go down into shelters. On 29 July she and fifty other women were sent to Hadamar; the family was merely informed that she had been taken to another asylum. The reason Minna H. was removed was that she was marked as a 'trouble-maker', i.e. she had asked for thimbles for herself and other patients whose fingers were bleeding as a result of sewing borders around floorcloths.[92] Despite this, when her son Helmut H. visited her at Langenhorn while on leave in the spring of 1943, he noted that she was in good physical condition. Following their own enquiries as to her whereabouts, on 16 May 1944 the family were informed that Minna H. had died of 'influenza' on 6 March.

From what has gone before, readers should have some idea of the desolate conditions prevailing in most German asylums during the years 1941–1945. They left intelligent and sensitive outside observers, such as Leon Jaworski, who in late 1945 walked around desolate wards, poking into medicine cupboards and reading death registers, profoundly despondent. In August 1945, Dr Elisabeth V. recorded her impressions of Eichberg, where she had worked for the previous three years. I wish to quote this extensively here, because some historians – much taken with what amounts to a minor academic 'insight' that has recently become fashionable – tend to relay the T–4 psychiatrists' 'modernising' rationalisations for the 'euthanasia' programme, while omitting any mention of the 'medieval' conditions they actually created.[93] Any discussion of 'modernisation' has to be considered in the light of such evidence. Dr V. wrote:

When I returned in 1942 to work in a provincial asylum after a break of about three years, I had to acknowledge that in the intervening period, the development of asylum-based psychiatric treatment had gone right down. As early as in 1937 or 1938 we had oral reports from doctors at Weilmünster about the so-called 'bunker' at Eichberg, which was used for the longterm containment of psychiatric offenders. Our criticism of a reversion to the psychiatry of the Middle Ages was considerable. I discovered that it was also totally justified, when during the first few days I saw this prison, which consisted of a mass bunker and two totally dark individual cells. After a prolonged period in these areas it would have been impossible to avoid damage to one's health or the lack of hygiene, especially since, as I heard later, not every patient had his own blanket, but rather was given a blanket in the evening, regardless of whether other patients there were covered in vermin. During my period of service there this 'bunker' was no longer used for its original purpose, i.e. for delinquent patients, but rather was filled with patients who in my opinion were chosen in accordance with no particular guidelines. The then chief doctor and asylum director, Schmidt, seems to have acted very arbitrarily and was not free from sudden changes of mood. During times when I had to deputise on the male wards, I objected to the fact that patients were being isolated in the bunker by the nursing staff without any orders from the doctors, and raised this issue during conferences.

The so-called 'bunker' on the women's wards was even worse in an hygienic sense. It consisted of two plain rooms in the cellar, one totally dark, the other with a small window. One of these rooms was very damp, since it remained unheated in winter; in both of them, patients were plagued by rats. A spell in the 'bunker' was accompanied by more or less lengthy periods without food. This last measure was illusory as far as the women were concerned, since those (mostly male) patients who could roam the asylum at liberty found ways of smuggling in food. In one case, a female patient was even sexually harassed or raped by a male patient during the night.

A new sight for me were the so–called transit wards in the female section. These housed women who should have fallen victim to the 'action', but who, in a sense, were left hanging in the air because of its sudden cessation. These wards were chronically overcrowded; most of the patients lacked a bed, sleeping instead on straw mattresses on the floor. As far as I can remember, there were no day rooms in these wards. The number of staff stood in stark contrast to the volume of patients. People frequently complained that one sister was alone with eighty or ninety patients in a ward. Levels of care and the condition of the patients corresponded with this. Most of them were physically reduced to a state bordering on the skeletal. This was a consequence of the fact that the food was quantitatively and qualitatively totally inadequate, whereby it should be stressed that at the time (1942/1943) the population as a whole still received relatively good rations. The then asylum director, Dr Mennecke, forbade the sort of forced feeding which was normal in the case of catatonic or depressed patients who refused food. During mealtimes, the patients were left to their own devices, which meant that weak, apathetic and helpless patients were subject to the sick and asocial thieving compulsions of certain individuals, thus losing their own food. Since the asylum's population greatly outstripped its resources, there was not enough bedlinen or underclothes, the result of which was that on the one hand, many patients went around naked at night and hence caught colds, while on the other hand there was a rise in dermatological and contagious diseases, which naturally spread like wildfire because of the high levels of occupancy. I was particularly upset by the fact that patients from other asylums had long numbers printed on their backs or upper arms in blue ink. I was never able to find out precisely what this was for. Naturally, I was able to put two and two together, i.e. that it had something to do with their transfer to Hadamar . . .

One heard nothing regarding the 'action' which had already been concluded. However, people often discussed the problem of killing mental patients, which was falsely confused with the question of 'euthanasia'. When he acquired an electro-shock apparatus, Director Mennecke raised the question of whether one could effect their deaths through high levels of electric current passed through their brains. He also set up a so–called nurse-free ward, in order to see how long mental patients would vegetate without any care and attention. He seems to have been encouraged to try this out by people in Heidelberg, since he set up the ward, and tried this out, shortly after going on a course for several weeks at Professor Schneider's Heidelberg psychiatric clinic . . .

From time to time we received mentally ill 'eastern workers'. Some of them came to my ward, where I examined them and looked after them like other patients. Sometimes, however, I never got to see them. Dr Schmidt said – I don't know whether spontaneously or in response to a question – that we had a special department for mentally ill 'eastern workers', and that it did not concern me. Through the overall situation and because of remarks made by the senior nurse, I could only conclude that the lives of these women had been prematurely terminated, if not by Dr Schmidt in person, then on his instructions. One day I found a pretext to raise the matter with him. At any rate, I made it very clear to him that as a doctor one should treat mentally ill foreigners exactly as one would treat mentally ill Germans, just as a doctor at the front would afford the same treatment to German and enemy wounded. However, he was strongly of the opinion that there was no room in Germany for mentally ill foreigners, especially Russians, and that he was acting as a soldier when he drew the consequences from this. I could not agree with this, and said that a soldier with a gun in his hand faced armed opponents, but that doctors had to behave in a completely different fashion. Dr Schmidt abruptly terminated the discussion with the remark that I was just a woman, and hence felt things like one, and that I would never be able to understand him regarding these matters.[94]

Let us be quite clear about what Dr V. described. Patients were being kept in deplorable and inhuman conditions, including being consigned to rat-infested bunkers by non-medical staff. Many of them were starving; many of them were being killed for no other reason than their 'race'. Doctors imagined that they were soldiers (this meant that the patients were the 'enemy'), and were encouraged by distinguished academics to see how one might best starve people to death, or use 'modern' therapies to electrocute them. As she said, psychiatry had reverted to the worst excesses of an earlier era.

As we saw above (p. 259), the 'euthanasia' programme threatened the entire institutional basis of psychiatry. About a third of available psychiatric beds were lost in a two-year period, along with most of the patients who had once occupied them. Moreover, a profession that had never basked in much public esteem was now openly associated in the public mind with mass murder. In July 1942, Nitsche organised a survey of the various regional asylums, soliciting views as to how psychiatry might overcome its image problem, i.e. that asylums were viewed with mistrust and horror. Several of the respondents recommended that asylums should become more like hospitals, with the emphasis upon treatment rather than containment.[95] To this end, a number of eminent T-4 psychiatrists floated schemes for the future reform of psychiatric provision. Nitsche himself spoke of a 'renaissance' of psychiatry, winning Bouhler to the idea that the money saved through the 'euthanasia' programme could be redeployed in the service of therapy-centred reform psychiatry. Allers confessed to killing this flight of fancy stone dead by simply telling Bouhler that there was no surplus money available.[96] Even existing new therapies, such as insulin-shock treatment, were halted because Linden put a stop to the supply of that commodity for non-diabetic uses. Schneider and others opened two observational research stations at Brandenburg-Görden and Wiesloch. In the eyes of those in the KdF, who footed the bill for these clinics, the latter were nothing more than a sop to ease professorial bad consciences about the 'euthanasia' programme, in the sense that the latter generated research 'materials'.[97] One should never take professional motivation at its face value, which in this case means uncritically relaying what amounted to a series of uneasy rationalisations of the 'euthanasia' programme in terms of putative 'modernisation'.

Nitsche, de Crinis, Schneider, Heinze, Rüdin and others produced various memoranda outlining the future of their discipline. The main mover here was probably Schneider, who in 1941 had addressed the Association of German Neurologists and Psychiatrists on how his discipline might accommodate itself to Nazi eugenic policies and what he ominously and obliquely called 'other measures'. Schneider's talk was a sort of *pièce justificative* for the benefit of 'many lay, even intelligent ... national comrades' who already thought there was no need for psychiatry. There were 'even' officials responsible for the funding of psychiatric institutions who were entertaining the heretical thought that psychiatry had become 'superfluous'.[98] What followed was a sort of preemptive strike against these 'slumbering dangers'. The state's eugenic policies were focussed on the longterm. It would take centuries to eradicate the endogenous psychoses; and in any case, accident, environment and mutation would continue to produce both endogenous and exogenous disorders. Stopping psychiatric research at this point would be like unilateral disarmament, or the abandonment of weapons development because of a vague prospect of global peace. These metaphors were as revealing as they were depressing.[99] Where there was a threat, 'one needed scientifically based defences and the necessary academic institutes, researchers, and people practically versed in defence'. One did not get rid of bacteriologists just because one had succeeded in stamping out certain epidemic diseases. Academics usually talk this language when they sense a challenge to their existence.

Many of Schneider's ideas resurfaced in the joint memorandum produced by the 'euthanasia' psychiatrists. What is actually interesting here is not their routine and self-interested subscription to the reformist idealism of the 1920s, or the 'modern' therapeutic techniques of the 1930s, but rather their attempts to combat lay and medical contempt for their discipline (the former stemming from their involvement in Nazi eugenic policies, the latter from the unscientific and hopeless nature of the entire enterprise), coupled with barely concealed efforts to secure continued funding for their squalid 'research' activities. There was nothing 'idealistic' about this; just a group of thoroughly amoral eggheads bent on continuing to access the honey-pot. For, despite all their sterling achievements, the rest of the medical profession still regarded them as defenders of lost outposts, and worse, because of the 'euthanasia' programme, some of the civil servants responsible for asylums were of the opinion that one would not need any more psychiatrists after the war. Indeed, this was already coming to pass, since there was a mass exodus of young psychiatrists from the profession.[100]

The reform proposals began with a number of organisational changes, of which their authors would naturally be the main beneficiaries. The entire asylum system would be subject to central psychiatric control, thus countering the wartime tendency for asylum economic administrators like Grossmann or Klein to succeed in elbowing the medical professionals to one side.[101] The asylums were to be closely bound to university research centres, providing the latter with, so to speak, their raw materials (points 4 and 5 of the proposals). Those asylums which had been put to other uses should revert to their original function. In keeping with the usual dictates of academic empire-building and the quest for 'relevance', asylums were to work closely with agencies concerned with youth or 'criminal biology' (point 10). Being professors, they were keen to incorporate perpetual refresher courses (which they would run) for asylum doctors into the new system (points 11 and 13). Conscious of their poor image, they inevitably insisted upon the outlawing of any public defamation of their profession in future (point 17).

Nitsche's correspondence with Schneider and others illustrates the type of 'research' to emerge from the close association of asylums and university research centres. Essentially, Schneider wanted the brains of victims of the 'euthanasia' programme. He sent lists of desiderata to Nitsche, requesting the brains of dwarfs, twins, and people suffering from idiocy and rare neurological abnormalities, presumably on the basis that abnormalities were the most scientifically revealing.[102] Nitsche in turn sent him copies of registration forms, from which Schneider could pick out the 'material' he wanted.[103] Schneider was advised of suitable cases by his colleagues and former pupils, such as Dr Hebold who wrote on 26 October 1942 with the intelligence that he had encountered three feebleminded individuals in the Katharinenhof, almost forgetting 'an imbecile, all of whose fingers ended at the first joint'.[104] Schneider was quite fussy about his brains, insisting that they be sent by courier rather than by freight or the postal system.[105] Schneider's eminent colleague, Professor Julius Hallervorden of the Kaiser Wilhelm Institute for Neurology, similarly assembled a collection of over 600 brains which he had acquired (or himself removed) from people killed by his friend Heinze at Brandenburg Görden.[106] Having decimated the asylum population and reduced a once-adequate system to absolute 'medieval' desolation, the T–4 psychiatrists, only belatedly realising that this might put them out of a job, vainly tried to salvage what they could through macabre experiments on the remains of their victims. The 'modernity' of this belated exercise in rationalising mass murder is actually not its most salient feature – unless of course, one feels uncomfortable with non-rationalistic explanations for this sort of human behaviour, in which case 'modernisation' theories probably fit the bill all too appropriately.

PART FOUR

AFTERMATHS

CHAPTER 9

HOW PROFESSOR HEYDE BECAME
DR SAWADE

IN THE course of this book we have repeatedly ventured into a series of encapsulated worlds, acquiring a sense of their distinct institutional character and domestic psychodramas. We have also seen something of the relationship between asylums and society as a whole. Ranged above the individual asylums, the covert KdF-cum-T–4-bureaucracy in Berlin also developed a house style, with its bigwigs and would-be professorial potentates, office wits, nicknames (the canteen waitress, an ex-dancer, was known as 'Terpsichore', the two Beckers as 'Rot' and 'Millionen'), and so forth. A sort of institutional culture emerged too in the death camps, based on bullying, heavy drinking, lachrymose sing-songs about the Carinthian *Heimat*, and a particularly black form of barracks humour. It is time now to see how some of these institutions were viewed through the eyes of strangers, and then to address the matter of reckonings. How did these places and people seem to decent people from Brooklyn, Leningrad, London or Texas? What was the eventual fate of men and women who had murdered tens of thousands of people?

In spring 1945, forensic pathologists attached to the invading Red Army were despatched to the asylum at Obrawalde to investigate disquieting reports from those troops who had been first on the scene. They interviewed ten of the surviving inmates. The latter testified that between thirty and fifty patients had been murdered there each day for several years. Upon inspecting the asylum buildings, the Russians discovered large quantities of morphia and scopolamine, syringes, and a store room with clothing and hundreds of pairs of shoes. They found a crematorium and a half-completed gas chamber. The place reminded them of Mauthausen; the difference was just one of scale. The cemetery area included several mass graves; the one the Russians opened for forensic reasons contained about a thousand corpses crudely arranged in four or five layers.

The Russian investigators worked through the death register, establishing that 18,232 people had died at Obrawalde in the previous three years. For example, of the 3,948 admissions in 1944, 3,814, or 97%, were

Plate 44. The cemetery area above the asylum at Hadamar shortly after the end of the Second World War. These mass graves contained several layers of victims of the second phase of the 'euthanasia' programme. This photograph was taken by American investigators in the course of preparing evidence for the Hadamar trial.

dead by the time the Russians arrived. They noted that not even cholera or the plague in more primitive hygienic circumstances would have resulted in such a high mortality rate.[1] The recorded causes of death were routinised and implausible: 'angina', 'exhaustion' and so forth. Patients who were still alive – like the dentist who was temporarily acting as asylum director – testified that they owed their survival solely to their specialist skills. Had this dentist not had the foresight to request a selection of his instruments from home, he would have been dead too. Survival was a matter of chance as well as inner resourcefulness. And so the Russians continued their work, gradually accustoming themselves to the ghastly jargon of 'Todeszimmer' and 'Todesspritzen' (death rooms and lethal injections), and interviewing medical staff personally responsible for killing 'over 1,500' people. They exhumed forty-two corpses of civilians, whose ages ranged from two to sixty years of age. Half of them bore signs of having been given injections, and in 95% of cases their organs revealed traces of morphia and scopolamine. Photographs taken during the exhumation resemble what one sees at Pompeii: an expressionist version of a classical frieze. People frozen artlessly in the positions they randomly fell in, swathed in shirts or vests, and partially merged with the backdrop of mud. The Russians decided there were not enough Soviet military victims to proceed any further.

On the western side of Germany, Major Herman Bolker, a pathologist from the Brooklyn Cancer Institute attached to the US Army Medical Corps, arrived at Hadamar on 2 April 1945. A very grim silent film entitled *Murder Mills Hadamar*,[2] shot by a military camera crew, shows young Bolker working on twelve recently disinterred corpses in the cemetery above the asylum, a *modus operandi* not uninfluenced by the fact that those who move the bodies backwards and forth are seen clutching handkerchiefs to their noses. A party of grim-faced and battle-worn US soldiers watch over him, smoking and casually holding their rifle straps. Bolker conducted complete autopsies upon six of those who had been exhumed, who, lacking a wooden identity disc attached to their toes, could be presumed to be non-German patients. Four of this group revealed signs of tuberculosis. Bolker discovered boxes containing glass tubes of morphine hydrochlorate, $2/100$ of a gramme per cc, labelled 'shake before use' and 'poison'. He noted that one does not administer a drug which reduces the respiratory rate to people suffering from a disease of the lungs, and that Hadamar had no X-ray facility or pneumonothorax machines, essential for the identification and treatment of tuberculosis.[3] Some of the bodies had tell-tale signs of morphine poisoning, notably pin-prick pupils.

Other parts of the same film show members of the Hadamar staff arriving in jeeps at an American interrogation centre in Wiesbaden. Leon Jaworski, a thirty-six-year-old Texan lawyer of Polish ancestry, was attached to the Judge Advocate General's Corps, the legal branch of the US Army. He began his military legal career prosecuting Nazi prisoners of war who had quietly murdered less ideologically committed comrades in detention centres like Camp Chaffee in Arkansas. At Christmas 1944 he flew to Paris, where, as a lieutenant-colonel, he began assembling evidence on war crimes. His first case was that of a civilian mob which had beaten to death six members of a downed American bomber crew in the streets of Rüsselheim. Jaworski then moved on to Hadamar, where members of staff were tried in connection with the murder of four hundred foreign nationals. There are several still photographs of the accused being interrogated by US war crimes investigators. With shorn heads and unshaven faces, they all look rather rough; a few of them have been punched about, a not unnatural reaction by US combat troops to their enduring arrogance and the gravity of their offences.[4]

The trial had many interesting legal aspects, not least that both the accused and their victims were civilians, the latter being foreign nationals.[5] The right to try German civilians was partially established by the Rüsselheim case. For jurisdictional reasons, charges concerning the deaths of over ten thousand German civilians were left to the reconstituted German authorities. Looking back over a long and immensely distinguished career – including his spell as Watergate prosecutor – Jaworski wrote:

Of all the experiences I had in trying war crimes, Hadamar was unquestionably the most depressing. I simply could not fathom the drastic changes that could take place in human beings over a brief period of years. . . . I felt, as I have not felt before or since, a cold rage as I made my closing argument to the court:

'In contrast to the fairness of this proceeding, let us pause to consider what sort of trial these accused gave to those unfortunate people who appeared before them at Hadamar between July 1944 and April 1945. There came person after person, weary, heavy-laden, some very sick. But they came thinking that they saw upon the horizon the dawn of a brighter day. And what sort of trial was given them, what sort of a hearing, what sort of an opportunity was accorded them at this place where they thought they might find some comfort? . . . They were brought into the death halls. They were given the promise that medication would be administered to them in their ailment. Oh, what a vicious falsehood, what a terrible lie, what an evil and wicked thing to do to a person who is already suffering and already carrying burdens, to build up false hope that a ray of sunshine was to enter their hearts. Yes, they were given medications, of poison that gripped their heart and closed their eyelids still. What sort of trial did they have? Upon them was forced the hush of death. Their bodies were taken to a bleak cellar. They were lumped together and dumped together in a common grave, buried without the benefit of clergy. Now, that, in substance, is the sort of trial that the accused gave to those who appeared before their Bar of Justice.'[6]

For seven days, commencing on 8 October, Jaworski took the accused step by step through their part in killing four hundred Polish and Russian foreign forced workers. In a sense this type of slow, dogged attempt to establish the bare facts of an individual's culpability was a more telling indictment than the practice used subsequently by West German courts, which dwelt more extensively upon motivation and the general outlook of the accused, the overall political context, and indeed the internal politics of each institution. Jaworski's technique left little scope for such diversionary evasions.

The verdicts in the US military trial were death sentences for Alfons Klein and two particularly sadistic orderlies, Heinrich Ruoff and Karl Willig; a sentence of life imprisonment for Adolf Wahlmann; thirty-five years' hard labour for Adolf Merkle; thirty years for Philipp Blum; and twenty-five years for Irmgard Huber.[7]

Klein, Ruoff and Willig were hanged in quick succession in the early afternoon of 14 March 1946 in the Bruchsal prison. The law, ritualised, routinised, and embodied in the hangman and two burly American military policemen, despatched these three men coldly and mechanically. The procedure took about thirty minutes from start to completion. The precisely recorded exchanges between the condemned and a party of American officers were banally perfunctory, with two of the condemned not unnaturally displaying signs of extreme nervousness as the presiding American Major read out, and had translated, the sentence of execution. Willig's penultimate utterance before all went black for him was: 'I did my duty as a German official. God is my witness.'[8]

A few of those most seriously implicated in the events we have been considering decided to call it a day either before the total capitulation of the regime, or shortly after entering Allied captivity. Philipp Bouhler and Herbert Linden (the two bureaucratic architects of the 'euthanasia' programme) Max de Crinis and Schneider committed suicide in 1945. Odilo Globocnik, the organisational mind behind 'Aktion Reinhard', followed the example set by his Reichsführer-SS, poisoning himself shortly after entering British captivity. Irmfried Eberl, the thirty-seven-year-old Bernburg doctor and first commandant of Treblinka, was arrested by the German authorities and held in prison. His attempts to deny his real identity were frustrated by fellow inmate Pauline K., who, upon being shown a photograph of him, exclaimed 'That is Dr Eberl.' Shortly afterwards, he failed to emerge one morning from his cell, and was discovered hanging in a corner from a heating pipe. Eberl and Bodo Gorgass were the only T-4 medical gassing experts (there were fourteen in all) to be arrested or tried in the four years following the cessation of hostilities.[9] Others would not follow them into the dock until the mid 1960s or late 1980s.

Karl Brandt and Viktor Brack were among the twenty-three accused in the Nuremberg Doctors' Trial in the summer of 1947, a laudably comprehensive attempt by the Americans to account for not only 'euthanasia' crimes, but also the whole complex of stomach-churning 'medical' and 'scientific' experiments.[10] For 133 days, the court heard testimony from the accused and thirty-two witnesses. The witnesses included Friedrich Mennecke, obliging now under the weight of a separate death sentence, and Hermann Pfannmüller. The latter occasionally forgot where he was and who he was talking to, announcing 'I am a doctor confronted with a lawyer and our points of view are completely divergent.' This attempt to establish zones of professional exclusivity cut little ice with the prosecuting counsel:

Just a moment, Doctor. Just a moment. I will ask the questions and you will answer them. If you do not choose to answer the question will you kindly say 'I refuse to answer the question.' Either answer the question or don't answer the question. I don't want to hear any more quibbling from you.[11]

The prosecutor used irony and understatement – which were probably lost on this witness – to query Pfannmüller's claim that he had been scrupulous in refereeing two thousand patient registration forms over a twenty-day period:

Now, can't you see how important it is to a layman like myself and the Tribunal to have you explain to us just what length of time is necessary for a psychiatrist, and a man with your experience, to study one of these questionnaires in order to determine whether or not this should be a plus case or a minus case. Do you understand the import of my questioning, the reason for it, now?[12]

Of all the accused we are concerned with, Brack's testimony was the most revealing. He had been arrested in Trauenstein and held in a camp at Moosburg. He was suffering from a stomach disorder, and his two children had tuberculosis.[13] Over several days he recalled what had impelled him to become involved in the 'euthanasia' programme. During the Depression he had chauffeured his doctor father about. Accompanying his father on house calls, Brack had noted a process whereby there was an 'automatic moving away of the family from the patient. That does not mean at all that this was malicious or unfeeling, but the relatives were often not able to cope spiritually with the length and extent of the sickness.'[14] Following Hitler's commission to Brandt and Bouhler, the latter had charged Brack with the operational arrangements. He read extensively on the subject: Thomas More, Binding and Hoche, Unger. He decided to visit some asylums since he had no previous experience of this area. He went to Buch and Brandenburg Görden:

What I saw there was terrible. Even I, who am only a layman, find it difficult to describe it, but I can remember some of the terrible cases clearly, because as the first ones which I had ever seen in my life, they made a lasting impression. In the institution Buch I saw a woman who was thirty-eight to forty years old approximately, who was wearing a heavy, tough shirt, and sitting in a kind of a cage on wooden shavings. She bared her teeth at people when they came near her and she was absolutely incapable of any contact. She took her food like an animal. She did indecent things with her excrement. She was constantly obscene, she was incapable of speaking, and as the nurse told me, she had been in that condition for eighteen or nineteen years.

In the same institution I saw a child. It was a girl of three or four years of age. It was simply a torso. It had no arms, no legs, a big head, albino, red inflamed eyes. And at that age, it was not able to speak a single word yet. It was a terrible sight – simply a body with a head and no possibility that a human being could develop from this creature.[15]

No one in court asked Brack whether these lurid cases were typical of the victims of the 'euthanasia' programme. He adopted a philosophical tone when answering questions from his defence counsel:

The life of the insane person has, for himself and for his relatives, lost all purpose, and consists only of pain and misery. Just as the soul belongs in the helping hands of the priest, so the body belongs in the helping hands of the physician. Only so can the sick person really be assisted. In that case, however, this means for the doctor that his duties, particularly in view of the person's spiritual life – it is his duty to free the person from his unworthy condition, so – I might even say – from his prison.[16]

This lofty tone was followed by several bruising sessions with the prosecuting counsel. Attempts to highlight Brack's alleged efforts to assist the occasional Jewish person, or his 'reluctant' involvement in the Final Solution, broke down as the prosecution refreshed his memory on such subjects as when he had first encountered Adolf Eichmann (he claimed to have heard the name after the war), or the personnel and technical assistance he had afforded Globocnik in carrying out 'Aktion Reinhard'. Why, it was asked (and not answered), if he thought what he had done was legally or morally justifiable, did he send urgent secret teletypes in 1944 ordering the immediate destruction of the facilities at Hartheim? Brack, alias 'Jennerwein', was sentenced to death and hanged in the Landsberg jail in 1948.

Equally stressing the theme of compassion, and thus implicitly excluding any baser economic motives, Karl Brandt struck a more self-righteous note in the witness box:

I do not feel that I am incriminated. I am convinced that what I did in this connection I can bear the responsibility for before my conscience. I was motivated by absolutely humane feelings. I never had any other intention. I never had any other belief than that those poor miserable creatures – that the painful lives of these creatures were to be shortened. The only thing that I regret in this connection is that external circumstances brought it about that pain was inflicted on the relatives. But I am convinced that these relatives have overcome this sorrow today and that they themselves feel that their dead relatives were freed from suffering.[17]

As for medical ethics, 'One may hang a copy of the Oath of Hippocrates in one's office but nobody pays any attention to it.'[18] This tall, aristocratic 'medical idealist' was also sentenced to death. As he geared himself up on the gallows for a further elegant disquisition, Brandt's attempts to denounce 'victors' justice' were abruptly stifled by the hood placed over his head.

Any sense of catharsis one may feel can be rapidly dispelled by following the fate of those convicted in other trials, who were sentenced to what were, given their age, literally life terms of imprisonment; or indeed, that of most of the other *dramatis personae* encountered in this book. In February 1947, twenty-five members of the Hadamar staff, including Gorgass, Wahlmann, Irmgard Huber and Paul R., were brought before a German court in Frankfurt am Main to answer charges of mass murder. The judgement was based upon the testimony of the accused, relatives of the victims and a handful of survivors, and such documentation as the accused had not yet destroyed. Unlike the US military lawyers, the

Plate 45. The accused in the dock during the second Hadamar trial before a German court in 1947. Front row: lawyers. Middle row, left to right: Irmgard Huber; Adolf Wahlmann; Bodo Gorgass. Back row: Agnes S.; Paul H.; Paul R.; Judith T.

German authorities were more concerned with motivation, and in drawing a finer distinction between murder and being an accessory to murder. Both Gorgass and Wahlmann were convicted of murdering 'at least' one thousand and nine hundred people, and were sentenced to death, commuted on appeal to terms of life imprisonment. Wahlmann was imprisoned until 1953; Gorgass was pardoned in 1958 and became an industrial pharmacist. The grounds given for this extraordinary decision by Minister President Zinn were that Gorgass was 'repentent' and 'physically broken'. Unlike his 'thousand or so' victims, Gorgass is still alive somewhere in Germany. Those nurses and orderlies who had been sentenced to imprisonment by the Americans did not then serve the sentences imposed by the German court for entirely separate offences.[19]

Other German trials concerned some of the individuals we have had cause to encounter rather repeatedly. Hermann Pfannmüller, whose patients once rhymed 'Der Pfannmüller und das Hitlerreich, die bringen uns alle ins Himmelreich',[20] received a five-year prison sentence in 1951. A few items of correspondence survive between Pfannmüller and his wife while he was in custody, including one in which Theresa Pfannmüller wrote: 'Yes, yes, it's humane all right that women and children are burned out of their homes, that thousands are freezing, that refugees have to live outside in the cold, but it's a crime against the state that someone like you put to sleep the sort of lumps of flesh (*Fleischklumpfen*) that you had there in the asylum.'[21] Not for the first or last time, the victims' suffering was relativised.

A fellow enthusiast for the starving of patients, 'Valo' Faltlhauser, was jailed for three years for having been what was euphemistically described as 'an accessory to manslaughter' in 'at least' three hundred cases. The one year and four months he had spent in an internment camp were deducted from the sentence.[22] Since Faltlhauser was an intelligent man (with Gustav Kolb he had coauthored the standard work on community care), rather than a callous thug like Mennecke or Pfannmüller, it may be instructive to review some of the arguments he used in his own defence. Describing himself as 'a supporter of euthanasia', he dwelt upon the influence of Binding and Hoche, being careful however to dismiss the idea that he killed people for 'reasons of utility'. No, he averred, 'for me the decisive motive was compassion'.[23] In his eyes, 'euthanasia' was not merely a matter of helping terminally ill people to die relatively painlessly, but encompassed 'the destruction of worthless life'. Faltlhauser regarded the lives of mental patients as being synonymous with torment. He had not troubled their relatives over the matter in question, lest it cause them 'conflicts of conscience'. As for the victims, they evinced no independent willpower for him to violate. In his own family, two of his grandchildren, who had been born with abnormalities, and his father, had had to be institutionalised because of neurological disorders. Only those who had experienced the same daily and nightly degree of anxiety could 'really understand' that killing these people was 'the opposite' of offences against humanity. (None of the foregoing had much to do with the murder of people like the 'gypsy' youth L., who, as we saw in the previous chapter, had an abundance of 'willpower'.)[24] Little of what Faltlhauser had to say was very enlightening. A Protestant pastor, Hans S., was more percipient when he remarked that 'Dr Faltlhauser seemed to me to be a typical example of what happens when a man abandons one principle, and then is unable to stop.'[25] That was the general problem.

The Eichberg trial resulted in a sentence of death upon Friedrich Mennecke for the murder of 'at least' two and half thousand people. Mennecke had left Eichberg under a cloud in 1943, following his row with Bernotat. The latter had vetoed Mennecke's plans for the 'modernisation' of the asylum's therapeutic facilities, and arranged the dcotor's immediate transfer to front-line duties. It was yet another demonstration of where power really lay in the relationship between bureaucrats and professionals. In characteristically craven fashion, Mennecke informed his wife that he was going to simulate heart trouble to facilitate a transfer to a military casualty station.[26] In his professional capacity, Mennecke usually made very short work of soldiers who tried similar evasive tactics. Ironically he *was* ill with goitre, or swelling of the thyroid gland – which probably explains his protruding eyes in photographs – and subsequently developed tuberculosis. His war ended as a patient in hospital. Imprisoned after his trial in Butzbach, Mennecke died on 28 January 1947, before his appointment with the hangman. The suddenness of his death, following a visit from Eva, gave grounds for suspicion.

Mennecke's superior, Bernotat, changed his name to 'Otto Kallweit', and became the owner of a tobacconist's. He died undetected in 1951 at Neuhof near Fulda.[27] His Bavarian equivalent, Walter 'Bubi' Schultze, received a three-year jail sentence after the war (which he never served), and, following an appeal by the state prosecutor, a four-year sentence in 1960 in connection with 'children's euthanasia'. Ludwig Sprauer, the former head of the Badenese health service, was sentenced to life imprisonment in 1948 by a court in Freiburg. This was reduced to eleven years on appeal in 1950. Shortly after, Sprauer was released.[28]

The fate of Mennecke's co-accused and successor at Eichberg, Walter Schmidt, is instructive. The latter was convicted on a specimen charge of 'at least' seventy murders and sentenced to death, which was soon commuted to life imprisonment with hard labour. Thanks to a carefully orchestrated clemency campaign by his friends, relatives and legal representatives, Schmidt was released in 1953, after six years in prison. First, Schmidt's apologists pointed to the incrementally milder sentences passed for similar offences in later German trials. Secondly, they organised a petition, signed by 250 citizens of Hattenheim, which stressed his role as concerned doctor to the local population. Apparently the fact that he refused to use a car in wartime, preferring to pedal around on a bicycle like some Teutonic Dr Finlay, was testament enough to his 'idealism'.[29] Further petitions were organised, and even the Central Association of those sterilised or whose health had been damaged by the Nazis felt moved to write on Schmidt's behalf.[30] The press took up the call, with one illustrated magazine grotesquely using the headline 'Ich klage an' to demand Schmidt's release. The illustrations included a sketch of a hydrocephalic baby (caption: 'Was the political leadership perhaps right?') and a photograph showing a man pretending to be Schmidt (replete with white coat and clipboard), dramatically trying to halt what was supposed to be one of the T–4 buses![31] A particularly tasteless touch – one can always rely upon journalists – was provided by a weekly paper which claimed that 'thousands' of people were dying because of Schmidt's imprisonment.

Allegedly, Schmidt – whose fate was described here as 'one of the greatest tragedies of our times' – had discovered a cure for multiple sclerosis, childhood paralysis and glandular disorders.[32] Apparently he had made these startling discoveries in an internment camp; apparently, the lame had tossed away their sticks and crutches, as this latter-day scientific Jesus enabled them to walk. In fact, he had plagiarised the pre-1914 research of a crank Viennese doctor, which involved massaging a salve derived from the ovaries of freshly slaughtered cows on to people's ears, backs and necks. Any 'results' could be attributed purely to Schmidt's powers of suggestion.[33] Preposterous though his claims were (and one should think about the hopes he raised in the minds of credulous and desperate people), in 1951 the authorities cut Schmidt's sentence to ten years. Continuing pressure resulted in his release in 1953. Schmidt was not officially permitted to continue practising medicine, but this did not prevent him from doing so.

Popular pressure also played a role in the proceedings against the personnel of the Idstein reformatory. Two doctors, Mathilde Weber and Hermann Wesse, and the director, Wilhelm Grossmann, were sentenced to death in January 1947. While the sentence against Wesse was confirmed, those imposed on Weber and Grossmann were rejected on appeal. One of the appeal court's subtler findings was that just because Grossmann had threatened to turn mentally handicapped children into 'angels', this merely bespoke a certain crudity in the way he expressed himself, as opposed to a deadly declaration of intent.[34] Systematic beatings with an oxhide whip could be excused on the grounds that they were 'controlled' – i.e. not carried out in a berserk fashion – and a form of delayed self-defence against 'dangerous' feebleminded patients. A re-trial of Grossmann and Weber, on the lesser charge of accessory to murder, resulted in sentences of respectively four and a half and three and a half years' imprisonment.[35] These extraordinary decisions were not uninfluenced by a massive campaign conducted by the citizens of Idstein on behalf of the convicted child-murderess Weber. Her husband was the local general practitioner. Weber was not even in prison yet, since her putative poor state of health served to delay the onset of her sentence. Having failed in her final appeal – she also had the temerity to demand that the state reimburse her legal costs – she went to jail on 11 October 1954, being released on parole on 16 November. She thus served just over a month in prison for being 'an accessory' to about 150 'proven' cases of murder.[36] Nor did Grossmann actually have to go to prison. The local magistracy testified as to his 'correct and orderly way of life', arguing that his conviction 'may' have been legally right, but that it was (yet another!) 'human tragedy'.[37] When the Wiesbaden communal authorities, who took over responsibility for the Kalmenhof, celebrated eighty years of their history in 1948, Idstein's Nazi past was not even mentioned.

So far we have been considering those who were actually brought before a court of law. Many of the perpetrators had this disagreeable experience rather late in life, managing usually to find a way of postponing or avoiding it.

After the war, Dr Horst Schumann, whose career included Grafeneck, Sonnenstein, and disgusting 'experimental' activities in Auschwitz, calmly registered with the police in Gladbeck, notwithstanding the fact that his name had come up repeatedly at the Nuremberg Doctors' Trial in connection with horrific 'medical' experiments. He made the transition from experimenting with X-ray sterilisation in Auschwitz, on 'subjects' who were killed or scarred for life, to post-war sports doctor and general practitioner relatively smoothly. Schumann erred only once, when in 1951 he applied for a hunting and fishing permit. Routine enquiries in his place of birth revealed that he was on the wanted list. It took two weeks before any action was taken to apprehend him. Since Schumann was a 'respected citizen', the police in Gladbeck interviewed various people connected with him, one of whom probably tipped him off about the lackadaisical police 'efforts' to apprehend him. By the time two policemen arrived at his doorstep, Schumann was en route to Japan, where he acquired documents from the German consulate in Osaka. During the mid 1950s, he fitfully came to the attention of the authorities in Egypt, Sudan and Congo, where he ran a leper colony. A naive German religious affairs journalist published a piece on him in *Christ und Welt*, wherein he was portrayed as a second Albert Schweitzer. By the time the extradition requests arrived, Schumann was off to Nigeria and Ghana, where he encountered Mr (and Mrs) Kallmeyer, the gas expert from the former Criminal Technical Institute.[38] Schumann worked in Ghana as head of a hospital, until the fall of Nkrumah resulted in extradition to Germany.

In between extradition and the commencement of his trial four years later in September 1970(!), Schumann entertained his fellow inmates with articles in the prison journal about whether 'Blacks actually have an intelligence', while finding the time to acquire a starting pistol for a future escape bid. Having thought better of such drastic measures, Schumann decided to rely upon his medical knowledge. This was more effective than any jail break. The first step was to get out of prison, to which end he decided to fake a haemorrhage, it being easier to escape from hospital. His cellmate, Hans-Joachim 'Millionen' Becker, subsequently testified that Schumann employed a convict trick of swallowing his own blood in order to dramatically spew it up again to simulate a sudden haemorrhage. 'Herr Dr. med.' Schumann – he had actually been struck off in 1961 – was quietly released from detention on medical grounds (headaches and dizziness rather than vomiting blood being the main symptoms) in 1972. He died eleven years later.[39]

By definition, doctors were well placed to fake medical conditions which would serve to delay or indefinitely postpone their trials. Laymen also had no difficulty in doing so. Hans Hefelmann, one of the senior bureaucrats in the Chancellory of the Führer, was an agronomist by training. In January 1945 he took over the running of a home for refugees established in the former asylum of Stadtroda. He knew its medical director, Kloos, because the latter had run one of the T-4 'paediatric clinics' there. Following the arrival of the Allies, Hefelmann successively relocated to Munich, Innsbrück and then far-away Buenos Aires. Along the way, he found work as a driver for a cheese wholesaler, in a brewery, on construction sites, as a carpenter, and finally managing a German-language bookshop in Argentina.[40] Returning to the Federal Republic in 1955, he lived undisturbed, running a business in Trauenstein called 'Susi Bekleidung', until the authorities began to close their rather frayed net on the surviving senior T-4 figures. Deciding that Spain, whither he fled, was not for him – he did not like the climate – Hefelmann returned to Germany and surrendered to the authorities who by this time (1960!) were looking for him. His trial commenced in 1964.

Attempts to fabricate unfitness for trial had begun in earnest a year earlier. A doctor specified the exact height of the armrests and the thickness of the upholstery on the accused's chair, and the time he would need to exercise his bad back after long sedentary spells in the courtroom. His friend Kloos, by now medical director of the Göttingen provincial hospital, then sent Hefelmann's lawyer and physician a report on the accused's health, helpfully drawing attention to memory lapses which would render Hefelmann unfit for trial. A physician appointed by the court confirmed that Hefelmann was suffering from an 'unknown' illness which, despite being 'unknown', was likely to be terminal. A second, more sceptical report was simply ignored. With the trial suspended, Hefelmann merely had to keep up a steady stream of medical reports. In October 1972 he was released and declared permanently unfit to face trial. In a minor concession to humanity Hefelmann (who, one recalls, could not sit for long periods and had lapses of concentration) was banned from driving a car. This was the sole penalty imposed upon a man accused of murdering 70,000 adults and 'at least' three thousand children. Nor, of course, did he have 'only two years' to live, since he was still alive in the late 1980s.[41]

Hefelmann's co-accused in the Frankfurt trial included Professor Werner Heyde. Before he was replaced by Paul Nitsche, Heyde was the medical supremo of the 'euthanasia' programme. In 1945, Heyde fled to Denmark, where he was interned by the British. He was subsequently delivered to the German authorities, appearing as a witness in both the Hadamar and Nuremberg Doctors' trials. Having been placed under arrest in consequence, on 25 July 1947 Heyde jumped off the back of an

American military lorry as it passed through his home town of Würzburg en route to Frankfurt's Hammelsgasse prison. For weeks, he hitch-hiked or walked and worked his way northwards to Schleswig-Holstein, acquiring identity papers on the black market, which were then obligingly endorsed by the British occupation authorities. The papers gave his place of birth as being across the river Neisse, which would frustrate any future enquiries. As 'Fritz Sawade' he could now register with the police. There were a few deft alterations to his hairline and type of spectacles.

After working as a gardener, 'Sawade' successfully applied for a job as a sports physician in Flensburg. The absence of a certificate to practise medicine does not seem to have exercised anyone in a region where Nazis were as thick as flies both before and after 1945.[42] Through social contacts with local and regional worthies, the former T–4 expert 'medical' referee was soon working as a referee for public insurance offices and on behalf of the courts. A busy fellow, 'Sawade' produced about 7,000 expert testimonies. He bought a modest semi-detached house and a Volkswagen Beetle. Werner Schlegelberger, the former State Secretary in the Ministry of Justice, lived in a house up the road. Heyde and his wife went on foreign holidays, notwithstanding the fact that Frau Heyde had been claiming payments as a widow and for her two 'orphans' since 1951. The immigration officials do not seem to have questioned her companion. Most of the local establishment, as well as the entire medical faculty of the University of Kiel, were aware that 'Sawade' was in fact Heyde. Thanks to Heyde's wife, one could not help knowing. In the course of a party for local academic dignitaries, Frau Dr Sawade became progressively irritated at the way in which the wives of professors snubbed her in her capacity of wife of a modest sports doctor. Her crushed *amour propre* eventually moved her to exclaim: 'Don't you know who I am? I am not just a mere Frau Doctor, but, just so you know, Frau Professor Heyde! Her husband no doubt wished on such occasions that he had remained steadfast to his earlier sexual inclinations, by sticking, so to speak, to young male students and soldiers.

Loose talk set off various obscure inter-collegial animosities, which led in turn to remarks from much further afield, such as 'I hear that Heyde, the murderer of the mad, has set up shop under the name Dr Sawade with you up in Schleswig-Holstein.'[43] Taking the precaution of going to Hamburg to check the possibility of sudden flight, Heyde also used a lawyer to pressure his professional foes into silence. His downfall had further elements of farce. The director of the university clinic brought an action against some noisy student neighbours. In the course of a conversation with a very senior official, the professor fulminated on several themes, mentioning that a Flensburg doctor using a false name was writing official reports. The search began for 'Sawade's' certificate to practise. Of

course, there was not one. Shortly after a manhunt began, albeit temporarily derailed by the fact that Heyde was alleged to be driving a VW, when
in reality he was behind the wheel of a Borgward-Isabella. Heyde eventually surrendered himself to the authorities.[44] A photograph shows him
sitting grim-faced in the back of a police car.

Ensconced in a comfy prison in Limburg, where he received *Le Figaro*
and the *Manchester Guardian, Die Zeit*, books, bottles of Riesling, cigarettes
and telephone access to his lawyer, Heyde also enjoyed the services of a
personal prisoner-cum-cleaner. Having failed in his attempts to claim
circulatory problems or temporary periods of blindness, Heyde resorted to
more desperate stratagems. A very dedicated team of public prosecutors
under Fritz Bauer had assembled several hundred volumes of evidence and
testimony, and a statement of charges concerning the organisation of the
murders of 'about 100,000' people, which alone runs to 833 pages. It is the
most complete investigation into the first part of the 'euthanasia' programme. Heyde realised that he was not going to slip out of this so easily.
He therefore suborned a twenty-four-year-old petty criminal into helping
him distract a guard, while he used a bar of soap to take a mould of the key
(there was only one) which opened all doors throughout the prison. The
guard had helpfully dumped the bunch of keys on Heyde's cell table.
Heyde then used his two-way radio(!) to arrange a meeting between friends
outside and his young convict associate, who regularly went on outside
work parties to pick up food for the prison kitchens.

Slipping his guard, the young man took a taxi from Limburg to
Frankfurt where he waited in a predesignated restaurant. The latter was
opposite the offices of Heyde's lawyer. Our young prisoner wore sunglasses, twiddling another pair in his fingers as a sign to his unknown
contacts. A Chandleresque 'fat man' eventually asked him: 'Do you have
greetings for me?' To which the appropriate answer was 'from uncle
Werner'. The young man was given 2,500DMs in cash – a fortune at the
time – and the promise of 20,000DMs more, to facilitate 'uncle Werner's'
escape from prison. There were a few cunning refinements, such as a
contact telephone number – 673 327 minus one per digit thus became 562
216 – and, a definite plus point for a young man fresh from jail, an
attractive blonde with a nice voice called Christa, who acted as his driver.
Despite the fact that her perfume drove him to distraction, young Christa
remained, alas, Teutonically 'sachlich'. She did volunteer the intelligence
that 'the influence of our friends extends to the highest levels of the State.
They sit in the ministries, in the prosecutors' offices, and in many police
stations.'[45]

Being even more seriously venal than the professor, the young prisoner
then sold this sensational tale to a gutter-press illustrated magazine. In the
meantime, Heyde had suddenly been moved on 31 August 1963 to another

prison at Butzbach. Bauer had got wind of an escape plan. The guards who searched Heyde before his departure found stenographic notes which spoke of a car with red flowers on display beneath the rear window shelf, which he would find in the Koblenz station car park. A thorough search of his cell unearthed the radio with notes on its frequency. At Butzbach, Heyde's defence lawyer asked for an urgent meeting with prosecutor Bauer. The former spoke of the imminence of the article concerning the adventure of the young prisoner, the drift of which would ruin him. The lawyer said that he often acted for large stores, including ones owned by Jewish people. After several hours the lawyer admitted that it was he who had met the young prisoner in the restaurant, that Christa was the daughter of a client, and that he was part of a conspiracy to spirit Heyde out of Germany in a packing case.

Following the publication of the article, which did not mention anything to do with the lawyer, Heyde's thoughts turned to suicide. He was probably encouraged along this desperate course by the fact that on 12 February 1964 one of his co-accused, the T–4 bureaucrat Tillmann – who for medical reasons was not in custody – jumped (or was pushed) out of the eighth-floor window of a building in Cologne. Heyde was put under more stringent observation. On the morning of 13 February, Heyde's prisoner-cleaner arrived to tidy his cell. Heyde was hanging by his belt(!) from a heating pipe. In a suicide note he said that he did not want to be an exhibit in a 'show trial', and that he did not consider himself either juridically or morally guilty of anything. In a typical reversal of roles, Heyde claimed that he and the German people were being persecuted by Bauer, who was a former concentration camp inmate. Heyde's family included the following line in the obituary: 'After an active life and after a long, troubling denial of liberty, Herr Prof. Dr med. Werner Heyde has been summoned at the age of 62 before his heavenly judge.'[46] Many of his professorial colleagues at dozens of universities no doubt breathed a profound sigh of relief, since Heyde knew enough to take them all down with him, and was embittered and vindictive enough to have done so.

In reality, apart from Paul Nitsche who was tried and executed in 1948 in Dresden, the T–4 professors did not have much to worry about. Hans Heinze became director of a clinic for juvenile psychiatry in 1954, only coming to the attention of the authorities in 1962. His alleged poor health kept him out of the dock until his death in 1983.[47] His co-referee on the Reich Committee, Werner Catel, fled from the Russians in 1946. A year later he was director of a paediatric hospital at Mammolshain in Taunus. By 1954, he had become professor of paediatric medicine at the University of Kiel. He published a book which advocated the 'mercy killing' of defective infants. In a surprisingly sympathetic 1964 interview in *Der Spiegel*, which spoke of his 'Europe-wide reputation', Catel endeavoured to defend his views on infanticide. 'Believe me,' he said, 'in every case it is possible to distinguish these creatures without a soul from those who will become human.' Doctors would have to tell parents that 'these creatures are beyond help, that they will never become a person'. These infants were 'not people, but simply beings produced by people'; 'monsters', in fact, whose visage was responsible for many a broken marriage. The journalist failed to question Catel's vivid language. Warming to his theme, Catel reviewed the many cases he had seen 'of [children with] water on the brain, with heads almost larger than their bodies; microcephalic cases [with heads] as small as a fist; open skulls, in which part of the brain is missing, with eyes in dislocated positions ...'. Full of righteous indignation, he related an anecdote redolent of past thinking. He knew a couple with two children, a healthy eight-year-old boy and a younger girl who 'moaned like an animal', could not recognise her parents, was bound to a sort of commode, and chewed the table. The boy had to tend his sister (both parents worked!) 'day in, day out' and was hence the 'victim'. He was 'spiritually ruined'. Statistics Catel had acquired from the Institute for Human Genetics in Münster suggested that every year there were 25,000 mentally retarded, and 2,000 seriously deformed, potential infant 'victims' who 'victimised' their families in the above-alleged fashion in the Federal Republic. Catel modestly wished to confine his 'euthanasia' measures to three categories of severe neurological abnormality. He made a few concessions to the new spirit of the times (Germany was after all a democracy of sorts), by allowing that a lawyer, theologian and token woman might be part of the panel which took the final decision. The hearings would be held in public. In time-honoured fashion, the journalist from *Der Spiegel* thanked the 'Herr Professor' for the interview.[48]

Although he was forced to retire in 1960 because of public outrage, Catel thoughtfully left the university half a million DMs in his will for a 'Werner Catel Prize' and eponymous Foundation. Further public outcry prevented the university from accepting the money.

If justice flew blindly past these professors, it stumbled by most of the T-4 bureaucrats. In a separate trial commencing in April 1967, four former T-4 officials, Dietrich Allers, Gerhard Bohne, Adolf Kaufmann and Reinhold Vorberg, went on trial for organising tens of thousands of murders. What happened was the judicial equivalent of the song 'ten green bottles', although none of these men 'fell'. Dr Gerhard Bohne had decided to flee the country in 1963, in view of the investigation into Werner Heyde. He essentially used prostate trouble as a means of escaping justice. Refusing point blank to allow the medical agents of a 'communist judiciary'(!) to operate, Bohne insisted upon his own choice of hospital. His lawyer, a former colleague of Roland Freisler, argued that the accused was sixty, without means, and very ill, hence not likely to make a run for it.

Actually, he was ill because a doctor, a fellow inmate, was overdosing him with caffeine and quinine. Bohne having been released on the grounds of ill health, his lawyer duly surrendered his client's passport, promising to watch over Bohne in his own house. Four months later the same lawyer informed the prosecutor that his client had 'gone abroad' to recuperate, notwithstanding the absence of a passport. By the time a belated official medical report had informed the court of Bohne's lack of drive, its 'will-less' object had rallied sufficiently to reach Argentina. It was relatively easy to leave the country when, notwithstanding charges concerning 15,000 murders, neither the police nor the prison authorities had bothered to take his fingerprints.[49]

Bohne lived in Argentina under the name Kurt Adolf Rüdinger. Since the Argentinian police had doubts as to his identity, he began to make plans to decamp to Egypt. Forestalled in this endeavour, in November 1966 he was escorted at gunpoint on to a plane bound for Germany. En route, he spent part of the flight regaling his two escorts with how his lawyer planned to organise his escape from custody. Within a month of touching down in Germany, Bohne was not in court or prison, but in hospital. Doctors advised that he could only manage four hours in court per day. Further medical reports led to the temporary suspension of proceedings, and then in July 1969 to their abandonment.[50]

The co-accused now included Allers, Kaufmann and Vorberg. Kaufmann had been responsible for setting up the six extermination facilities used under 'Aktion T-4'. Arrested in 1965, he initially tried to use his wife's alleged bedridden immobility to worm his way out of the dock, a tactic ruined by the discovery of a letter from her which dwelt at length on how she had painted the entire house in his absence. Kaufmann no doubt also wished he had remained a bachelor. The trial against him was abandoned on the grounds that stress might precipitate a heart attack.

That left Vorberg and Allers. Vorberg had escaped in 1947 from the same internment camp which housed his cousin Viktor Brack. (Brack did not fancy the prospect of being shot at, and so was hanged instead.) Various jobs followed, one thoughtfully provided by another cousin who had been in charge of the synthetic chemical division of the Four-Year Plan; the last was with a Bonn construction company. The authorities had this information through an interrogation of another suspect. By the time the police decided to arrest him, Vorberg had exchanged Bonn for the charms of Barcelona. Although, after a visit to Madrid, prosecutor Bauer was sceptical whether Franco's regime would extradite Vorberg, he used a German bishop to exercise moral suasion upon a very eminent Spanish cleric. Vorberg was arrested and then extradited to Germany in March 1963. In prison he took up painting tin figures, and reading homiletic tomes such as one entitled 'Don't Take Life Too Seriously'. Although he was a little portly, there was nothing to suggest unfitness to stand trial. In 1968, Reinhold Vorberg was sentenced to ten years' imprisonment in connection with organising over 70,000 murders. By the time his appeal was rejected in 1972, he was already a free man, since the time he had served both in custody in Spain and under arrest in Germany was discounted against the sentence.

The last of the accused, Dietrich Allers, whom we last encountered walking about with a riding crop at Trieste (p. 234 above), was detained by the British, who sent him to an internment camp at Neuengamme. Released in 1947, Allers worked in various menial jobs, advancing rapidly to the position of manager. In 1948 he was arrested by the Americans and turned over to the German authorities; they set him free shortly afterwards. Brack's former lawyer from T-4 times testified that Allers was merely Brack's office boy. Allers went to work in the Hamburg dockyards as a company lawyer, managing to stand as a candidate for the quasi-fascist 'Socialist Reich Party' in 1951. He kept in regular contact with such friends as Werner Blankenburg, alias 'Werner Bieleke', who died peacefully in Stuttgart in 1957. Indeed, Blankenburg himself had a sort of Stuttgart circle of ex-T-4 personnel, including Erwin Lambert – now in paving stones rather than pipes – and Frau Lambert's gynaecologist, Dr Aquilin Ullrich, whom we shall shortly encounter in greater detail. Blankenburg's funeral was a get-together of old comrades.[51]

As a man of renewed influence, Allers did several favours for more humble T-4 personnel, offering to find one a job as a policeman, since he was on such excellent terms with the relevant Hamburg senator. He described the city itself as 'an oasis' for men like himself, for the highest court there had effectively put a bar on the trial of Nazi criminals. Eventually detained in connection with the 'euthanasia' programme, Allers was sentenced to eight years' imprisonment in December 1968. Like Vorberg he served very little of it, since the time he had spent in internment after the war was deducted from the sentence.

These miscarriages of justice, which could easily be multiplied, ran parallel with something like official indifference towards those who had been compulsorily sterilised or whose relatives had been murdered. In 1960–1961, people who had been compulsorily sterilised were excluded from the provisions of the Federal Compensation Law, on the grounds that the Nazis' eugenic legislation was 'legitimate' and not specifically National Socialist. It merely built upon measures first essayed in the last stages of the Weimar Republic. This was analogous with attempts to deny compensation to Sinti and Roma on the grounds that measures taken against 'gypsies' were part of the on-going fight against crime. From the late 1960s, a great deal of research on crimes committed by the Nazis against Germans gradually broke through the pattern first established at

Nuremberg, with its inherent preoccupation with crimes committed against Jews or non-German nationals. In 1981 the Federal German government eventually conceded one-off payments of up to 5,000DMs to those persons who had been compulsorily sterilised.[52] The maximum payment was derisory in relation to compensation granted in (for example) cases involving loss of earnings, let alone in relation to the massive sums transferred to Israel for reasons of atonement and foreign policy. It was also conditional upon completion of a long and complex claim form and, should one want to establish permanent disability, an intrusive and potentially traumatic medical examination.[53] This had unfortunate past associations for people denied the chance to reproduce by doctors. In 1984 a psychiatric lobby group based in Gütersloh urged the Federal Parliament to acknowledge formally that some five hundred thousand families had been persecuted through sterilisation or 'euthanasia'. Two years later, Klara Nowak – who had herself been compulsorily sterilised – founded the League of those harmed by compulsory sterilisation and 'euthanasia' (the address is Meiersfelder Strasse 7, 4930 Detmold, Germany), a national self-help group for those whose lives had been ruined by these policies. This has provided a forum in which elderly and often isolated people can discuss profoundly painful experiences which are still a cause of shame, in the double sense that they have no direct descendants and that other people might think that there 'must have been something wrong with them' for them to have been affected by these Nazi policies.[54] Unfortunately, there is no academic industry devoted to exploring the psychological suffering of victims of Nazi doctors. The more active members of the League endeavour to help those who have all but become hermits, fearful of any contact with human – as opposed to animal – society. Many members of the League demonstrate a high level of commitment and an amazing energy in keeping public consciousness of these events alive. They are often driven by the fear that after their own deaths, these events will become just an historical footnote.

Naturally, the surviving perpetrators and former victims do not exist on separate planets. Many of the victims have attended the post-war trials, either as observers or latterly as co-plaintiffs. In a few cases, such as Josef S., nowadays a retired Mannheim policeman, and Paul R. the former Hadamar orderly, there is less formal contact, born of the desire of the relatives of victims to get at a truth they feel they have been denied by official evasions, uncooperative archives, and an indifferent and theory-obsessed academic historical profession. It undoubtedly helps to comprehend these events if one can put a human face to them.

In the mid 1960s Josef S. attended the trial of Drs Bunke, Endruweit and Ullrich. All three were practising physicians; moves to have them struck off were thwarted by petitions signed by thousands of their patients.

All three were found guilty of being accessories to murder (in Ullrich's case involving 'at least 1,815' victims), but were acquitted on the extenuating grounds that they had not known that what they did was illegal, and were also under the misapprehension that their victims lacked normal human willpower. Upon hearing this remarkable verdict, their supporters broke into frenetic applause, with the three doctors finding it difficult to shake the many hands proffered them. Josef S. wept with anger, and cried out 'You murderers, you criminals!'[55] Three years later, the court of appeal in Karlsruhe overturned the verdict, although it was not until 1986 that Josef S. saw the three doctors in court again.

During the early 1970s attempts were made to put the four men on trial (for reasons of economy they had been joined in the dock by Dr Kurt Borm), attempts which were frustrated by the fact that all three of the original accused suffered, or were (allegedly) in imminent danger of, heart attacks, which (allegedly) rendered them unfit to stand trial. Inevitably, none of the three was declared unfit to practise medicine. Judging by what happened to Borm, who was not ill, they had little to fear from the courts. Although he was found guilty in 1972 of being an accessory to the murder of 'at least 6,652' psychiatric patients, the court could not prove that he was aware of the illegality of his actions. A large number of prominent people, including the artist Joseph Beuys and the writers Heinrich Böll and Günter Grass, found this verdict disgraceful.[56]

In 1986, what will probably prove to have been the last major trial of those involved in the 'euthanasia' programme commenced in Frankfurt. After one day, Endruweit managed to have himself excused by being declared unfit for trial. This left Bunke and Ullrich, who, after much medico–legal wrangling, were declared fit enough to appear in court for only two or three hours a week, a process which meant that the trial had already gone on for sixteen months by 1989. Josef S. was now a co–plaintiff and hence entitled to receive much of the trial documentation, upon which this account is largely based. His rather diminished faith in German justice was severely taxed by the revealing rhetorical infelicities of the defence counsel. One of the latter spoke of the victims as 'people whose lives had no content, almost like people in a dream, whom one could describe as burned-out human husks'.[57] A deeply religious man, Josef S. was also offended in other ways by Ullrich's insistence during the trial that 'I have nothing to repent, I killed these patients out of love and pity.' Although Josef S.'s local Roman Catholic priest had refused in 1941 to bless his mother's ashes or offer a decent place of burial on the grounds that she had been cremated (an offer by his grandmother to bring the ashes in a basket to Mass for indirect blessing was also refused), the same Church had seen fit to readmit Ullrich in 1962 to the faithful, despite his demonstrative and opportunistic exit from it in 1939. Attempts by Josef S. to clear up how the

Church could readmit and continue to provide spiritual solace to the (self-proclaimed) unrepentant doctor have so far remained unsuccessful, as have his efforts to shed light on why priests secretly wrote to the court on Ullrich's behalf during his trial. Letters to his diocesan bishop and the Pope have never been answered.[58] No doubt this, like the Roman Catholic Church's regular provision of religious solace to murderers in Northern Ireland, is a matter too mysterious for mere laymen to divine. To add insult to injury, Josef S.'s local priest proffered the rather unhelpful, and in the circumstances tactless, advice, 'Don't make yourself crazy on account of these doctors.'[59]

Eventually, on 28 May 1987, Bunke and Ullrich were convicted of having been accessories to the murder of respectively 11,000 and 4,500 people. They received four-year jail sentences, i.e. one year more than the statutory minimum sentence for the same offence involving one victim. In December 1988, the Federal court of appeal decided that since Bunke and Ullrich must have taken holidays and leave while working in extermination centres, the number of victims must have been 'only' 9,200 and 2,340, or nearly 16% and 50% fewer than originally established. Their sentences were therefore cut to three years in prison. Nearly thirty years after proceedings began against them, both men did go to prison. In Ullrich's case this meant an open establishment near Lake Constance, with weekend home visits, virtually unlimited visiting rights and, by reliable accounts, the opportunity to tend ailing fellow inmates, notwithstanding his having been struck off the medical register in 1984.[60] They currently live in retirement in Celle and Stuttgart. Josef S. lives an active and rich life, clouded by the feeling that the fate of people like his mother will slip from memory, and with foreboding regarding the future of a united Germany.[61]

CHAPTER 10

LEARNING FROM THE PAST?
THE SINGER DEBATE

THIS BRIEF afterword is designed to show how others have charted the same waters. Following an evanescent flurry of activity after 1945, silence descended upon the subject of the Nazi 'euthanasia' programme until the early 1980s. A decade of intensive scholarship has recently eventuated in the Singer 'debate', with which this chapter closes. First, however, we must return to the scene the Allies found in 1945.

The earliest studies of the Nazi 'euthanasia' programme appeared in the immediate aftermath of the Second World War. The American psychiatrist Major Leo Alexander was commissioned by the Combined Intelligence Objectives Sub-Committee to write a report on Nazi compulsory sterilisation and 'euthanasia' murders. Compiling a telling range of documentation concerning the asylum at Eglfing-Haar, Alexander was sensitive to such details as the different tone adopted by the asylum's director, Hermann Pfannmüller, in written communications with various anxious relatives of patients. Alexander also recorded his immediate impressions of the psychiatrists he visited in the course of compiling his report. Thus, on 9 June 1945 he and a Major Baruch paid a call on Dr Wilhelm Möckel of Wiesloch, who 'presented the obvious appearance of a frightened man. He was pale, there was perspiration on his forehead, and he showed generalized tremor.' Reassured as to the purpose of the visit, Möckel immediately telephoned his daughter, 'telling her in German that it was not what he had feared and that there was no need for her any longer to stand by'.[1]

The Nuremberg Doctors' Trial of 1946–1947 furnished a wealth of testimony and evidence, particularly regarding aberrant medical experiments in the concentration camps.[2] Alexander Mitscherlich, a young lecturer, attended the trial as a representative of the German medical association. No senior medical figure would undertake the task, and Mitscherlich was aware that doing so would mean the end of his career. Together with Fred Mielke, Mitscherlich produced a brochure, which received hostile criticism, and then a report, 'Science without Humanity', ten thousand copies of which were bought up and pulped by the German medical association. This report was never mentioned or reviewed in medical circles. The report was eventually published in book form as 'Medicine without Humanity' in 1960.[3] Paradoxically, this actually did the German medical profession a good turn by concentrating on a couple of dozen semi-deviant figures, whose obviously barbaric activities could be distanced from the lower-key collusion of thousands of their colleagues who had never been put on trial.

Other early post-war German discussion of the 'euthanasia' programme included a short book by Alice Platen-Hallermund, and Walter Schmidt's remarkable study of eight Bavarian asylums, written in 1945, shortly after he became commissary director of Eglfing-Haar following the arrest of Herman Pfannmüller. In 1946 Schmidt tried to publish his work. Distinguished professors told him 'not to fuel the flames'. He presented the manuscript to the medical faculty of the University of Hamburg; it circulated for two years and then disappeared. Another version was eventually published by a religious publishing house in 1965, sinking without trace.[4] Alice Platen-Hallermund's rather perceptive short book went into immediate critical oblivion.[5] Although German academics, and especially historians, totally neglected the subject, foreigners produced some valuable memoirs and studies. These included François Bayle, a French naval physician, Earl Kintner and Leon Jaworski, whose memoirs we have already encountered. The books of Bayle, Kintner and Jaworski were never translated into German.[6]

Despite massive media interest in the arrest and suicide of Werner Heyde, and the controversial publications of a re-established Werner Catel, virtually no studies of either compulsory sterilisation or the 'euthanasia' programme were produced in the 1960s, with the exception of a key article by psychiatrist Klaus Dörner, who has since gone on to publish extensively in the margins between history and reform psychiatry.[7] In the 1970s, two academic historians, Lothar Gruchmann and Karl Dietrich Erdmann, produced a handful of articles on the subject, including the former's studies of Lothar Kreyssig.[8] Ecclesiastical historians were content to integrate leading church figures into a largely mythical history of German resistance, a tendency first challenged by the Leipzig historian Kurt Nowak in his important study of the churches and 'euthanasia', published in 1978.[9] Nowak's book has in turn been augmented by other fine studies of individual clerics, notably Martin Höllen's outstanding studies of Bishop Heinrich Wienken.[10]

Matters improved in the early 1980s, when doctors, psychiatrists and medical historians of a different generation began to probe the past of their respective professions. There were too many of them to be dismissed in the manner with which the medical profession had dealt with earlier alleged *Nestbeschmützer*. The key figures in both West and, to a lesser extent, East

Germany were Gerhard Baader, Klaus Dörner, Christian Pross, Rolf Winau, Walter Wuttke and Achim Thom.[11]

However, the first full-scale and massively documented study of the 'euthanasia' programme was produced by the freelance journalist and filmmaker Ernst Klee.[12] A trained theologian, in 1986 he published what is still the benchmark for studies of the 'euthanasia' programme, based as it is upon a vast quantity of documentation and a journalist's eye for the telling detail. Nothing produced before or since measures up to Klee's pioneering study, although a great deal of work by others has rounded out his picture. While history professors swapped theories of fascism or increasingly arcane theoretical explanations of the origins of the Holocaust, local historians, groups of students, and people who worked in institutions involved in the 'euthanasia' programme began publishing detailed studies of particular regions, towns or institutions. This was an implicit rejection of the often rather abstract and sterile product emanating from the universities.

The same approach informed freelance historians loosely grouped in Hamburg and Berlin, including Götz Aly and Karl-Heinz Roth, respectively a journalist and a psychiatrist. Together with others, they have produced a stream of detailed research, and often compelling conclusions, about this most radical attempt to 'solve the social question', a notion that is not unproblematic.[13] Although one may not agree with the emphasis they place on the role of 'expertocracies', or their literal reading of Nazi expert claims to be engaged in a very brutal form of 'modernisation', their archival research alone would embarrass most professional historians.[14] Apart from its intrinsic significance, the work of Aly had led, *inter alia*, to German universities ceasing to instruct medical students with anatomical specimens derived from victims of the 'euthanasia' programme, and to a very critical reading of the life and work of such founding fathers of German clinical psychiatry as Karl Bonhoeffer.[15] Some of their work is now in turn being subjected to a revisionist critique, albeit around the margins.[16]

Non-German historians have tended to concentrate on the origins of the ideologies which informed these policies. Building on a tradition first essayed by, for example, George Mosse in America and Peter Pulzer in Britain, which temporarily went out of fashion in the 'structuralist'-dominated German historical scene of the 1970s and 1980s, younger British and North American scholars such as Proctor and Weindling have explored the complex strands that made up medicalised Nazi racism.[17] Weindling, in particular, has produced a large body of detailed and subtle work which explores the different tendencies within German 'eugenicist' thought, revealing how health and fertility became identified with German nationalism, and how nationalism fed back into medicine. Along the way, he frequently decouples those who advocated compulsory sterilisation from antisemites and extreme 'Nordic' ethnocentric racists, pointing out too that advocacy of compulsory sterilisation did not necessarily entail subscription to 'euthanasia'. Nor were these manifestations of Social Darwinism confined to the political right. A labour movement hostile to the *Lumpenproletariat* was also sometimes susceptible to the allures of this highly interventionist form of secular scientific 'progress'. Like the German historian Detlev Peukert, Weindling has also explored the thin dividing line separating the burgeoning Wilhelmine and Weimar *Sozialstaat* from various sinister forms of eugenic social engineering.[18] Unfortunately, little of this intellectually sophisticated work has fed into the mainstream of academic literature on National Socialism, which is still frequently dominated by an agenda set by various kinds of Marxist thirty years ago. Growing student indifference to these questions will probably result in some sort of academic sea change to catch up with current political realities, particularly as the ranks of those British and American historians of modern German history become rather more politically pluralistic than has been the case in the last couple of decades.

Some of the same ground discussed by Weindling is covered by the German scholars Weingart, Kroll, and Bayertz, and Hans-Walter Schmuhl.[19] Although the first part of the latter's synthesis is a valuable discussion of the longterm origins of Nazi medicalised murder, the book has little new to offer on the 'euthanasia' programme, and suffers from its dogmatic attempt to fit the subject into what has become a rather tired 'structure-functionalist' framework. It is thus a one-dimensional form of sociological theorising, rather than a research-led study of either compulsory sterilisation or 'euthanasia'. The former has, in any case, been explored in great detail from a feminist perspective by Gisela Bock, and in a number of detailed and original local case studies.[20]

Although it attracted considerable press attention, and has inspired a short novel by Martin Amis, *Time's Arrow*, Robert Jay Lifton's *Nazi Doctors* was not taken very seriously by many of those who know about these subjects.[21] Psychohistory over coffee and cake with mass murderers seems a rather feeble way of attempting to penetrate the carapace of self-exculpation which his subjects had rehearsed to perfection for their rather more taxing encounters with state prosecutors and judges. Apart from the rather distasteful way in which Lifton writes himself into the story (despite the paucity of the research, the credits have a cast of thousands), and barely conceals the *frisson* of sitting face to face with devious delinquents, the terms on which he met them -- recommended by the head of the Max Planck Institute for a chat about the stresses of doctors in Nazi Germany – hardly had them squirming in their armchairs. The portentous and evocative chapter headings – 'Doubling: the Faustian

Bargain' being among the less pretentious – bear very little resemblance to the characters that emerge from the historical record. Talk of the 'idealism' of a Brandt, Catel or Schneider ignores both their lack of pity (never a quality much prized in German intellectual circles since Nietzsche), and the coldly ruthless way they went about gassing or starving their own patients for the basest careerist, economic or political motives.

Apart from a steady stream of local studies, latterly including ones concerned with Austria and the former GDR, there have also been a number of worthwhile films and television documentaries about the 'euthanasia' programme. These include a worthy ÖRF documentary about Hartheim, and some profoundly moving studies of patient life by Harmut Schoen, such as 'Fritz. Die zweite Beachtung', or his humbling ZDF documentary about present-day life in Grafeneck. Channel 4 have also broadcast my own efforts in this direction, namely 'Selling Murder: The Killing Films of the "Third Reich"', an analytical examination of the arguments deployed in Nazi 'euthanasia' film propaganda set against the reality of it.[22]

Very little has been done to study those who were killed, which is a sad comment upon how we all think and operate. Such studies of patients as do exist tend to use computers to tot up the proportions of epileptics to schizophrenics among the murdered, an approach I find depressing and worrying. A conspicuous exception is Ullrich Dapp's moving account of the life and death of his grandmother, Emma Zeller-Dapp, which shows what one can achieve with a limited range of crucial documentation about the conflicts and tensions within a particular family.[23]

Although relatively scant attention has been paid to the history of 'euthanasia' as an issue after 1945, one exception is Ernst Klee's recent investigation of the German Society for Humane Dying, the equivalent of those rather sinister 'self-help' groups which 'assist' people to kill themselves in circumstances which are often rather dubious. The controversy periodically generated by such groups pales into insignificance beside the storm which in recent years has accompanied the attempts of the Australian moral philosopher, Peter Singer, to gain a hearing for his utilitarian 'practical ethics'.

Singer teaches 'bioethics' at Monash University in Australia. Judging from his books, he seems a man with impeccable, albeit predictable, liberal credentials, with 'right-on' stances about animals, civil disobedience and the Third World. Hitherto best known for his impassioned advocacy of animal rights and concern for the world's starving, he has increasingly become identified with equalising the status of some animals and some humans, by re-drawing the circle around the concept of what constitutes a person. One offshoot of this endeavour has been to suggest the sanctioning of consensual infanticide in case of anencephaly, major chromosomal disorders, or severe forms of Down's Syndrome and spina bifida, as well as voluntary euthanasia.[24] These views are not considered particularly controversial in international philosophical circles.

In 1989, Singer was invited to Marburg to address a high-powered symposium on 'Bioengineering, Ethics, and Mental Disability'. Singer accepted the invitation, and also agreed to speak at Dortmund on the question – he has a penchant for provocative titles – 'Do severely disabled newborn infants have a right to life?' Singer was then 'disinvited' from the Marburg symposium on the grounds that it was one thing to discuss his ideas behind closed doors with a group of academics, another to propagate them in a public lecture in Dortmund. There was the real risk of demonstrations by self-help groups, such as Franz Christoph's self-styled Cripples Movement, and other heterogeneous groups opposed to genetic engineering and reproductive technologies.[25] Both lectures were subsequently cancelled. A lecture Singer subsequently attempted to deliver in Saarbrücken, at the invitation of Professor Georg Meggle, who was determined to prove that one was free to discuss bioethics in Germany, was repeatedly interrupted by protesters, who refused to allow him to expound his view on voluntary euthanasia, preferring instead to confuse him with the Nazis. Singer rejected this (erroneous) charge with the *non sequitur* that three of his Austrian-Jewish grandparents had died in concentration camps. His opponents' cries of 'Singer raus' reminded him of the Nazis' 'Juden raus'.[26]

Clearly disconcerted by his experiences in Germany, Singer has converted them into at least two published attacks upon what he describes as 'a peculiar tone of fanaticism about some sections of the German debate over euthanasia that goes beyond normal opposition to Nazism, and instead begins to seem like the very mentality that made Nazism possible'. Apart from difficulties in making himself heard in lecture theatres, Singer claims that attempts were made to secure the dismissal of the professors who invited him to Germany, on the grounds that they were supporting the propagation of unconstitutional views; that various forms of jiggery-pokery have been employed to rig the appointment of philosophy lecturers so as to exclude specialists in bioethics; and that publishers have engaged in a form of sinister self-censorship by not accepting Singer's book *Should the Baby Live?*

There are thus two further debates in addition to the one Singer wished to stimulate, or provoke, regarding consensual infanticide and euthanasia: one concerning academic freedom in Germany, and another concerning the extent to which Singer's views share common ground with those of the Nazis and their intellectual progenitors. Before taking any of this at face value, it is important to stress, first that the entire Singer debate is of minor import beside the enormities of the Nazi 'euthanasia' programme, and second that Singer and his legion of German detractors have produced a small library of books and articles on the back of it. Singer himself also tends to conflate the views of his many critics, normally picking the most extreme to demonstrate the formulaic and hysterical quality of their arguments. Only German philosophers of his own persuasion are deemed capable of a rational discussion of his opinions.[27] A cynic might argue that as an English-speaking philosopher, Singer is lucky that anything he has to say might rouse mass interest, let alone generate feature articles and entire television programmes.

Although it is true that Singer would have few difficulties in airing his view in, say, Britain or the Netherlands, he is guilty of wishful thinking if he thinks that anxiety about reproductive technology is confined to Germany, or indeed to those on the left of the political spectrum, who in this instance find themselves in a 'conservative' intellectual position. Nor is Germany peculiar with regard to instances of attempting to deny the right to speak to people with controversial views. A few years ago, the University of Oxford witnessed attempts to 'disinvite' the historian Ernst Nolte; and as any reader of the *New York Review of Books* (where Singer published his 'On Being Silenced in Germany') will know, in the United States entire campuses seem to be slipping under the control of a bureaucratically entrenched thought-police with the power to censor behaviour, humour and language. Deplorable though they are, such problems are general to the modern academy, rather than local to Germany. This does not, of course, make such sinister notions as freedom of speech being a form of 'repressive tolerance' any more palatable to those who believe in the life of the mind.[28]

Apart from these unattractive features of modern academic life in general, how justified are Singer's numerous German critics in seeing linkages between his brand of utilitarianism (which as a tradition alien to Germany may in itself be the source of the disagreement) and the views of the Nazis? One key theme in Singer's thought, and in the history of moral philosophy in general (at least since Nietzsche), is that our present attitudes towards the sanctity of human life stem from the coming of Christianity, and hence would have been alien to, say, the Greeks and Romans. Accurately enough, Singer observes: 'Today the doctrines are no longer generally accepted, but the ethical attitudes to which they gave rise fit in with the deep-seated Western belief in the uniqueness and special privileges of our species, and have survived.'[29]

Following on from this, he rejects what he calls speciesist distinctions between persons and non-human animals. Pointing to the conceptual capabilities of chimpanzees and dolphins, which he feels give them a claim to 'personhood', Singer writes: 'some members of other species are persons; some members of our own species are not ... So it seems that killing, say, a chimpanzee is worse than the killing of a gravely defective human who is not a person.'[30] In other words, he denies the human attributes of some members of our own species. In effect, if not in intent, he arrives at the same point as many of the intellectual progenitors of the Nazi 'euthanasia' programme.

Dealing directly with the charge, first made by Leo Alexander in connection with the Nuremberg Doctors' Trial, that the Nazi 'euthanasia' programme started 'from small beginnings' (i.e. the 'slippery slope' argument), Singer writes, 'The Nazis committed horrendous crimes; but this does not mean that everything the Nazis did was horrendous. We cannot condemn euthanasia just because the Nazis did it, any more than we can condemn the building of new roads for this reason.'[31] Quite rightly, Singer points to the economistic and racial motivation behind the Nazis' killing of the mentally ill and handicapped, and, of course, its non-consensual character. However, rather surprisingly for a professional teacher of philosophy, he omits the entire philosophical background to the Nazis' policies, notably the writings of Binding and Hoche and their various imitators. There one can easily discover an attempt to relativise prevailing morality through reference to ancient or primitive alternatives; the radical redefinition of what constitutes a 'person' as opposed to 'beings' or 'creatures', i.e. the denial of human attributes; and the purposive use of analogies with animals. Perhaps more worrying than these rather academic issues is Singer's optimistic assertion regarding the practical side of what he envisages: 'If acts of euthanasia could only be carried out by a member of the medical profession, with the concurrence of a second doctor, it is not likely that the propensity to kill would spread unchecked throughout the community.'[32] Many people might not find this scenario very reassuring. Looked at in the shadow of the enormities discussed in this book the affair amounts to little more than a temporarily distracting extended footnote.

NOTES

I WINTER LANDSCAPES: PSYCHIATRIC REFORM AND RETRENCHMENT DURING THE WEIMAR REPUBLIC

The following abbreviations are used in the notes:

BDC	Berlin Document Center
BkH JB	*Bezirkskrankenhaus Haar: Jahresbericht*
HHStAW	Hessisches Hauptstaatsarchiv, Wiesbaden
IWM	Imperial War Museum, London
NAW	National Archives, Washington
StAM	Staatsarchiv, Munich
StAAug	Staatsarchiv, Augsburg
ZSL	Zentrale Sstelle der Landesjustizverwaltungen

1 Hans-Ludwig Siemen, *Menschen blieben auf der Strecke ... Psychiatrie zwischen Reform und Nationalsozialismus* (Gütersloh 1987), pp. 29–30. This subject remains otherwise virtually unexplored.

2 Heinz Faulstich, *Von der Irrenfürsorge zur 'Euthanasie'* (Freiburg im Breisgau 1993), p. 77.

3 Georg Illberg, 'Die Sterblichkeit der geisteskranken in den sächsischen Anstalten während des Krieges', *Allgemeine Zeitschrift für Psychiatrie* (1922), 78, p. 58.

4 Dr Mathes, 'Die Entwicklungsstufen der badischen praktischen Anstaltspsychiatrie bis zur Eröffnung der Anstalt Emmendingen und deren 40 jährige Tätigkeit', *Allgemeine Zeitschrift für Psychiatrie* (1929), 91, pp. 349–350.

5 E. Bratz, 'Kann die Versorgung der Geisteskranken billiger gestaltet werden und wie?', *Allgemeine Zeitschrift für Psychiatrie* (1932), 98, p. 7.

6 Adolf Gross, 'Zeitgemässe Betrachtungen zum wirtschaftlichen Betrieb der Irrenanstalten', *Allgemeine Zeitschrift für Psychiatrie* (1922), 79, p. 62.

7 A. Richter, 'Über die Ernährungsverhältnisse in der Irrenanstalt Buch während des Krieges 1914/18 und deren Folgen', *Allgemeine Zeitschrift für Psychiatrie* (1919), 75, p. 414, and p. 417 for mortality rates at Berlin-Buch.

8 Karl Bonhoeffer, opening address to the German Psychiatric Association, *Allgemeine Zeitschrift für Psychiatrie* (1920/21), 76, p. 600.

9 Ursula Grell, 'Karl Bonhoeffer und die Rassenhygiene', in Arbeitsgruppe zur Erforschung der Karl-Bonhoeffer-Nervenklinik (ed.), *Totgeschwiegen 1933–1945. Zur Geschichte der Wittenauer Heilstätten. Seit 1957 Karl-Bonhoeffer-*

Nervenklinik (2nd edn Berlin 1989), pp. 208–209; Martin Seidel and Klaus-Jürgen Neumarker, 'Karl Bonhoeffer und seine Stellung zue Sterilisierungs-gesetzgebung', ibid., pp. 274ff.

10 Christoph Hoffmann, 'Der Inhalt des Begriffes "Euthanasie" im 19. Jahrhundert und seine Wandlung in der Zeit bis 1920', Medical Dissertation, Humboldt Universität Berlin (1969), fols. 33–35.

11 Ibid., p. 65.

12 Douglas Walton, *Slippery Slope Arguments* (Oxford 1992).

13 Hoffmann, 'Der Inhalt', p. 75, citing C. W. Hufeland, 'Die Verhältnisse des Ärztes', *Journal der praktischen Ärzneykunde und Wundärzneykunst* (1806), 23, pp. 15–16.

14 Walter Schmuhl, *Rassenhygiene, Nationalsozialismus, Euthanasie. Von der Verhütung zur Vernichtung 'lebensunwerten Lebens' 1890–1945* (Göttingen 1987), p. 109.

15 Ernst Haeckel, *Natürliche Schöpfungsgeschichte* (Berlin 1868), p. 177. Alleged ancient precursors were central to the ideas – and post-war defence – of many of those accused of 'euthanasia' murders. Recourse to classical antiquity primarily enabled them to relativise the more recent Christian doctrine of the sanctity of human life. Hitler also referred approvingly in *Mein Kampf* to what he imagined to be the ancient Spartan practice of killing unfit infants. The more complex ancient reality is discussed in Martin Schmidt, 'Hephaistos lebt – Untersuchungen zur Frage der Behandlung behinderter Kinder in der Antike', *Hephaistos. Kritische Zeitschrift zu Theorie und Praxis der Archäologie, Kunstwissenschaft und angrenzender Gebiete* (1983/1984), 5/6, pp. 133–161. I am grateful to Götz Aly for this reference.

16 Roland Gerkan, 'Euthanasie', *Das monistische Jahrhundert* (1913), 2, p. 172.

17 Ibid., p. 173.

18 Ibid., pp. 170–171.

19 Ibid., 'Epilog' (R. Gerkan to W. Ostwald), p. 174.

20 Ibid., p. 174.

21 Wilhelm Borner, 'Euthanasie', *Das monistische Jahrhundert* (1913), 2, pp. 251–254.

22 Ibid., p. 339.

23 Alfred Bozi, 'Euthanasie und Recht', *Das monistische Jahrhundert* (1913), 2, p. 579.

24 M. Beer, *Ein schöner Tod. Ein Wort zur Euthanasiefrage* (Barmen 1914), p. 9.

25 The most systematic analysis of Binding and Hoche is Karl Heinz Hafner and Rolf Winau, 'Die Freigabe der Vernichtung lebensunwerten Lebens. Eine Untersuchung zu der Schrift von Karl Binding und Alfred Hoche', *Medizinhistorisches Journal* (1974), 9, p. 234; see also Rolf Winau, 'Die Freigabe der Vernichtung "lebensunwerten Lebens"', J. Bleker, N. Jachertz (eds.), *Medizin im Dritten Reich* (Cologne 1989), pp. 76–85; Michael Opielka, 'Psychiatrie in Deutschland auf dem Weg zur Vernichtung', Walter Wuttke (ed.), *Heilen und Vernichten im Nationalsozialismus* (Giessen 1988), pp. 127ff. See Jürgen Schmidt, 'Darstellung, Analyse und Wertung der Euthanasiedebatte in der deutschen Psychiatrie von 1920–1933', Medical Dissertation, University of Leipzig (1983), for an exhaustive discussion of the reception of Binding and Hoche's tract in the psychiatric profession.

26 Eduard Seidler, 'Alfred Hoche (1865–1943). Versuch einer Standortsbestimmung', *Freiburger Universität Blätter* (1986), 25, p. 75, is a sensitive account of Hoche's life and work.
27 See Roderich Wald, 'Deutsche Nervenärzte als Dichter und Denker. II. Alfred Erich Hoche', *Psychiatrisch-Neurologische Wochenschrift* (1936), 38, pp. 104–107, for several examples of his rather plangent poetry.
28 For example, Robert Gaupp, 'Alfred Erich Hoche', *Zeitschrift für die gesamte Neurologie und Psychiatrie* (1943), 176, pp. 1–6.
29 Seidler, 'Alfred Hoche', p. 75.
30 Karl Binding and Alfred Hoche, *Die Freigabe der Vernichtung lebensunwerten Lebens. Ihr Mass und ihre Form* (Leipzig 1920), p. 6.
31 Ibid., p. 16.
32 Ibid., pp. 16–18.
33 Ibid., p. 27.
34 Ibid., p. 27.
35 Ibid., pp. 28–29.
36 Ibid., p. 32.
37 Ibid., p. 33.
38 Ibid., pp. 35–37.
39 Ibid., p. 40.
40 Ibid., pp. 46–49.
41 Ibid., p. 57.
42 Ibid., p. 54.
43 Ibid., pp. 59–60.
44 Ibid., p. 62.
45 Robert Gaupp, 'Die Freigabe der Vernichtung lebensunwerten Lebens', *Deutsche Strafrechts-Zeitung* (1920), 7, pp. 336–337.
46 K. Klee, 'Die Freigabe der Vernichtung lebensunwerten Lebens', *Aerztliche Sachverständigen-Zeitung* (1921), 27, p. 4.
47 Ibid., p. 6.
48 Stadtrat Borchardt, 'Die Freigabe der Vernichtung lebensunwerten Lebens', *Deutsche Strafrechts-Zeitung* (1922), 9, p. 208.
49 E. Mann, *Die Erlösung der Menschheit vom Elend* (Weimar 1922), pp. 50ff.
50 F. Brennecke, 'Kritische Bemerkungen zu den Forderungen Binding-Hoches "Die Freigabe der Vernichtung lebensunwerten Lebens"', *Psychiatrisch-Neurologische Wochenschrift* (1921), 4, pp. 7–9.
51 Waschkuhn, 'Die Freigabe der Vernichtung lebensunwerten Lebens', *Psychiatrisch-Neurologische Wochenschrift* (1922), 24, p. 217.
52 Schmuhl, *Rassenhygiene*, p.121.
53 Ewald Meltzer, *Das Problem der Abkürzung 'lebensunwerten' Lebens* (Halle 1925), p. 55 and p. 63.
54 Ibid., p. vii.
55 Ibid., pp. 102–103.
56 Ibid., p. 110.
57 Ibid., pp. 50–53.
58 Ibid., p. 52.
59 Ibid., pp. 51–52 and p. 68.

60 Ibid., p. 87.

61 Ibid., p. 87.

62 Ibid., pp. 95–96.

63 Ibid., p. 101.

64 Ibid., p. 88.

65 Ibid., p. 90 and pp. 98–99.

66 Ibid., p. 92.

67 Ibid., p. 93.

68 Ibid., p. 98.

69 Schmidt, 'Darstellung', pp. 36–37.

70 Meltzer, *Das Problem*, p. 69; for the fate of Meltzer's former patients (he died in 1940), see Jürgen Trögisch, 'Bericht über Euthanasie-Massnahmen im "Katherinenhof" Grosshennersdorf', *Fröhlich Helfen* (1986), 1, pp. 40–42.

71 Paul Weindling, *Health, Race and German Politics between National Unification and Nazism 1870–1945* (Cambridge, 1989), p. 396.

72 The conference minutes are reproduced in the *Allgemeine Zeitschrift für Psychiatrie* (1923), 79, p. 438.

73 Ibid., p. 441.

74 Christoph Sachsse and Florian Tennstedt, *Geschichte der Armenfürsorge in Deutschland*, vols. 1–3 (Stuttgart 1980–1991), vol.1, pp. 227–232.

75 K. Nowak, *'Euthanasie' und Sterilisation im 'Dritten Reich'. Die Konfrontation der evangelischen und katholischen Kirche mit dem 'Gesetz zur Verhütung erbkranken Nachwuchses' und der 'Euthanasie'-Aktion* (Göttingen 1978, 2rd edn 1984), pp. 58–59.

76 Meltzer, *Das Problem*, pp. 76–77.

77 Ibid., pp. 78–79.

78 Ibid., pp. 82–85.

79 Ibid., p. 77.

80 Siemen, *Menschen blieben auf der Strecke*, p. 33. For a fascinating study of nineteenth-century German asylums, see Dirk Blasius, *Der verwaltete Wahnsinn. Eine Sozialgeschichte des Irrenhauses* (Frankfurt am Main 1980). See also the comparative essays by Günter Herzog, 'Heilung, Erziehung, Sicherung. Englische und deutsche Irrenhäuser in der ersten Hälfte des 19. Jahrhunderts', in Jürgen Kocka (ed.), *Bürgertum im 19. Jahrhundert. Deutschland im europäischen Vergleich* (Munich 1988), vol. 3, pp. 418–446, and Roy Porter, 'Madness and its Institutions', in Andrew Wear (ed.), *Medicine in Society* (Cambridge 1992), pp. 277–301; for a straightforward account of the architectural evolution of the asylum in Germany and Europe see Dieter Jetter, *Grundzüge der Geschichte des Irrenhauses* (Darmstadt 1981).

81 Gross, 'Zeitgemässe Betrachtungen', p. 61.

82 Ibid., pp. 62–63.

83 On the abuse of psychiatric casualties during the First World War see Peter Riedesser and Axel Verderber, *Aufrüstung der Seelen. Militärpsychiatrie und Militärpsychologie in Deutschland und Amerika* (Freiburg 1985), pp. 11ff.; for an unsympathetic contemporary account of psychiatric-reform pressure groups in the early 1920s, see Ernst Rittershaus, *Die Irrengesetzgebung in Deutschland* (Berlin 1927), p. 25.

84 Siegfried Grubitzsch, 'Revolutions- und Rätezeit 1918/19 aus der Sicht Deutscher Psychiater', *Psychologie & Gesellschaftskritik* (1985), pp. 35–38.

85 Gustav Kolb, conference paper ('Referat') in *Allgemeine Zeitschrift für Psychiatrie* (1920), 76, pp. 254ff. See also his 'Reform der Irrenfürsorge', *Zeitschrift für die gesamte Neurologie und Psychiatrie* (1919), 47, pp. 137ff. The latter was explicitly designed to anticipate (and preempt) reforms likely to be introduced by (hostile) Social Democrat governments.

86 Siemen, *Menschen blieben auf der Strecke*, p. 39.

87 See the discussion in *Allgemeine Zeitschrift für Psychiatrie* (1926), 83, p. 368.

88 B. Richarz, *Heilen, Pflegen, Töten. Zur Alltagsgeschichte einer Heil- und Pflegeanstalt bis zum Ende des Nationalsozialismus* (Göttingen 1987), p. 78.

89 Hans Roemer, 'Die sozialen Aufgaben des Irrenarztes in der Gegenwart', *Psychiatrisch-Neurologische Wochenschrift* (1920), 45, p. 343.

90 Valentin Faltlhauser, 'Erfahrungen des Erlanger Fürsorgearztes', *Allgemeine Zeitschrift für Psychiatrie* (1925), 80, p. 102. See Chapter 8 for Faltlhauser's involvement in the 'euthanasia' programme.

91 Dr Kuhne, 'Offene Fürsorge für entlassene Geisteskranke der Heil- und Pflegeanstalt Emmendigen', *Allgemeine Zeitschrift für Psychiatrie* (1929), 91, pp. 356–357.

92 Faltlhauser, 'Erfahrungen', p. 104.

93 Ibid., p. 115.

94 Ibid., p. 112.

95 Kuhne, 'Offene Fürsorge', p. 359; Faltlhauser, 'Erfahrungen', p. 121.

96 Sachsse and Tennstedt, *Geschichte der Armenfürsorge*, vol. 2, pp. 136–137.

97 Faltlhauser, 'Erfahrungen', p. 112; Kuhne, 'Offene Fürsorge', p. 361.

98 Faltlhauser, 'Erfahrungen', p. 109.

99 Ibid., pp. 116–117.

100 Ibid., p. 108.

101 On this see above all Karl-Heinz Roth, 'Erbbiologische Bestandsaufnahme – ein Aspekt "ausmerzender" Erfassung vor der Entfesselung des Zweiten Weltkrieges', in Roth (ed.), *Erfassung zur Vernichtung. Von der Sozialhygiene zum 'Gesetz über Sterbehilfe'* (Berlin 1984), pp. 59ff.

102 Helmut Hildebrandt, 'Offene Fürsorge und Psychische Hygiene in der Weimarer Republik: Die Zwei Gesichte eines sozialpsychiatrischen Versuchs', *Psychologie & Gesellschaftskritik* (1986), 10, pp. 21–22. See also Roth, 'Erbbiologische Bestandsaufnahme', pp. 57ff.

103 Siemen, *Menschen blieben auf der Strecke*, p. 63.

104 Hermann Simon, 'Aktivere Krankenbehandlung in der Irrenanstalt', Part I, *Allgemeine Zeitschrift für Psychiatrie* (1927), 87, p. 98 and pp. 104–105.

105 Ibid., p. 100.

106 Ibid., p. 106.

107 Hermann Simon, 'Aktivere Krankenbehandlung in der Irrenanstalt', Part II, *Allgemeine Zeitschrift für Psychiatrie* (1929), 90, p. 90.

108 Ibid., p. 95.

109 Ibid., p. 103.

110 Simon, 'Aktivere Krankenbehandlung', Part I, p. 103.

111 Ibid., p. 114.

112 Ibid., pp. 121–123.
113 Ibid., p. 128.
114 Simon, 'Aktivere Krankenbehandlung', Part II, p. 256.
115 Ibid., pp. 267ff.
116 Ibid., pp. 114–115.
117 M. Thumm, 'Milieugestaltung im Rahmen der aktiveren Therapie und ihre Auswirkungen auf freie Behandlung und offene Fürsorge', paper, *Allgemeine Zeitschrift für Psychiatrie* (1928), 88, p. 65.
118 Sachsse and Tennstedt, *Geschichte der Armenfürsorge*, vol. 3, pp. 43–49. For an excellent discussion of the impact of the Depression upon psychiatric thinking see Hans-Ludwig Siemen, 'Reform und Radikalisierung. Veränderungen der Psychiatrie in der Weltwirtschaftskrise', in Norbert Frei (ed.), *Medizin und Gesundheitspolitik in der NS-Zeit* (Munich 1991), pp. 191ff.
119 Harald James, *The German Slump. Politics and Economics 1924–1936* (Oxford 1986); see also Weindling, *Health, Race and German Politics*, p. 444.
120 Achim Thom, 'Die Entwicklung der Psychiatrie und die Schicksale psychisch Kranker sowie geistig Behinderter unter der Bedingung der faschistischen Diktatur', in *Medizin unterm Hakenkreuz'*, p. 130. See also the discussion of the case of Josef S.'s mother in the following chapter for an example of the impact of the Depression upon chronically sick members of families.
121 Report of the Reichssparkommissar concerning asylums in Hesse, reprinted in *Psychiatrisch-Neurologische Wochenschrift* (1930), 32, p. 137.
122 Siemen, *Menschen blieben auf der Strecke*, pp. 99–101.
123 E. Bratz, 'Kann die Versorgung der Geisteskranken billiger gestaltet werden und wie?', pp. 31–35.
124 Sabine Damm and Norbert Emmerich, 'Die Irrenanstalt Dalldorf-Wittenau bis 1933', in Arbeitsgruppe (ed.), *Totgeschwiegen 1933–1945*, pp. 41–42.
125 Ibid., pp. 37–38.
126 Erich Friedländer, 'Eine Gefahr für die deutsche Irrenpflege', *Allgemeine Zeitschrift für Psychiatrie* (1930), 93, p. 197.
127 Bratz, 'Kann die Versorgung', pp. 4–9.
128 Ibid., pp. 17–20.
129 Ibid., pp. 21–22.
130 Erich Friedländer, 'Kann die Versorgung der Geisteskranken billiger gestaltet werden und wie?', *Psychiatrisch-Neurologische Wochenschrift* (1932), 34, p. 379.
131 R. Carriere, 'Gründe der Überfüllung der Anstalten und Vorschläge zur Abhilfe - besonders der Freistaat Sachsen', *Allgemeine Zeitschrift für Psychiatrie* (1931), 94, p. 154.
132 Weindling, *Health, Race and German Politics*, pp. 389–392.
133 Robert Gaupp, 'Die Unfruchtbarmachung geistig und sittlich Minderwertiger', paper, *Allgemeine Zeitschrift für Psychiatrie* (1926), 83, p. 376.
134 Ibid., p. 379.
135 Ibid., p. 380.
136 Ibid., pp. 386–387.
137 Ibid., p. 390.
138 Hans Luxenburger, 'Grundsätzliches zur kausalen Prophylaxe der erblichen Geisteskrankheiten', *Zeitschrift für psychische Hygiene* (1929), 2, p. 169.

139 Bratz, 'Kann die Versorgung', p. 26.
140 Bertold Kihn, 'Die Ausschaltung der Minderwertigen aus der Gesellschaft', *Allgemeine Zeitschrift für Psychiatrie* (1932), 98, p. 389.
141 Ibid., p. 391.
142 Ibid., p. 391.
143 Ibid., p. 394.
144 Ibid., p. 396.
145 Ibid., p. 401.
146 Ibid., pp. 403–404.
147 Faltlhauser, conference paper, *Allgemeine Zeitschrift für Psychiatrie* (1932), 96, p. 371.
148 Ibid., Bumke, conference paper, p. 372.
149 Ibid., p. 373.
150 Ibid., p. 373.
151 Steve Jones, *The Language of the Genes. Biology, History and the Evolutionary Future* (London 1993), p. 8.
152 Hans-Georg Güse and Norbert Schmacke, *Psychiatrie zwischen bürgerlichen Revolution und Faschismus* (Giessen 1974), vol. 2, pp. 361–363.
153 Luxenburger, conference paper, p. 374.
154 Ibid., p. 375.
155 Ernst Rüdin, address to second annual conference for mental hygiene, *Zeitschrift für psychische Hygiene* (1932), 5, p. 68.
156 Ibid.; Luxenburger, paper p. 70.
157 Ibid., p. 74.
158 Nowak, *'Euthanasie' und Sterilisation*, pp. 91–92. See also his 'Die Kirche und das "Gesetz zur Verhütung erbkranken Nachwuchses" vom 14 Juli 1933', in J. Tuchel (ed.), *'Kein Recht auf Leben'. Beiträge und Dokumente zur Entrechtung und Vernichtung 'lebensunwerten Lebens' im Nationalsozialismus* (Berlin 1984), pp. 101–119; 'Sterilisation, Krankenmord und Innere Mission im "Dritten Reich", in Achim Thom and G. Cargorodcev (eds.), *Medizin unterm Hakenkreuz* pp. 167ff.
159 Hans Harmsen, paper, *Zeitschrift für psychische Hygiene* (1932), 5, p. 75; on Harmsen see Sabine Schleiermacher, 'Die Innere Mission und ihr bevölkerungspolitisches Programm', in Heidrun Kaupen-Haas (ed.), *Der Griff nach der Bevölkerung. Aktualität und Kontinuität nazistischer Bevölkerungspolitik* (Nordlingen 1986), pp. 78ff., and her 'Der Centralausschuss für Innere Mission und die Eugenik am Vorabend des "Dritten Reichs"' in T. Strohm and J. Thierfelder (eds.), *Diakonie im 'Dritten Reich'* (Heidelberg 1990), pp. 60–77.
160 Nowak, *'Euthanasie' und Sterilisation*, p. 110.
161 Ibid., p. 75.
162 Ibid., p. 108.
163 Struve, conference paper, *Zeitschrift für psychische Hygiene* (1932), 5, p. 77.
164 Weindling, *Health, Race and German Politics*, pp. 523–525.
165 On the background to the Law, see above all Gisela Bock, *Zwangssterilisation im Nationalsozialismus. Studien zur Rassenpolitik und Frauenpolitik* (Opladen 1986); see also Jeremy Noakes, 'Nazism and Eugenics: the Background to the Nazi Sterilisation Law of 14 July 1933', in R. J. Bullen *et al.* (eds.), *Ideas into*

Politics (London, 1984), pp. 75–94; Paul Weindling, 'Compulsory Sterilisation in National Socialist Germany', *German History* (1987), 5, pp. 10–24; Christian Ganssmüller, *Die Erbgesundheitspolitik des Dritten Reiches* (Cologne, Vienna 1987).

2 HOPE AND HARD TIMES: ASYLUMS IN THE 1930S

1 Hendrik Graf, 'Die Situation der Patienten und des Pflegepersonals der rheinischen Provinzial- Heil- und Pflegeanstalten in der Zeit des Nationalsozialismus' in M. Leipert, R. Styrnal and W. Schwarzer (eds.), *Verlegt nach unbekannt. Sterilisation und Euthanasie in Galkhausen 1933–1945. Dokumente und Darstellungen zur Geschichte der rheinischen Provinzialverwaltung und des Landschaftsverbandes Rheinland* (Cologne 1987), p. 45.

2 *BkH JB*, 1935, p. 23.

3 *BkH JB* 1936, pp. 26–28.

4 Gerhard Schmidt, *Selektion in der Heilanstalt 1939–1945* (Frankfurt am Main 1983), p. 26.

5 *BkH JB* 1934, p. 28.

6 Anon., 'Wir besuchen Geisteskranke in ihren Anstalten. Erschütternde Eindrücke bei einer Pressefahrt nach Eglfing-Haar und Schönbrunn', *Münchner neueste Nachrichten*, 23 February 1934, p. 15.

7 Anon., 'Lebendig und doch tot!', *Münchner Zeitung*, 23 February 1934, p. 6. See also Bernhard Richarz, *Heilen, Pflegen, Töten*, p. 60.

8 Anon., 'Die Lehre von Eglfing: Sterilisation ein Gebot der Humanität und Selbsterhaltung der Nation', *Völkischer Beobachter*, 23 February 1934.

9 'Ein mütiger Schritt', *Das schwarze Korps*, 11 March 1937, p. 18.

10 'Zum Thema: Gnadentod', *Das schwarze Korps*, 18 March 1937, p. 9.

11 J. Enge, 'Das Gesetz zur Verhütung erbkranken Nachwuchses in Laienbetrachtung und ärztliche Erfahrungen als Gutachter im Erbgesundheitsverfahren', *Psychiatrisch-Neurologische Wochenschrift* (1937), 39, p. 10.

12 Ernst Klee, *'Euthanasie' im NS-Staat. Die 'Vernichtung lebensunwerten Lebens'* (Frankfurt am Main 1983), pp. 76–77.

13 Staatsarchiv, Munich (hereafter StAM), Staatsanwaltschaft Nr 17460 1/2, Trial of Hermann Pfannmüller, vol. 1, testimony of Dr Karl Steichele, p. 7.

14 Ibid., enclosing NO–863, testimony of Ludwig Lehner. See also A. Mitscherlich and F. Mielke (eds.), *Medizin ohne Menschlichkeit. Dokumente des Nürnberger Ärzteprozesses* (2nd edn Frankfurt am Main 1978), p. 193.

15 Walter Wuttke, 'Medizin, Ärzte, Gesundheitspolitik', in Otto Borst (ed.), *Das Dritte Reich in Baden und Württemberg* (Stuttgart 1988) pp. 229–230.

16 Fritz Ast, 'Der Ärztemangel in den Heilanstalten und Vorschläge zu dessen Behebung, insbesondere hinsichtlich der den Heilanstalten erwachsenden neuen Aufgaben', *Zeitschrift für psychische Hygiene* (1936), 9, p. 9.

17 HHStAW Abt. 461 Nr 32442 (Eichberg Trial), vol. 4, p. 2 (Hinsen testimony).

18 'Anstaltskosten müssen gesenkt werden', speech by Bernotat on 24 September 1937, in Horst Dickel, *'Die sind doch alle unheilbar'. Zwangssterilisation und Tötung der 'Minderwertigen' im Rheingau, 1934–1945* (Wiesbaden 1988), pp. 68–69.

19 Peter Chroust (ed.), *Friedrich Mennecke. Innenansichten eines medizinischen Täters im Nationalsozialismus. Eine Edition seiner Briefe 1935–1947* (Hamburg 1988), vol. 2, Nr. 246, pp. 917–918.

20 HHStAW Abt. 461 Nr 32442 (Eichberg Trial), vol. 2, p. 4 (Mennecke testimony).

21 Dickel, *'Die sind doch alle unheilbar'*, p. 84.

22 HHStAW Abt. 461 Nr 32442 (Eichberg Trial), vol. 4, p. 3 (Hinsen testimony).

23 Heidi Schmidt von Blittersdorff, Dieter Debus and Birgit Kalkowsky, 'Die Geschichte der Anstalt Hadamar von 1933–1945 und ihre Funktion im Rahmen von T-4', in Dorothee Roer and Dieter Henkel (eds.), *Psychiatrie im Faschismus. Die Anstalt Hadamar 1933–1945* (Bonn 1986), p. 74.

24 Ibid., pp. 74–75.

25 Peter Chroust *et al.* (eds.), *'Soll nach Hadamar überführt werden'. Den Opfern der Euthanasiemorde 1939 bis 1945. Gedenkausstellung in Hadamar* (Frankfurt am Main 1989), p. 25.

26 Manfred Klüppel, *'Euthanasie' und Lebensvernichtung am Beispiel der Landesheilanstalten Haina und Merxhausen. Eine Chronik der Ereignisse 1933–1945* (3rd edn Kassel 1985), pp. 17–18.

27 Dorothea Sick, *'Euthanasie' im Nationalsozialismus am Beispiel des Kalmenhofs in Idstein im Taunus. Materialien zur Sozialarbeit und Sozialpolitik*, vol. 9 (2nd edn Frankfurt am Main 1983), p. 32. See also Martin Wisskirchen, 'Idiotenanstalt – Heilerziehungsanstalt – Lazarett. Die Entwicklung des Kalmenhofs 1888–1945', in Christian Schrapper and Dieter Sengling (eds.), *Die Idee der Bildbarkeit. 100 Jahre sozialpädagogische Praxis in der Heilerziehungsanstalt Kalmenhof* (Weinheim and Munich 1988), pp. 120ff.

28 W. Möckel and E. Schweickert, 'Die wirtschaftlichen Aufgaben der Heil- und Pflegeanstalten im neuen Vierjahresplan', *Psychiatrisch-Neurologische Wochenschrift* (1937), 39, pp. 425–428.

29 Klee, *'Euthanasie' im NS-Staat*, p. 67.

30 Manfred Klüppel, *'Euthanasie' und Lebensvernichtung*, pp. 19–20; Klee, *'Euthanasie'*, p. 74.

31 Imperial War Museum, London, CIOSC File Nr xxviii–50. Leo Alexander (ed.), *Public Mental Health Practices in Germany. Sterilization and Execution of Patients Suffering from Nervous or Mental Diseases*, Appendix 6, pp. 155ff.

32 Ibid., p. 169.

33 Sick, *'Euthanasie'*, p. 29.

34 HHStAW Abt. 461 Nr 31526 (Idstein Trial), vol. 3, p. 31 (Emil Spornhauer testimony). See also Wisskirchen, 'Idiotenanstalt', pp. 114–119.

35 'Betriebsgrundsätze' and 'Betriebsordnung', reprinted in Sick, *'Euthanasie'*, p. 30–31.

36 Helmut Sorg, '"Euthanasie" in den evangelischen Heilanstalten in Württemberg im Dritten Reich', Magisterhausarbeit (FU-Berlin 1987), pp. 55–57. I am grateful to Wolfgang Wippermann for a copy of his pupil's dissertation.

37 Hans Rössler, 'Die "Euthanasie" – Diskussion in Neuendettelsau 1937–1939', *Zeitschrift für bayerische Kirchengeschichte* (1986), 55, pp. 199–208. See also Hans Rössler, 'Ein neues Dokument zur "Euthanasie" – Diskussion in Neuendettelsau 1939', *Zeitschrift für bayerische Kirchengeschichte* (1988), 57, pp. 87–91.

38 HHStAW Abt. 461 Nr 32442 (Eichberg Trial), vol. 4, pp. 101–103 (Hinsen testimony); Chroust, *Mennecke, Briefe*, vol. 1, pp. 4–8; see also Peter Chroust, 'Friedrich Mennecke', in Götz Aly *et al.* (eds.), *Beiträge zur nationalsozialistischen Gesundheits- und Sozialpolitik* (Berlin 1987), 4, pp. 67ff. and Peter Chroust, 'Ärzteschaft und "Euthanasie" – unter besondere Berücksichtigung Friedrich Menneckes', in Christina Vanja (ed.), *Euthanasie in Hadamar. Die nationalsozialistische Vernichtungspolitik in hessischen Anstalten* (Kassel 1991), pp. 123ff. for biographical sketches of Mennecke.

39 Valentin Faltlhauser, 'Jahresbericht der Kreis-Heil und Pflegeanstalt Kaufbeuren-Irsee über das Jahr 1934', *Psychiatrisch-Neurologische Wochenschrift* (1935), 37, p. 372.

40 Ast, 'Der Ärztemangel', p. 16.

41 Richarz, *Heilen, Pflegen, Töten*, pp. 46–47.

42 *BkH JB* 1937, pp. 4–6.

43 Graf, 'Die Situation der Patienten', p. 43.

44 Peter Delius, *Das Ende von Strecknitz. Die Lübecker Heilanstalt und ihre Auflösung 1941. Ein Beitrag zur Sozialgeschichte der Psychiatrie im Nationalsozialismus* (Kiel 1988), p. 39.

45 See, for example, Antje Wettlaufer, 'Die Beteiligung von Schwestern und Pflegern an den Morden in Hadamar', in D. Roer and D. Henkel (eds.), *Psychiatrie im Faschismus*, pp. 300–304. The standard work on nursing in Germany under the National Socialists is Hilde Steppe (ed.), *Krankenpflege im Nationalsozialismus* (5th edn, Frankfurt am Main 1989).

46 Ibid., pp. 303–304.

47 Hilde Steppe, 'Mit Tränen in den Augen zogen wir dann die Spritzen auf . . . ', in Steppe (ed.), *Krankenpflege im Nationalsozialismus*, pp. 140–141.

48 HHStAW Abt 461 Nr 32061 (Hadamar Trial), vol. 7, p. 17; I am grateful to Paul R. for a series of interviews between 1991 and 1993 regarding his activities at Hadamar.

49 Ganssmüller, *Erbgesundheitspolitik*, pp. 42–43.

50 Gisela Bock, 'Sterilisationspolitik im Nationalsozialismus: die Planung einer heilen Gesellschaft durch Prävention', in Klaus Dörner (ed.), *Fortschritte der Psychiatrie im Umgang mit Menschen. Wert und Verwertung des Menschen im 20. Jahrhundert* (Rehburg-Loccum 1984), p. 88; see also Bock's *Zwangssterilisation im Nationalsozialismus*, p. 238, and her 'Zwangssterilisation im Nationalsozialismus', in Vanja (ed.), *Euthanasie in Hadamar*, p. 69 for the figure of 400,000. Studies of compulsory sterilisation include Achim Thom, 'Die rassenhygienischen Leitideen der faschistischen Gesundheitspolitik – die Zwangssterilisierungen als Beginn ihrer antihumanen Verwirklichung', in Thom and Caregorodcev (eds.), *Medizin unterm Hakenkreuz*, pp. 65ff.

51 Dr Matzner, 'Das Verfahren vor den Erbgesundheitsgerichten', *Der Öffentliche Gesundheitsdienst* (1935–1936), 1, pp. 281–289.

52 Ibid., p. 286.

53 Hermann Nobbe, 'Das Gesetz zur Verhütung erbkranken Nachwuchses, Irrenanstalten, Aussenfürsorge und Familienpflege', *Psychiatrisch-Neurologische Wochenschrift* (1934), 36, p. 473; Wilhelm Lange, 'Ergebnisse, Lehren und Wünsche, die sich aus der Jahresarbeit (1934) eines Erbgesundheitsgerichtes

(Chemnitz) ergeben', *Psychiatrisch-Neurologische Wochenschrift* (1935), 37, pp. 81–82.

54 Faltlhauser, 'Jahresbericht', p. 332.

55 'Merkblatt über die Unfruchtbarmachung', *Reichsgesetzblatt* 1 (1935), p. 1021.

56 Arthur Gütt, Ernst Rüdin and Falk Ruttke, *Gesetz zur Verhütung erbkranken Nachwuchses vom 14. Juli 1933 mit Auszug aus dem Gesetz gegen gefährliche Gewohnheitsverbrecher und über Massnahmen der Sicherung und Besserung vom 24. November 1933* (2nd edn, Munich 1936), p. 73.

57 'Gesetz zur Änderung des GveN vom 26 Juni 1935', *Reichsgesetzblatt* 1 (1935), p. 773.

58 For the surgical techniques see Erich Lexer, 'Die Eingriffe zur Unfruchtbarmachung des Mannes und zur Entmannung' and H. Eymer, 'Die Unfruchtbarmachung der Frau', in Gütt, Rüdin and Ruttke, *Gesetz zur Verhütung*, pp. 319ff. and 327ff.

59 *BkH JB* 1934, p. 20.

60 Faltlhauser, 'Jahresbericht', p. 335.

61 'Fünfte Verordnung zur Ausführung des Gesetzes zur Verhütung erbkranken Nachwuchses 25 Februar 1936', *Reichsgesetzblatt* 1, p. 122.

62 *BkH JB* 1935, p. 18.

63 *BkH JB* 1936, p. 17.

64 *BkH JB* 1933, p. 17.

65 Faltlhauser, 'Jahresbericht', p. 330.

66 Karl Hermann Heydecke, 'Unsere Erfahrungen über den Einfluss der Sterilisierung auf die psychische Gesamthaltung der Sterilisierten', *Psychiatrisch-Neurologische Wochenschrift* (1936), 38, pp. 284–285; for similar claims, see Karl Kolb, 'Postoperative psychische Reaktionen bei Sterilisierten in der Heilanstalt', *Münchener Medizinische Wochenschrift* (1935), 83, pp. 1641–1642.

67 Interview with Klara Nowak, Hadamar 1991.

68 Useful, although obviously *parti pris*, sources for deficiencies in the Law are articles in psychiatric and public health journals by doctors who served on the Hereditary Health Courts; see, for example, Straub, 'Die Verantwortung des Ärztes als Mitglied des Erbgesundheitsgerichts', *Psychiatrisch-Neurologische Wochenschrift* (1935), 37, pp. 68–69; Wilhelm Lange, 'Ergebnisse, Lehren und Wünsche'; Dr Neubelt, 'Einige Mitteilungen zur Durchführung des Gesetzes zur Verhütung erbkranken Nachwuchses', *Der Öffentliche Gesundheitsdienst* (1935–1936), 1, pp. 420–423; Falk Ruttke, 'Beispiele aus der Rechtsprechung zum Begriff "schweren erblichen körperlichen Missbildung"', ibid., pp. 573–576; Erich Wirth, 'Erfordert bei der Erbbegutachtung die Diagnose der erblichen Taubheit unbedingt den Nachweis der erblichen Belastung?', *Münchener Medizinische Wochenschrift* (1936), 83, pp. 1304ff.; O. Marchesani, 'Über erbliche Blindheit', *Münchener Medizinische Wochenschrift* (1936), 83, pp. 1167–1171.

69 For the reasons why haemophilia was omitted see C. H. Schröder, 'Beitrag zur Vererbung und Behandlung der Hämophilie', *Münchener Medizinische Wochenschrift* (1935), 83, pp. 1281–1284; Schmuhl, *Rassenhygiene, Nationalsozialismus, Euthanasie*, p. 156. The effectiveness of Schmuhl's competent survey of the literature on 'euthanasia' – the book rests on practically no original archival

research – is largely vitiated by his insistence upon fitting what is a very complex subject into a predictable and simpleminded 'structure-functionalist' framework.

70 'Begründung zum GVeN vom 26 Juli 1933', Nr 172.

71 Kurt Kolle, 'Die Unfruchtbarmachung bei Alkoholismus', *Allgemeine Zeitschrift für Psychiatrie* (1939), 112, pp. 401–402.

72 Güse and Schmacke, *Psychiatrie zwischen bürgerlicher Revolution und Faschismus*, vol. 2, pp. 403–408.

73 Hellmuth Eckhardt, 'Die sog. angeborene Huftverrenkung und das Gesetz zur Verhütung erbkranken Nachwuchses', *Der Öffentliche Gesundheitsdienst* (1935–1936), 1, pp. 321ff.

74 Ruttke, 'Beispiele aus der Rechtsprechung', pp. 573ff.

75 Hans-Ullrich Brändle, 'Aufartung und Ausmerze. NS-Rassen- und Bevölkerungspolitik im Kräftefeld zwischen Wissenschaft, Partei und Staat am Beispiel des "angeborenen Schwachsinns"', in Walter Wuttke (ed.), *Volk und Gesundheit. Heilen und Vernichten im Nationalsozialismus* (Frankfurt am Main 1988), pp. 154–156.

76 W. Weygandt, 'Talentierte Schwachsinnige und ihre erbgesetzliche Bedeutung', *Zeitschrift für die gesamte Neurologie und Psychiatrie* (1938), 161, pp. 532–535.

77 G. Friese, 'Erbkrankheit, Begabung und Unfruchtbarmachung', *Der Öffentliche Gesundheitsdienst* (1935), 1, pp. 899ff.

78 Enge, 'Das Gesetz zur Verhütung erbkranken Nachwuchses', p. 8.

79 Brändle, 'Aufartung und Ausmerze', pp. 157–158.

80 Günter Liermann, 'Der Intelligenzprüfungsbogen nach Anlage 5a der ersten Verordnung zur Durchführung des Gesetzes zur Verhütung erbkranken Nachwuchses in seiner Anwendung bei Jugendlichen in der Stadt Königsberg i. Pr. und dem Samland im Alter von 14–18 Jahren', *Der Öffentliche Gesundheitsdienst* (1935–1936), 1, pp. 244–254.

81 *BkH JB* 1934, p. 16.

82 Faltlhauser, 'Jahrsbericht', pp. 331–332.

83 *BkH JB* 1934, pp. 21–22.

84 HHStAW Abt. 401/1 Nr 12845 (Eichberg Verwaltungsakten); *BkH JB* 1938, p. 35.

85 *BkH JB* 1934, pp. 16–17.

86 On Astel see BDC, files on Karl Astel, especially 'Bericht über die Tätigkeit des Thür. Landesamt für Rassewesen' (1933–1934); 'Lebenslauf' (1934). On hereditary health databanks see above all Roth, 'Erbbiologische Bestandsaufnahme', pp. 62–68; Paul Weindling, '"Mustergau" Thüringen. Rassenhygiene zwischen Ideologie und Machtpolitik', in Norbert Frei (ed.), *Medizin und Gesundheitspolitik*, pp. 84ff.

87 Norbert Emmerich, 'Die Wittenauer Heilstätten 1933–1945', in Arbeitsgruppe zur Erforschung der Geschichte der Karl-Bonhoeffer-Nervenklinik (eds.), *Totgeschwiegen 1933–1945. Zur Geschichte der Wittenauer Heilstätten. Seit 1957 Karl-Bonhoeffer-Nervenklinik* (2nd edn, Berlin 1989), p. 82; Richarz, *Heilen, Pflegen, Töten*, pp. 134–135; Winter, 'Die Geschichte der NS-"Euthanasie" Anstalt Hadamar', p. 46, for further examples from various asylums.

88 Dr Reich, 'Einiges über erbbiologische Ermittlungstätigkeit', *Der Öffentliche Gesundheitsdienst* (1935–1936), 1, p. 130.
89 Hans Burkhardt, 'Was kann die psychiatrische offene Fürsorge für Erbforschung und Rassenhygiene leisten?', *Psychiatrisch-Neurologische Wochenschrift* (1934), 36, p. 242. See also Karl Knab, 'Erbbiologische Bestandsaufnahme der Insassen der öffentlichen Heil- und Pflegeanstalten und offene Fürsorge für Geisteskranke', *Psychiatrisch-Neurologische Wochenschrift* (1936), 38, pp. 211–212.
90 Faltlhauser, 'Jahresbericht', p. 346.
91 Ibid., p. 372.
92 Ibid., p. 372.
93 Burkhardt, 'Was kann die psychiatrische offene Fürsorge', p. 342. For the wider manipulation of population censuses see Götz Aly and Karl-Heinz Roth, *Die restlose Erfassung. Volkszählen, Identifizieren, Aussondern im Nationalsozialismus* (Berlin 1984).
94 Burkhardt, 'Was kann die psychiatrische offene Fürsorge', p. 234.
95 Ibid., p. 235.
96 Reich, 'Einiges über erbbiologische Ermittlungstätigkeit', pp. 130–132.
97 Details from Judgement of the Hereditary Health Court, Krefeld, 19 August 1936, reprinted in Leipert *et al.* (eds.), *Verlegt nach unbekannt*, Dok. 26, pp. 142–144.
98 Ibid., p. 143.
99 Ibid., Dok. 31, Meldung der Städtischen Krankenanstalt Wuppertal-Barmen vom 23 Juli 1937, p. 149.
100 Judgement of the Hereditary Health Court in Frankfurt am Main in the case of Anna V. on 26 November 1937, reprinted in Bettina Winter, 'Die Geschichte der NS–"Euthanasie"-Anstalt Hadamar', in Winter (ed.), *'Verlegt nach Hadamar'* (Kassel 1991), p. 53.
101 Director of the Landesheilanstalt Hadamar to the Hereditary Health Court, Frankfurt am Main, 28 December 1937, reprinted in Winter, 'Die Geschichte', p. 54.
102 Judgement of the Hereditary Health Court, Frankfurt am Main in the case of Anna V. on 18 March 1938, reprinted in Winter, 'Die Geschichte', p. 50.
103 Erving Goffmann, 'The Underlife of a Public Institution: A Study of Ways of Making Out in a Mental Hospital', in Goffman, *Asylums. Essays on the Social Situation of Mental Patients and Other Inmates* (Harmondsworth 1961), pp. 157ff.
104 Richarz, *Heilen, Pflegen, Töten*, p. 53.
105 *BkH JB* 1933, pp. 6–7.
106 *BkH JB* 1933, pp. 34–37.
107 Author's own archive, Josef S., 'Mein Lebenslauf' (unpublished manuscript dated 30 May 1992), fols. 1–2. I am grateful to Josef S. for agreeing to record his own experiences in a more formal way than through our many conversations.
108 HHStAW Abt. 461 Nr 32061 (Hadamar Trial), vol. 7, p. 153 (Testimony of Klara S.).
109 Berndt-Michael Becker, 'Der Zeitzeuge Fritz N.', in Arbeitsgruppe (ed.), *Totgeschwiegen*, pp. 177–183.

110 HHStAW Abt. 430/1 Nr 11462, Lina C's patient file, report on her admission to Eichberg on 10 April 1941.
111 Ibid., 'Meldebogen 1', no date.
112 Ibid., 'Krankheitsverlauf', entry for 5 April 1942.
113 HHStAW Abt. 430/1 Nr 11472, Wilhelm B., 'Auszug aus den Strafprozessakten d. Staatsanwaltschaft bei dem Landgericht Wiesbaden über Wilhelm B.' (24 November 1941), pp. 1–3.
114 Ibid., copy of Wilhelm B.'s death certificate dated 8 August 1942 and letter to Frau M. dated 8 August 1942, informing her that Wilhelm B. had succumbed to 'his incurable illness'.
115 StAM, RA 3761 Nr 57693, Bezirksarzt der Hauptstadt der Bewegung, 'Gutachten' on Maria Z., dated 3 March 1936; and Gestapo memo on Maria Z. dated 11 November 1940.
116 Richarz, *Heilen, Pflegen, Töten*, p. 59.
117 Horst Dickel, 'Alltag in einer Landesheilanstalt im Nationalsozialismus – das Beispiel Eichberg', in Landeswohlfahrtsverband Hessen (ed.), *Euthanasie in Hadamar. Die nationalsozialistische Vernichtungspolitik in hessischen Anstalten* (Kassel 1991), p. 106.
118 *BkH JB* 1932, p. 19.
119 *BkH JB* 1933, p. 19; 1936, p. 23.
120 Monika Daum, 'Arbeit und Zwang, das Leben der Hadamarer Patienten im Schatten des Todes', in Roer and Henkel (eds.), *Psychiatrie im Faschismus*, p. 191.
121 Dickel, 'Alltag in einer Landesheilanstalt im Nationalsozialismus', p. 108.
122 HHStAW Abt. 461 Nr 32442 (Eichberg Trial), p. 18.
123 HHStAW Abt. 461 Nr 32442 (Eichberg Trial), vol. 2, testimony of E.B. on 6 June 1946.
124 Ibid., testimony of L.H. on 29 June 1946.
125 Ibid., testimony of I.H. on 2 July 1946 and testimony of Frau K. on 21 July 1946.
126 On the 'Packsack' treatment see Sabine Damm and Norbert Emmerich 'Die Irrenanstalt Dalldorf-Wittenau bis 1933', in Arbeitsgruppe (ed.), *Totgeschwiegen*, p. 23; Delius, *Das Ende von Strecknitz*, p. 37.
127 Berndt-Michael Becker, 'Der Zeitzeuge Fritz N.', in Arbeitsgruppe (ed.), *Totgeschwiegen*, p. 178.
128 *BkH JB* 1933, p. 17.
129 *BkH JB* 1934, pp. 26–27.
130 HHStAW Abt. 430/1 Nr 11002, Paul S.'s patient file. Biographical details from admission document dated 25 February 1941 and death certificate dated 7 July 1941.
131 Ibid.; all details taken from Paul S.'s patient record from the Erziehungs- und Pflegeanstalt Scheuern bei Nassau, beginning with his admission on 1 October 1930 from the Krüppelheim at Bad Kreuznach, where he had lived from 1921 to 1930.
132 Ibid., Eichberg 'Aufnahmebefund,' p. 1.
133 Ibid.; all biographical details from Paul S.'s Eichberg patient record with dated entries.

134 Ibid., entry for 3 February 1941 recording his transfer to Eichberg and entry for 8 July 1941 recording his death.
135 HHStAW Abt. 430/1 Nr 11258, Johanne B.'s patient file. Death certificate 15 May 1941.
136 See ibid., 'Ärztliche Gutachten' dated 28 December 1931, for this account.
137 Ibid., Johanne B.'s patient record from the Provinzial- Heil- und Pflegeanstalt zu Hildesheim.
138 Ibid., entry for 24 January 1933.
139 Ibid., entry for 16 November 1936.
140 Ibid., entry for 17 April 1941.
141 Ibid., Eichberg continuation of her patient record, entry for 22 April 1941.
142 HHStAW Abt. 430/1 Nr 113746, Wilhelm D.'s patient record. 'Aussagen der Frau des Patienten D', dated 31 December 1919; and 'Auszug aus dem Diziplinärstrafverzeichnis der Gefängnisakte', entries from August 1919 onwards.
143 Ibid., 'Ärztliches Gutachten' dated 6 December 1925.
144 Ibid., p. 2.
145 Ibid.; there are hundreds of drawings in his patient file.
146 Ibid., 'Geschichte der Krankheit' entry for 7 February 1920.
147 Ibid., entry for 5 March 1920.
148 Ibid., entry concerning an interview with Dr K. on 24 April 1925.
149 Ibid., Eichberg asylum to the Sozialverwaltung in Hamburg dated 27 April 1940.
150 Ibid., Dr F. Mennecke to Frau G., dated 20 October 1942.
151 Faltlhauser, 'Jahresbericht', pp. 322–323.
152 Richarz, *Heilen, Pflegen, Töten*, p. 73.
153 *BkH JB* 1931, p. 17.
154 Hans-Ludwig Siemen, *Das Grauen ist vorprogrammiert. Psychiatrie zwischen Faschismus und Atomkrieg* (Gütersloh 1987), p. 159; see also Siemen, *Menschen blieben auf der Strecke*, pp. 152ff.
155 Karl Knab, 'Was ist für die Anstaltspsychiatrie wichtiger: die medikamentose Behandlung oder die Psychotherapie?', *Psychiatrisch-Neurologische Wochenschrift* (1935), 37, p. 367.
156 Faltlhauser, 'Jahresbericht', pp. 321–323.
157 David Schöne and Dieter Schöne, 'Zur Entwicklung und klinischen Anwendung neuer somatischer Therapiemethoden der Psychiatrie in den 30er Jahren des 20. Jahrhunderts unter besonderer Berücksichtigung der Schocktherapien und deren Nutzung in den deutschen Heil- und Pflegeanstalten', Medical Dissertation, University of Leipzig (1986), fols. 15ff. For a good overview of the main trends in clinical psychiatry during the 1930s, see Thom, 'Die Entwicklung', especially pp. 137–138 for the new somatic therapies.
158 For procedure see Anton von Braunmühl, 'Insulinschockbehandlung der Schizophrenie', *Münchener Medizinische Wochenschrift* (1937), 84, pp. 8ff. For examples of complications see Marianne Feldhofen, 'Schwierigkeiten und Gefahren der Insulinschockbehandlung der Schizophrenie', *Allgemeine Zeitschrift für Psychiatrie* (1937), 105, pp. 281ff., and Richard Müller, 'Krampfbehandlung der Schizophrenie und Schenkelhalsfraktur', *Münchener Medizinische Wochenschrift* (1939), 86, pp. 525–526.
159 Peter Hays, *New Horizons in Psychiatry* (Harmondsworth 1971), p. 114.

160 Anton von Braunmühl, 'Über die Insulinschockbehandlung', *Psychiatrisch-Neurologische Wochenschrift* (1937), 39, p. 156.

161 Ibid., p. 163.

162 *BkH JB* 1936, p. 21.

163 Hans Roemer, 'Die Praktische Einführung der Insulin- und Cardiazolbehandlung in den Heil- und Pflegeanstalten', *Allgemeine Zeitschrift für Psychiatrie* (1938), 107, p. 122.

164 L. Ziegelroth, 'Bericht über die Besichtigung der Insulinstation in der Heilanstalt Eglfing', *Psychiatrisch-Neurologische Wochenschrift* (1937), 39, pp. 496–498.

165 Anton von Braunmühl, 'Über die Insulinschockbehandlung der Schizophrenie', p. 10.

166 *BkH JB* 1936, pp. 18–19.

167 Anton von Braunmühl, 'Schocklinie und Hypoglykamielinie', *Zeitschrift für die gesamte Neurologie und Psychiatrie* (1940), 169, pp. 413ff., especially p. 417.

168 Braunmühl, 'Über die Insulinschockbehandlung', pp. 162–163.

169 HHStAW Abt. 430/1 Nr 10613, Karl H.'s patient file. 'Abschrift der Krankengeschichte aus der Nervenklinik der Stadt und Universität Frankfurt am Main' dated 8 May 1937.

170 Ibid., p. 4.

171 Ibid., p. 14.

172 Ibid., p. 15.

173 Ibid., p. 16.

174 Ibid., Eichberg patient record showing Karl H.'s admission and death on 2 June 1940.

175 Siemen, *Menschen blieben auf der Strecke*, p. 156.

176 Richard Müller, 'Krampfbehandlung der Schizophrenie und Schenkelhalsfraktur', *Münchener Medizinische Wochenschrift* (1939), 86, pp. 525–526; Anton von Braunmühl, 'Aus der Praxis der Krampftherapie', *Allgemeine Zeitschrift für Psychiatrie* (1942), 120, pp. 146–157.

177 R. Carriere, 'Ein Jahr Cardiazolbehandlung auf der unruhigen Frauenabteilung', *Allgemeine Zeitschrift für Psychiatrie* (1939), 113, pp. 347ff.

178 G. Ewald and S. Haddenbrock, 'Die Elektrokrampftherapie. Ihre Grundlagen und ihre Erfolge', *Zeitschrift für die gesamte Neurologie und Psychiatrie* (1942), 174, p. 639.

179 Anton von Braunmühl, 'Die kombinierte Schock-Krampfbehandlung', *Zeitschrift für die gesamte Neurologie und Psychiatrie* (1938), 164, pp. 72–73.

180 Schmidt, *Selektion in der Heilanstalt*, p. 21.

181 IWM, CIOSC File Nr xxviii–50, Kleist report on Herborn dated 24 March 1938, p. 169. For Kleist's comments on Bernotat see HHStAW Abt. 461 Nr 32061 (Hadamar Trial), vol. 7, p. 13.

3 'WHEELS MUST ROLL FOR VICTORY!' CHILDREN'S 'EUTHANASIA' AND 'AKTION T–4'

1 Zentrale Stelle der Landesjustizverwaltungen, Ludwigsburg (hereafter ZSL) 'Euthanasie' (alphabetically arranged volumes), Hea–Heq, interrogation of Richard von Hegener, 30 March 1960, pp. 4–5.

2 On the Chancellory of the Führer as an example of Nazi resort to prerogative agencies to expedite the implementation of policies while by-passing normative bureaucratic channels, see above all Jeremy Noakes, 'Philipp Bouhler und die Kanzlei des Führers der NSDAP', in Dieter Rebentisch and Karl Teppe (eds.), *Verwaltung contra Menschenführung im Staat Hitlers* (Göttingen 1986), p. 210.

3 BDC, personal files on Philipp Bouhler; Bundesarchiv Dokumentationszentrale (Berlin) personal file on Philipp Bouhler.

4 Klee, *'Euthanasie' im NS-Staat*, pp. 77–79.

5 HHStAW Abt. 631a/92, Hans Hefelmann, 'Ergänzungen zum Problem der Euthanasie-Massnahmen während des Hitler-Regimes' (1961), p. 3.

6 For Brandt's background, see his BDC personal file, and IWM *Medical Trial*, Case 1, US versus Karl Brandt *et al.* (1947), especially vol. 5, pp. 2301ff. for Brandt's account of his background and entry into Hitler's inner court.

7 IWM *Medical Trial*, Case 1, US versus Karl Brandt *et al.* (1947), vol. 6, pp. 2396ff.

8 HHStAW Abt. 631a Nr 293, interrogation of Werner Catel on 15 May 1962, p. 21.

9 Ibid., pp. 23–24.

10 For an excellent, if selfconsciously academic, account of these older debates about Nazism, see Ian Kershaw, *The Nazi Dictatorship* (3rd edn London 1993), pp. 8off. The new directions taken by research since the late 1970s, when these older debates had already peaked, are discussed and evaluated in M. Burleigh and W. Wippermann, *The Racial State: Germany 1933–1945* (2nd edn Cambridge 1992).

11 HHStAW Abt. 631a Nr 301, interrogation of Hans Heinrich Lammers dated 21 March 1961, p. 2.

12 IWM *Medical Trial*, Case 1, vol. 6, p. 2397. See also Mitscherlich and Mielke (eds.), *Medizin ohne Menschlichkeit*, p. 184.

13 IWM *Medical Trial*, Case 1, vol. 6, pp. 2396ff.

14 ZSL 'Euthanasie', Hea-Heq, interrogation of Richard von Hegener dated 30 March 1960, p. 5.

15 For a largely derivative attempt to fit the complexities of the 'euthanasia' programme into an orthodox 'structure-fuctionalist' straitjacket, see Schmuhl, *Rassenhygiene*.

16 See the important study of Karl-Heinz Roth and Götz Aly, 'Das "Gesetz über die Sterbehilfe bei unheilbar Kranken". Protokolle der Diskussion über die Legalisierung der nationalsozialistischen Anstaltsmorde in den Jahren 1938–1941', in Roth (ed.), *Erfassung zur Vernichtung*, especially pp. 104–105.

17 NAW T–253, Roll 44, Morell files, Nr 81. I am grateful to Desmond King for acquiring this film for me.

18 Ibid.

19 Roth and Aly, 'Das "Gesetz über die Sterbehilfe"', p. 108.

20 Klee, *'Euthanasie'*, pp. 80–81.

21 See HHStAW Abt. 631a Nr 297, interrogation of Ernst Wentzler dated 8 October 1963, p. 5 and p. 11, for these details.

22 Ibid., p. 10.

23 Ibid., pp. 13–14.

24 Ibid., p. 15.

25 Ibid., interrogation of Hans Heinze, 5 April 1950, p. 2. See also ZSL 'Euthanasie', Hea–Heq for interrogations of Heinze dated 24 February 1958; 10 March 1958; 31 March 1958; 22 April 1958; 2 May 1960; 22 February 1961; 27 September 1961 (pp. 1–50); 9 November 1961; and 16 May 1962.

26 HHStAW Abt. 631a Nr 293, interrogation of Werner Catel dated 14 May 1962, pp. 7–8.

27 Ibid., p. 13.

28 Klee, *'Euthanasie'*, p. 301; for a good summary of the activities of these clinics, see Hans Mausbach and Barbara Bromberger, 'Kinder als Opfer der NS-Medizin, unter besonderer Berücksichtigung der Kinderfachabteilungen in der Psychiatrie', in Vanja (ed.), *Euthanasie in Hadamar*, pp. 145ff. For a good detailed study, albeit one denied the benefit of access to the records of the Landesarchiv in Schleswig-Holstein, see Klaus Bästlein, 'Die "Kinderfachabteilung" Schleswig 1941 bis 1945', Arbeitskreis zur Erforschung des Nationalsozialismus in Schleswig-Holstein (ed.), *Informationen zur Schleswig-Holsteinischen Zeitgeschichte* (1993), 20, pp. 16–45. I am grateful to my former pupil, Jürgen Jürgensen of Kiel, for this reference. See also Richarz, *Heilen, Pflegen, Töten*, pp. 177ff.; Susanne Scholz and Reinhard Singer, 'Die Kinder in Hadamar', in Roer and Henkel (eds.), *Psychiatrie im Faschismus*, pp. 214ff.; Andrea Berger and Thomas Oelschlager 'Ich habe sie eines natürlichen Todes sterben lassen', in Christian Schrapper and Dieter Sengling (eds.), *Die Idee der Bildbarkeit. 100 Jahre sozialpädagogischer Praxis in der Heilerziehungsanstalt Kalmenhof* (Weinheim and Munich 1988), pp. 310ff. for studies of individual clinics.

29 See the collection of photographs in StAM, Staatsanwaltschaften Nr 17460 1/2.

30 On the offer of free 'treatment', see HHStAW 631a/Nr 364, the Amtsarzt to Stefan H., dated 10 May 1941.

31 HHStAW Abt. 631a Nr 364, Reichsausschuss to the Gesundheitsamt Biberach, dated 26 February 1941.

32 Ibid., Gesundheitsamt Biberach to the Reichsausschuss, dated 17 February 1941.

33 Ibid., Nr 366b, Landespolizei-Kommissariat Ludwigsburg interview with Emma J., including references to documentation dated 12 June 1942.

34 Ibid., Nr 364, the Amtsarzt to the Reichsausschuss, dated 10 May 1944; and Landespolizei Württemberg-Hohenzollern to the Amstgericht Münsingen, dated 12 June 1948, with transcript of interview with the mother.

35 Ibid., Nr 363, Kriminal-Kommissariat Waldshut interview with Margarethe F., dated 18 April 1962.

36 Bästlein, 'Die "Kinderfachabteilung"', p. 29.

37 For the former see HHStAW Abt. 631a Nr 366a, Landespolizei Württemberg-Hohenzollern to the Amtsgericht Münsingen, dated 6 June 1948; for the latter see ibid. Nr 364, interview with the former mayor of Dietmanns dated 9 June 1948, and interview with Paula W., dated 21 June 1948, for the role of NSV 'community' nurses.

38 Ibid., Landespolizei Württemberg-Hohenzollern, interview with Maria H. dated 6 June 1948.

39 Ibid., Landespolizei Württemberg-Hohenzollern, interview with Alfons T. dated 9 June 1948.
40 Bästlein, 'Die "Kinderfachabteilung"', p. 39.
41 Richarz, *Heilen, Pflegen, Töten*, p. 178.
42 StAM, Staatsanwaltschaften Nr 19031, Trial of Emma D. *et al.*, p. 10; interrogation of Emma L. for the *modus operandi*.
43 Richarz, *Heilen, Pflegen, Töten*, p. 179.
44 For similar procedures at Kaufbeuren-Irsee, see StAAug Staatsanwaltschaften Ks 1/49, Trial of Valentin Faltlhauser *et al.*, vol. 1, p. 43, interrogation of Faltlhauser dated 21 April 1948.
45 StAM, Staatsanwaltschaften Nr 17460 1/2, vol. 1, testimony of Dr Moritz S. (1949).
46 StAM, Staatsanwaltschaften Nr 19031, trial of Emma D.,, p. 17, testimony of Dr Franz S.
47 StAM, Staatsanwaltschaften Nr 17460 1/2, vol. 2, p. 71, testimony of Heinz H.
48 Ibid., p. 36, testimony of Dr Karl S.
49 Ibid., 'Protokoll', pp. 10–12 for the reference to 'human husks' and p. 7 for his general attitudes towards 'euthanasia'.
50 IWM *Medical Trial*, Case 1, US versus Karl Brandt *et al.*, vol. 4, p. 159 (NO–1313), Friedrich Hölzel to Hermann Pfannmüller, dated 20 August 1940.
51 StAM, Staatsanwaltschaften Nr 19031, Trial of Emma D. *et al*, p. 10, interrogation of Emma L.
52 Ibid., p. 8, text of the oath sworn on 26 April 1941.
53 Ibid., p. 10, testimony of Emma L., and p. 11, that of Maria S.
54 Berger and Oelschlager, 'Ich habe sie eines natürlichen Todes sterben lassen', p. 312.
55 'Interview mit einem Augenzeugen– dem Totengräber', reproduced in Sick, *'Euthanasie' im Nationalsozialismus*, p. 91.
56 Ibid., p. 73, undated standard letter bearing Grossmann's signature.
57 HHStAW Abt. 631a Nr 366a, Landespolizei Württemberg to the Amtsgericht Münsingen, dated 6 June 1948.
58 Ibid., Valentin Faltlhauser to Rosa E., dated 3 November 1942.
59 Ibid., death certificate for Margot E., dated 8 November 1942.
60 Ibid., Landespolizei Württemberg to the Amtsgericht Münsingen, dated 6 June 1948.
61 HHStAW Abt. 361a Nr 366b, director of Eichberg to Frau S., dated 3 September 1941.
62 Ibid., director of Eichberg to Herr and Frau S., dated 14 November 1941.
63 Ibid., Nr 368, testimony of Julie S., dated 15 June 1948.
64 Ibid., Nr 364, director of Eichberg to the mayor of Oberjesingen, dated 29 September 1941.
65 HHStAW Abt. 430/1, patient record number 10998 containing all the above materials on Anna Maria R.
66 Klee, *'Euthanasie'*, p. 380.
67 HHStAW Abt. 631a Nr 424, patient record with all materials (including photographs and X-ray plates), on Horst L.
68 Roth and Aly, 'Das "Gesetz über die Sterbehilfe"', p. 102.

69 See Burleigh and Wippermann, *The Racial State*, Part II, for a comprehensive discussion of the links between all areas of persecution. See the section on the Rummelsburg workhouse in Chapter 8 for how different sorts of 'racial' expertise were brought to bear upon the heterogeneous inmates of one institution.

70 HHStAW Abt. 631a Nr 79, 'Anklageschrift' against Heyde, pp. 55–56 incorporating Lammers's testimony before the Military Tribunal at Nuremberg on 7 February 1947.

71 Ibid., pp. 180–181, testimony of Hans Hefelmann dated 31 August 1961.

72 Mitscherlich and Mielke, *Medizin ohne Menschlichkeit*, pp. 184–185; Nowak, *'Euthanasie' und Sterilisation im 'Dritten Reich'*, p. 79.

73 HHStAW Abt. 631a Nr 301, testimony of Hans Heinrich Lammers dated 21 March 1961, p. 4.

74 Mitscherlich and Mielke, *Medizin ohne Menschlichkeit*, p. 184.

75 The note is reproduced in Burleigh and Wippermann, *The Racial State*, p. 143.

76 ZSL 'Euthanasie', Li–Lz, testimony of Ilse L. dated 16 June 1961, p. 3.

77 Nowak, *'Euthanasie'*, p. 80.

78 ZSL 'Euthanasie', La–Le, interrogation of Hans Heinrich Lammers dated 18 July 1960, p. 3. In other words, Hitler's authorisation did not even correspond with the terms of the Third Reich's own dictatorial version of German legal positivism, i.e. the conversion of decrees into law. Defence claims in post-war trials that the 'euthanasia' programme was 'legal' thus had no factual basis at all.

79 ZSL 'Euthanasie', Heyde, interrogation of Werner Heyde dated 22 December 1961, pp. 22–36.

80 H. Hennermann, 'Werner Heyde und seine Würzburger Zeit', in G. Nissen and G. Keil (eds.), *Psychiatrie auf dem Wege zur Wissenschaft. Psyhchiatrie-historisches Symposium anlässlich des 90. Jahrestages der Eröffnung der Psychiatrischen Klinik der Königlichen Universität Würzburg* (Stuttgart 1985), pp. 55–57.

81 ZSL 'Euthanasie', Heyde, interrogation of Werner Heyde dated 22 December 1961, p. 39.

82 Ibid., interrogation of Werner Heyde dated 22 September 1961, pp. 62–66.

83 Ibid., p. 168.

84 See Christine Teller, 'Carl Schneider. Zur Biographie eines deutschen Wissenschaftlers', *Geschichte und Gesellschaft* (1990), 16, pp. 465ff. for the most informed study of Schneider.

85 Peta Becker von Rose, 'Carl Schneider – wissenschaftlicher Schrittmacher der Euthanasie und Universitätspsychiater in Heidelberg 1933–1945', Gerrit Hohendorf and Achim Magull-Seltenreich (eds.), *Von der Heilkunde zur Massentötung. Medizin im Nationalsozialismus* (Heidelberg 1990), p. 100.

86 Klaus Dörner, 'Klassische Texte – neu gelesen', pp. 112ff.

87 See Hinrich Jasper, *Maximinian de Crinis (1889–1945). Eine Studie zur Psychiatrie im Nationalsozialismus* (Husum 1991), pp. 30ff., for an excellent study of de Crinis's early life in Austria and scientific work that is slightly disappointing on his activities within the 'euthanasia' programme.

88 Ibid., pp. 57–64.

89 See M. de Crinis, 'Die deutsche Psychiatrie', *Psychiatrisch-Neurologische Wochenschrift* (1939), 41, pp. 1–5 for the text of the lecture.

90 Jasper, *Maximinian de Crinis*, pp. 101–102.

91 Ibid., p. 121.

92 Klee, *'Euthanasie'* p. 87.

93 HHStAW Abt. 631a Nr 310a, interrogation of Albert Widmann dated 19 May 1960, pp. 2–3.

94 Ibid., pp. 5–6.

95 On Grafeneck see Otto Frey, *Gedenkstätte Grafeneck* (Grafeneck 1990) and Karl Morlok, *Wo bringt ihr uns hin? 'Geheime Reichssache' Grafeneck* (2nd edn Stuttgart 1990).

96 Morlok, *Wo bringt ihr uns hin?*, pp. 7–10.

97 Ibid., pp. 24ff. The descriptions of the physical location of T-4's installations are based upon exhibition materials (and a walk around the grounds) in the present Samaritans' home.

98 ZSL 'Euthanasie', Baa–Bh, interrogation of Hans-Joachim Becker dated 22 June 1961, p. 5.

99 Götz Aly (ed.), *Aktion T–4 1939–1945. Die 'Euthanasie'-Zentrale in der Tiergartenstrasse 4* (2nd edn Berlin 1989), pp. 11–12.

100 BDC personal files on Viktor Brack; ZSL 'Euthanasie' Bra–Bz, NO–426 dated 12 October 1946, pp. 1–2; IWM Case 1, *Medical Trial*, US versus Karl Brandt *et al.* (including Viktor Brack), vol. 15, pp. 7413ff., for Brack's detailed account of his life.

101 ZSL 'Euthanasie', Maa–Me, testimony of Hildegard M. dated 14 October 1965, p. 3.

102 ZSL 'Euthanasie', A, interrogation of Dietrich Allers dated 18 August 1949, p. 4.

103 ZSL 'Euthanasie', Schr–Schz, interrogation of Hermann Schweninger dated 9 April 1963, p. 1.

104 ZSL 'Euthanasie', A, interrogation of Dietrich Allers dated 28 June 1961, p. 2.

105 ZSL 'Euthanasie', Kaa–Ki, interrogation of Adolf Kaufmann dated 21 July 1965, p. 9; Li–Lz, interrogation of Robert Lorent dated 8 January 1962, p. 2, and Hefelmann volume, interrogation of Hans Hefelmann dated 4 January 1961, p. 1, for Brack and Tillmann. See A, interrogation of Dietrich Allers dated 7 May 1963, p. 3, and Bi–Bq, interrogation of Gerhard Bohne dated 6 December 1960, p. 1, for these manifold personal relationships. These examples could be effortlessly repeated.

106 ZSL 'Euthanasie', Bi–Bq, interrogation of Gerhard Bohne dated 10 April 1961, pp. 5–7.

107 ZSL 'Euthanasie', Maa–Me, testimony of Hildegard M. dated 14 October 1945, p. 2.

108 ZSL 'Euthanasie', Maa–Me, testimony of Kurt M. dated 3 December 1965, p. 7.

109 ZSL 'Euthanasie', A, interrogation of Dietrich Allers dated 2 September 1965, p. 4.

110 ZSL 'Euthanasie', Haa–Hd, testimony of Hedwig H. dated 1 March 1966, p. 6.

111 ZSL 'Euthanasie', Li–Lz, interrogation of Robert Lorent dated 18 October 1965, p. 32.

112 ZSL 'Euthanasie', Na–Oz, interrogation of Josef Oberhauser dated 15 June 1960, p. 1 and 22 July 1960, p. 1.
113 ZSL 'Euthanasie', F, interrogation of Kurt Franz dated 5 December 1962, p. 2.
114 ZSL 'Euthanasie', Baa–Bh, interrogation of Erich Bauer dated 12 December 1960, p. 2 and 9 January 1962, p. 2.
115 ZSL 'Euthanasie', Haa–Hd, testimony of Emil H. dated 3 March 1966, p. 2.
116 ZSL 'Euthanasie', Na–Oz, testimony of Vincent N. dated 4 September 1945, p. 3.
117 ZSL 'Euthanasie', Bra–Bz, interrogation of Viktor Brack dated 21 May 1948, p. 2, where Brack 'fingered' Linden.
118 ZSL LG Freiburg, Urteil 1 Ks 5/1948, Ludwig Sprauer, p. 32.
119 ZSL 'Euthanasie', Hefelmann, interrogation of Hans Hefelmann dated 7 November 1960, p. 19.
120 ZSL 'Euthanasie', Ta–U, interrogation of Aquilin Ullrich dated 10 October 1962, pp. 6–8.
121 ZSL 'Euthanasie', Kaa–Ki, interrogation of Werner Kirchert dated 16 February 1960, pp. 2–4.
122 ZSL 'Euthanasie', Kaa–Ki, interrogation of Werner Kirchert dated 2 May 1960.
123 Author's own archive, Generalstaatsanwaltschaft Frankfurt am Main v. Aquilin Ullrich and others, 'Anklageschrift' dated 15 January 1965, pp. 77–79. Examples of these forms are normally reproduced in the 'Anklageschriften' relating to most prosecutions of those involved in the 'euthanasia' programme.
124 Ibid., 'Merkblatt', p. 78.
125 Ibid., Reich Ministry of the Interior to the Oberpräsident of Hanover, dated 26 July 1940.
126 Ibid., p. 82.
127 Klee, *'Euthanasie'*, p. 99.
128 Ernst Klee (ed.), *Dokumente zur 'Euthanasie'* (Frankfurt am Main 1986), Nr 29, p. 99.
129 StAM, Staatsanwaltschaften Nr 17460 1/2, containing NO–1130, i.e. carbon copies of notes of acknowledgement regarding packages of forms from Pfannmüller to Heyde bearing the dates given in the text.
130 StAM, Staatsanwaltschaften Nr 17460 1/2 p. 23, letter from Pfannmüller to Theresa Pfannmüller dated 22 April 1947.
131 See IWM Case 1, *Medical Trial*, US versus Karl Brandt *et al.*, vol. 15, pp. 7319ff., for Pfannmüller's bruising encounter with the prosecutor regarding how rapidly he processed these forms.
132 ZSL 'Euthanasie', W, testimony of Klara W. dated 19 September 1962, p. 4.
133 See Christina Vanja and Martin Vogt, 'Zu melden sind sämtliche Patienten …', in Vanja (ed.), *Euthanasie in Hadamar*, p. 29 for the rates of payment.

4 'THE PSYCHOPATHS' CLUB'

1 ZSL V 203 AR–Nr 1101/1962 (LG Hannover 2 Ks 2/1967), judgement upon Kurt Eimann, p. 3.

2 ZSL V 203 AR–Nr 452/1964, Trial of Dr Kurt Bode, vol. 1, letter from Günter Grass to the State Prosecutor dated 23 November 1965.

3 BDC, personal file on Kurt Eimann, Höhere SS- und Polizeiführer Danzig-Westpreussen, 'Bericht über Aufstellung, Einsatz und Tätigkeit des SS-Wachsturmbann E' dated 9 January 1940, pp. 1–3.

4 Klee, *'Euthanasie'*, p. 95.

5 ZSL V 203 AR–Nr 1101/1962, Eimann Trial, pp. 58–59, including testimony from the former Leader of SS-Section Baltic Sea on 9 January 1963.

6 ZSL V 203 AR–Nr 1101/1962, Eimann Trial, 'Lebenslauf', p. 7. After his activities in Poland, Eimann went on to soldier with the II–SS Panzerkorps in Normandy and the Ardennes, winning the Iron Cross First and Second Class. Following a brief period in captivity, he worked as a builder's labourer, and then as a travelling salesman in soap. In 1968 he received a four-year prison sentence for his part in killing 1,200 psychiatric patients.

7 ZSL V 203 AR–Nr 1101/1962, interrogation of Kurt Eimann dated 20 December 1968, p. 12.

8 Klee, *Dokumente zur 'Euthanasie'*, Nr 18, pp. 70–71, extract from final judgement against Kurt Eimann.

9 ZSL V 203 AR–Nr 1101/1962, testimony of Kurt Eimann, pp. 10–11.

10 BDC personal file on Kurt Eimann, Höhere SS- und Polizeiführer Danzig-Westpreussen, 'Bericht', p. 3.

11 ZSL 203 AR–Z 69/1959, vol. 8, pp. 15–17, for Lange's biography.

12 ZSL 203 AR–Z 69/1959, investigation of Wilhelm Koppe, vol. 4, p. 556.

13 ZSL 'Euthanasie', Re–Rz, testimony of Dr Hans-Hermann Renfranz dated 20 March 1963, p. 7.

14 BDC personal file on Herbert Lange, letter from Wilhelm Koppe to the Höhere SS- und Polizeiführer Nordost, SS-Gruppenführer Sporrenberg, dated 18 October 1940; Höhere SS- und Polizeiführer beim Reichskommissar für die besetzten norwegischen Gebiete (Rediess) to Karl Wolff dated 7 November 1940.

15 Klee, *'Euthanasie'*, p. 193.

16 Ian Kershaw, 'Improvised Genocide? The Final Solution in the Warthegau', *Transactions of the Royal Historical Society* (1922), 6th Series, 2, pp. 66–67.

17 Walter Grode, 'Deutsche "Euthanasie"-Politik in Polen während des Zweiten Weltkriegs', *Psychiatrie & Gesellschaftskritik* (1992), 16, p. 6; see also Z. Jaroszewski, 'Die Vernichtung psychisch Kranker unter deutscher Besatzung', *Sozialpsychiatrische Informationen* (1982), 12, p. 12.

18 HHStAW Abt. 631a Nr 1643, Z. Jaroszewski, 'Das Schicksal des psychiatrischen Krankenhauses in Owinskie während des Krieges', report dated 30 October 1945, pp. 1–7.

19 HHStAW 631a Nr 1643 'Biuletyn Głownej Komisji Badania Zbrodni Niemieckich w Polsce' (Warsaw 1947), vol. 3, p. 3.

20 ZSL 'Euthanasie', Baa–Bh, interrogation of August Becker dated 10 March 1960, p. 1.

21 For these details, see HHStAW Abt. 361a Nr 291, interrogation of August Becker dated 20 June 1961, p. 4. On the involvement of Brack and Conti see Klee, *'Euthanasie'*, p. 110. For a good detailed portrait of Conti, see Michael

Kater, 'Doctor Leonardo Conti and his Nemesis: the Failure of Centralized Medicine in the Third Reich', *Central European History* (1985), 18, pp. 299–325.

22 HHStAW Abt. 631a Nr 291, interrogation of August Becker dated 4 April 1960, pp. 5–6.

23 Ibid.

24 On Sprauer see ZSL Urteil LG Freiburg IKs 5/1948, pp. 15–16.

25 On Mauthe see ZSL IV 449 AR-Nr 2811/1967, including Urteil LG Tübingen Ks 6/1949, pp. 13–14, for his areas of responsibility.

26 HHStAW Abt. 631a Nr 335, reports on interrogation sessions of Egon Stähle between 6 November 1947 and 30 June 1948.

27 StAM Staatsanwaltschaft Nr 1905 1/2, Trial of Walter Schultze, vol. 1, p. 23 for his 'Lebenslauf' (biography).

28 Klee, *'Euthanasie'*, p. 47.

29 Author's own archive, Generalstaatsanwaltschaft Frankfurt am Main, 'Anklageschrift' against Dr Aquilin Ullrich *et al.*, 15 January 1965, p. 24, testimony of Professor Bohm.

30 Ralf Seidel and Thorsten Suesse, 'Werkzeuge der Vernichtung. Zum Verhalten von Verwaltungsbeamten und Ärzten bei der 'Euthanasie', in Norbert Frei (ed.), *Medizin und Gesundheitspolitik in der NS-Zeit*, pp. 254–257.

31 On Creutz, see the relatively sympathetic account in Matthias Leipert, 'Die Beteiligung der Provinzial-Heil- und Pflegeanstalt Galkhausen an der Vernichtung psychisch Kranker und Behinderter im Nationalsozialismus', in Leipert, Styrnal and W. Schwarzer (eds.), *Verlegt nach unbekannt*, pp. 28ff.; for a more critical view, see Siemen, *Das Grauen ist vorprogrammiert*, pp. 188–191.

32 HHStAW Abt. 631a Nr 359, testimony of Dr Hans Koch dated 3 March 1948.

33 HHStAW Abt. 631a Nr 353, testimony of Dr Josef Wrede in the case against Egon Stähle on 10/11 December 1947, p. 2.

34 ZSL 'Euthanasie', Re–Rz, interrogation of Johannes Recktenwald dated 12 August 1947, p. 11.

35 HHStAW Abt. 631a Nr 359, testimony of Dr Ritter dated May 1948, p. 1.

36 For an example of attempts to delay the registration procedure by Dr Ilsabe Gestering of Ursberg, see Gernot Römer, *Die grauen Busse in Schwaben. Wie das Dritte Reich mit Geisteskranken und Schwangeren umging* (Augsburg 1986), pp. 8off.

37 ZSL 'Euthanasie', Pa–Ra, testimony of Dr Werner Philipps dated 7 December 1961, p. 3; and 'Euthanasie', Na–Oz, testimony of Adolf Nell, no date, p. 2.

38 Schmidt, *Selektion in der Heilanstalt*, p. 52.

39 Ibid., p. 53.

40 Römer, *Die grauen Busse*, pp. 72–73.

41 HHStAW Abt. 631a Nr 354, director of Göppingen to the Ministry of the Interior in Württemberg, dated 21 December 1940.

42 Ibid., testimony, of Dr K. John to the Spruchkammer Göppingen, dated 23 August 1946.

43 See the memorandum reproduced in Klüppel, *'Euthanasie' und Lebensvernichtung am Beispiel der Landesheilanstalten Haina und Merxhausen*, pp. 34–35.

44 Helmut Sorg, '"Euthanasie" in den evangelischen Heilanstalten in Württemberg im Dritten Reich', dissertation, Freie Universität Berlin (1987), fols. 74–77.

45 HHStAW Abt. 631a Nr 355, Landesfürsorgeanstalt Markgröningen to the Landesfürsorgebehörde Stuttgart, dated 2 September 1940.

46 HHStAW Abt. 631a Nr 355, testimony of Heinrich Scholder, Nurse Maria S. and others, dated 15 April 1948.

47 For examples, see HHStAW Abt. 631a Nr 359, Minister of the Interior, Württemberg, to the Pflegeanstalt Liebenau, dated 9 September 1940.

48 Ibid., testimony of Dr Hugo Götz dated 16 July 1948, pp. 4–5.

49 ZSL 'Euthanasie', Na–Oz, testimony of Adolf Nell, no date, p. 2.

50 Sorg, '"Euthanasie" in den evangelischen Heilanstalten', fols. 90–91.

51 This point was made explicitly by Gebhard Ritter of Liebenau in HHStAW Abt. 631a Nr 359, testimony bearing no date, p. 10.

52 ZSL 'Euthanasie', Ta–U, testimony of Karl Todt dated 10 January 1948, p. 1.

53 Römer, *Die grauen Busse*, p. 70.

54 ZSL 'Euthanasie', Na–Oz, testimony of Adolf Nell, p. 4.

55 HHStAW Abt. 631a Nr 357, letter from Ludwig Schlaich to P. Frick dated 5 November 1940. See also Ludwig Schlaich, *Vernichtung und Neuanfang. Das Schicksal der Heil- und Pflegeanstalt in Stetten i. R.* (Stuttgart 1946), p. 5.

56 Klüppel, *'Euthanasie' und Lebensvernichtung*, p. 41.

57 Römer, *Die grauen Busse*, p. 59.

58 ZSL 'Euthanasie', Pa–Ra, testimony of Anton Pfänder dated 19 January 1959.

59 HHStAW Abt. 631a Nr 359, testimony of Walter M. dated 3 February 1948 with copy of Helene M.'s final letter to him.

60 Ibid., testimony of Paul Morstatt dated 3 March 1948, p. 7.

61 Sorg, '"Euthanasie" in den evangelischen Heilanstalten', fol. 89.

62 Bettina Winter, 'Die Geschichte der NS-"Euthanasie"-Anstalt Hadamar', in Winter (ed.), *Verlegt nach Hadamar*, p. 79.

63 See ibid., p. 87, for a map showing the asylum's catchment area and the ring of holding asylums.

64 ZSL 'Euthanasie', Hu–Jz, testimony of Michael H. dated 19 December 1947.

65 Testimony of Benedikt H. dated 16 January 1966, reproduced in Armin Trus, '... für die Gesundung des deutschen Volkskörpers. Von der Asylierung zur "Vernichtung lebensunwerten Lebens" (2nd revised edn, Giessen 1991), source section 2.2.7 (no page).

66 Winter, 'Die Geschichte der NS-"Euthanasie"-Anstalt Hadamar', pp. 29ff.

67 Monika Daum, 'Arbeit und Zwang, das Leben der Hadamarer Patienten im Schatten des Todes', in D. Roer and D. Henkel (eds.), *Psychiatrie im Faschismus. Die Anstalt Hadamar 1933–1945* (Bonn 1986), pp. 176–177.

68 HHStAW Abt. 461 Nr 32061 (Hadamar Trial), vol. 2, testimony of Fritz Scherwing dated 3 March 1946. Since these trial records were erratically paginated (and are in an advanced state of deterioration), I have given the date when the witness spoke in court. Each daily session is clearly dated.

69 ZSL 'Euthanasie', Haa–Hd, testimony of Emil H. dated 3 March 1966, p. 3.

70 Heidi Schmidt von Blittersdorf, Dieter Debus and Birgit Kalkowsky, 'Die Geschichte der Anstalt Hadamar von 1933 bis 1945 und ihre Funktion im

Rahmen von T–4', in Roer and Henkel (eds.), *Psychiatrie und Faschismus*, pp. 58ff. On Hadamar see also three important memorial exhibition catalogues: Peter Chroust *et al.* (eds.), *'Soll nach Hadamar überführt werden'. Den Opfern der Euthanasiemorde 1939 bis 1945* (Frankfurt am Main 1989); Vanja (ed.), *Euthanasie in Hadamar*; and Winter (ed.), *Verlegt nach Hadamar*. I have also drawn upon the immense knowledge of Trus's '... für die Gesundung des deutschen Volkskörpers'. Gerhard Kneuker and W. Steglich, *Begegnungen mit der Euthanasie in Hadamar* (Rehburg-Loccum 1985) is essentially a form of printed psychotherapy by two Hadamar psychiatrists, rather than a serious study of the asylum. One hopes that in the coming years similarly lavish resources will be devoted to the study of Nazi extermination centres in the former GDR, notably Brandenburg, Bernburg and Sonnenstein.

71 ZSL 'Euthanasie', Haa–Hd, testimony of Emil H. dated 3 March 1966, p. 3. Much of my account of the *modus operandi* relies upon several interviews with the former Hadamar T–4 orderly Paul R. between 1991 and 1993.

72 Interview with Paula S. in Hadamar in 1991; HHStAW Abt. 461 Nr 32061, Hadamar Trial, vol. 2, p. 9, testimony of Else M. dated 19 February 1946.

73 ZSL 'Euthanasie', Na–Oz, testimony of Fritz Neumann dated 22 October 1969, p. 2.

74 BDC personal files on Christian Wirth and Gottlieb Hering; on the connections between the 'Euthanasia' programme and 'Aktion Reinhard' see Part III.

75 See ZSL 'Euthanasie', Hea–Heq, testimony of Elfriede H. dated 9 May 1949, pp. 1ff. for an example of this procedure.

76 HHStAW Abt. 631a Nr 56, undated list of suitable causes of death, including meningitis (p. 13); pneumonia (p. 56); strokes (p. 16).

77 Winter (ed.), *Verlegt nach Hadamar*, p. 108.

78 HHStAW Abt. 461 Nr 32061, Hadamar Trial, vol. 7, testimony of Bodo Gorgass dated 24 February 1947, p. 4.

79 Ibid., p. 5.

80 Ibid., pp. 1–2.

81 Ibid., p. 10.

82 Ibid., p. 37.

83 Ibid., p. 12.

84 Ibid., p. 13.

85 Ibid., p. 14.

86 Ibid., p. 17.

87 For an intelligent collection of essays on this subject, see Hohendorf and Magull-Seltenreich (eds.), *Von der Heilkunde zur Massentötung*.

88 Notably Robert Jay Lifton's *The Nazi Doctors. A Study in the Psychology of Evil* (London 1986). This book is not taken very seriously by most German historians of the Nazi 'Euthanasia' programme, as distinct from *bien pensant* media circles in Britain or America.

89 Antje Wettlaufer, 'Die Beteiligung von Schwestern und Pflegern an den Morden in Hadamar', in Roer and Henkel (eds.), *Psychiatrie und Faschismus*, pp. 300–304. See also the valuable collection of essays, Hilde Steppe (ed.), *Krankenpflege im Nationalsozialismus* (5th edn, Frankfurt am Main 1989).

90 Interview with Paul R. dated 12 September 1990.
91 Interview with Paul R. dated 1991.
92 HHStAW Abt. 461 Nr 32061, Hadamar Trial, vol. 2, testimony of Paul R. dated 6 March 1946.
93 Interview with Paul R. dated 1991.
94 Interview with Paul R. dated 1991.
95 HHStAW Abt. 461 Nr 32061, Hadamar Trial, vol. 2, testimony of Paul R., p. 65.
96 Ibid., Paul R., pp. 68–69.
97 Interview with Paul R. dated 1991.
98 ZSL 'Euthanasie', Ku–Kz, interrogation of Pauline K. dated 15 June 1948, pp. 1–2.
99 ZSL 'Euthanasie', Ka–Kz, interrogation of Pauline K. dated 24 October 1946, p. 1.
100 Antje Wettlaufer, 'Die Beteiligung', p. 319.
101 Winter, *Verlegt nach Hadamar*, p. 180.
102 Aly (ed.), *Aktion T–4*, p. 17. Apart from the studies of Hadamar mentioned above, there are a few short studies of other extermination centres. These include Hugo Jensch, *Euthanasie-Aktion 'T–4'. Verbrechen in den Jahren 1940 und 1941 auf dem Sonnenstein in Pirna* (Pirna, no date), and various information sheets produced by the Gedenkstätte Bernburg.
103 NAW T1021, Roll 18, Hartheim Statistics, pp. 1–3.
104 Ibid., p. 4.
105 Ibid., p. 22.

5 'GENTLEMEN'S AGREEMENTS'? RESPONSES TO THE 'EUTHANASIA' PROGRAMME

1 ZSL 'Euthanasie', A, interrogation of Hans Dietrich Allers dated 28 June, p. 13.
2 ZSL 'Euthanasie', Li–Lz, testimony of Ilse L. dated 16 June 1961, p. 4.
3 Ibid., p. 7.
4 Klee, *'Euthanasie'*, p. 160.
5 HHStAW Abt. 631a Nr 1281, copy of a letter from Dr W. Weskott to Egon Stähle dated 12 July 1940, p. 2.
6 BDC, 0.041 'Euthanasia', general documentation, Gaustabsamtsleiter Sellmer to Hans Hefelmann, dated 25 February 1941.
7 ZSL 'Euthanasie', Maa–Me, testimony of Robert M. dated 17 November 1947, p. 1. For a sensitive discussion of popular responses to the 'euthanasia' programme, see Kurt Nowak, 'Widerstand, Zustimmung, Hinnahme. Das Verhalten der Bevölkerung zur "Euthanasie"', in Frei (ed.), *Medizin und Gesundheitspolitik in der NS-Zeit*, pp. 235–251.
8 BDC, 0.041 'Euthanasia', general documentation, Else von Löwes to Frau Walter Buch, dated 25 November 1940, pp. 1–3.
9 Ibid., Walter Buch to Heinrich Himmler, dated 7 December 1940; and Heinrich Himmler to Walter Buch, dated 19 December 1940.
10 Ibid., Standartenführer Schiele to Obergruppenführer Jüttner, dated 22

November 1940, enclosing 'Planwirtschaftliche Massnahmen in Heil- und Pflegeanstalten', pp. 1–5.

11 Ibid., Alice K. to the Ministry of the Interior (Stuttgart) dated 5 November 1940. The quality of response from asylums to enquiries regarding the whereabouts of patients depended very much on who one was. Jewish people were excluded from the already sparse range of social courtesies at the disposal of German bureaucrats. At Eglfing-Haar, director Pfannmüller used a gradated series of responses: from no response at all, to a terse and unhelpful 'sent to another institution, location unknown'; then 'is no longer in the institution but was transferred on 20 September 1940 with a collection of Jewish patients'; and so on up to quite courtly exchanges of correspondence with people who had shown the necessary deference. Even the Dresdner Bank got the brush-off when a branch tried to locate a man called Oswald F. At first their mail was returned unprocessed. The Bank was then told that Oswald F. was no longer at Eglfing-Haar and that his whereabouts were unknown. On 27 December 1940 the Bank again wrote, asking pointedly whether Oswald F. was alive or dead. On 30 December 1940, Pfannmüller wrote that 'Oswald F. was transferred to another asylum on 20 September 1940. Nothing further is known.' For this correspondence see IWM CIOSC File Nr xxviii–50, Leo Alexander, 'Public Mental Health in Germany. Sterilization and Execution of Patients Suffering from Nervous or Mental Diseases', Combined Intelligence Objectives Sub-Committee, pp. 24ff. and documents reproduced pp. 134ff.

12 Interview with Pastor Siegfried Birschel in Hadamar (1991).

13 For these examples, see BDC, 0.041 'Euthanasia', general documentation, Security Police report on Franconia (no date).

14 BDC, 0.041 'Euthanasia', general documentation, Marie K. to the asylum at Sonnenstein, dated 27 November 1940.

15 Ibid., T–4 to the Gaustabsamtsleiter Sellmer, 1940.

16 Ibid., p. 6.

17 Klee, *'Euthanasie'*, p. 317.

18 HHStAW Abt. 731a Nr 60, testimony of Elsbeth R., no date.

19 Ibid., Nr 1155, testimony of Dr Wilhelm F. dated 8 June 1946.

20 Nowak, 'Sterilisation, Krankenmord und Innere Mission im 'Dritten Reich', p. 167.

21 Nowak, *'Euthanasie'*, pp. 133ff. Nowak's book remains the most intelligent study of the churches and the 'euthanasia' programme.

22 Klee (ed.), *Dokumente zur 'Euthanasie'* Nr 59, 'Denkschrift des Pastor Paul Gerhard Braune für Adolf Hitler', dated 9 July 1940, p. 162.

23 Nowak, *'Euthanasie'* pp. 136–137.

24 Klee, *Dokumente*, Nr 60, Landesbischof Theophil Wurm to the Reich Minister of the Interior, dated 19 July 1940, p. 166.

25 Ibid., p. 167.

26 Schmuhl, *Rassenhygiene*, pp. 331–332.

27 Jörg Thierfelder, 'Karsten Jaspersens Kampf gegen die NS–Krankenmorde', in T. Strohm and J. Thierfelder (eds.), *Diakonie in 'Dritten Reich'* (Heidelberg 1990), pp. 229–235; Klee, *Dokumente*, Nr 64, letter from Pastor Fritz von Bodelschwingh to Minister of the Interior Frick dated 28 September 1940, p. 174.

28 Klee, *Dokumente*, Nr 71a, selection criteria used by Dr Gerhard Schorsch, dated 20 January 1941, pp. 188–189.

29 NAW, T1021, Heidelberger Dokumente, Roll 11, p. 126867, 'Bericht über die Planungsbesichtigung der Anstalt für Epileptische Bethel', dated 20 May 1942.

30 On Kreyssig see above all Lothar Gruchmann, 'Ein unbequemer Amtsrichter im Dritten Reich. Aus den Personalakten des Dr. Lothar Kreyssig', *Vierteljahresheft für Zeitgeschichte* (1984), 32, p. 469.

31 Klee, *Dokumente*, Nr 73, letter from Kreyssig to the Reich Minister of Justice dated 8 July 1940, pp. 201–204.

32 Lothar Gruchmann, *Justiz im Dritten Reich 1933–1940. Anpassung und Unterwerfung in der Ära Gürtner* (Munich 1988) is the definitive account of the politics of the legal system under Nazism. Citation p. 507.

33 Klee, *Dokumente*, p. 199.

34 Ibid., Nr 77, Generalstaatsanwalt Stuttgart to the Minister of Justice, dated 12 October 1940, pp. 210–212.

35 Gruchmann, *Justiz im Dritten Reich*, p. 514ff.

36 Klee, *Dokumente*, Nr 74, Kreyssig's 'Stellungnahme' dated 1 March 1963, p. 205.

37 Gruchmann, *Justiz im Dritten Reich*, p. 511.

38 Klee, *Dokumente*, Nr 74, p. 207.

39 For the details see Gruchmann, 'Ein unbequemer Amstrichter', pp. 471–472.

40 ZSL 'Euthanasie', Hefelmann, interrogation of Hans Hefelmann dated 6 September 1960; 'Euthanasie', Pa–Ra, interrogation of Irmgard R. dated 24 August 1961, p. 3.

41 Ibid.

42 Karl-Heinz Roth and Götz Aly, 'Das "Gesetz über die Sterbehilfe bei unheilbar Kranken". Protokolle der Diskussion über die Legalisierung der nazionalsozialistischen Anstaltsmorde in den Jahren 1938–1941', in Karl-Heinz Roth (ed.), *Erfassung zur Vernichtung. Von der Sozialhygiene zum 'Gesetz über Sterbehilfe'* (Berlin 1984), pp. 113–115.

43 ZSL 'Euthanasie', Hefelmann, interrogation of Hans Hefelmann dated 14 September 1960, pp. 35–36.

44 Roth and Aly, 'Das "Gesetz über die Sterbehilfe"', pp. 130ff.

45 Ibid., p. 137.

46 NAW T–1021, Roll 11, Heidelberger Dokumente, pp. 126659ff.

47 Roth and Aly, 'Das "Gesetz über die Sterbehilfe"', p. 116.

48 Klee, *Dokumente*, Nr 79, 'Protokoll der Arbeitstagung der Oberlandesgerichtspräsidenten und Generalstaatsanwälte' on 23 and 24 April 1941 in Berlin, pp. 216–218.

49 HHStAW Abt. 631a Nr 305, interrogation of Franz Schlegelberger dated 4 May 1960, p. 4.

50 ZSL 'Euthanasie', Haa–He, interrogation of Franz Hagemann dated 6 December 1961, Anlage, p. 2.

51 Klee, *Dokumente*, Nr 80, notes of Dr Alexander Bergmann on the talks by Brack and Heyde dated 23 April 1941, pp. 219–220.

52 Martin Höllen, 'Katholische Kirche und NS-"Euthanasie"', *Zeitschrift für Kirchengeschichte* (1980), 91, p. 64; the second letter is printed in Klee,

Dokumente, Nr 61, Archbishop Conrad of Freising to Lammers, dated 1 August 1940, pp. 167–168. On the Roman Catholic episcopate, see also Martin Höllen, 'Episkopat und T–4', in Aly (ed.), *Aktion T–4*, pp. 84–91; Kurt Nowak, 'Kirchliche Widerstand gegen die "Euthanasie"', in Vanja (ed.), *Euthanasie in Hadamar*, pp. 157–164. Studies in asylums and homes run by the Roman Catholic charitable network are in their infancy; see Hans-Josef Wollasch, 'Caritas und Euthanasie im Dritten Reich', in Wollasch (ed.), *Beiträge zur Geschichte der deutschen Caritas in der Zeit der Weltkriege* (Freiburg 1978), pp. 208ff., and Carl Becker, 'Die Durchführung der Euthanasie in den katholischen caritativen Heimen für geistig Behinderte', *Jahrbuch der Caritaswissenschaft* (1968), pp. 104–119.

53 Höllen, 'Katholische Kirche', p. 66, note 58.

54 See Gitta Sereny, *Into that Darkness* (London 1974), pp. 64ff.

55 ZSL 'Euthanasie', Haa–Hd, interrogation of Albert Hartl dated 22 March 1966, p. 12.

56 Sereny, *Into that Darkness*, p. 70.

57 Höllen, 'Katholische Kirche', p. 59.

58 ZSL 'Euthanasie', Haa–Hd, interrogation of Albert Hartl dated 22 March 1966, p. 5.

59 Ibid., 30 January 1961, pp. 11–12.

60 Ibid., 7 December 1960, p. 21.

61 Ibid., 29 May 1961, p. 9.

62 Ibid., 30 January 1961, pp. 11–12.

63 Höllen, 'Katholische Kirche', p. 78.

64 Klee, *Dokumente*, Nr 68, letter from Cardinal Faulhaber to Bishop Wienken dated 18 November 1940, pp. 183–184.

65 ZSL 'Euthanasie', Hefelmann, interrogation of Hans Hefelmann dated 7 December 1960, p. 22.

66 Klee, *Dokumente*, Nr 69, papal prohibition of direct killing of the physically or mentally handicapped dated 2 December 1940.

67 Joachim Kuropka (ed.), *Clemens August Graf von Galen. Sein Leben und Wirken in Bildern und Dokumenten* (Cloppenburg 1992), p. 54. On Galen see also the older hagiographical study by Heinrich Portmann, *Kardinal von Galen: Ein Gottesmann seiner Zeit* (Münster 1961), and Joachim Kuropka (ed.), *Clemens August Graf von Galen. Neue Forschungen zum Leben und Wirken des Bischofs von Münster* (Münster 1992).

68 Kuropka, *Clemens August Graf von Galen*, pp. 112–133.

69 Peter Löffler (ed.), *Clemens August Graf von Galen: Akten, Briefe und Predigten 1933–1946* (Mainz 1988), vol. 2, p. 543.

70 Klee, *Dokumente*, p. 193.

71 Löffler, *Galen: Akten*, vol. 2, p. 878.

72 Kuropka, *Clemens August Graf von Galen*, p. 212.

73 H. Trevor-Roper (ed.), *Hitler's Table-Talk* (Oxford 1988), p. 555.

74 Interview with Paula S. in Hadamar, 1991.

75 Höllen, 'Katholische Kirche', p. 80.

76 ZSL 'Euthanasie', Bra–Bz, NO–426, testimony of Viktor Brack dated 12 October 1946, p. 6.

77 ZSL 'Euthanasie', Hefelmann, interrogation of Hans Hefelmann dated 14 September 1960, p. 32.
78 Klee, *Dokumente*, Nr 98, Viktor Brack to Heinrich Himmler dated 23 June 1942, pp. 274–275. In the course of cross-examination during the Nuremberg Medical Trial, Brack recalled meeting Himmler some time after the autumn of 1941. The conversation turned from corruption in the SS to the need for old SS members for 'the most heavy tasks'. Brack continued, 'Then he [Himmler] suddenly stopped and told me that Hitler had some time ago given him the order for the extermination of the Jews. He said that preparations had already been made, and I think that he used the expression that for reasons of camouflage one would have to work as quickly as possible. He seemed to say these things quite without any inner approval of them, but he also said them as if they were a matter of course.' IMW Case 1, *Medical Trial*, US versus Karl Brandt *et al.*, vol. 16, p. 7508 (May 1947).

6 SELLING MURDER: THE KILLING FILMS OF THE THIRD REICH

1 Bundesarchiv Koblenz, *Erbkrank* (1936).
2 *Erbkrank*. I am grateful to Linden Burleigh for helping to transcribe the captions from the film.
3 Karl-Heinz Roth, 'Filmpropaganda für die Vernichtung der Geisteskranken und Behinderten im "Dritten Reich"', Götz Aly *et al.* (eds.), *Reform und Gewissen. 'Euthanasie' im Dienst des Fortschritts. Beiträge zur nationalsozialistischen Gesundheits- und Sozialpolitik* (Berlin 1985), vol. 2, p. 126.
4 See 'Die furchtbare Erbe einer Trinkerin', exhibition poster of the Reich Food Estate.
5 Former Institut für den wissenschaftlichen Film der DDR (now Bundesarchiv, Filmarchiv Aussenstelle Potsdam), *Opfer der Vergangenheit* (1937).
6 *Opfer*. I am grateful to Linden Burleigh for helping to transcribe the commentary.
7 *Opfer* commentary.
8 Ibid.
9 Ibid.
10 Ibid.
11 Institut für den wissenschaftlichen Film der DDR, *Das Erbe* (1935).
12 See the discussion of T–4 films below.
13 Again, this technique was taken over from earlier Nazi graphics. See especially plate 30, the poster 'Hier trägst Du mit!'.
14 Uncut film footage actually reveals the technique in action, although this would have been edited out before the films were shown. See plate 31 for an example.
15 This 'Willy Horton' approach to penology is evident in *Opfer der Vergangenheit*, where the commentary dilates upon jaunty-looking bankrobbers and rather sinister-looking rapist-murderers.
16 See especially *Das Erbe* for the use of animals.
17 Institut für den wissenschaftlichen Film der DDR, *Was du ererbt . . .* (no date). The film teems with babies.
18 See above all Karl Ludwig Rost, *Sterilisation und Euthanasie im Film des 'Dritten*

Reiches'. Nationalsozialistische Propaganda in ihrer Beziehung zu rassenhygienischen Massnahmen des NS-Staates (Husum 1987), p. 82.

19 ZSL 'Euthanasie', F, interrogation of Kurt Franz dated 5 December 1962, p. 9. Brack was in charge of the film show.

20 ZSL 'Euthanasie', Sch–Schq, Hermann Schweninger's statement dated 2 October 1966, pp. 5ff.

21 NAW T–1021, Heidelberger Dokumente, Roll 12, p. 127270, dated May 1940.

22 Ibid.

23 Ibid., p. 127273, 'Ausscheidung der Lebensunwerten'.

24 Ibid., p. 127173, Hefelmann memo for Heyde dated 11 December 1940.

25 Rost, *Sterilisation und Euthanasie*, p. 130.

26 NAW T–1021, Heidelberger Dokumente, Roll 12, p. 127353, memo by Schneider dated 13 March 1942. Apart from commenting upon the score, Schneider suggested showing the film to an invited audience of lay persons, including women, with a view to testing the reactions of a more emotionally responsive audience.

27 The film rolls were misleadingly catalogued under the title 'laws of heredity'. They include a series of remarkable sound interviews with individual patients, whose 'revealed delusions' – notably a woman who 'tastes her own murdered head' – match up precisely with those interview subjects mentioned in the T–4 draft treatments. What was filmed elsewhere, e.g. various forms of active therapy, also corresponds with the content of these treatments.

28 NAW T–1021, Heidelberger Dokumente, Roll 12, pp. 127182ff., *Dasein ohne Leben.*

29 Ibid., p. 127194.

30 Ibid., pp. 127176ff.

31 Ibid., pp. 127333ff. Paul Nitsche, 'Änderungsvorschläge zu diesem Film'.

32 Ibid., p. 127165, Hermann Schweninger, 'Entwurf für den wissenschaftlichen Dokumentarfilm G.K.' dated 29 October 1942.

33 Ibid., p. 127167.

34 Ibid., pp. 127167–127168.

35 Ibid., pp. 127170–127171.

36 Rost, *Sterilisation und Euthanasie*, pp. 122–123.

37 NAW T–1021, Heidelberger Dokumente, Roll 12, *Drei Menschen. Ein Film um das Gesetz des Herzens*, p. 124801.

38 Ibid., p. 124860ff.

39 NAW T–1021, Heidelberger Dokumente, Roll 12, pp. 127195–127204.

40 Unger was born in 1891. Some of his books, such as his biography of Robert Koch, were filmed.

41 Hellmuth Unger, *Sendung und Gewissen* (Berlin 1926, 2nd edn 1942).

42 NAW T–1021, Heidelberger Dokumente, Roll 12, *Ich klage an*, draft script, pp. 127274ff.

43 Ibid., pp. 127291.

44 Ibid., p. 127309.

45 Ibid., pp. 127322–127323.

46 See Rost, *Sterilisation und Euthanasie*, pp. 166ff. for the best account of *Ich klage an.*

47 I am grateful to Ludwig Rost for making a copy for me of Liebeneiner's own working script of *Ich klage an*.
48 *Illustrierte Filmkurier* brochure (no date) on *Ich klage an*.
49 British Film Institute Film Archive, *Ich klage an*, is the copy of the film upon which these comments are based.
50 Author's archive, Wolfgang Liebeneiner, *Ich klage an*, 'Geschworenenszene' (unpaginated).
51 Ibid., p 274.
52 Rost, *Sterilisation und Euthanasie*, pp. 208ff.
53 See Heinz Boberach (ed.), *Meldungen aus dem Reich. Die geheimen Lageberichte des Sicherheitsdienstes der SS (1938–1945)* (Herrsching 1984), vol. 9, pp. 3175–3178 for report dated 15 January 1942. The text is also in Erwin Leiser, *Nazi Cinema* (London 1974), which remains the best short account of Nazi film propaganda.
54 Rost, *Sterilisation und Euthanasie*, p. 212.
55 Ibid., pp. 212–213.
56 Ibid., p. 213.
57 Boberach, *Meldungen aus dem Reich*, vol. 9, pp. 3175–3178.
58 Ibid., p. 3178.

7 EVIL EMPIRES: FROM 'AKTION 14F13' TO TRIESTE

1 BDC, personal file on Viktor Brack, containing NO–018, Heinrich Himmler to Viktor Brack, dated 19 December 1940.
2 Klee, *'Euthanasie'*, p. 345.
3 HHStAW Abt. 631a Nr 295, testimony of Rudolf G. dated 14 November 1960, p. 1. Studies of 'Aktion 14f13' include Walter Grode, *Die 'Sonderbehandlung 14f13' in den Konzentrationslagern des Dritten Reiches. Ein Beitrag zur Dynamik faschistischer Vernichtungspolitik* (Frankfurt am Main 1987), and his '"Euthanasie"-Ärzte in den NS-Konzentrationslagern. Verlauf und Entwicklung der "Sonderbehandlung 14f13"', *Psychologie & Gesellschaftskritik* (1989), 13, pp. 73–86; Stanisław Kłodzinski, 'Die "Aktion 14f13". Der Transport von 575 Häftlingen von Auschwitz in das "Sanatorium Dresden"', in Aly (ed.), *Aktion T–4 1939–1945* (Berlin 1987), pp. 136–146.
4 Klee, *'Euthanasie'*, p. 347.
5 ZSL 'Euthanasie', F, testimony of Władysław F. dated 12 March 1968, pp. 1–2.
6 For an account of 'Aktion 14f13' in Mauthausen/Hartheim, see Gordon J. Horowitz, *In the Shadow of Death. Living Outside the Gates of Mauthausen* (London 1989), pp. 56ff.
7 Grode, '"Euthanasie"-Ärzte', pp. 74–75.
8 HHStAW Abt. 631a Nr 295, testimony of Rudolf G. dated 14 November 1960, p. 3.
9 Grode, '"Euthanasie"-Ärzte', p. 82.
10 Lutz Raphael, 'Euthanasie und Judenvernichtung', in Vanja (ed.), *Euthanasie in Hadamar*, pp. 79–81; on the fate of Jewish psychiatric patients see Henry Friedländer, 'Jüdische Anstaltspatienten im NS-Deutschland', in Aly (ed.), *Aktion T–4 1939–1945* (Berlin 1987), pp. 34ff.

11 Chroust (ed.), *Mennecke, Briefe*, vol. 1, p. 10. On Mennecke see also Chroust, 'Ärzteschaft und "Euthanasie"', pp. 123ff.

12 Chroust, 'Ärzteschaft und "Euthanasie"', pp. 128–129.

13 HHStAW Abt. 461 Nr 32442, Eichberg Trial, testimony of Dr Wilhelm Hinsen dated 10 December 1946, p. 1.

14 Chroust (ed.), *Mennecke, Briefe*, vol. 1, p. 243.

15 Ibid., pp. 242–243.

16 Ibid., p. 245.

17 Klee, *'Euthanasie'*, p. 349.

18 Chroust, *Mennecke, Briefe*, vol. 1, p. 262.

19 HHStAW Abt. 631a Nr 1319, photographs with comments on reverse.

20 Ibid., Nr 300, testimony of Karl K. dated 27 August 1960.

21 Ibid., Nr 298, testimony of Hans H. dated 12 January 1960.

22 Ibid., 21 September 1961.

23 ZSL, 'Euthanasie', Baa–Be, testimony of Walter B. dated 11 October 1963, p. 3.

24 IWM Case 1, *Medical Trial*, US versus Karl Brandt *et al.*, vol. 4, p. 1753, SS–WVHA to commanders of the concentration camps, dated 27 April 1943.

25 Angelika Ebbinghaus and Gerd Preissler (eds.), 'Die Ermordung psychisch kranker Menschen in der Sowjetunion', in Aly *et al.* (eds.), *Reform und Gewissen*, vol. 1, pp. 80–82.

26 On the Einsatzgruppen, see the detailed standard work of Helmut Krausnick, *Hitlers Einsatzgruppen. Die Truppen des Weltanschauungskrieges 1938–1942* (Frankfurt am Main 1985).

27 Ebbinghaus and Preissler, 'Die Ermordung', pp. 84–88; see also ZSL 'Euthanasie', Scha–Schq, interrogation of Hans Scheidt dated 6 April 1960, p. 2 for the murders at Mogilew.

28 BBC TV interview with a former interpreter for the Einsatzgruppen (BBC 1 'The People's Century?' programme 'Master Race') for the gardening metaphor. Other favourites were drawn from the imagery of disease, plague and vermin.

29 Gerald Fleming, *Hitler and the Final Solution* (Oxford 1986), pp. 81–83; Raul Hilberg, *Die Vernichtung der europäischen Juden* (revised second German edition Frankfurt am Main 1990), vol. 2, pp. 937ff. See also Philippe Burrin, *Hitler and the Jews* (London 1994) for the most recent discussion of the origins of the 'Final Solution'.

30 ZSL 'Euthanasie', Bra–Bz, NO–426, interrogation of Viktor Brack dated 12 October 1946, p. 7.

31 Chroust, *Mennecke, Briefe*, vol. 1, 14 January 1942, p. 329.

32 HHStAW Abt. 631a Nr 309, interrogation of Hans Otto G. dated 18 July 1961, p. 6.

33 ZSL, 'Euthanasie', Mi–Mz, testimony of Dr Adolf M. dated 20 September 1962, p. 2.

34 StAAug, Staatsanwaltschaften Ks 1/49, Trial of Valentin Faltlhauser *et al.*, testimony of Heinrich Wolff dated 20 May 1948, p. 8.

35 On 'Aktion Reinhard' see Raul Hilberg, 'Aktion Reinhard', in Eberhard Jäckel and Jürgen Rohwer (eds.), *Der Mord an den Juden im Zweiten Weltkrieg*

(Frankfurt am Main 1987), pp. 175ff.; Ernst Klee, 'Von der "T–4" zur Judenvernichtung', in Aly (ed.), *Aktion T–4*, pp. 147ff.; Eugen Kogon *et al.* (eds.), *Nationalsozialistische Massentötungen durch Giftgas* (Frankfurt am Main 1986); and Yitzhak Arad, *Belzec, Sobibor, Treblinka: The Operation Reinhard Death Camps* (Bloomington, Indiana 1987). For further reading on other aspects of the Holocaust see the excellent synthesis by Michael Marrus, *The Holocaust in History* (London 1988).

36 Sereny, *Into that Darkness*, pp. 102ff.

37 See ZSL 'Euthanasie', Na–Oz, interrogation of Josef Oberhauser dated 4 February 1963, pp. 6–7 for the idea of T–4 personnel being 'loaned' to Globocnik.

38 ZSL 'Euthanasie', Ga–Go, interrogation of Heinrich Gley dated 4 December 1962, p. 5.

39 ZSL 'Euthanasie', Li–Lz, interrogation of Robert Lorent dated 18 October 1965, p. 28.

40 ZSL 'Euthanasie', Bi–Bq, interrogation of Kurt Bollender dated 8 July 1965, p. 4. Structural-functionalist historians tend not to bother with such obvious motives as sheer greed, lest it get in the way of the idea of a step-by-step progression – rather than a headlong rush – over this particular moral abyss.

41 BDC, SS–HO, Viktor Brack to Heinrich Himmler dated 23 June 1942. In his testimony at the Nuremberg Medical Trial Brack also stressed Himmler's concern that his men should do the work as expeditiously as possible. In 1924, Hoess had been given ten years' hard labour for clubbing a political opponent, slitting his throat and shooting him in the head. See Martin Broszat (ed.), *Kommandant in Auschwitz* (Munich 1987), p. 37, note 1.

42 ZSL 'Euthanasie', Na–Oz, interrogation of Josef Oberhauser dated 26 February 1960, p. 1.

43 ZSL 'Euthanasie', Baa–Bh, interrogation of Erich Bauer dated 9 January 1962, p. 2.

44 Sereny, *Into that Darkness*, p. 138 and pp. 160ff.

45 See Hilberg, *Die Vernichtung*, vol. 2, p. 956, for these 'statistics'.

46 BDC, 0.401 'Euthanasia', Globocnik's 'Bericht über die Verwaltungsmässige Abwicklung der Aktion Reinhard', with enclosed detailed accounts.

47 BDC, 0.401 'Euthanasia', Reichsführer-SS (Adjutantur) to the SS-Personal-hauptamt Berlin, dated 19 August 1943, with these recommendations for promotion.

48 ZSL 'Euthanasie', A, interrogation of Hans Dietrich Allers dated 16 May 1963, pp. 1–4.

49 Sereny, *Into that Darkness*, pp. 260–263.

50 HHStAW Abt. 631a Nr 1318, judgement of the court in Trieste dated 29 April 1976, p. 11.

51 Carlo Schiffrer, *La Risiera* (Trieste 1961), p. 10, with photographs of the graffiti on the cell walls, and groundplans of the warehouse during the Nazi occupation of the Dalmatian coast.

52 HHStAW Abt. 631a Nr 1318, judgement, p. 4.

53 HHStAW Abt. 631a Nr 1318, judgement, pp. 3–5.

8 'MEDIEVAL' OR MODERN? 'EUTHANASIA' PROGRAMMES 1941–1945

1 Heidi Schmidt von Blittersdorf, Dieter Debus and Birgit Kalkowsky, 'Die Geschichte der Anstalt Hadamar von 1933 bis 1945 und ihre Funktion im Rahmen von T–4', in Roer and Henkel (eds.), *Psychiatrie im Faschismus*, pp. 102–103; on the children's 'euthanasia' programme see Anon., 'Reichsausschusskinder. Eine Dokumentation', in Aly (ed.), *Aktion T–4*, pp. 121ff.

2 StAM, Staatsanwaltschaften Nr 17460, Trial of Hermann Pfannmüller, vol. 1, testimony of Dr Franz G., p. 7.

3 Ibid., Hermann Pfannmüller, 'Stellungnahme des Direktors der Heil- und Pflegeanstalt Eglfing-Haar zum Bericht des Bayerischen Prüfungsverbandes öffentlicher Kassen, Prüfungsamt München, vom 23 November 1938', dated 1 November 1939, p. 5.

4 Ibid., p. 8.

5 Ibid., p. 9.

6 Ibid., p. 10.

7 StAM, RA 3761 Nr 57693, letter from the Oberstaatsanwalt to Pfannmüller dated 9 May 1940.

8 StAM, RA 3761 Nr 57693, letter from Pfannmüller to the Regierungspräsidenten in Munich dated 30 May 1940.

9 StAAug, Staatsanwaltschaften Ks 1/49, Trial of Valentin Faltlhauser, vol. 7, testimony of Dr Albert S. dated 19 July 1949, p. 83.

10 Ibid., testimony of Valentin Faltlhauser dated 9 July 1949, p. 17.

11 StAM, Staatsanwaltschaften Nr 17460, Trial of Hermann Pfannmüller, vol. 1, testimony of Dr Josef Entres, pp. 150ff.

12 Klee (ed.), *Dokumente zur Euthanasie*, Nr 102, 'Hungerkost', p. 286.

13 StAAug, Staatsanwaltschaften Ks 1/49, Trial of Valentin Faltlhauser, vol. 1, 'Wochen-Speisezettel der Heil- und Pflegeanstalt Kaufbeuren' dated November/December 1942.

14 StAM, Staatsanwaltschaften Nr 19051/2, Trial of Walter Schultze, vol. 1.

15 StAM, Staatsanwaltschaften Nr 17460, Trial of Hermann Pfannmüller, vol. 1, testimony of the Roman Catholic priest Josef Raedecker, p. 5.

16 Ibid., testimony of Wilhelm M., p. 5.

17 Ibid., testimony of Babette K., p. 86.

18 Ibid., testimony of Pfarrer Josef Raedecker, p. 5.

19 Richarz, *Heilen, Pflegen, Töten*, p. 177.

20 StAAug, Staatsanwaltschaften Ks 1/49, Trial of Valentin Faltlhauser, vol. 7, testimony of Georg Frick dated 14 July 1949, p. 50.

21 Ibid., vol. 2, testimony of Willi B. dated 24 September 1947, p. 2.

22 Ibid., Josef Wille, 'Bericht über die Vorkommnisse in der Anstalt Irsee während des Hitlerregierung', dated 4 December 1946, p. 4.

23 Ibid., vol. 7, testimony of Josef Wille dated 19 July 1949, p. 78.

24 HHStAW Abt. 461 Nr 32061 (Hadamar Trial), vol. 2, testimony of Lydia T. dated 8 March 1946.

25 Ibid., vol. 7, testimony of Adolf Wahlmann dated 24 February 1947, p. 28.

26 Monika Daum, 'Arbeit und Zwang, das Leben der Hadamarer Patienten im

Schatten des Todes', in Roer and Henkel (eds.), *Psychiatrie und Faschismus*, pp. 208–209.

27 Winter (ed.), *Verlegt nach Hadamar*, p. 125.

28 Dickel, *'Die sind doch alle unheilbar'*, p. 90, Elisabeth L. to Dr Conrad, dated 25 May 1940.

29 HHStAW Abt. 461 Nr 32442 (Eichberg Trial), vol. 2, testimony of Friedrich Mennecke dated 3 May 1946, p. 30.

30 Dickel, *'Die sind doch alle unheilbar'*, p. 89, Lippert to Rödel, dated 15 January 1945.

31 HHStAW Abt. 461 Nr 31526 (Idstein Trial), vol. 1, report by the public prosecutor in Frankfurt am Main regarding deputy director Wilhelm Grossmann dated 21 January 1945, pp. 1–6.

32 NAW T-1021, Heidelberger Dokumente, Roll 12, p. 127418, Carl Schneider's testimonial on behalf of Friedrich Mennecke dated 18 July 1942.

33 Chroust (ed.), *Mennecke, Briefe*, vol. 1, Nr 120, p. 356, letter dated 15 June 1942.

34 Ibid., Nr 118, p. 348, letter dated 9 June 1942.

35 Ibid., Nr 120, p. 359, letter dated 15 June 1942.

36 Ibid., Nr 131, p. 407, letter dated 30 June 1942.

37 Ibid., Nr 136, p. 424, letter dated 1 July 1942.

38 HHStAW Abt. 461 Nr 32061 (Hadamar Trial), vol. 7, testimony of Dr Adolf Wahlmann dated 24 February 1947, p. 27.

39 See NAW T-1021, Heidelberger Dokumente, Roll 12, pp. 127895ff., for T–4 invoices concerning deliveries of over 10,000 ampoules of morphia and scopolamine in January 1944.

40 HHStAW Abt. 461 Nr 32061 (Hadamar Trial), vol. 7, testimony of Irmgard Huber dated 25 February 1947, p. 3; testimony of B. dated 25 February 1947, p. 9; testimony of Lydia T. dated 25 February 1947, p. 14; testimony of Paul R. dated 25 February 1947, p. 22; etc.

41 StAAug, Staatsanwaltschaften Ks 1/49, vol. 2, testimony of Max R. dated 1 May 1947, p. 4.

42 Ibid.

43 Ibid.; see also vol. 7, pp. 46–47 for various testimonies regarding the death of L.

44 Daum, 'Arbeit und Zwang', p. 197.

45 HHStAW Abt. 461 Nr 32442 (Eichberg Trial), vol. 3, testimony of Friedrich J. dated 12 September 1946, p. 4.

46 Daum, 'Arbeit und Zwang', p. 207.

47 The prohibition of corporal punishment: *Haus-Ordnung der Heilerziehungsanstalt Kalmenhof zu Idstein i. Ts.* (Frankfurt 1925), p. 13, clause 4; HHStAW Abt. 461 Nr 31526 (Idstein Trial), vol. 1, testimony of Karlheinz L. dated 27 January 1947, p. 35; interrogation of Maria M. dated 27 April 1945, pp. 1–3.

48 Rainer Scheer, 'Die nach Paragraph 42b RStGB verurteilten Menschen in Hadamar', in Roer and Henkel (eds.), *Psychiatrie im Faschismus*, pp. 246–247.

49 HHStAW Abt. 430/1 Nr 11332, patient record of Friedrich K., Eichberg questionnaire dated 29 July 1942. For the persecution of the deaf and dumb during the Third Reich, see Horst Biesold, *Klagende Hände. Betroffenheit und*

Spätfolgen in Bezug auf das Gesetz zur Verhütung erbkranken Nachwuchses, dargestellt am Beispiel der 'Taubstummen' (Solms 1988).

50 HHStAW Abt. 430/1 Nr 11332, patient record of Friedrich K., undated autobiographical account.

51 Ibid., Kriminalpolizei Frankfurt to Dr Friedrich Mennecke, dated 18 May 1942.

52 Chroust, *Mennecke, Briefe*, vol. 1, Nr 138, p. 434, letter dated 7 July 1942.

53 HHStAW Abt. 430/1 Nr 11332, patient record of Friedrich K., Walter Schmidt to the Reich Committee, dated 15 July 1942.

54 Ibid., Friedrich Mennecke to Herr S., dated 29 September 1942.

55 Ibid., note recording the cause of death.

56 HHStAW Abt. 430/1 Nr 11440, patient record of Marianna D. Entries in patient's case notes, and letter from Friedrich Mennecke to Josefa D. dated 13 June 1942.

57 Burleigh and Wippermann, *The Racial State*, Chapter 6, pp. 172ff.

58 NAW T-1021, Heidelberger Dokumente, Roll 12, p. 128269, Paul Nitsche's handwritten aide-memoire for Hans Hefelmann, dated 15 December 1941, with recommended names.

59 On Robert Ritter see Ute Brücker-Boroujerdi and Wolfgang Wippermann, 'Die Rassenhygienische und Erbbiologische Forschungsstelle im Reichsgesundheitsamt', *Bundesgesundheitsblatt* (1989), 32, pp. 13–19; Reiner Gilsenbach, 'Wie Lolitschai zur Doktorwürde kam', in Aly (ed.), *Feinderklärung und Prävention, Beiträge zur nationalsozialistischen Gesundheits- und Sozialpolitik* (1988), vol. 6, pp. 101–152.

60 NAW T-1021, Heidelberger Dokumente, Roll 12, p. 127494, notes by Paul Nitsche dated 16 February 1942 recording the final 'tally'.

61 Götz Aly, 'Medizin gegen Unbrauchbare', in Aly *et al.* (eds.), *Reform und Gewissen*, vol. 1, pp. 45–55.

62 HHStAW Abt. 461 Nr 32061 (Hadamar Trial), vol. 7, testimony of Irmgard Huber dated 25 February 1947, p. 4.

63 Earl W. Kintner (ed.), *The Hadamar Trial* (London and Edinburgh 1949), p. 159. This is an edited version of the proceedings of US versus Alfons Klein *et al.* For the complete version see NAW M-1078, Rolls 1–3.

64 Ibid., p. 159.

65 HHStAW Abt. 461 Nr 32061 (Hadamar Trial), vol. 7, testimony of Margarete Borkowski dated 25 February 1947, p. 8.

66 Ibid., pp. 10–11.

67 Ibid., testimony of Lydia T. dated 25 February 1947, p. 15.

68 StAM, Staatsanwaltschaften Nr 19031, Trial of Emma D. *et al.*, copy of the oath taken on 26 April 1941, p. 8.

69 Ibid., testimony of Emma L., p. 10.

70 Ibid.

71 Ibid., testimony of Josef R. dated 21 July 1948, p. 38.

72 NAW T-1021, Heidelberger Dokumente, Roll 12, p. 127963, Hans Dietrich Allers to Paul Nitsche, dated 15 January 1944, enclosing a list of 'suitable' personnel, including (p. 127966) Pauline K.

73 StAAug, Staatsanwaltschaften Ks 1/49, Trial of Valentin Faltlhauser *et al.*, vol. 7, testimony of Pauline K. dated 20 July 1949, pp. 95ff.

74 Ibid., graphs depicting monthly patient mortality rates in vol. 2, testimony of Sister Gualberta dated 11 May 1948, p. 10.
75 Ibid., vol. 7, testimony of Sister Berthilla dated 19 July 1949, p. 85.
76 Ibid., testimony of Heinrich W. dated 18 July 1949, pp. 66–68.
77 Ibid., vol. 2, testimony of Afra K. dated 21 May 1948.
78 Mathias Hamann, 'Die Morde an polnischen und sowjetischen Zwangsarbeitern in deutschen Anstalten', in Aly *et al.* (eds.), *Beiträge zur nationalsozialistischen Gesundheits- und Sozialpolitik* (2nd edn 1987), 1, pp. 123–124.
79 Holker Kaufmann and Klaus Schulmeyer, 'Die polnischen und sowjetischen Zwangsarbeiter in Hadamar', in Roer and Henkel (eds.), *Psychiatrie im Faschismus*, pp. 257–260.
80 Hamann, 'Die Morde', pp. 133–135.
81 HHStAW Abt. 430/1 Nr 11598, patient records concerning Wassil P., letter from the director of Eichberg to the Labour Office in Wiesbaden dated 25 February 1941.
82 Ibid., Nr 11635, patient records of Anna P., including her 'Nachlass'.
83 Ibid., Nr 31841, patient records of Alexander M., entries for 23 June 1943 and 19 July 1943; Nr 11635, patient records of Anna P., entry for 28 June 1943.
84 Ibid., Nr 11671, patient records of Anna B., entry for 8 April 1943; Nr. 11664, patient records of Beloskowa M.
85 Ibid., Nr 11664, patient records of Belowskowa M., letter from Walter Schmidt to the Labour Office in Frankfurt am Main dated 15 June 1943.
86 Ibid., entry for 15 July 1943; 'acute circulatory collapse resulted in death'.
87 Kintner (ed.), *The Hadamar Trial*, session on 9 October 1945, pp. 35–36. See also Leon Jaworski, *Confession and Avoidance*, pp. 107ff.
88 Daum, 'Arbeit und Zwang', pp. 184–186.
89 Peter von Rönn, 'Auf der Suche nach einem anderen Paradigma', *Recht und Psychiatrie* (1991), 9, pp. 50–51.
90 NAW T-1021, Heidelberger Dokumente, Roll 12, pp. 126846ff., 'Übersicht über die Verteilung der in Heil- und Pflegeanstalten nicht mehr für Geisteskranke verwendeten Betten', dated 10 October 1942.
91 Götz Aly, 'Die "Aktion Brandt" – Bombenkrieg, Bettenbedarf und "Euthanasie"', in Aly (ed.), *Aktion T-4*, pp. 168ff.
92 Interview with Helmut H. in Hadamar (1991). I am also grateful to Helmut H. for a written autobiographical account of these events and for documents and photographs concerning his mother.
93 Hans-Walter Schmuhl, 'Reformpsychiatrie und Massenmord', in Michael Prinz and Rainer Zitelmann (eds.), *Nationalsozialismus und Modernisierung* (Darmstadt 1991), pp. 239ff. My criticisms of this type of argument are not rooted in moral outrage, but in the fact that they reflect a literal, one-sided, and uncritical reading of the sources; an incapacity to see a larger human truth looming beyond the minor academic 'truth' that is being so dogmatically propounded; and last but not least, quite bad taste in the face of so much evidence of human suffering.
94 HHStAW Abt. 461 Nr 32442 (Eichberg Trial), vol. 1, Elisabeth V.'s 'Bericht' dated 9 August 1945, pp. 1–15.

95 NAW T-1021, Heidelberger Dokumente, Roll 12, p. 128159ff., for the responses to Nitsche's survey dated 11 July 1942.

96 ZSL, 'Euthanasie', A, interrogation of Hans Dietrich Allers dated 28 June 1961, p. 12.

97 ZSL, 'Euthanasie', Li–Lz, interrogation of Robert Lorent dated 18 October 1965, p. 57.

98 Bundesarchiv, Koblenz, R96 1/9, Carl Schneider, 'Schlussbemerkungen' (1941), p. 127587.

99 Ibid., pp. 127588–127589.

100 BA R96 1/9, 'Gedanken und Anregungen', pp. 126422ff.; also NAW T-1021, Heidelberger Dokumente, Roll 12, pp. 127702ff.

101 For this tendency, see NAW T-1021, Heidelberger Dokumente, Roll 12, letter from Max de Crinis to Paul Nitsche dated 25 January 1943.

102 Ibid., letter from Carl Schneider to Paul Nitsche dated 1 October 1942.

103 NAW T-1021, Heidelberger Dokumente, Roll 12, p. 128038, letter from Carl Schneider to Paul Nitsche dated 19 June 1943, requesting copies of the forms, and p. 128030, Nitsche's letter to Schneider dated July 1943, obliging him.

104 Ibid., p. 122835, Hebold to Schneider dated 26 October 1942.

105 Ibid., p. 127876, 'Nachtragsbericht' dated 2 February 1944.

106 Götz Aly, 'Forschen an Opfern. Das Kaiser-Wilhelm-Institut für Hirnforschung und die "T-4"', in Aly (ed.), *Aktion T-4*, pp. 154ff. See also Götz Aly, 'Der saubere und der schmutzige Fortschritt', in Aly (ed.), *Beiträge zur nationalsozialistischen Gesundheits- und Sozialpolitik* (1985), vol. 2, especially pp. 48ff.

9 HOW PROFESSOR HEYDE BECAME DR SAWADE

1 Klee (ed.), *Dokumente zur 'Euthanasie'*, Nr 114, 'Erklärung des gerichtsmedizinischen Hauptexperten der 1. Weissrussischen Front über die Massenvernichtung der Patienten in Meseritz-Obrawalde', p. 312.

2 NAW (Sound and Motion Picture Division), III ADC 3832–3833, 'Murder Mills: Hadamar' (1945).

3 NAW T-1078, Rolls 1–3 (Hadamar Trial), Roll 1, frames 000616–617, for Bolker's report; and Roll 2, no page or frame number for Bolker's evidence on 8 October 1945. See also Kintner (ed.), *The Hadamar Trial*, pp. 61–62.

4 Leon Jaworski, *Confession and Avoidance. A Memoir* (New York 1979), pp. 98ff.

5 The international legal ramifications of the trial are lucidly discussed by Julie Masal, 'The Hadamar Trial', MSc dissertation, London School of Economics (1993). See also Heinz Boberach, 'Die strafrechtliche Verfolgung der Ermordung von Patienten in nassauischen Heil- und Pflegeanstalten nach 1945', in Vanja (ed.), *"Euthanasia in Hadamar"*, pp. 165ff. For the verdicts in many post-war German trials, see Seminarium voor Strafrecht en Strafrechtspleging Van Hamel der Universiteit van Amsterdam (ed.), *Justiz und NS-Verbrechen. Sammlung deutscher Strafurteile wegen nationalsozialistischer Tötungsverbrechen 1945–1966* (Amsterdam 1968–1981), vols. 1–50.

6 Jaworski, *Confession and Avoidance*, pp. 112–113.

7 Kintner, *Hadamar Trial*, p. 247.

8 NAW T–1078, Hadamar Trial, Roll 2, no page number, report on executions by hanging in the Bruchsal prison dated 14 March 1946.

9 Ernst Klee, *Was sie taten – was sie wurden. Ärzte, Juristen und andere Beteiligte am Kranken- oder Judenmord* (Frankfurt am Main 1988), p. 95.

10 For extracts from the trial, see Mitscherlich and Mielke, *Medizin ohne Menschlichkeit*, and Trials of War Criminals before the Nuremberg Military Tribunals, Nuremberg, October 1946 – April 1949, vol. 1, *The Medical Case*. For the complete twenty-five volumes of transcripts of the proceedings see note 11 below.

11 IWM Case 1, *Medical Trial*, US versus Karl Brandt *et al.*, vol. 15, 9 May 1947, p. 7349. Apart from the light they shed upon the 'euthanasia' programme and 'medical' experiments, these records are also interesting in terms of the creative fantasy of the various defence counsels.

12 Ibid., p. 7385.

13 Ibid., 12 May 1947, p. 7420.

14 Ibid., p. 7616.

15 Ibid., vol. 16, 13 May 1947, p. 7567.

16 Ibid., p. 7637.

17 Ibid., vol. 6, 4 February 1947, p. 2349.

18 Ibid., p. 2436.

19 Chroust *et al.* (eds.), *'Soll nach Hadamar überführt werden'*, p. 111.

20 StAM, Staatsanwaltschaften Nr 17460, Trial of Hermann Pfannmüller, vol. 2, testimony of Josef Radecker dated 24 October 1949, p. 50; Klee, *Was sie taten*, p. 310, note 8.

21 StAM, Staatsanwaltschaften Nr 17460, Trial of Hermann Pfannmüller, Theresa Pfannmüller's letter to Hermann Pfannmüller dated 21 January 1946.

22 Staatsanwaltschaften Ks 1/49, Trial of Valentin Faltlhauser, vol. 7, 30 July 1949, p. 156.

23 Ibid., 7 July 1949, p. 6.

24 Ibid., 7–8 July 1949, pp. 5–11.

25 Ibid., vol. 2, p. 11.

26 Chroust (ed.), *Mennecke, Briefe*, vol. 1, p. 7.

27 Dickel, *'Die sind doch alle unheilbar'*, *p. 39*.

28 Klee, *Was sie taten*, p. 90.

29 Dickel, *'Die sind doch alle unheilbar'*, p. 140.

30 Ibid., p. 142.

31 Reproduced in Winter (ed.), *Verlegt nach Hadamar*, pp. 176–177.

32 Ibid., p. 178.

33 Dickel, *'Die sind doch alle unheilbar'*, *p. 145*.

34 Klee, *Was sie taten*, p. 203.

35 Ekkehard Maasz, 'Verschweigen, Vergessen, Erinnern. Vergangenheitsbewältigung in Idstein', in Schrapper and Sengling (eds.), *Die Idee der Bildbarkeit*, p. 341.

36 Ibid., p. 346.

37 Klee, *Was sie taten*, p. 205.

38 See Anon., 'KZ-Arzt vor Ghanas Richtern', *Die Zeit* Nr 34, 19 August 1966, on the extradiction proceedings.

39 Klee, *Was sie taten*, pp. 102–107.
40 ZSL 'Euthanasie', Hefelmann, interrogation of Hans Hefelmann dated 31 August 1960, pp. 2ff.
41 Klee, *Was sie taten*, pp. 50–55.
42 ZSL 'Euthanasie', Heyde, interrogation of Werner Heyde dated 12 October 1961–22 December 1961 (pp. 1–227); see pp. 56ff. for his life after 1945.
43 Klee, *Was sie taten*, p. 24.
44 See 'NS-Verbrechen', *Der Spiegel*, Nr 8 (1964), pp. 28ff., for a detailed account of the unmasking of Dr Sawade.
45 'Heyde kam nicht durch', *Revue Report* (no date), p. 105.
46 Klee, *Was sie taten*, p. 50.
47 Ibid., p. 138.
48 'Aus Menschlichkeit töten?', interview with Werner Catel, *Der Spiegel*, Nr 8 (1964), pp. 41ff.
49 Klee, *Was sie taten*, p. 45.
50 Ibid., pp. 71–74.
51 ZSL 'Euthanasie', V, testimony of Elly V. dated 2 April 1963, p. 1–2.
52 Klaus Dörner, 'Entschädigung für die Opfer von Zwangssterilisation und Euthanasie', in Vanja (ed.), *Euthanasie in Hadamar*, pp. 175ff. For an exhaustive parliamentary discussion of these issues see Deutsche Bundestag (ed.), *Wiedergutmachung und Entschädigung für nationalsozialistisches Unrecht* (24 June 1987).
53 Author's archive, 'Antrag auf laufende Beihilfen nach den Richtlinien der Bundesregierung über Härteleistung an Opfer von NS-Unrechtsmassnahmen im Rahmen des Allgemeinen Kriegsfolgengesetzes vom 7 März 1988.'
54 Klara Nowak, *Ich klage an* (Detmold 1989).
55 Author's archive, private letter from Josef S. dated 18 October 1989, p. 5.
56 *Frankfurter Allgemeine Zeitung*, 10 June 1974.
57 Author's archive, formal complaint from Josef S. to the Landgericht Frankfurt am Main dated 16 June 1986.
58 Author's archive, letter from Josef S. dated 18 October 1989.
59 'Offiziell kein Thema', *Die Zeit*, 19 June 1992.
60 Author's archive, Josef S. to the Bundesjustizminister dated 13 August 1990, detailing several unsatisfactory aspects of the terms of confinement.
61 Author's archive, several letters from Josef S. to the author between 1991 and 1993.

10   LEARNING FROM THE PAST? THE SINGER DEBATE

1 IWM CIOSC file Nr xxviii–50, Leo Alexander, 'Public Mental Health Practices in Germany. Sterilisation and Execution of Patients Suffering from Nervous or Mental Diseases', Combined Intelligence Objectives Sub-Committee (no date). (This chapter is a revised version of my ' "Euthanasia" in the Third Reich: Some Recent Literature', *Social History of Medicine*, 1991, 4, pp. 317–318.)
2 See IWM (formerly PRO 646), Case 1, *Medical Trial*, US versus Karl Brandt *et al.* (1947), vols. 1–25 for transcripts of the trial.

3 Mitscherlich and Mielke, *Medizin ohne Menschlichkeit*. The book was translated into English by J. Cleugh as *The Death Doctors* (London 1962).

4 See Walter Schmidt, *Selektion in der Heilanstalt 1939–1945* (Stuttgart 1965, Frankfurt am Main 1983), pp. 157ff. for the history of the book.

5 Alice Platen-Hallermund, *Die Tötung Geisteskranker in Deutschland. Aus der Deutschen Ärztekommission beim amerikanischen Militärgericht* (Frankfurt am Main 1948).

6 F. Bayle, *Croix gammée contre caducée. Les expériences humaines en Allemagne pendant la Deuxième Guerre Mondiale* (Neustadt 1955); E. Kintner (ed.), *The Hadamar Trial*. D. M. Fyfe (ed.), *War Crimes Trials* (London 1949); Leon Jaworski, *After Fifteen Years* (Houston 1961).

7 K. Dörner, 'Nationalsozialismus und Lebensvernichtung', *Vierteljahreshefte für Zeitgeschichte* (1967), 15, pp. 121–152.

8 Lothar Gruchmann, 'Euthanasie und Justiz im Dritten Reich', *Vierteljahreshefte für Zeitgeschichte* (1972), 20, pp. 235–279; Karl Dietrich Erdmann, '"Lebensunwertes Leben". Totalitäre Lebensvernichtung und das Problem der Euthanasie', *Geschichte im Wissenschaft und Unterricht* (1975), 4, pp. 215–225.

9 Nowak, *'Euthanasie' und Sterilisation im 'Dritten Reich'*.

10 Martin Höllen, 'Katholische Kirche und NS-"Euthanasie"'.

11 G. Baader and U. Schultz (eds.), *Medizin und Nationalsozialismus. Tabuisierte Vergangenheit – ungebrochene Tradition?* (Berlin 1908); W. Wuttke-Groneberg, *Medizin im Nationalsozialismus. Ein Arbeitsbuch* (Tübingen 1982); Thom and Caregorodcev (eds.), *Medizin unterm Hakenkreuz*. In this connection one should mention Benno Müller-Hill's *Murderous Science. Elimination by Scientific Selection of Jews, Gypsies, and Others, Germany 1933–1945* (Oxford 1988).

12 Klee, *'Euthanasie'*. See also his collection of documents, *Dokumente zur 'Euthanasie'*.

13 K. H. Roth (ed.), *Erfassung zur Vernichtung. Von der Sozialhygiene zum 'Gesetz über Sterbehilfe'* (Berlin 1984); Aly (ed.), *Aktion T-4*; Aly et al. (eds.), *Beiträge zur nationalsozialistischen Gesundheits- und Sozialpolitik* (Berlin 1985–), vols. 1–11 so far. There are also important local studies such as Angelika Ebbinghaus et al. (eds.), *Heilen und Vernichten im Mustergau Hamburg* (Hamburg 1984).

14 For a useful introduction to some of the critiques of this work, see Wolfgang Schneider (ed.), *'Vernichtungspolitik'. Eine Debatte über den Zusammenhang von Sozialpolitik und Genozid im nationalsozialistischen Deutschland* (Hamburg 1991).

15 Arbeitsgruppe (ed.) *Totgeschwiegen 1933–1945*.

16 Notably by Peter von Rönn, 'Auf der Suche nach einem anderen Paradigma', *Recht und Psychiatrie* (1991), 9, pp. 8–13.

17 G. Mosse, *Towards the Final Solution. A History of European Racism* (London 1978); P. Pulzer, *Political Antisemitism in Germany and Austria* (London 1968). The latter was pioneering in the sense of trying to fuse electoral sociology and psychology with a more conventional form of Teutonic *Ideengeschichte*.

18 Paul Weindling, *Health, Race and German Politics*. See also Robert Proctor, *Racial Hygiene. Medicine under the Nazis* (Cambridge, Massachusetts 1988).

19 P. Weingart, J. Kroll and K. Bayertz, *Rasse, Blut und Gene. Geschichte der*

Eugenik und Rassenhygiene in Deutschland (Frankfurt am Main 1988); Schmuhl, *Rassenhygiene, Nationalsozialismus, Euthanasie.*

20 Gisela Bock, *Zwangssterilisation und Nationalsozialismus. Studien zur Rassenpolitik und Frauenpolitik* (Opladen 1986).

21 Robert Jay Lifton, *The Nazi Doctors. A Study in the Psychology of Evil* (London 1986).

22 ÖRF 'Life and Death in the Castle'; Harmut Schoen, 'Fritz. Die zweite Beachtung', and his ZDF documentary on Grafeneck; Domino Films/Channel 4 'Selling Murder: The Killing Films of the "Third Reich"' (1992).

23 H.-U. Dapp, *Emma Z. Ein Opfer der Euthanasie* (Stuttgart 1990).

24 Peter Singer, 'Silenced in Germany', *New York Review of Books* (1991), 38, pp. 34ff. See also his 'Bioethics and Academic Freedom', *Bioethics* (1990), 4, pp. 33–34.

25 Franz Christoph, *Tödliche Zeitgeist. Notwehr gegen Euthanasie* (Cologne 1990).

26 Singer, 'Silenced in Germany', p. 40.

27 The most sustained attempt to defend Singer is Rainer Hegselmann and Reinhard Merkel (eds.), *Zur Debatte über Euthanasie* (Frankfurt am Main 1991); among the most effective critiques of Singer are Till Bastian (ed.), *Denken – Schreiben – Töten. Zur neuen 'Euthanasie'-Diskussion* (Stuttgart 1990), and Theo Bruns, Ulla Penselin and Udo Sierck (eds.), *Tödliche Ethik. Beiträge gegen Eugenik und 'Euthanasie'* (2nd edn Hamburg 1993).

28 Bruns *et al.* (eds.), *Tödliche Ethik*, p. 15.

29 Peter Singer, *Practical Ethics* (Cambridge 1979), pp. 77–78.

30 Ibid., p. 97. Singer's claim that some form of legalised euthanasia would not be analogous with the Nazis' economically and racially driven murder of 'useless mouths' may well be perfectly sound. What is worrying about his book is the constant and systematic efforts to exclude certain people from the category of 'person', the latter being solely defined in terms of simple conceptual functions or the capacity to comprehend one's own future. There is also what I see as a worrying insensitivity to language and metaphor, as when he argues: 'Suppose that we apply the test of imagining living the life of the weed I am about to pull out of my garden. I then have to imagine living a life with no conscious experiences at all. Such a life is a complete blank; I would not in the least regret the shortening of this subjectively barren form of existence. This test suggests, therefore, that the life of a being that has no conscious experiences is of no intrinsic value' (*Practical Ethics*, p. 92).

31 Ibid., p. 154.

32 Ibid., p. 156.

BIBLIOGRAPHY

The bibliography excludes some works cited in passing, but includes relevant primary and secondary sources in addition to those directly cited.

ARCHIVAL SOURCES

(1) Hessisches Hauptstaatsarchiv, Wiesbaden:

(a) (4Kls 7/47) Abt. 461 Nr 32061 (Hadamar Trial), Landgericht Frankfurt am Main 1947, volumes 1–50.

(b) Abt. 461 Nr 31526 (Kalmenhof [Idstein] Trial), Landgericht Frankfurt am Main 1947, volumes 1–30.

(c) (4a 1s 13/46 Frankfurt) Abt. 461 Nr 32442 (Eichberg Trial), Landgericht Frankfurt am Main 1946, volumes 1–19.

(d) Abt. 463 Nr 1154, Weilmünster investigation, Landgericht Frankfurt am Main, volumes 1–7.

(e) (Ks 2/63 Frankfurt) Abt. 631a, case against Werner Heyde *et al.*, volumes 1–453. This investigation, conducted by a team of assiduous and dedicated German state prosecutors under Generalstaatsanwalt Bauer, constitutes the most detailed attempt to unravel the activities of one of the major figures involved in organising and carrying out the 'euthanasia' programme. Since Heyde was pushed out of T–4 in 1941–1942, on the pretext of his earlier homosexual activities, these records are necessarily most enlightening about the period 1939–1941, i.e. regarding the 'children's euthanasia' programme, 'Aktion T–4' and 'Aktion 14f13' in the concentration camps. Heyde committed suicide before he could be brought to trial.

(f) Abt. 430/1, Administrative and patient records of the former Landesheilanstalt Eichberg Nrs: 11044; 10985; 11111; 11144; 11168; 11109; 11063; 11112; 11113; 11053; 11094; 11213; 11062; 11093; 11469; 11456; 11455; 11426; 11407; 11405; 11475; 11474; 11471; 11470; 11475; 11404; 11354; 11371; 11378; 11498; 11497; 11496; 11454; 11453; 11408; 11409; 11396; 11403; 16141; 11475; 11002; 10989; 11102; 10949; 10851; 11152; 11104; 11047; 11155; 11186; 10852; 10998; 10969; 10894; 11000; 11013; 10878; 11110; 11051; 11100; 11101; 10975; 11156; 10967; 11024; 11108; 11114; 11125;

11257; 11258; 11243; 11231; 11253; 10930; 11221; 11019; 11247; 11084;
11036; 11268; 11139; 10882; 10887; 11037; 11273; 10883; 11035; 10901;
11143; 10961; 11108; 11164; 11214; 11090; 11691; 11226; 10610; 10785;
10823; 10633; 10637; 10564; 11153; 10938; 10968; 11189; 11154; 11191;
11193; 10922; 11151; 10709; 10625; 10541; 10613; 10828; 10628; 10849;
10531; 11108; 11164; 11214; 11090; 11091; 11226; 10610; 10785; 10823;
10633; 10637; .10564; 11153; 10938; 10968; 11189; 11154; 11191; 11193;
10922; 11151; 10709; 10625; 10541; 10613; 10828; 10849; 10531; 11502;
11472; 11447; 11431; 11000; 11354; 11491; 11494; 11478; 11461; 11396;
11174; 10894; 10892; 10986; 10938; 11311; 11292; 11294; 11295; 11330;
11297; 11365; 11296; 11293; 11329; 11326; 11309; 11325; 11359; 11464;
11445; 11480; 11285; 11695; 11565; 11658; 11598; 11630; 11711; 11757;
11767; 11653; 11762; 11665; 11662; 11518; 11666; 11753; 11818; 11576;
11787; 11762; 11785; 11554; 11716; 11805; 11769; 11855; 11856; 11681;
11673; 11680; 11671; 11568; 11646; 11722; 11649; 11664; 11797; 11635;
11598; 11510; 11844; 11607; 11654; 11579; 11782; 31841; 11598; 11607;
11635; 11654; 11664; 11671; 11753; 11649; 11345; 12613; 12628; 12530;
12528; 12613; 12590; 12591; 12630; 12826; 12505; 12513; 12505; 12593;
12845; 12826; 12667.

(2) National Archives, Washington DC:

(a) M–1078, Rolls 1–3, United States of America v. Alfons Klein *et al*. The records of the first trial of Hadamar personnel in connection with the murder of about 400 foreign nationals.

(b) T–1021, Rolls 1–18, including the Heidelberger Dokumente, i.e. correspondence to and from Werner Heyde's successor as medical supremo of T–4, Professor Paul Nitsche, which the US Army Headquarters War Crimes Branch at Heidelberg originally assembled on 'euthanasia' in the context of the Nuremberg Doctors' Trial. Nitsche himself was executed following a separate trial in Dresden.

(c) T–253, Roll 44, Morell-Akte.

(3) Staatsarchiv, Munich:

(a) (IKs 10/49) Staatsanwaltschaft Nr 17460 1/2, Trial of Dr Hermann Pfannmüller.

(b) (I KLs 158/48) Staatsanwaltschaft Nr 19051, Trial of Professor Walter 'Bubi' Schultze, volumes 1–4 and Sonderbände 1–3.

(c) Staatsanwaltschaft Nr 19031, Trial of Emma D. *et al*.

(d) Akten der Regierung von Oberbayern: (RA) 3761 (Gesundheitswesen) Nrs 57686–57693, 'Beschwerden von Geisteskranken gegen Artikel 80 des P. Str. G. B.' 1933–1941.

(e) Landratsämter (LRA) Ebersberg Nr 66550
Berchtesgaden Nrs 30015–30016

Bibliography

(4) Bezirkskrankenhaus Haar:

Jahresberichte der Heil- und Pflegeanstalt Eglfing-Haar 1930–1946.

(5) Staatsarchiv, Augsburg:

(a) (Ks 1/49) Trial of Valentin Faltlhauser and others, volumes 1–7.
(b) Jahresberichte des Heil- und Pflegeanstalt Kaufbeuren-Irsee, 1933–1945.

(6) Bundesarchiv, Koblenz:

(a) R96 I Reichsarbeitsgemeinschaft für Heil- und Pflegeanstalten
(b) Filmarchiv.
  Sünden der Vater (b/w silent 16mm film, 141m).
  Das Erbe (b/w sound 35mm film, 330m).
  Erbkrank (b/w silent 16mm film, 265m).

(7) Bundesarchiv, Aussenstelle Potsdam-Babelsberg (former GDR Institut für den wissenschaftlichen Film):

Opfer der Vergangenheit (b/w sound 35mm film, 726m)
Was du ererbt ... (b/w silent 16mm film, 273m)
Eight rolls of uncut film material shot in various asylums, containing scenes of 'active' and somatic therapies and interviews with patients.

(7) Imperial War Museum, London:

(a) (formerly PRO 646) Case 1, *Medical Trial*, US versus Karl Brandt *et al.* (1947), volumes 1–25.
(b) CIOSC file Nr xxviii–50, Leo Alexander, 'Public Mental Health Practices in Germany. Sterilisation and Execution of Patients Suffering from Nervous or Mental Diseases.' Combined Intelligence Objectives Sub-Committee (no date), containing important documents on Eglfing-Haar and the Kleist reports on asylums in 1938.

(8) Zentrale Stelle der Landesjustizverwaltungen, Ludwigsburg:

(a) 'Euthanasie' A– Wi–Z, c. 30 volumes of alphabetically organised files containing interrogations and witness depositions from all major 'euthanasia' trials between c. 1946 and c. 1970. Individual volumes are devoted to the successive interrogations of Dietrich Allers, Hans Hefelmann and Werner Heyde.
(b) 9 AR–Z 340/1956, investigation of Werner Blankenburg, volumes 1–15.
(c) 203 AR–Z 69/59, investigation of Wilhelm Koppe and Gustav Laabs, (Kulmhof and Soldau), volumes 1–9.
(d) 203 AR–Nr 452/1964, investigation of Dr Kurt Bode (Danzig), volumes 1–4.

Bibliography

(e) V 203–AR Nr 1101/1962, investigation of Kurt Eimann, Georg Ebracht (Danzig-Neustadt).
(f) Urteil LG Freiburg 1 Ks 5/1948, Ludwig Sprauer and Josef Schreck.
(g) Urteil LG Düsseldorf 8 Kls 8/1948, Walter Creutz et al.
(h) Urteil LG Tübingen Ks 6/1949, Otto Mauthe, Max Eyrich et al.
(i) 439 AR–251/1962, investigation of Professor Berthold Kihn.
(j) VI 449 AR 2497/1966, Dr Hilde Wernicke et al.

(9) Berlin Document Center:

(a) Personal files on:
Karl Astel
Viktor Brack
Karl Brandt
Philipp Bouhler
Bodo Gorgass
Werner Heyde
Gottlieb Hering
Paul Nitsche
Hermann Pfannmüller
Franz Stangl
Christian Wirth
(b) general documentation of 'euthanasia' and SS records.

(10) British Film Institute, London:

Ich klage an (1941 sound 35mm feature film, 3,340m).

(11) Private Archives:

(a) Elvira M. (patient record)
(b) Josef S. (documents relating to the trial of Aquilin Ullrich et al.; private correspondence; correspondence with lawyers and government agencies c. 1986–1990)
(c) Klara Nowak (patient record and documents relating to the Bund der Zwangs-sterilisierten und 'Euthanasie'geschädigten)
(d) Helmut Heinze (documents relating to the murder of his mother)

(12) Taperecorded interviews with:

Klara Nowak, Detmold (1991)
Josef S., Oggersheim and Hadamar (1991–1993)
Paul R., W. and Hadamar (1990–1993)
Elvira M., Lübeck and Hadamar (1991)
Paula S., Hadamar (1991)
Siegfried Birschel, Hadamar (1991)
Helmut Heinze, Hamburg and Hadamar (1991)

Bibliography

BIBLIOGRAPHIES

Beck, Christoph, *Sozialdarwinismus, Rassenhygiene, Zwangssterilisation und Vernichtung 'lebensunwerten' Lebens. Eine Bibliographie zum Umgang mit behinderten Menschen im 'Dritten Reich'* – *und heute* (Bonn 1992)

Koch, Gerhard, *Euthanasie, Sterbehilfe. Eine dokumentierte Bibliographie* (2nd edn Erlangen 1990)

PUBLISHED PRIMARY SOURCES AND COLLECTIONS OF DOCUMENTS

Ast, Fritz, 'Die Problematik der Sparmassnahmen in der Geisteskrankenfürsorge', *Allgemeine Zeitschrift für Psychiatrie* (1933), 100, pp. 235–266.

'Sterilisierung und Anstaltsbestände', *Psychiatrisch-Neurologische Wochenschrift* (1933), 35, pp. 539–540.

'Der Ärztemangel in den Heilanstalten und Vorschläge zu dessen Behebung, insbesondere hinsichtlich der den Heilstätten', *Zeitschrift für Psychische Hygiene* (1936), 9, pp. 8–20.

'Erfahrungen über den Nachweis der Schizophrenie im Erbgesundheitsgerichtsverfahren', *Allgemeine Zeitschrift für Psychiatrie* (1939), 112, pp. 360–390.

Bauer, Elisabeth, 'Mittel zur Bekämpfung der Komplikationen bei der Insulinschock- und Elektrokrampfbehandlung', *Psychiatrisch-Neurologische Wochenschrift* (1943), 45, pp. 140–142.

Baumann, Friedrich and Rein, Oskar, 'Zur Reform der Irrenfürsorge', *Allgemeine Zeitschrift für Psychiatrie* (1920/1921), 76, pp. 122–124.

Becker, Karl, 'Erfahrungen bei der Durchführung des Sterilisierungsgesetzes in der Heil- und Pflegeanstalt Langenhagen bei Hannover', *Psychiatrisch-Neurologische Wochenschrift* (1935), 37, pp. 277–279.

Behmsen, Dr, 'Zur Frage der Unfruchtbarmachung bei Alkoholismus', *Psychiatrisch-Neurologische Wochenschrift* (1934), 36, pp. 282–283.

Bender, Wilhelm, 'Arbeitstherapie, besonders bei alten Schizophrenen', *Allgemeine Zeitschrift für Psychiatrie* (1927), 87, pp. 402–409.

Berg, Dr, 'Zur Krise der Offenen Fürsorge', *Psychiatrisch-Neurologische Wochenschrift* (1932), 34, pp. 548–549.

Berterermann, Helmuth, 'Zur Frage der Unfruchtbarmachung wegen Schwachsinns', *Münchener Medizinische Wochenschrift* (1938), 85, pp. 1135–1136.

Binding, Karl and Hoche, Alfred, *Die Freigabe der Vernichtung lebensunwerten Lebens. Ihr Mass und ihre Form* (Leipzig 1920).

Bingel, A., 'Über die psychischen und chirurgischen Komplikationen des Elektrokrampfes', *Allgemeine Zeitschrift für Psychiatrie* (1940), 115, pp. 325–343.

and Meggendorfer, F., 'Über die ersten deutschen Versuche einer Elektrokrampfbehandlung der Geisteskrankheiten', *Psychiatrisch-Neurologische Wochenschrift* (1940), 42, pp. 41–43.

Blume, Gustav, 'Über die Einrichtung psychiatrischer Krankheitsgeschichten', *Allgemeine Zeitschrift für Psychiatrie* (1933), 99, pp. 84–97.

Borchardt, Stadtrat, 'Die Freigabe der Vernichtung lebensunwerten Lebens', *Deutsche Strafrechts-Zeitung* (1922), 9, pp. 206–210.

Borner, Wilhelm, 'Euthanasie', *Das monistische Jahrbuch* (1913), 2, pp. 249–254.

Bozi, Alfred, 'Euthanasie und Recht', *Das monistische Jahrhundert* (1913), 2, pp. 576–580.

Bratz, E., 'Kann die Versorgung der Geisteskranken billiger gestaltet werden und wie?', *Allgemeine Zeitschrift für Psychiatrie* (1932), 98, pp. 1–40.

Braune, A., 'Euthanasie und Arzt', *Das monistische Jahrhundert* (1913), 2, pp. 871–873.

Braunmühl, Anton von, 'Über die Insulinschockbehandlung der Schizophrenie', *Psychiatrisch-Neurologische Wochenschrift* (1937), 39, pp. 156–163.

'Die Insulinschockbehandlung der Schizophrenie', *Münchener Medizinische Wochenschrift* (1937), 84, pp. 8–11.

'Das "Azoman" bei der Krampfbehandlung der Schizophrenie', *Psychiatrisch-Neurologische Wochenschrift* (1938), 40, pp. 515–519.

'Die kombinierte Schock-Krampfbehandlung der Schizophrenie am Beispiel der "Blockmethode"', *Zeitschrift für die gesamte Neurologie und Psychiatrie* (1938), 164, pp. 69–92.

'Shocklinie und Hypoglykämielinie', *Zeitschrift für die gesamte Neurologie und Psychiatrie* (1940), 169, pp. 413–436.

'Einige grundsätzliche Bermerkungen zur Schock- und Krampfbehandlung der Psychosen', *Allgemeine Zeitschrift für Psychiatrie* (1941), 118, pp. 67–79.

'Fünf Jahre Schock- und Krampfbehandlung in Eglfing-Haar', *Archiv für Psychiatrie* (1941), 114, pp. 410–440.

'Aus der Praxis der Krampftherapie', *Allgemeine Zeitschrift für Psychiatrie* (1942), 120, pp. 146–157.

Bresler, J., 'Deutsche Erbforschung in grösster materieller Not!' *Psychiatrisch-Neurologische Wochenschrift* (1934), 36, pp. 625–634.

'Die Zehn wichtigsten Kulturaufgaben der Anstalten für Geisteskranke', *Psychiatrisch-Neurologische Wochenschrift* (1935), 37, pp. 409–417.

'Insulin in der Psychiatrie', *Psychiatrisch-Neurologische Wochenschrift* (1937), 39, pp. 14–15.

'Wirtschaftstüchtigkeit unserer Anstalten', *Psychiatrisch-Neurologische Wochenschrift* (1942), 44, pp. 25–27 and 35–37.

Buchner, Otto, 'Erfahrungen bei über 1500 Elektroschockfällen', *Psychiatrisch-Neurologische Wochenschrift* (1942), 44, pp. 97–100.

Bufe, E., 'Zur Krise der Familienpflege', *Psychiatrisch-Neurologische Wochenschrift* (1932), 34, pp. 545–547.

Burkhardt, Hans, 'Was kann die psychiatrische Offene Fürsorge für Erbforschung und Rassenhygiene leisten?', *Psychiatrisch-Neurologische Wochenschrift* (1934), 36, pp. 232–236.

Busse, Walter, 'Erbbiologische Arbeit an Heil- und Pflegeanstalten', *Psychiatrisch-Neurologische Wochenschrift* (1935), 37, pp. 207–211.

Carriere, R., 'Sparmassnahmen und Anstaltsniveau', *Psychiatrisch-Neurologische Wochenschrift* (1930), 32, pp. 329–331.

'Ein Jahr Cardiazolbehandlung auf der unruhigen Frauenabteilung', *Allgemeine Zeitschrift für Psychiatrie* (1939), 113, pp. 347–354.

Chroust, Peter (ed.), *Friedrich Mennecke. Innenansichten eines medizinischen Täters im Nationalsozialismus. Eine Edition seiner Briefe 1935–1947* (Hamburg 1988), vols. 1 and 2.

Bibliography

Creutz, W., 'Die Ausbildung des Pflegepersonals für Geisteskranke', *Zeitschrift für psychische Hygiene* (1939), 12, pp. 95–119.

Crinis, Max de 'Die deutsche Psychiatrie', *Psychiatrisch-Neurologische Wochenschrift* (1939), 41, pp. 1–5.

Demme, H., 'Die Stellung der Epilepsie im Rahmen des Gesetzes zur Verhütung erbkranken Nachwuchses', *Münchener Medizinische Wochenschrift* (1935), 28, pp. 1567–1571.

Donalies, Gustav, 'Der "Fall" Jan H.', *Psychiatrisch-Neurologische Wochenschrift* (1942), 44, pp. 76–78.

Ebbinghaus, Angelika, and Preissler, Gerd, 'Die Ermordung psychisch kranker Menschen in der Sowjetunion', in Aly, Götz *et al.* (eds.), *Beiträge zur national-sozialistischen Gesundheits- und Sozialpolitik* (2nd edn Berlin 1987), vol. 1, pp. 75–107.

Eckhardt, Hellmut, 'Die sog. angeborene Hüftverrenkung und das Gesetz zur Verhütung erbkranken Nachwuchses', *Der Öffentliche Gesundheitsdienst* (1935–1936), 1, pp. 321–328.

Enge, J., 'Wirtschaftliche und soziale Lage des Irrenpflegepersonals', *Allgemeine Zeitschrift für Psychiatrie* (1919), 75, pp. 373–387.

'Die erweiterte Heilanstalt Strecknitz-Lübeck', *Psychiatrisch-Neurologische Wochenschrift* (1931), 33, pp. 1–5.

'Fehlschlüsse und Irrtümer bei Sparmassnahmen', *Psychiatrisch-Neurologische Wochenschrift* (1932), 34, pp. 569–572.

'Erfolge psychiatrischer Aufklärungsarbeit', *Psychiatrisch-Neurologische Wochenschrift* (1933), 34, pp. 307–310.

'Klinisch-diagnostische Richtlinien für die Praxis der Durchführung des Gesetzes zur Verhütung erbkranken Nachwuchses', *Psychiatrisch-Neurologische Wochenschrift* (1935), 37, pp. 622–626.

'Das Gesetz zur Verhütung erbkranken Nachwuchses in Laienbetrachtung und ärztliche Erfahrungen als Gutachter im Erbgesundheitsverfahren', *Psychiatrisch-Neurologische Wochenschrift* (1937), 39, pp. 8–13.

'Die Zukunft der Psychiatrie', *Psychiatrisch-Neurologische Wochenschrift* (1942), 44, pp. 425–428.

Ernst, Konrad, 'Von der Bedeutung der Irrenanstalten', *Psychiatrisch-Neurologische Wochenschrift* (1939), 41, pp. 251–252.

Ewald, Gottfried, 'Zur Theorie der Schizophrenie und der Insulinschockbehandlung', *Allgemeine Zeitschrift für Psychiatrie* (1939), 110, pp. 153–170.

Ewald, G., and Haddenbruck, S., 'Die Elektrokrampftherapie. Ihre Grundlagen und ihre Erfolge', *Zeitschrift für die gesamte Neurologie und Psychiatrie* (1942), 174, pp. 635–669.

Faltlhauser, Valentin, 'Erfahrungen des Erlanger Fürsorgearztes' *Allgemeine Zeitschrift für Psychiatrie* (1925), 80, pp. 102–125.

'Die wirtschaftliche Unentbehrlichkeit und die wirtschaftliche Gestaltung der offenen Geisteskrankenfürsorge der Gegenwart unter besonderer Berücksichtigung der Fürsorge in der Stadt', *Zeitschrift für psychische Hygiene* (1932), 5, pp. 84–98.

'Irrenanstalten und nationalsozialistische Bevölkerungspolitik', *Psychiatrisch-Neurologische Wochenschrift* (1939), 41, pp. 179–183.

Bibliography

Feldhofen, Marianne, 'Schwierigkeiten und Gefahren der Insulinschockbehandlung der Schizophrenie', *Allgemeine Zeitschrift für Psychiatrie* (1937), 105, pp. 281–298.

Fischer, Max, 'Erblichkeitsforschung an den Heil- und Pflegeanstalten für Geisteskranke', *Psychiatrisch-Neurologische Wochenschrift* (1931), 33, pp. 268–271.

'Das Sterilisierungsgesetz', *Psychiatrisch-Neurologische Wochenschrift* (1933), 35, pp. 484–487.

'Adolf Hitler und die Rassenhygiene', *Psychiatrisch-Neurologische Wochenschrift* (1939), 41, pp. 177–178.

Flinker, R., 'Zur Frage der Wirkungsmechanismus bei der Insulin-, Cardiazol-, und Dauerschlafbehandlung der Schizophrenie', *Allgemeine Zeitschrift für Psychiatrie* (1938), 109, pp. 111–115.

Franke, Gerhard, 'Gedanken über eine wirksamere Handhabung der ausmerzenden Erbpflege', *Psychiatrisch-Neurologische Wochenschrift* (1942), 44, pp. 305–307.

Friedländer, A. A., 'Psychiatrie und "öffentliche Meinung"', *Psychiatrisch-Neurologische Wochenschrift* (1933), 34, pp. 301–307.

Friedländer, Erich, 'Eine Gefahr für die deutsche Irrenpflege', *Allgemeine Zeitschrift für Psychiatrie* (1930), 93, pp. 194–205.

'Neue Wege der Irrenfürsorge?' *Psychiatrisch-Neurologische Wochenschrift* (1931), 33, pp. 327–329.

'Kann die Versorgung der Geisteskranken billiger gestaltet werden und wie?', *Psychiatrisch-Neurologische Wochenschrift* (1932), 34, pp. 373–381.

Friedlaender, Karl, 'Insulin-Schockbehandlung der Schizophrenie', *Psychiatrisch-Neurologische Wochenschrift* (1936), 38, p. 520.

Friese, G., 'Erbkrankheit, Begabung und Unfruchtbarmachung', *Der Öffentliche Gesundheitsdienst* (1935–1936), 1, pp. 899–903.

Fumarola, G., 'Eine neue Methode der Krampfbehandlung in der Psychiatrie: Der Elektroschock', *Psychiatrisch-Neurologische Wochenschrift* (1939), 41, pp. 87–88.

Gaupp, R., 'Die Freigabe der Vernichtung lebensunwerten Lebens', *Deutsche Strafrechts-Zeitung* (1920), 7, pp. 332–338.

Referat, 'Die Unfruchtbarmachung geistig und sittlich Minderwertiger', *Jahresversammlung des Deutschen Vereins für Psychiatrie am 1 und 2 September 1925 in Cassel, Allgemeine Zeitschrift für Psychiatrie* (1926), 83, pp. 371–390.

'Alfred Erich Hoche', *Zeitschrift für die gesamte Neurologie und Psychiatrie* (1943), 176, pp. 1–6.

Geller, Walter, 'Erfahrungen mit der Insulinbehandlung der Schizophrenie nach Sakel', *Psychiatrisch-Neurologische Wochenschrift* (1936), 38, pp. 528–633.

Gerhardt, Margarethe, 'Ergebnisse und Beobachtungen bei der Cariazol-Krampfbehandlung von Schizophrenien und anderen Psychosen', *Allgemeine Zeitschrift für Psychiatrie* (1938), 109, pp. 141–162.

Gerkan, Roland, 'Euthanasie', *Das monistische Jahrhundert* (1913), 2, pp. 169–173.

Glatzel, F., 'Unsere bisherigen Erfahrungen mit dem Sterilisierungsgesetz', *Psychiatrisch-Neurologische Wochenschrift* (1934), 36, pp. 236–240.

Gross, Adolf, 'Zeitgemässe Betrachtungen zum wirtschaftlichen Betrieb der Irrenanstalten', *Allgemeine Zeitschrift für Psychiatrie* (1922), 79, pp. 60–74.

Bibliography

Gütt, Arthur, 'Der öffentliche Gesundheitsdienst im Dritten Reich', *Der Öffentliche gesundheitsdienst* (1935–1936), 1, pp. 84–94.

Gütt, Arthur, Rüdin, Ernst and Ruttke, Falk, *Gesetz zur Verhütung erbkranken Nachwuchses vom 14. Juli 1933 mit Auszug aus dem Gesetz gegen gefährliche Gewohnheitsverbrecher und über Massnahmen der Sicherung und Besserung vom 24. November 1933* (2nd edn Munich 1936).

Häfner, Wilhelm, 'Zur Frage der sogenannten eugenischen Sterilisation beim vererbten Schwachsinn', *Psychiatrisch-Neurologische Wochenschrift* (1932), 34, pp. 315–320.

Harmsen, Hans, 'Die Durchführung des Gesetzes zur Verhütung erbkranken Nachwuchses in den Anstalten der Inneren Mission', *Zeitschrift für psychische Hygiene* (1936), 9, pp. 20–22.

'Ewald Meltzer', *Psychiatrisch-Neurologische Wochenschrift* (1936), 38, pp. 613–615.

Harrasser, A., 'Konstitution und Rasse bei oberbayrischen endogenen Psychotikern', *Zeitschrift für die gesamte Neurologie und Psychiatrie* (1937), 158, pp. 471–480.

Henle, F., 'Euthanasie', *Das monistische Jahrhundert* (1913), 2, pp. 309ff.

Hermkes, Karl, 'Schulunterricht im Rahmen der Anstaltsbehandlung', *Allgemeine Zeitschrift für Psychiatrie* (1935), 103, pp. 26–36.

Heydecke, Karl Hermann, 'Unsere Erfahrungen über den Einfluss der Sterilisierung auf die psychische Gesamthaltung der Sterilisierten', *Psychiatrisch-Neurologische Wochenschrift* (1936), 38, pp. 283–286.

Hildenbrand, G., 'Monismus und sittliches Bewusstsein', *Das monistische Jahrhundert* (1913), 2, pp. 491–496.

Hirschmann, Johannes, 'Über Insulinbehandlung bei Schizophrenie', *Psychiatrisch-Neurologische Wochenschrift* (1937), 39, pp. 13–14.

Hoffmann, Hans, 'Allgemeines zur Durchführung des Gesetzes zur Verhütung erbkranken Nachwuchses', *Der Öffentliche Gesundheitsdienst* (1937), 3, pp. 49–70.

Holthaus, B., 'Die erbbiologische Bestandsaufnahme in den Heilanstalten Westfalens', *Zeitschrift für psychische Hygiene* (1938), 11, pp. 49–57.

Horn, Walter, 'Untersuchungen und Beobachtungen an geisteskranken Juden', *Allgemeine Zeitschrift für Psychiatrie* (1941), 117, pp. 167–180.

Hürten, Ferdinand, 'Die ersten Hundert auf Grund des Gesetzes vom 24. November 1933 in der westfälischen Provinzial-Heilanstalt Eickelborn untergebrachten geistig abnormen Rechtsbrecher', *Allgemeine Zeitschrift für Psychiatrie* (1937), 106, pp. 255–338.

'Die erbbiologische Bestandsaufnahme in den Provinzial-Heilanstalten', *Psychiatrisch-Neurologische Wochenschrift* (1937), 39, pp. 135–139.

Illberg, Georg, 'Die Sterblichkeit der Geisteskranken in den sachsischen Anstalten während des Krieges', *Allgemeine Zeitschrift für Psychiatrie* (1922), 78, pp. 58–63.

Kaminski, Joachim, 'Die Heil- und Pflegeanstalten im Vierjahresplan', *Psychiatrisch-Neurologische Wochenschrift* (1939), 41, pp. 68–72.

Kehrer, F., 'Zur Frage der Kann-Vorschrift des §1 des Gesetzes', *Psychiatrisch-Neurologische Wochenschrift* (1934), 36, pp. 301–302.

Bibliography

Kihn, B., 'Die Ausschaltung der Minderwertigen aus der Gesellschaft', *Allgemeine Zeitschrift für Psychiatrie* (1932), 98, pp. 387–404.

Kintner, Earl W. (ed.), *The Hadamar Trial* (London and Edinburgh 1949).

Kirchhof, Johannes, 'Bedeutung und Formgebung des Films in Neurologie und Psychiatrie', *Psychiatrisch-Neurologische Wochenschrift* (1943), 45, pp. 181–185.

Klee, Ernst (ed.), *Dokumente zur 'Euthanasie'* (Frankfurt am Main 1986).

Klee, K., 'Die Freigabe der Vernichtung lebensunwerten Lebens', *Aerztliche Sachverständigen-Zeitung* (1921), 27, pp. 1–7.

Kleist, Karl, 'Die gegenwärtigen Strömungen in der Psychiatrie', *Allgemeine Zeitschrift für Psychiatrie* (1925), 82, pp. 1–41.

Klinkenberg, K., 'Zur Frage der Unfruchtbarmachung geistig Minderwertiger insbesondere nach eugenischen Gesichtspunkten', *Allgemeine Zeitschrift für Psychiatrie* (1927), 87, pp. 410–438.

Knab, Karl, 'Ein Beitrag zum Problem der Familienpflege als billigste Versorgungsart chronisch Geisteskranker und asozialer psychischer Grenzzustände', *Psychiatrisch-Neurologische Wochenschrift* (1930), 32, pp. 467–473.

'Entwicklungsstand der Tapiauer Familienpflege', *Allgemeine Zeitschrift für Psychiatrie* (1932), 96, pp. 339–347.

'Die Auswirkung des Sterilisierungsgesetzes in der Heil- und Pflegeanstalt Tapiau', *Psychiatrisch-Neurologische Wochenschrift* (1934), 36, pp. 268–269.

'Sind Familienpflege und pflegeloser Abteilungen veraltet und verfehlte Einrichtungen in der öffentlichen Geisteskrankenversorgung?', *Psychiatrisch-Neurologische Wochenschrift* (1934), 36, pp. 505–508.

'Die Bedeutung der Familienpflege im deutschen Geisteskrankenversorgungssystem', *Psychiatrisch-Neurologische Wochenschrift* (1935), 37, pp. 265–269.

'Was ist für die Anstaltspsychiatrie wichtiger: die medikamentöse Behandlung oder die Psychotherapie?', *Psychiatrische-Neurologische Wochenschrift* (1935), 37, pp. 365–367.

'Erbbiologische Bestandsaufnahme der Insassen der öffentlichen Heil- und Pflegeanstalten und offene Fürsorge für Geisteskranke', *Psychiatrisch-Neurologische Wochenschrift* (1936), 38, pp. 210–212.

Kolb, Gustav, 'Reform der Irrenfürsorge', *Zeitschrift für die gesamte Neurologie und Psychiatrie* (1919), 47, pp. 137–172.

'Was wir in der Anstalt Erlangen erreicht haben', *Psychiatrisch-Neurologische Wochenschrift* (1931), 33, pp. 571–572.

Kolb, Karl, 'Postoperative psychische Reaktionen bei Sterilisierten in der Heilanstalt', *Münchener Medizinische Wochenschrift* (1935), 28, pp. 1641–1642.

Kolle, Kurt, 'Die Unfruchtbarmachung bei Alkoholismus', *Allgemeine Zeitschrift für Psychiatrie* (1939), 112, pp. 397–404.

Kraepelin, Emil, 'Ziele und Wege der psychiatrischen Forschung', *Zeitschrift für die gesamte Neurologie und Psychiatrie* (1918), 42, pp. 169–205.

Kuhne, Dr, 'Offene Fürsorge für entlassene Geisteskranke der Heil- und Pflegeanstalt Emmendingen', *Allgemeine Zeitschrift für Psychiatrie* (1929), 91, pp. 355–368.

Kuhne, K., 'Beköstigung, Bekleidung und Wäsche in der Landesheilanstalt', *Psychiatrisch-Neurologische Wochenschrift* (1936), 38, pp. 529–533.

Bibliography

Kuppers, E., 'Die Schockbehandlung des manisch-depressiven Irreseins', *Allgemeine Zeitschrift für Psychiatrie* (1939), 112, pp. 436–445.

Lange, Wilhelm, 'Ergebnisse, Lehren und Wünsche, die sich aus der Jahresarbeit (1934) eines Erbgesundheitsgerichtes (Chemnitz) ergeben', *Psychiatrisch-Neurologische Wochenschrift* (1935), 37, pp. 75–82.

Lemme, Hansjoachim, 'Die Rechtssprechung in Erbgesundheitsgerichtssachen', *Der Öffentliche Gesundheitsdienst* (1935–1936), 1, pp. 789–797.

Liermann, Gunter, 'Der Intelligenzprüfungsbogen nach Anlage 5a der ersten Verordnung zur Durchführung des Gesetzes zur Verhütung erbkranken Nachwuchses in seiner Anwendung bei Jugendlichen in der Stadt Königsberg i. Pr. und dem Samland im Alter von 14–18 Jahren', *Der Öffentliche Gesundheitsdienst* (1935–1936), 1, pp. 244–254.

Liers, Hans, 'Die Verwendung der Heil- und Pflegeanstalt Kreuzburg OS. als Arbeitsanstalt', *Psychiatrisch-Neurologische Wochenschrift* (1939), 41, pp. 394–396.

Linden, H., 'Die weltanschaulichen und wissenschaftlichen Grundlagen des Gesetzes zur Verhütung erbkranken Nachwuchses', *Der Öffentliche Gesundheitsdienst* (1937), 3, pp. 808–820.

Loew, H., 'Das Verhalten der Körpergewichte von Geisteskranken während der Kriegszeit', *Allgemeine Zeitschrift für Psychiatrie* (1922), 78, pp. 1–57.

Luxenburger, Hans, 'Grundsätzliches zur kausalen Prophylaxe der erblichen Geisteskrankheiten', *Zeitschrift für psychische Hygiene* (1929), 2, pp. 164–172.

'Die praktische Mitarbeit der Heil- und Pflegeanstalten in der psychiatrischen Erblichkeitsforschung', *Psychiatrisch-Neurologische Wochenschrift* (1930), 32, pp. 406–410.

'Die praktische Mitarbeit der Heil- und Pflegeanstalten in der psychiatrischen Erblichkeitsforschung', *Allgemeine Zeitschrift für Psychiatrie* (1930), 93, pp. 349–352.

Marchesani, O., 'Über erbliche Blindheit', *Münchener Medizinische Wochenschrift* (1936), 83, pp. 1167–1171.

Mathes, Dr, 'Die Entwicklungsstufen der badischen praktischen Anstaltspsychiatrie bis zur Eröffnung der Anstalt Emmendingen und deren 40 jährige Tätigkeit', *Allgemeine Zeitschrift für Psychiatrie* (1929), 91, pp. 337–355.

Matzner, Dr, 'Das Verfahren vor den Erbgesundheitsgerichten', *Der Öffentliche Gesundheitsdienst* (1935–1936), 1, pp. 281–289.

Meduna, Ladislaus von, 'Die Konvulsionstherapie der Schizophrenie', *Psychiatrisch-Neurologische Wochenschrift* (1935), 37, pp. 317–319.

'Die Bedeutung des epileptischen Anfalls in der Insulin- und Cardiazolbehandlung der Schizophrenie', *Psychiatrisch-Neurologische Wochenschrift* (1937), 39, pp. 331–334.

'Die Konvulsionstherapie der Schizophrenie', *Psychiatrisch-Neurologische Wochenschrift* (1939), 41, pp. 165–169.

Meltzer, Ewald, *Das Problem der Abkürzung 'lebensunwerten' Lebens* (Halle 1925).

'Die Frage des unwerten Lebens (Vita non iam vitalis) und die Jetztzeit', *Psychiatrisch-Neurologische Wochenschrift* (1932), 34, pp. 584–591.

'Fünf-Jahresbericht über die Anstalt der Inneren Mission "Katharinenhof",

Grosshennersdorf (Sa.)', *Psychiatrisch-Neurologische Wochenschrift* (1939), 41, pp. 359–362 and 372–374.

Meyer, E., 'Neue und alte Strömungen in der praktischen Psychiatrie', *Allgemeine Zeitschrift für Psychiatrie* (1926), 83, pp. 191–200.

Möckel, W. and Schweickert, E., 'Die wirtschaftlichen Aufgaben der Heil- und Pflegeanstalten im neuen Vierjahresplan', *Psychiatrisch-Neurologische Wochenschrift* (1937), 39, pp. 425–428.

'Die Aufgaben der Heil- und Pflegeanstalten im Vierjahresplan und in der Kriegswirtschaft', *Allgemeine Zeitschrift für Psychiatrie* (1939), 113, pp. 373–386.

'Die Behandlung der Kranken in der Heil- und Pflegeanstalt Wiesloch (Baden) im Jahre 1939', *Psychiatrisch-Neurologische Wochenschrift* (1940), 42, pp. 77–79 and 449–451.

'Die Krankenbehandlung in der Heil- und Pflegeanstalt Wiesloch (Baden)', *Psychiatrisch-Neurologische Wochenschrift* (1942), 44, pp. 45–46.

'Anstaltskost und Vitamine', *Psychiatrisch-Neurologische Wochenschrift* (1942), 44, pp. 257–261.

Müller, Richard, 'Krampfbehandlung der Schizophrenie und Schenkelhalsfraktur', *Münchener Medizinische Wochenschrift* (1939), 86, pp. 525–526.

Neubelt, Dr, 'Einige Mitteilungen zur Durchführung des Gesetzes zur Verhütung erbkranken Nachwuchses', *Der Öffentliche Gesundheitsdienst* (1935–1936), 1, pp. 420–423.

Neukamp, Franz, 'Zum Problem des Gnadentodes oder der Sterbehilfe', *Zeitschrift für psychische Hygiene* (1937), 10, pp. 161–167.

Nieper, Ferdinand, 'Über Massnahmen und bisherige Erfahrungen bei der Durchführung des Erbgesundheitsgesetzes an den Wahrendorff'schen Privat Heil- und Pflegeanstalten Ilten', *Psychiatrisch-Neurologische Wochenschrift* (1934), 36, pp. 454–456.

Nobbe, Hermann, 'Das Gesetz zur Verhütung erbkranken Nachwuchses, Irrenanstalten, Aussenfürsorge und Familienpflege', *Psychiatrisch-Neurologische Wochenschrift* (1934), 36, pp. 471–474.

Ortleb, Dr, 'Mangel der Anstaltsbehandlung und Vorschläge zur Abhilfe', *Allgemeine Zeitschrift für Psychiatrie* (1926), 83, pp. 118–126.

Ostwald, Wilhelm, 'Euthanasie', *Das monistische Jahrhundert* (1913), 2, pp. 337–341.

'Wissenschaftliche oder Gefühlsethik?', *Das monistische Jahrhundert* (1913), 2, pp. 173–174.

Overhamm, G., 'Zur Technik der Intelligenzprüfung bei der Begutachtung Schwachsinniger', *Psychiatrisch-Neurologische Wochenschrift* (1936), 38, pp. 643–648.

Panse, Friedrich, 'Einrichtungen für die erbbiologische und sonstige Auswertung der Wittenauer Krankheitsgeschichten', *Allgemeine Zeitschrift für Psychiatrie* (1933), 99, pp. 98–102.

Papst, Pius, 'Herrn Obermedizinalrat Dr. Fritz Ast', *Psychiatrisch-Neurologische Wochenschrift* (1932), 34, pp. 469–471.

Reich, Dr, 'Einiges über erbbiologische Ermittlungstätigkeit', *Der Öffentliche Gesundheitsdienst* (1935–1936), 1, pp. 129–132.

Bibliography

Repkewitz, Dr, 'Die Offene Geisteskrankenfürsorge im Rahmen der Sparmass-nahmen', *Psychiatrisch-Neurologische Wochenschrift* (1933), 34, pp. 433–437.

Richter, A., 'Über die Ernährungsverhältnisse in der Irrenanstalt Buch während des Krieges 1914/18 und deren Folgen', *Allgemeine Zeitschrift für Psychiatrie* (1919), 75, pp. 407–423.

Roemer, Hans, 'Zur beruflichen Ausbildung des Pflegepersonals', *Allgemeine Zeitschrift für Psychiatrie* (1927), 85, pp. 16–34.

'Der Stand der offenen Fürsorge und Geisteskrankenfürsorge in Baden', *Allgemeine Zeitschrift für Psychiatrie* (1928), 88, pp. 460–468.

'Die Sparprogramme für die offene Gesundheitsfürsorge und die offene Geis-teskrankenfürsorge', *Zeitschrift für psychische Hygiene* (1932), 5, pp. 47–50.

'Die Leistungen der psychiatrischen Kliniken und der öffentlichen Heil- und Pflegeanstalten bei der Durchführung des Gesetzes zur Verhütung erb-kranken Nachwuchses im ersten Jahr des Vollzuges (1934)', *Zeitschrift für psychische Hygiene* (1936), 9, pp. 47–52.

'Zur Durchführung der erbbiologischen Bestandsaufnahme in den Heil- und Pflegeanstalten', *Zeitschrift für psychische Hygiene* (1936), 9, pp. 110–120.

'Die praktische Einführung der Insulin- und Cardiazolbehandlung in den Heil-und Pflegeanstalten', *Allgemeine Zeitschrift für Psychiatrie* (1938), 107, pp. 121–128.

Rohden, von, 'Über die rassenhygienischen Aufgaben des Anstaltspsychiaters', *Psychiatrisch-Neurologische Wochenschrift* (1933), 35, pp. 473–479.

Rüdin, Ernst, 'Bedingungen und Rolle der Eugenik in der Prophylaxe der Geistesstorungen', *Zeitschrift für psychische Hygiene* (1937), 10, pp. 99–108.

'Die empirische Erbprognose, die Zwillingsmethode und die Sippenforschung in ihrer Bedeutung für die psychiatrische Erbforschung und für die Psychia-trie überhaupt', *Allgemeine Zeitschrift für Psychiatrie* (1938), 107, pp. 3–20.

'Bedeutung der Forschung und Mitarbeit von Neurologen und Psychiatern im nationalsozialistischen Staat', *Zeitschrift für die gesamte Neurologie und Psychia-trie* (1939), 165, pp. 7–17.

Ruttke, Falk, 'Beispiele aus der Rechtsprechung zum Begriff der "schweren erblichen körperlichen Missbildung"', *Der Öffentliche Gesundheitsdienst* (1935–1936), 1, pp. 573–576.

Sack, 'Die Heil- und Pflegeanstalten, ihre wirtschaftlichen, finanziellen und sonstigen Verhältnisse', *Psychiatrisch-Neurologische Wochenschrift* (1938), 40, pp. 245–248 and 256–259.

Salm, Heinrich, 'Zur Frage der Sterilisierung Geisteskranker', *Münchener Medizi-nische Wochenschrift* (1935), 28, pp. 947–948.

'Behandlung und Verpflegung der Kranken in der Schwäbischen Kreis- Heil-und Pflegeanstalt Kaufbeuren-Irsee im Jahre 1937', *Psychiatrisch-Neurologi-sche Wochenschrift* (1938), 40, pp. 420–422 and 429–432.

'Das Schicksal von 133 in den Jahren 1928 bis 1930 zum ersten Mal in Anstaltsbehandlung getretenen Schizophrenen', *Psychiatrisch-Neurologische Wochenschrift* (1939), 40, pp. 197–199.

'Erfahrungen mit Neospiran und Azoman bei der Krampfbehandlung von Schizophrenen', *Psychiatrisch-Neurologische Wochenschrift* (1939), 41, pp. 469–472.

Bibliography

'Die Therapie in der Heil- und Pflegeanstalt Kaufbeuren (Schwaben) im Jahre 1938', *Psychiatrisch-Neurologische Wochenschrift* (1940), 42, pp. 1–4.

Schlaich, Ludwig, *Vernichtung und Neuanfang. Das Schicksal der Heil- und Pflegeanstalten in Stetten i. R.* (Stuttgart 1946).

Schlenke, Walburga, 'Bericht über zweienhalbjährige Elektroschockbehandlung', *Psychiatrisch-Neurologische Wochenschrift* (1943), 45, pp. 162–167.

Schlotmann, W., 'Insulin- und Cardiazolbehandlung in der Landes- Heil- und Pflegeanstalt Alzey', *Psychiatrisch-Neurologische Wochenschrift* (1938), 40, pp. 189–190.

Schmidt, Heinrich, 'Tätigkeitsbericht der Aussenfürsorgestelle für Geisteskranke an der Heil- und Pflegeanstalt Klingenmünster, Pfalz, während des Kalenderjahres 1929', pp. 577–582.

Schmidt, Dr, 'Aus der Praxis eines Erbgesundheitsobergerichts', *Psychiatrisch-Neurologische Wochenschrift* (1935), 37, pp. 328–330.

Schmieder, Fritz, 'Über Krampfschäden bei der Cardiazolbehandlung', *Allgemeine Zeitschrift für Psychiatrie* (1939), 113, pp. 341–346.

Schnidtmann, Moritz, 'Fürsorgeerziehung und Rassenhygiene', *Psychiatrisch-Neurologische Wochenschrift* (1933), 35, pp. 587–590.

Schottky, Johannes, 'Psychiatrische und kriminalbiologische Fragen bei der Unterbringung in einer Heil- oder Pflegeanstalt nach §42b und c des Strafgesetzbuches', *Allgemeine Zeitschrift für Psychiatrie* (1941), 117, pp. 287–355.

Schröder, C. H., 'Beitrag zur Vererbung und Behandlung der Hamophilie', *Münchener Medizinische Wochenschrift* (1935), 28, pp. 1281–1284.

Schuch, H., 'Ist die Aufhebung oder Einschränkung der offenen psychiatrischen Fürsorge eine wirksame Sparmassnahme?', *Zeitschrift für psychische Hygiene* (1932), 5, pp. 35–47.

Schulz, Dr, 'Die erbbiologische Arbeit an der Heil- und Pflegeanstalt Kaufbeuren, Schwaben im Jahre 1938', *Psychiatrisch-Neurologische Wochenschrift* (1940), 42, pp. 55–57.

Schulze, Paul, 'Über Anstaltsartefakte bei Geisteskranken und ihre Beseitigung', *Psychiatrisch-Neurologische Wochenschrift* (1930), 32, pp. 541–546.

Seidel, J., 'Kernfragen der Euthanasie', *Das monistische Jahrhundert* (1913), 2, pp. 580–584.

Sereny, Gitta, *Into that Darkness* (London, 1974).

Simon, Hermann, 'Aktivere Krankenbehandlung in der Irrenanstalt', Part I, *Allgemeine Zeitschrift für Psychiatrie* (1927), 87, pp. 97–145 and Part II, *Allgemeine Zeitschrift für Psychiatrie* (1929), 90, pp. 69–121 and 245–309.

Simon, Martin, 'Ein halbes Jahrhundert Familienpflege der Anstalt Ilten', *Psychiatrisch-Neurologische Wochenschrift* (1934), 36, pp. 451–454.

Stark, E., 'Zur Nachbehandlung Sterilisierter', *Münchener Medizinische Wochenschrift* (1935), 28, pp. 134–135.

Steinwaller, Bruno, '2 Jahre Erbgesundheitsgesetz – 1 1/2 Jahre Erbgesundheitsgerichtsbarkeit', *Psychiatrisch-Neurologische Wochenschrift* (1935), 37, pp. 325–328.

'Das finnische Erbgesundheitsgesetz von 1935', *Allgemeine Zeitschrift für Psychiatrie* (1936), 104, pp. 251–252.

Bibliography

'Zur Frage der Sterilisierung in England', *Allgemeine Zeitschrift für Psychiatrie* (1936), 104, pp. 252–253.

'Über den Stand der Gesundheitsgesetzgebung anderer Länder', *Allgemeine Zeitschrift für Psychiatrie* (1936), 104, pp. 412–413.

'Geplante polnische Erbgesundheitsgesetzgebung', *Allgemeine Zeitschrift für Psychiatrie* (1936), 104, pp. 413–415.

'Geplante Zulassung der Sterbehilfe in England', *Allgemeine Zeitschrift für Psychiatrie* (1936), 104, p. 415.

'Mexikanische Erb- und Geistesgesundheitspflege', *Allgemeine Zeitschrift für Psychiatrie* (1937), 106, pp. 251–254.

Stemmler, W., 'Die Unfruchtbarmachung Geisteskranker, Schwachsinniger und Verbrecher aus Anlage unter Erhaltung der Keimdrüsen (Vasektomie und Salpingektomie)', *Allgemeine Zeitschrift für Psychiatrie* (1925), 80, pp. 437–467.

'Der erbbiologische Bestandsaufnahme', *Allgemeine Zeitschrift für Psychiatrie* (1937), 106, pp. 84–90.

Stoerring, W., 'Prüfungsmethoden intellektueller Minderbegabung', *Psychiatrisch-Neurologische Wochenschrift* (1939), 41, pp. 47–53.

Strassmann, F., 'Erhaltung oder Vernichtung lebensunwerten Lebens', *Die Medizinische Welt* (1929), 31, pp. 500–502.

Straub, Dr, 'Landesamt für Erbgesundheitspflege in Kiel', *Psychiatrisch-Neurologische Wochenschrift* (1933), 35, pp. 367–368.

'Die Verantwortung des Arztes als Mitglied des Erbgesundheitsgerichts', *Psychiatrisch-Neurologische Wochenschrift* (1935), 37, pp. 68–69.

Titius, 'Zum Ausbau der Arbeitstherapie', *Psychiatrisch-Neurologische Wochenschrift* (1930), 32, pp. 426–427.

Wald, Roderich, Deutsche Nervenärzte als Dichter und Denker', *Psychiatrisch-Neurologische Wochenschrift* (1936), 38, pp. 104–107.

Weygandt, W., 'Hysterie als Erbkrankheit', *Zeitschrift für die gesamte Neurologie und Psychiatrie* (1936), 155, pp. 758–782.

'Talentierte Schwachsinnige und ihre erbgesetzliche Bedeutung', *Zeitschrift für die gesamte Neurologie und Psychiatrie* (1938), 161, pp. 532–535.

Wickel, 'Übersicht über Entwicklung und Stand der Aus- und Fortbildung des Pflegepersonals in den Krankenanstalten für Geisteskranken', *Zeitschrift für psychische Hygiene* (1936), 9, pp. 64–82.

Willige, Hans, 'Geschichte, Entwicklung und gegenwartiger Stand der Dr. Ferdinand Wahrendorff'schen Heil- und Pflegeanstalten in Ilten', *Psychiatrisch-Neurologische Wochenschrift* (1934), 36, pp. 445–451.

Wirth, Erich, 'Erfordert bei der Erbbegutachtung die Diagnose der erblichen Taubheit unbedingt den Nachweis der erblichen Belastung?', *Münchener Medizinische Wochenschrift* (1936), 83, pp. 1304–1306.

Wolfsdorf, Eugen, 'Euthanasie und Monismus', *Das monistische Jahrhundert* (1913), 2, pp. 305–311.

Wuth, Otto, 'Die medikamentöse Therapie der Psychosen', *Allgemeine Zeitschrift für Psychiatrie* (1931), 94, pp. 1–78.

Ziegelroth, L., 'Bericht über die Besichtigung der Insulinstation in der Heilanstalt Eglfing', *Psychiatrisch-Neurologische Wochenschrift* (1937), 39, pp. 496–498.

Bibliography

SECONDARY SOURCES

Ackerknecht, E. H., *A Short History of Psychiatry* (2nd edn New York, 1969).

Aly, Götz, 'Anstaltsmord und Katastrophenmedizin 1943–1945. Die Aktion Brandt', in Dörner, K. (ed.), *Fortschritte der Psychiatrie im Umgang mit Menschen* (Rehburg-Loccum 1984), pp. 33–55.

'Der Mord an behinderten Kindern zwischen 1939 und 1945', in Ebbinghaus A., Roth, K.-H. and Kaupen-Haas, H. (eds.), *Heilen und Vernichten im Mustergau Hamburg* (Hamburg 1984), pp. 147–155.

'Der saubere und der schmutzige Fortschritt', in Aly, G. *et al.* (eds.), *Reform und Gewissen' 'Euthanasie' im Dienst des Fortschritts. Beiträge zur national-sozialistischen Gesundheits- und Sozialpolitik*, vol. 2 (Berlin 1985), pp. 9–78.

(ed.), *Aktion T-4 1939–1945. Die 'Euthanasie'-Zentrale in der Tiergartenstrasse 4* (2nd edn Berlin 1989).

and Susanne Heim, *Vordenker der Vernichtung. Auschwitz und die deutschen Pläne für eine neue europäische Ordnung* (Hamburg 1991).

Tuberkulose und "Euthanasie"', in Pfeiffer, Jürgen (ed.), *Menschenverachtung und Opportunismus. Zur Medizin im Dritten Reich* (Tübingen 1992), pp. 131–146.

Annas, George and Grodin, Michael (eds.), *The Nazi Doctors and the Nuremberg Code* (New York 1992).

Arbeitsgruppe zur Erforschung der Geschichte der Karl-Bonhoeffer-Nerven-klinik (ed.), *Totgeschwiegen 1933–1945. Zur Geschichte der Wittenauer Heil-stätten. Seit 1957 Karl-Bonhoeffer-Nervenklinik* (2nd edn Berlin 1989).

Baader, Gerhard and Schultz, Ullrich (eds.), *Medizin und Nationalsozialismus. Tabuisierte Vergangenheit – ungebrochene Tradition?* (Frankfurt am Main 1987).

'Rassenhygiene und Eugenik', in Bleker, Johanna and Jachertz, Norbert (eds.), *Medizin im Dritten Reich* (Cologne 1989), pp. 22–29.

Bach, Otto, 'Zur Zwangssterilisierungspraxis in der Zeit des Faschismus im Bereich der Gesundheitsämter Leipzig und Grimma', in Thom, Achim and Spaar, Horst (eds.), *Medizin im Faschismus. Symposium über das Schicksal der Medizin in der Zeit des Faschismus in Deutschland 1933–1945* (Berlin 1985), pp. 157–161.

Baier, Lothar, 'Töten als heilen: Ärzte im Dritten Reich', *Merkur* (1989), 4, pp. 275–291.

Barham, Peter, *Schizophrenia and Human Value. Chronic Schizophrenia, Science and Society* (Oxford 1984).

Bastian, Till, *Von der Eugenik zur Euthanasie* (Bad Worishofen 1981).

(ed.), *Denken–Schreiben–Töten. Zur neuen 'Euthanasie'-Diskussion* (Stuttgart 1990).

Bästlein, Klaus, 'Die "Kinderfachabteilung" Schleswig 1941 bis 1945', in Arbeitskreis zur Erforschung des Nationalsozialismus in Schleswig-Holstein (ed.), *Informationen zur Schleswig-Holsteinischen Zeitgeschichte* (1993), 20, pp. 16–45.

Bäumer, Änne, *NS-Biologie* (Stuttgart 1990).

Becker, Carl, 'Die Durchführung der Euthanasie in den katholischen caritativen

Bibliography

Heimen für geistig Behinderte', *Jahrbuch der Caritaswissenschaft* (1968), pp. 104–119.

Behr, Heinrich, '"Euthanasie" und das Marienstift 1933–1945', *Fröhlich Helfen* (1986), 1, pp. 38–40.

Biesold, Horst, *Klagende Hände. Betroffenheit und Spätfolgen in Bezug auf das Gesetz zur Verhütung erbkranken Nachwuchses dargestellt am Beispiel der 'Taubstummen'* (Solms 1988).

Blasius, Dirk, *Der verwaltete Wahnsinn. Eine Sozialgeschichte des Irrenhauses* (Frankfurt am Main 1980).

'Psychiatrischer Alltag im Nationalsozialismus', in Peukert, Detlev and Reulecke, Jürgen (eds.), *Die Reihen fast geschlossen* (Wuppertal 1981), pp. 367–380.

'Die Ordnung der Gesellschaft. Zum historischen Stellenwert der NS-Psychiatrie', in Dörner, K. (ed.), *Fortschritte der Psychiatrie im Umgang mit Menschen* (Rehburg-Loccum 1984), pp. 11–22.

'The Asylum in Germany before 1860', in Spierenburg, P. (ed.), *The Emergence of Carceral Institutions. Prisons, Galleys and Lunatic Asylums* (Rotterdam 1984), pp. 148–164.

Umgang mit Unheilbaren. Studien zur Sozialgeschichte der Psychiatrie (Bonn 1986).

'Das Ende der Humanität. Psychiatrie und Krankenmord in der NS-Zeit', in Walter H. Pehle (ed.), *Der historische Ort des Nationalsozialismus* (Frankfurt am Main 1990), pp. 47–70.

'Die "Maskerade des Bösen". Psychiatrische Forschung in der NS-Zeit', in Frei, Norbert (ed.), *Medizin und Gesundheitspolitik in der NS-Zeit* (Munich 1991), pp. 265–285.

Bloch, Sidney and Chodoff, Paul (eds.), *Psychiatric Ethics* (2nd edn Oxford 1991).

Bock, Gisela, 'Sterilisationspolitik im Nationalsozialismus: die Planung einer heilen Gesellschaft durch Prävention', in Dörner, K. (ed.), *Fortschritte der Psychiatrie im Umgang mit Menschen* (Rehburg-Loccum 1984), pp. 88–104.

Zwangssterilisation im Nationalsozialismus. Studien zur Rassenpolitik und Frauenpolitik (Opladen 1986).

'Zwangssterilisation im Nationalsozialismus', in Christine Vanja (ed.), *Euthanasie in Hadamar. Die nationalsozialistische Vernichtungspolitik in hessischen Anstalten* (Kassel 1991), pp. 69–78.

Boland, Karl and Kowolik, Dagmar, *Heillose Zeiten. Zur lokalen Sozial- und gesundheitspolitik in Mönchengladbach und Rheydt von der Zeit der Wirtschaftskrise 1928 bis in die ersten Jahre der NS-Herrschaft* (Mönchengladbach 1991).

Bromberger, Barbara and Mausbacher, Hans, *Feinde des Lebens. NS-Verbrechen an Kindern* (Cologne 1987).

Bruns, Theo, Penselin, Ulla and Sierck, Udo (eds.), *Tödliche Ethik. Beiträge gegen Eugenik und 'Euthanasie'* (2nd edn Hamburg 1993).

Bund der 'Euthanasie'-Geschädigten und Zwangssterilisierten e.V. (ed.), *Ich klage an. Tatsachen und Erlebnisberichte der 'Euthanasie'-Geschädigten und Zwangssterilisierten* (Detmold 1989).

Burleigh, Michael, 'Euthanasia and the Cinema in the Third Reich', *History Today*, (1990), 40, pp. 11–16.

Bibliography

'"Euthanasia" in the Third Reich: Some Recent Literature', *Social History of Medicine* (1991), pp. 317–328.

'Racism as Social Policy: The Nazi "Euthanasia" Programme 1939–1945', *Ethnic and Racial Studies* (1991), 14, pp. 453–473.

and Wippermann, Wolfgang, 'Hilfloser Historismus. Warum die deutsche Geschichtswissenschaft bei der Erforschung der Euthanasie versagt hat', in Rost, K. L., Bastian, T. and Bonhoeffer, K. (eds.), *Thema: Behinderte. Wege zu einer sozial verpflichteten Medizin* (Stuttgart 1991), pp. 11–23.

and Wippermann, Wolfgang, *The Racial State: Germany 1933–1945* (2nd edn Cambridge 1992)

Burrin, Philippe, *Hitler and the Jews* (London 1994).

Christoph, Franz, *Tödlicher Zeitgeist. Notwehr gegen Euthanasie* (Cologne 1990).

Chroust, Peter, '"Ärzteschaft und "Euthanasie" – unter besonderer Berücksichtigung Friedrich Menneckes', in Landeswohlfahrtsverbandes Hessen (ed.) *Euthanasie in Hadamar. Die nationalsozialistische Vernichtungspolitik in hessischen Anstalten* (Kassel 1991), pp. 123–133.

Cohen, Cynthia '"Quality of Life" and the Analogy with the Nazis', *Journal of Medicine and Philosophy* (1983), 8, pp. 113–135.

Gross, Herwig, Hamman, Matthias and Sorensen, Jan (eds.), *'Soll nach Hadamar überführt werden'. Den Opfern der Euthanasiemorde 1939 bis 1945* (Frankfurt am Main 1989).

Cocks, Geoffrey, *Psychotherapy in the Third Reich. The Göring Institute* (New York 1985).

'Repressing, Remembering, Working Through: German Psychiatry, Psychotherapy, Psychoanalysis, and the "Missed Resistance" in the Third Reich', *Journal of Modern History* (1992), 64, supplement volume, pp. 204–216.

Damm, Sabine and Emmerich, Norbert, 'Die Irrenanstalt Dalldorf-Wittenau bis 1933', in Arbeitsgruppe zur Erforschung der Geschichte der Karl-Bonhoeffer-Nervenklinik (ed.), *Totgeschwiegen 1933–1945* (2nd revised edn Berlin 1989), pp. 11–47.

Dapp, Hans-Ulrich, *Emma Z. Ein Opfer der Euthanasie* (Stuttgart 1990).

Daub, Ute, '"Krankenhaus-Sonderlage Aktion Brandt in Koppern im Taunus" – Die letzte Phase der 'Euthanasie' im Frankfurt am Main', *Psychologie & Gesellschaftskritik* (1992), 16, pp. 39–67.

Daum, Monika, 'Arbeit und Zwang, das Leben der Hadamarer Patienten im Schatten des Todes', in Roer, D. and Henkel, D. (eds.), *Psychiatrie im Faschismus. Die Anstalt Hadamar 1933–1945* (Bonn 1986), pp. 173–213.

Delius, Peter, *Das Ende von Strecknitz. Die Lübecker Heilanstalt und ihre Auflösung 1941. Ein Beitrag zur Sozialgeschichte der Psychiatrie im Nazionalsozialismus* (Kiel 1988).

Dickel, Horst, *'Die sind doch alle unheilbar'. Zwangssterilisation und Tötung der 'Minderwertigen' im Rheingau 1934–1945* (Wiesbaden 1988).

'Alltag in einer Landesheilanstalt im Nationalsozialismus – Das Beispiel Eichberg', in Landeswohlfahrtsverband Hessen (ed.), *Euthanasie in Hadamar. Die nationalsozialistische Vernichtungspolitik in hessischen Anstalten* (Kassel 1991), pp. 105–113.

Bibliography

Dörner, Klaus, 'Nationalsozialismus und Lebensvernichtung', *Vierteljahreshefte für Zeitgeschichte* (1967), 15, pp. 121–152.

'NS-Euthanasie: Zur Normalisierung des therapeutischen Tötens', in Dörner, K. (ed.), *Fortschritte der Psychiatrie im Umgang mit Menschen* (Rehburg-Loccum 1984), pp. 105–116.

(ed.) *Der Krieg gegen die psychisch Kranken* (2nd edn Frankfurt am Main 1989).

Bürger und Irre. Zur Sozialgeschichte und Wissenschaftssoziologie der Psychiatrie (Frankfurt am Main 1984).

Tödliches Mitleid – Zur Frage der Unerträglichkeit des Lebens (2nd edn Gütersloh 1989).

'Anstaltsalltag in der Psychiatrie und NS-Euthanasie', in Bleker, Johanna and Jachertz, Norbert (eds.), *Medizin im Dritten Reich* (Cologne 1989), pp. 94–102.

'Entschädigung für die Opfer von Zwangssterilisationen und Euthanasie', in Christine Vanja (ed.), *Euthanasie in Hadamar. Die nationalsozialistische Vernichtungspolitik in hessischen Anstalten 1933–1945* (Kassel 1991), pp. 175–178.

and Plog, Ursula, *Irren ist Menschlich. Lehrbuch der Psychiatrie/Psychotherapie* (Bonn 1986).

Dressen, Willi, 'L'élimination des malades mentaux', in Bedarida, François (ed.), *La Politique nazi d'extermination* (Paris 1989), pp. 245–256.

Dworkin, Ronald, *Life's Dominion. An Argument about Abortion and Euthanasia* (London 1993).

Ebbinghaus, Angelika (ed.), *Öpfer und Täterinnen* (Nordlingen 1987).

Erdmann, Karl Dietrich, '"Lebensunwertes Leben". Totalitäre Lebensvernichtung und das Problem der Euthanasie', *Geschichte im Wissenschaft und Unterricht* (1975), 4, pp. 215–225.

Fallend, K., Handlbauer, B. and Kienreich, W. (eds.), *Der Einmarsch in die Psyche. Psychoanalyse, Psychologie und Psychiatrie im Nationalsozialismus und die Folgen* (Vienna 1989).

Finzen, Asmus, *Auf dem Dienstweg. Die Verstrickung einer Anstalt in der Tötung psychisch Kranker* (Rehburg-Loccum 1984).

Foucault, Michel, *Madness and Civilization. A History of Insanity in the Age of Reason* (London 1989).

The Birth of the Clinic (London 1989).

Frei, Norbert (ed.), *Medizin und Gesundheitspolitik in der NS-Zeit* (Munich 1991).

Frey, Otto, *Gedenkstätte Grafeneck* (Grafeneck 1990).

Friedländer, Henry, 'Jüdische Anstaltspatienten im NS-Deutschland', in Aly, G. (ed.), *Aktion T-4 1939–1945* (Berlin 1987), pp. 34–44.

Ganssmüller, Christian, *Die Erbgesundheitspolitik des Dritten Reiches* (Cologne, Vienna 1987).

Glover, Jonathan, *Causing Death and Saving Lives* (London 1977).

(ed.), *Utilitarianism and its Critics* (London and New York 1990).

Göbel, Peter and Thormann, Helmut, *Verlegt – vernichtet – vergessen? Leidenswege von Menschen aus Hephata im Dritten Reich. Eine Dokumentation* (Schwalmstadt 1985).

Bibliography

Goffman, Erving, *Asylums. Essays on the Social Situation of Mental Patients and Other Inmates* (London 1991).

Gould, Stephen Jay, *Ever Since Darwin. Reflections in Natural History* (London 1978).

The Mismeasure of Man (London 1981).

Graf, Hendrik, 'Die Situation der Patienten und des Pflegepersonals der rheinischen Provinzial- Heil- und Pflegeanstalten in der Zeit des Nationalsozialismus', in Leipert, M., Styrnal, R. and Schwarzer, W. (eds.), *Verlegt nach unbekannt. Sterilisation und Euthanasie in Galkhausen 1933–1945. Dokumente und Darstellungen zur Geschichte der Rheinischen Provinzialverwaltung und des Landschaftsverbandes Rheinland* (Cologne 1987), vol. 1, pp. 39–52.

Grell, Ursula, 'Karl Bonhoeffer und die Rassenhygiene', in Arbeitsgruppe zur Erforschung der Geschichte der Karl-Bonhoeffer-Nervenklinik (ed.), *Totgeschwiegen 1933–1945* (2nd edn Berlin 1989), pp. 207–218.

Grode, Walter, *Die 'Sonderbehandlung 14f13' in den Konzentrationslagern des Dritten Reiches. Ein Beitrag zur Dynamik faschistischer Vernichtungspolitik* (Frankfurt am Main 1987).

'"Euthanasie"–Ärzte in den NS-Konzentrationslagern. Verlauf und Entwicklung der "Sonderbehandlung 14f13"', *Psychologie & Gesellschaftskritik* (1989), 13, pp. 73–86.

'Deutsche "Euthanasie"-Politik in Polen während des Zweiten Weltkriegs', *Psychologie & Gesellschaftskritik* (1992), 16, pp. 5–13.

Grubitzsch, Siegfried, 'Revolutions- und Rätezeit 1918/19 aus der Sicht deutscher Psychiater', *Psychologie & Gesellschaftskritik* (1985), 9, pp. 23–47.

Gruchmann, Lothar, 'Euthanasie und Justiz im Dritten Reich', *Vierteljahreshefte für Zeitgeschichte* (1972), 20, pp. 235–279.

'Ein unbequemer Amtsrichter im Dritten Reich. Aus den Personalakten des Dr. Lothar Kreyssig', *Vierteljahreshefte für Zeitgeschichte* (1984), 32, pp. 463–488.

Justiz im Dritten Reich 1933–1940 – Anpassung und Unterwerfung in der Ära Gürtner (Munich 1988).

Güse, Hans-Georg and Schmacke, Norbert, *Psychiatrie zwischen bürgerlichen Revolution und Faschismus* (Giessen 1974), 2 volumes.

Hafner, Karl Heinz and Winau, Rolf, '"Die Freigabe der Vernichtung lebensunwerten Lebens". Eine Untersuchung zu der Schrift von Karl Binding und Alfred Hoche', *Medizinhistorisches Journal* (1974), 9, pp. 227–254.

Hamann, Matthias, 'Die Ermordung psychisch kranker polnischer und sowjetischer Zwangsarbeiter', in Aly, Götz (ed.), *Aktion T-4* (Berlin 1987), pp. 161–166.

'Die Morde an polnischen und sowjetischen Zwangsarbeitern in deutschen Anstalten', in Aly, Götz et al. (eds.), *Beiträge zur nationalsozialistischen Gesundheits- und Sozialpolitik* (2nd edn Berlin 1987), vol. 1, pp. 121–187.

Hartel, Christiana, 'Transporte in den Tod', in Arbeitsgruppe zur Erforschung der Geschichte der Karl-Bonhoeffer-Nervenklinik (ed.), *Totgeschwiegen 1933–1945* (2nd edn Berlin 1989), pp. 191–206.

Marianne Emmerich and Norbert Frei, 'Krankenmorde in den Wittenauer Heilstätten', in Arbeitsgruppe zur Erforschung der Geschichte der Karl-

Bibliography

Bonhoeffer-Nervenklinik (ed.), *Totgeschwiegen 1933–1945. Zur Geschichte der Wittenauer Heilstätten* (2nd edn Berlin 1989), pp. 185–189.

Hegselmann, Rainer and Merkel, Reinhard (eds.), *Zur Debatte über Euthanasie* (Frankfurt am Main 1991).

Hennermann, H., 'Werner Heyde und seine Würzburger Zeit', in Nissen, Gerhardt and Keil, Gundolf (eds.), *Psychiatrie auf dem Wege zur Wissenschaft. Psychiatrie-historisches Symposium anlässlich des 90. Jahrestages der Eröffnung der 'Psychiatrischen Klinik der Königlichen Universität Wurzburg'* (Stuttgart 1985), pp. 55–61.

Hentschel, Völker, *Geschichte der deutschen Sozialpolitik 1880–1980* (Frankfurt am Main 1983).

Herzog, Günter, 'Gründerjahre der Psychiatrie', in Dörner, K. (ed.), *Fortschritte der Psychiatrie im Umgang mit Menschen* (Rehburg-Loccum 1984), pp. 64–76.

'Heilung, Erziehung, Sicherung. Englische und deutsche Irrenhäuser in der ersten Hälfte des 19. Jahrhunderts', in Kocka, Jürgen (ed.), *Bürgertum im 19. Jahrhundert. Deutschland im europäischen Vergleich* (Munich 1988), vol. 3, pp. 418–446.

Hildebrandt, Helmut, 'Offene Fürsorge und Psychische Hygiene in der Weimarer Republik: die zwei Gesichter eines sozialpsychiatrischen Versuchs', *Psychologie & Gesellschaftskritik* (1986), 10, pp. 7–31.

'Das Bild der Psychiatrie zwischen 1880 und 1910: "Überwachen und Strafen" oder Gesundheits- und sozialpolitische Degeneration?', *Psychologie & Gesellschaftskritik* (1987), 11, pp. 21–44.

Hochmuth, Anneliese (ed.), *Bethel in den Jahren 1939–1943. Eine Dokumentation zur Vernichtung lebensunwerten Lebens* (Bielefeld 1979).

Hoffmann, Christoph, 'Der Inhalt des Begriffes "Euthanasie" im 19. Jahrhundert und seine Wandlung in der Zeit bis 1920', Medical Dissertation, Humboldt-Universität Berlin (1969).

Hohendorf, Gerrit and Magull-Seltenreich, Achim (eds.), *Von der Heilkunde zur Massentötung. Medizin im Nationalsozialismus* (Heidelberg 1990).

Höllen, Martin, 'Katholische Kirche und NS-"Euthanasie"', *Zeitschrift für Kirchengeschichte* (1980), 91, pp. 53–82.

Hoser, Cornelia and Weber-Diekmann, 'Zwangssterilisation an Hadamarer Anstaltsinsassen', in Roer, D. and Henkel, D. (eds.), *Psychiatrie im Faschismus. Die Anstalt Hadamar 1933 bis 1945* (Bonn 1986), pp. 121–172.

Huhn, Marianne, 'Psychiatrie im Nationalsozialismus am Beispiel der Wittenauer Heilstätten', in Aly, Götz (ed.), *Aktion T-4* (Berlin 1987), pp. 183–197.

James, Harold, *The German Slump. Politics and Economics 1924–1936* (Oxford 1986).

Jaroszewski, Zdzislaw, 'Die Vernichtung psychisch Kranker unter deutscher Besatzung', *Sozialpsychiatrische Informationen* (1982), 12, pp. 6–17.

Jasper, Hinrich, *Maximinian de Crinis (1889–1945). Eine Studie zur Psychiatrie im Nationalsozialismus*, in Winau, Rolf and Müller-Dietz, Heinz (eds.), *Abhandlungen zur Geschichte der Medizin und der Naturwissenschaften*, Heft 63 (Husum 1991).

Jensch, Hugo, *Euthanasie-Aktion T-4. Verbrechen in den Jahren 1940 und 1941 auf dem Sonnenstein in Pirna* (Pirna 1990).

Jetter, Dieter, *Grundzüge der Geschichte des Irrenhauses* (Darmstadt 1981).

Bibliography

Jodelet, Denise, *Madness and Social Representations* (Hemel Hempstead 1991).

Jones, Steve, *The Language of the Genes. Biology, History and the Evolutionary Future* (London 1993).

Kater, Michael H., *Doctors under Hitler* (North Carolina 1989).

'Doctor Leonardo Conti and his Nemesis: the Failure of Centralized Medicine in the Third Reich', *Central European History* (1985), 18, pp. 299–325.

Kelly, Alfred, *The Descent of Darwin. The Popularization of Darwinism in Germany, 1860–1914* (Chapel Hill 1981).

Klaus, Barbara and Brilla, Gunter, 'Politik in Biologiebüchern', in Poggeler, Franz (ed.), *Politik im Schulbuch* (Bonn 1985), pp. 144–191 and pp. 445–479.

Klee, Ernst, *'Euthanasie' im NS-Staat. Die 'Vernichtung lebensunwerten Lebens'* (Frankfurt am Main 1983).

Was sie taten – was sie wurden. Ärzte, Juristen und andere Beteiligte am Kranken- und Judenmord (Frankfurt am Main 1986).

'Von der "T–4" zur Judenvernichtung. Die "Aktion Reinhard" in den Vernichtungslagern Belzec, Sobibor und Treblinka', in Aly, Götz (ed.), *Aktion T–4* (Berlin 1987), pp. 147–152.

"Den Hahn aufzudrehen war ja keine grosse Sache." Vergasungsärzte während der NS-Zeit und danach', *Dachauer Hefte* (1988), 4, pp. 1–21.

(ed.), *'Schöne Zeiten'. Judenmord aus der Sicht der Täter und Gaffer* (Frankfurt am Main 1988).

'Die SA Jesu Christi'. Die Kirche im Banne Hitlers (Frankfurt am Main 1989).

'Durch Zyankali erlöst'. Sterbehilfe und Euthanasie heute (Frankfurt am Main 1990).

Persilscheine und falsche Pässe. Wie die Kirchen den Nazis halfen (Frankfurt am Main 1992).

'Die "Euthanasie" als Vorstufe zur Judenvernichtung', in Pfeiffer, Jürgen (ed.), *Menschenverachtung und Opportunismus. Zur Medizin im Dritten Reich* (Tübingen 1992), pp. 147–156.

and Dressen, Willy, 'Nationalsozialistische Gesundheits- und Rassenpolitik', in Benz, Wolfgang (ed.), *Sozialisation und Traumatisierung. Kinder in der Zeit des Nationalsozialismus* (Frankfurt am Main 1992), pp. 103–116.

Kłodzinski, Stanisław, 'Die "Aktion 14f13". Der Transport von 575 Häftlingen von Auschwitz in das "Sanatorium Dresden"', in Aly, G. (ed.), *Aktion T–4 1939–1945* (Berlin 1987), pp. 136–146.

Klüppel, Manfred, '"Euthanasie" und Lebensvernichtung 1933–1945 – Auswirkungen auf die Landesheilanstalten Haina und Merxhausen', in Heinemeyer, Walter and Punder, Tilman (eds.), *450 Jahre Psychiatrie in Hessen. Veroffentlichungen des Historischen Kommission für Hessen* (Marburg 1983), vol. 47, pp. 321–348.

'Euthanasie' und Lebensvernichtung am Beispiel der Landesheilanstalten Haina und Merxhausen. Eine Chronik der Ereignisse 1933–1945 (3rd edn Kassel 1985).

Kneuker, Gerd and Steglich, Wulf, *Begegnungen mit der Euthanasie in Hadamar* (Rehburg-Loccum 1985).

Koch, Gerhard, *Euthanasie, Sterbehilfe. Eine dokumentierte Bibliographie* (2nd edn Erlangen 1990).

Koonz, Claudia, 'Ethical Dilemmas and Nazi Eugenics: Single-Issue Dissent in

Religious Contexts', *Journal of Modern History* (1992), 64, supplement volume, pp. 8–31.

Kottow, M. H., 'Euthanasia after the Holocaust – Is it possible?: A Report from the Federal Republic of Germany', *Bioethics* (1988), 2, pp. 58–69.

Krüger, Martina, 'Kinderfachabteilung Wiesengrund. Die Tötung behinderte Kinder in Wittenau', in Arbeitsgruppe zur Erforschung der Geschichte der Karl-Bonhoeffer-Nervenklinik (ed.), *Totgeschwiegen 1933–1945* (2nd revised edn Berlin 1989), pp. 151–176.

Kuhse, Helga, *The Sanctity of Life Doctrine in Medicine. A Critique* (Oxford 1987).

Kuropka, Joachim (ed.), *Clemens August Graf von Galen. Neue Forschungen zum Leben und Wirken des Bischofs von Münster* (Cloppenburg 1992).

(ed.), *Clemens August Graf von Galen. Sein Leben und Wirken in Bildern und Dokumenten* (Cloppenburg 1992).

Landeswohlfahrtsverbandes Hessen (ed.), *Mensch achte den Menschen. Frühe Texte über die Euthanasieverbrechen der Nationalsozialisten in Hessen* (2nd edn Kassel 1987).

(ed.), *Psychiatrie im Nationalsozialismus* (Kassel 1989).

(ed.), *Euthanasie in Hadamar. Die nationalsozialistische Vernichtungspolitik in hessischen Anstalten* (Kassel 1991).

(ed.), *'Verlegt nach Hadamar'. Die Geschichte einer NS-'Euthanasie'-Anstalt* (Kassel 1991).

Leipert, Matthias, Styrnal, Rudolf and Schwarzer, Winfried (eds.), *Verlegt nach unbekannt. Sterilisation und Euthanasie in Galkhausen 1933–1945. Dokumente und Darstellung zur Geschichte der Rheinischen Provinzialverwaltung und des Landschaftsverbandes Rheinland*, vol. 1 (Cologne 1987).

Leiser, Erwin, *Nazi Cinema* (London 1974).

Lifton, Robert Jay, *The Nazi Doctors. A Study in the Psychology of Evil* (London 1986).

Mader, Ernst, *Das erzwungene Sterben von Patienten der Heil- und Pflegeanstalt Kaufbeuren-Irsee zwischen 1940 und 1945* (Blöcktach 1982).

Meier, Kurt, *Kreuz und Hakenkreuz. Die evangelische Kirche im Dritten Reich* (Munich 1992).

Meixner, Michael and Schwerdtner, Hans-Bodo, 'Das "Gesetz zur Verhütung erbkranken Nachwuchses", seine wissenschaftlichen und politischen Voraussetzungen und Folgewirkungen', Thom, Achim and Spaar, Horst (eds.), *Medizin im Faschismus. Symposium über das Schicksal der Medizin in der Zeit des faschismus in Deutschland 1933–1945* (Berlin 1985), pp. 152–156.

Menges, Jan, *'Euthanasie' in het derde Rijk* (Haarlem 1972).

Mildner, Karl-Heinz, 'Die Arbeitstherapie unter besonderer Berücksichtigung ihrer Entwicklung im Psychiatrischen Krankenhaus Haina', in Heinemeyer, Walter and Punder, Tilman (eds.), *450 Jahre Psychiatrie in Hessen. Veröffentlichungen der Historischen Kommission für Hessen* (Marburg 1983), vol. 47, pp. 375–381.

Mitscherlich, Alexander and Mielke, Fred (eds.), *Medizin ohne Menschlichkeit. Dokumente des Nürnberger Ärzteprozesses* (2nd edn Frankfurt am Main 1978).

Morlok, Karl, *Wo bringt ihr uns hin? 'Geheime Reichssache' Grafeneck* (2nd edn Stuttgart 1990).

Bibliography

Müller-Hill, Benno, *Murderous Science. Elimination by Scientific Selection of Jews, Gypsies and Others: Germany 1933–1945* (Oxford 1988).

Müller-Kuppers, Manfred, 'Kinderpsychiatrie und Euthanasie – Staatlich angeordnete und sanktionierte Kindesmisshandlung und Kindestötung zwischen 1933 und 1945', in Martinius, Joest and Frank, Reiner (eds.), *Vernachlässigung, Missbrauch und Misshandlung von Kindern. Erkennen, Bewusstmachen, Helfen* (Bern 1990), pp. 103–119.

Noakes, Jeremy, 'Nazism and Eugenics: The Background to the Nazi Sterilisation Law of 14 July 1933', in R. J. Bullen *et al.* (eds.), *Ideas into Politics* (London 1984), pp. 75–94.

'Philipp Bouhler und die Kanzlei des Führers der NSDAP', in Rebentisch, Dieter and Teppe, Karl (eds.), *Verwaltung contra Menschenführung im Staat Hitlers* (Göttingen 1989), pp. 209–236.

'Social Outcasts in the Third Reich', in Bessel, Richard (ed.), *Life in the Third Reich* (Oxford 1987), pp. 83–96.

Nowak, Kurt, *'Euthanasie' und Sterilisation im 'Dritten Reich'. Die Konfrontation der evangelischen und katholischen Kirche mit dem 'Gesetz zur Verhütung Erbkranken Nachwuchses' und der 'Euthanasie'-Aktion* (2nd edn Göttingen 1984).

'Die Kirche und das "Gesetz zur Verhütung erbkranken Nachwuchses" vom 14. Juli 1933', in Tuchel, Johannes (ed.), *'Kein Recht auf Leben'. Beiträge und Dokumente zur Entrechtung und Vernichtung 'lebensunwerten Lebens' im Nationalsozialismus* (Berlin 1984), pp. 101–119.

'Stimmen aus evangelischer Theologie und Kirche zur Vernichtung "lebensunwerten Lebens"', *Fröhlich Helfen* (1986), 1, pp. 32–38.

'Sterilisation, Krankenmord und Innere Mission im "Dritten Reich"', in Thom, A. and Caregorodcev, G. I. (eds.), *Medizin unterm Hakenkreuz* (East Berlin 1989), pp. 167–179.

'Widerstand, Zustimmung, Hinnahme. Das Verhalten der Bevölkerung zur "Euthanasie"', in Frei, Norbert (ed.), *Medizin und Gesundheitspolitik in der NS-Zeit* (Munich 1991), pp. 235–251.

Oosthuizen, G. C., Shapiro, H. A. and Strauss, S. A. (eds.), *Euthanasia* (Cape Town 1978).

Orth, Linca, *Die Transport Kinder aus Bonn* (Cologne 1989).

Pagel, Karl, 'Das Wirken von Pastor Paul Braune und sein Widerstand im Heim 'Gottesschutz' in Erkner', *Fröhlich Helfen* (1986), 1, pp. 45–51.

Pfürtner, Stephen H. *et al.*, *Ethik in der europäischen Geschichte* (Stuttgart 1988), vol. 2, *Reformation und Neuzeit*.

Pick, Daniel, *Faces of Degeneration. A European Disorder c. 1848–c. 1918* (Cambridge 1989).

Platen-Hallermund, Alice, *Die Tötung Geisteskranker in Deutschland* (Frankfurt am Main 1948).

Porter, Roy, *A Social History of Madness. Stories of the Insane* (London 1987).

Mind-Forg'd Manacles. A History of Madness in England from the Restoration to the Regency (London 1987).

'Madness and its Institutions', in Wear, Andrew (ed.), *Medicine in Society* (Cambridge 1992), pp. 277–301.

Portmann, Heinrich, *Kardinal von Galen. Ein Gottesmann seiner Zeit* (Münster 1961).

Proctor, Robert, *Racial Hygiene. Medicine under the Nazis* (Cambridge, Massachusetts 1988).

Richarz, Bernhard, *Heilen, Pflegen, Töten. Zur Alltagsgeschichte einer Heil- und Pflegeanstalt bis zum Ende des Nationalsozialismus* (Göttingen 1987).

Riedesser, Peter and Verderber, Axel, *Aufrüstung der Seelen. Militärpsychiatrie und Militärpsychologie in Deutschland und Amerika* (Freiburg 1985).

Römer, Gernot, *Die grauen Busse in Schwaben. Wie das Dritte Reich mit Geisteskranken und Schwangeren umging* (Augsburg 1986).

Rönn, Peter von, 'Zum indirekten Nachweis von Totungsaktivitäten während der zweiten Phase der NS-"Euthanasie"', *Recht und Psychiatrie* (1991), 9, pp. 8–13.

'Auf der Suche nach einem anderen Paradigma', *Recht und Psychiatrie* (1991), 9, pp. 50–56.

et al., Wege in den Tod. Hamburgs Anstalt Langenhorn und die Euthanasie in der Zeit des Nationalsozialismus (Hamburg 1993).

Roer, Dorothee and Henkel, Dieter (eds.), *Psychiatrie im Faschismus. Die Anstalt Hadamar 1933–1945* (Bonn 1986).

Rössler, Hans, 'Die "Euthanasie"-Diskussion in Neuendettelsau 1937–1939', *Zeitschrift für bayerische Kirchengeschichte* (1986), 55, pp. 199–208.

'Ein neues Dokument zur "Euthanasie"-Diskussion in Neuendettelsau 1939', *Zeitschrift für bayerische Kirchengeschichte* (1988), 57, pp. 87–91.

Rost, Karl Ludwig, *Sterilisation und Euthanasie im Film des 'Dritten Reiches'. Nationalsozialistische Propaganda in ihrer Beziehung zu rassenhygienischen Massnahmen des NS-Staates* (Husum 1987).

Roth, Karl-Heinz (ed.), *Erfassung zur Vernichtung. Von der Sozialhygiene zum 'Gesetz über Sterbehilfe'* (Berlin 1984).

'"Erbbiologische Bestandsaufnahme" – ein Aspekt "ausmerzender" Erfassung vor der Entfesselung des Zweiten Weltkrieges', in Roth, Karl-Heinz (ed.), *Erfassung zur Vernichtung. Von der Sozialhygiene zum 'Gesetz über Sterbehilfe'* (Berlin 1984), pp. 57–100.

'Filmpropaganda für die Vernichtung der Geisteskranken und Behinderten im "Dritten Reich"', in Aly, G. *et al.* (eds.), *Reform und Gewissen. 'Euthanasie' im Dienst des Fortschritts. Beiträge zur nationalsozialistischen Gesundheits- und Sozialpolitik*, vol. 2 (Berlin 1985), pp. 125–193.

'"Ich klage an" – Aus der Entstehungsgeschichte eines Propaganda-Films', in Aly, Götz (ed.), *Aktion T-4* (Berlin 1987), pp. 93–116.

and Aly, Götz, 'Das "Gesetz über die Sterbehilfe bei unheilbar Kranken". Protokolle der Diskussion über die Legalisierung der nationalsozialistischen Anstaltsmorde in den Jahren 1938–1941', in Roth, Karl-Heinz (ed.), *Erfassung zur Vernichtung. Von der Sozialhygiene zum 'Gesetz über Sterbehilfe'* (Berlin 1984), pp. 101–179.

Rothmaler, Christiane, 'Zwangssterilisationen nach dem "Gesetz zur Verhütung erbkranken Nachwuchses"', in Bleker, Johanna and Jachertz, Norbert (eds.), *Medizin im Dritten Reich* (Cologne 1989), pp. 68–75.

Rückleben, Hermann, *Deportation und Tötung von Geisteskranken aus den badischen Anstalten der Inneren Mission Kork und Mosbach* (Karlsruhe 1981).

Bibliography

Rudnick, Martin, *Behinderte in Nationalsozialismus. Von der Ausgrenzung und der Zwangssterilisation zur 'Euthanasie'* (Weinheim/Basel 1985).
(ed.), *Aussondern – Sterilisation – Liquidieren* (Berlin 1990).

Sachsse, Christoph and Tennstedt, Florian, *Geschichte der Armenfürsorge in Deutschland*, vols. 1–3 (Stuttgart 1980–1992).

Scheer, Rainer, 'Die nach Paragraph 42b RStGB verurteilten Menschen in Hadamar', in Roer, D. and Henkel, D. (eds.), *Psychiatrie im Faschismus. Die Anstalt Hadamar 1933 bis 1945* (Bonn 1986), pp. 237–255.

Schleiermacher, Sabine, 'Die Innere Mission und ihr bevölkerungspolitisches Programm', in Heidrun Kaupen-Haas (ed.), *Der Griff nach der Bevölkerung: Aktualität und Kontinuität nazistischer Bevölkerungspolitik* (Nordlingen 1986), pp. 73–89.

'Der Centralausschuss für die innere Mission und die Eugenik am Vorabend des "Dritten Reichs"', in Strohm, Theodor and Thierfelder, Jörg (eds.), *Diakonie im 'Dritten Reich'* (Heidelberg 1990), pp. 60–77.

'Die Innere Mission zwischen Initiative und Anwendung sozialpolitischer Massnahmen in den 30er Jahren', in Büttner, M., Krolzick, U. and Waschkies, H.-J. (eds.), *Religion and Environment. Proceedings of the Symposium of the XVIIIth International Congress of History of Science at Hamburg-Munich* (Bochum 1990), pp. 225–235.

Schleunes, Karl, 'Nationalsozialistische Entschlussbildung und die Aktion T-4', in Jäckel, Eberhard and Rohwer, Jürgen (eds.), *Der Mord an den Juden im Zweiten Weltkrieg* (Frankfurt am Main 1987), pp. 70–83.

Schmidt, Gerhard, *Selektion in der Heilanstalt 1939–1945* (Frankfurt am Main 1983).

Schmidt, Jürgen, 'Darstellung, Analyse und Wertung der Euthanasiedebatte in der deutschen Psychiatrie von 1920–1933', Medical Dissertation, University of Leipzig (1983).

Schmidt, Martin, 'Hephaistos Lebt – Untersuchungen zur Frage der Behandlung behinderter Kinder in der Antike', *Hephaistos. Kritische Zeitschrift zu Theorie und Praxis der Archäologie, Kunstwissenschaft und angrenzender Gebiete* (1983/1984), 5/6, pp. 133–161.

Schmuhl, Walter, *Rassenhygiene, Nationalsozialismus, Euthanasie. Von der Verhütung zur Vernichtung 'lebensunwerten Lebens' 1890–1945* (Göttingen 1987).

'Die Selbstverständlichkeit des Tötens. Psychiater im Nationalsozialismus', *Geschichte und Gesellschaft* (1990), 16, pp. 411–439.

'Reformpsychiatrie und Massenmord', in Prinz, Michael and Zitelmann, Rainer (eds.), *Nationalsozialismus und Modernisierung* (Darmstadt 1991), pp. 239–266.

Schneider, Wolfgang (ed.), *Vernichtungspolitik. Eine Debatte über den Zusammenhang von Sozialpolitik und Genozid im nationalsozialistischen Deutschland* (Hamburg 1991).

Scholz, Susanne and Singer, Reinhard, 'Die Kinder in Hadamar', in Roer, D. and Henkel, D. (eds.), *Psychiatrie im Faschismus. Die Anstalt Hadamar 1933 bis 1945* (Bonn 1986), pp. 214–236.

Schöne, David and Schöne, Dieter, 'Zur Entwicklung und klinischen Anwendung neuer somatischer Therapiemethoden der Psychiatrie in den 30er Jahren des

20. Jahrhunderts unter besonderer Berücksichtigung der Schocktherapien und deren Nutzung in den deutschen Heil- und Pflegeanstalten', Medical Dissertation, University of Leipzig (1987).

Schonhagen, Benigna, *Tübingen unterm Hakenkreuz. Eine Universitätsstadt in der Zeit des Nationalsozialismus. Beiträge zur Tübinger Geschichte*, vol. 4 (Stuttgart 1991).

Schrapper, Christian and Sengling, Dieter (eds.), *Die Idee der Bildbarkeit. 100 Jahre sozialpädagogischer Praxis in der Heilerziehungsanstalt Kalmenhof* (Weinheim and Munich 1988).

Schreiber, Bernhard, *The Men Behind Hitler* (London 1972).

Schultz, Ulrich, 'Dichtkunst, Heilkunst, Forschung: Der Kinderarzt Werner Catel', in Aly, Götz (ed.), *Beiträge zur nationalsozialistischen Gesundheits- und Sozialpolitik* (Berlin 1985), 2, pp. 107–124.

Schulze, Dietmar, 'Zur Geschichte der Landes- Heil- und Pflegeanstalt Bernburg/Anhaltischen Nervenklinik in der Zeit von 1934 bis 1945', dissertation, Martin-Luther-Universität Halle-Wittenberg (1993).

Schwann, Hannelore and Wilke, Joachim, 'Zur Frage der Zwangssterilisierung bei ererbter Taubheit', in Thom, Achim and Spaar, Horst (eds.), *Medizin im Faschismus. Symposium über das Schicksal der Medizin in der Zeit des Faschismus in Deutschland* (Berlin 1985), pp. 162–166.

Seibert, Horst, 'Hitlers T4–Aktion und die Innere Mission', *Pastoraltheologie* (1990), 79, pp. 399–417.

Seidler, Eduard, 'Alfred Hoche (1865–1943). Versuch einer Standortbestimmung', *Freiburger Universitätblätter* (1986), 25, pp. 65–75.

Sick, Dorothea, *'Euthanasie' im Nationalsozialismus am Beispiel des Kalmenhofs in Idstein im Taunus. Materialien zur Sozialarbeit und Sozialpolitik*, vol. 9 (2nd edn Frankfurt am Main 1983).

Siemen, Hans-Ludwig, *Das Grauen ist vorprogrammiert. Psychiatrie zwischen Faschismus und Atomkrieg* (Giessen 1982).

Menschen blieben auf der Strecke … Psychiatrie zwischen Reform und Nationalsozialismus (Gütersloh 1987).

'Reform und Radikalisierung. Veränderungen der Psychiatrie in der Weltwirtschaftskrise', in Frei, Norbert (ed.), *Medizin und Gesundheitspolitik in der NS-Zeit* (Munich 1991), pp. 191–200.

Simon-Pelanda, Hans, 'Medizin und Trinkerfürsorge', *Dachauer Hefte* (1988), 4, pp. 215–224.

Singer, Peter, *Practical Ethics* (Cambridge 1979).

(ed.) *Applied Ethics. Oxford Readings in Philosophy* (Oxford 1986).

'Bioethics and Academic Freedom', *Bioethics* (1990), 4, pp. 33–44.

(ed.) *A Companion to Ethics* (Oxford 1991).

Sorg, Helmut, '"Euthanasie" in den evangelischen Heilanstalten in Württemberg im Dritten Reich', dissertation, Freie Universität Berlin (1987).

Steinfels, Peter and Levine, Carol (eds.), *Biomedical Ethics and the Shadow of Nazism. A Conference on the Proper Use of the Nazi Analogy in Ethical Debate.* The Hastings Center Special Supplement (1976).

Steppe, Hilde (ed.), *Krankenpflege im Nationalsozialismus* (5th edn Frankfurt am Main 1989).

Steurer, Leopold, *Ein vergessenes Kapital Südtiroler Geschichte. Die Umsiedlung und Vernichtung der Südtiroler Geisteskranken im Rahmen des nationalsozialistischen Euthanasieprogrammes* (Bozen 1982).

Stöffler, Friedrich, 'Die "Euthanasie" und die Haltung der Bischöfe in hessischen Raum 1940–1945', *Archiv für mittelrheinische Kirchengeschichte* (1961), p. 13.

Stolz, Peter, 'Die Rolle der Irrenanstalten im Faschisierungsprozess der deutschen Psychiatrie', *Recht und Psychiatrie* (1983), 2, pp. 65–70.

Suesse, Thomas and Meyer, Heinrich, *Abtransport des 'Lebensunwerten'. Die Konfrontation niedersächsischer Anstalten mit der NS-'Euthanasie'* (Hanover 1988).

Teller, Christine, 'Die "aktivere Heilbehandlung" der 20er und 30er Jahre: z.B. Hermann Simon und Carl Schneider', in Dörner, K. (ed.), *Fortschritte der Psychiatrie im Umgang mit Menschen* (Rehburg-Loccum 1985), pp. 77–87.

'Carl Schneider. Zur Biographie eines deutschen Wissenschaftlers', *Geschichte und Gesellschaft* (1990), 16, pp. 464–478.

Teppe, Karl, *Massenmord auf dem Dienstweg. Hitlers 'Euthanasie'-Erlass und seine Durchführung in den Westfälischen Provinzialheilanstalten* (Münster 1989).

Thierfelder, Jörg, 'Karsten Jespersens Kampf gegen die NS-Krankenmorde', in Strohm, T. and Thierfelder, J. (eds.), *Diakonie im 'Dritten Reich'* (Heidelberg 1990), pp. 229–235.

Thom, Achim, 'Die Durchsetzung des faschistischen Herrschaftsanspruches in der Medizin und der Aufbau eines zentralistisch organisierten Medizinalwesens', in Thom, A. and Caregorodcev, G. I. (eds.), *Medizin unterm Hakenkreuz* (East Berlin 1989), pp. 35–62.

'Die rassenhygienischen Leitideen der faschistischen Gesundheitspolitik – die Zwangssterilisierungen als Beginn ihrer antihumanen Verwirklichung', in Thom, A. and Caregorodcev, G. I. (eds.), *Medizin unterm Hakenkreuz* (East Berlin 1989), pp. 63–90.

'Die Entwicklung der Psychiatrie und die Schicksale psychisch Kranker sowie geistig Behinderter unter der Bedingung der faschistischen Diktatur', in Thom, A. and Caregorodcev, G. I. (eds.), *Medizin unterm Hakenkreuz* (East Berlin 1989), pp. 127–165.

'Kriegsopfer der Psychiatrie. Das Beispiel der Heil- und Pflegeanstalten Sachsens', in Frei, Norbert (ed.), *Medizin und Gesundheitspolitik in der NS-Zeit* (Munich 1991), pp. 201–216.

and Caregorodcev, Genadij Ivanovic (eds.), *Medizin unterm Hakenkreuz* (East Berlin 1989).

Trögisch, Jürgen, 'Bericht über Euthanasie-Massnahmen im "Katherinenhof" Grosshennersdorf', *Fröhlich Helfen* (1986), 1, pp. 40–43.

Vanja, Christine, (ed.), *Euthanasie in Hadamar. Die nazionalsozialistische Vernichtungspolitik in hessischen Anstalten* (Kassel 1991).

Walter, Bernd, 'Anstaltsleben als Schicksal. Die nationalsozialistische Erb- und Rassenpflege an Psychiatrie-Patienten', in Frei, Norbert (ed.), *Medizin und Gesundheitspolitik in der NS-Zeit* (Munich 1991), pp. 217–233.

Weindling, Paul, 'Soziale Hygiene: Eugenik und medizinische Praxis – Der Fall Alfred Grotjahn', *Jahrbuch für kritische Medizin* (1984), 10, pp. 6–20.

'Weimar Eugenics: The Kaiser Wilhelm Institute for Anthropology, Human

Bibliography

Heredity and Eugenics in Social Context', *Annals of Science* (1985), 42, pp. 303–318.
'Medicine and Modernization: The Social History of German Health and Medicine', History of Science (1986), 24, pp. 277–301.
'Compulsory Sterilisation in National Socialist Germany', *German History* (1987), 5, pp. 10–24.
'Die Verbreitung rassenhygienischen/eugenischen Gedankengutes in bürgerlichen und sozialistischen Kreisen in der Weimarer Republik', *Medizinhistorisches Journal* (1987), 22, pp. 352–368.
'The Medical Profession, Social Hygiene and the Birth Rate in Germany, 1914–18', in Wall and Winter (eds.), *The Upheaval of War* (Cambridge 1988), pp. 417–437.
'Referat', Institut für Zeitgeschichte (ed.), *Medizin im Nationalsozialismus* (Munich 1988), pp. 28–33.
Health, Race and German Politics between National Unification and Nazism 1870–1945 (Cambridge 1989).
'The "sonderweg" of German Eugenics: Nationalism and Scientific Internationalism', *British Journal of the History of Science* (1989), 22, pp. 321–333.
'Psychiatry and the Holocaust', *Psychological Medicine* (1992), 22, pp. 1–3.
'"Mustergau" Thüringen. Rassenhygiene zwischen Ideologie und Machtpolitik', in Frei, Norbert (ed.), *Medizin und Gesundheitspolitik in der NS-Zeit* (Munich 1991), pp. 84ff.
'Bourgeois Values, Doctors and the State: The Professionalization of Medicine in Germany 1848–1933', in Blackbourn, David and Evans, Richard (eds.), *The German Bourgeoisie. Essays on the Social History of the German Middle Class from the Late Eighteenth to the Early Twentieth Century* (London 1991), pp. 198–223.
Weingart, P., Kroll, J. and Bayertz, K., *Rasse, Blut und Gene. Geschichte der Eugenik und Rassenhygiene in Deutschland* (Frankfurt am Main 1988).
Werner, Wolfgang, 'Rheinprovinz und die Tötungsanstalt Hadamar', in Vanja, Christine (ed.), *Euthanasie in Hadamar. Die nationalsozialistische Vernichtungspolitik in hessischen Anstalten* (Kassel 1991), pp. 135–143.
Wettlaufer, Antje, 'Die Beteiligung von Schwestern und Pflegern an den Morden in Hadamar', in Roer, D. and Henkel, D. (eds.), *Psychiatrie im Faschismus. Die Anstalt Hadamar 1933–1945* (Bonn 1986), pp. 283–330.
Winau, Rolf, 'Die Freigabe der Vernichtung "lebensunwerten Lebens": Euthanasie – Wandlung eines Begriffes', in Bleker, Johanna and Jachertz, Norbert (eds.), *Medizin im Dritten Reich* (Cologne 1989), pp. 76–85.
Winter, Bettina, 'Hadamar als T4 Anstalt 1941–1945', in Vanja, Christine (ed.), *Euthanasie in Hadamar. Die nationalsozialistische Vernichtungspolitik in hessischen Anstalten* (Kassel 1991), pp. 91–104.
Wollasch, Hans-Josef, 'Caritas und Euthanasie im Dritten Reich', *Beiträge zur Geschichte der deutschen Caritas in der Zeit der Weltkriege* (Freiburg 1978), pp. 208–225.
Wuttke, Walter, 'Heilen und Vernichten. Ärzte und Medizin im Nationalsozialismus', in Leipert, M., Styrnal, R. and Schwarzer, W. (eds.), *Verlegt nach*

unbekannt. Sterilisation und Euthanasie in Galkhausen 1933–1945. Dokumente und Darstellungen zur Geschichte der Rheinischen Provinzialverwaltung und des Landschaftsverbandes Rheinland (Cologne 1987), vol. 1, pp. 12–21.

'Medizin, Ärzte, Gesundheitspolitik', in Borst, Otto (ed.), *Das Dritte Reich in Baden und Württemberg* (Stuttgart 1988), vol. 1, pp. 211–235.

'Ideologien der NS-Medizin', in Pfeiffer, Jürgen (ed.), *Menschenverachtung und Opportunismus. Zur Medizin im Dritten Reich* (Tübingen 1992), pp. 157–171.

(ed.), *Medizin im Nationalsozialismus. Ein Arbeitsbuch* (Tübingen 1980).

Zehethofer, Florian, 'Das Euthanasieproblem im Dritten Reich am Beispiel Schloss Hartheim', *Oberösterreichische Heimatblätter* (1978), 32, pp. 46–62.

INDEX

Index

Index

Index

Index